*I Was Born Poor, I was Born Black,
And I Was Born In Mississippi...
When You've Been Through That
You Can Deal With Anything*

Ron Anderson

Copyright © Ron Anderson 2024

All Rights Reserved

No part of this publication may be reproduced, distributed, or transmitted in any form or by any means, including photocopying, recording, or other electronic or mechanical methods, without the author's prior written permission, except in the case of brief quotations embodied in critical reviews and certain other non-commercial uses permitted by copyright law. For permission requests, please get in touch with the author.

Contents

Dedication i

Acknowledgments ii

Contributors iv

About the Author vi

Introduction 1

Chapter 1 Prelude to Poverty 16

Chapter 2 Whatever the Terms the Landlord Offered 54

Chapter 3 The Blues Come Out of The Fields, Baby 93

Chapter 4 Jim Crow's Alive and Well 131

Chapter 5 Bloodstained Whitewash 162

Chapter 6 The Tryout 197

Chapter 7 The Great Wall of Boston 247

Chapter 8 Boston, The Little Rock of the North 288

Chapter 9 Post Jackie Robinson – Baseball's Non-acceptance 328

Chapter 10 Dick Williams 365

Chapter 11 An Impossible Nightmare 398

Chapter 12 A Moral Victory 423

Chapter 13 Cultural Deprivation 456

Chapter 14 Scott Keeps Booming 481

Chapter 15 The Intractable Jim Baumer 506

Chapter 16 Now He's Your Headache 532

Chapter 17 Racial Injustice Persists After All These Years 561

Chapter 18 Stonewalled 591

Photo Album 620

Index 635

Dedication

For my wife Gail, as always…

Acknowledgments

There are so many who made invaluable contributions to this work and whom I gratefully acknowledge, from George Scott, his boyhood friends, acquaintances, teammates, neighbors, coaches, mentors, town historians, to numerous baseball historians, SABRites and the many former major leaguers who were teammates –or opponents - who kindly gave of their time to be interviewed.

Also, a debt of gratitude is owed to Princella Wilkerson Nowell, a notable Greenville, Mississippi and Washington County historian, past president of the Mississippi Historical Society, and whose legacy dates back to the distinguished Mississippi Wilkerson family of yesteryear, who made inestimable contributions with details, and who shared with me important documents about Greenville and its early years.

To Nadine Ferrero, a graduate of Boston University's Genealogy Studies Program with a certificate in their vaunted Certificate in Genealogical Research program, who laid the genealogical foundation for me for this story; a research challenge indeed attempting to uncover Deep South details on Mississippi's African American past.

I owe special thanks to Hodding Carter III for his sage perspective on the history of Greenville, Mississippi, his insightful views on the political and social structure of the town and its relevance to the boyhood days and challenges confronting George Scott and African American athletes like him; to Dorothy Williams, PhD, for her likewise articulate description of what it was like for an African American growing up in Greenville – and, to be living in a turbulent racist Mississippi - of the 50s and 60s; Mississippi's social justice activist Betty Jo Boyd, and in numerous ways of the Deep South, for her perspective on the town of Greenville, its people, the all-black institution known as Coleman High, and of the times in the racially conflicted Mississippi Delta; and Beverly Gardner for his historical views on Greenville, its racial climate, and the history of venerable Sportsman's Park, the seat of semipro baseball in the Delta, where major league baseball, Negro Leagues, The House of David, and the likes of Roy Campanella, Jackie Robinson, Bob Feller, and Don Newcombe once played.

My heartfelt thanks go out to the late Ed Scott, the Red Sox scout who signed George Scott, for his multiple hours of interviews with me delving into the history of his time and experiences with the Red Sox, his Negro League days, his discovery of George Scott and Henry Aaron, and of the numerous stories he shared with me on his life in baseball.

To Carlos Fragoso, who was of enormous help to me with Scott's Mexican League years, scouring the newspaper stories of the day, interviewing key Mexican League baseball people, and altogether helping with many loose ends on Scott's five seasons south of the border; and to Edward Almada, who helped with information on the Mexican and Mexican Pacific [Winter] Leagues; Almada's father, Mel Almada, was the first Mexican National to play in the Major Leagues [1933-1939].

Contributors

George Scott	John Provenza	Andrew Jackson
Milt Bolling	Davis Weathersby	E. T. Davis
Jay Acton	Sam McDowell	Beatrice Scott
Mike Babcock	John Wathan	Bob Scranton
Stan Block	Joseph Barthell, Jr.	W. C. Gorden
Mike Kardamis	Ed Scott	Beverly Gardner
Jim Mudcat Grant	Bob Veale	Betty Jo Boyd
Marty Pattin	Eddie Dennis	Alex Grammas
Gene Martin	Edsel Neal	Clark Viegas
Whitey Herzog	Bobby Doerr	Darrell Brandon
Frank Sanders	Fred Beene	George Digby
Diego Segui	Jonathan Fleisig	Merv Rettenmund
Lenny Green	John Thomas	Luis Tiant
Rico Petrocelli	Zelma Kelly	Tommy Harper
Jim Gosger	Bill Slack	Gloster Richardson
Mary Haynes	Elijah Moore	Hodding Carter III

Fred Patek

Leonia Collins Dorsey

Doctor Dorothy Williams

Doctor Robert Young

John Hawkins

A.C. Thomas

Willie Richardson

Charles "Chuck" Prophet

Doctor William Ware

Carlos Fragoso

Debbie Matson

Bill Nowlin

Dan Desrochers

David Laurila

David Vincent

Martha Reagan

Janice Brown

Greg Rybarczyk

Mary Dayle

Princella Nowell

Elisabeth Keppler

Aaron Schmidt

Noel Workman

Charlie Blanks

Brenda Fulton-Poke

Thomas Van Hyning

Edwin Fernandez

Alfredo Ortiz

Alfonso Araujo

Manuel Cazarin

Porfirio Mendoza

Jose Pena

Tommy Morales

Benjamin "Papelero" Valenzuela

Gene Phillips

Lee Sigman

Jose Luis Gutierrez

Jacob Cruz

Edward Almada

Leonte Landino

Jorge Colón-Delgado

Tom Larwin

Bill Jenkinson

Phil Lowry

Miles Wolff

Pam Ganley

Doug Adams

Mary Russell Baucom

Arthur Pollock

Pat Kelly

Allison Midgley

David Smith

Nadine Ferrero

About the Author

Ron Anderson grew up in the Boston area following their 1950s era major league baseball teams, with allegiance initially rooted in the crosstown club, the Braves, and then morphing permanently to the vicissitudes of a Red Sox team in 1953 upon the Braves departure from the city. He was a contributing writer to several Society for American Baseball Research (SABR) biographies: *'75: The Red Sox Team That Saved Baseball; The 1967 Impossible Dream Red Sox: Pandemonium on the Field; When Boston Still Had the Babe: The 1918 World Series Champion Red Sox; Spahn, Sain and Teddy Ballgame: Boston's almost Perfect Baseball Summer of 1948; Go-Go to Glory: The 1959 Chicago White Sox*. A contributing author of several articles for SABR's Baseball Biography Project. And, his full-length baseball biography of former Red Sox All-Star first baseman George Scott - *Long Taters: A Baseball Biography of George "Boomer" Scott*, McFarland Publishing, which was released in the fall of 2011. He lives with his wife, Gail, in Concord, NH.

Introduction

Some who read my biography of George "Boomer" Scott, the ballplayer, published by McFarland in 2011, asked me whether *Long Taters* was the entire story: a legitimate question and they sensed there was more and yearned to hear about it. It was the complete baseball narrative for George, but there is more underpinning to his story nonetheless.

There is a compelling racial element that permeates the George Scott narrative. Though unquestionably intersecting with his sporting achievements, which are the basis for *Long Taters*, it speaks for a much larger story. When *Long Taters* was published, George was delighted that I had finally written his baseball story and pleased with its account. It reflected on racial bigotry, though it was not the central theme – baseball was - and he was good with that. But he also was quick to admonish, surprisingly, in the first few days of its publication that there was more to this, a broader message, and astonishingly insisted on a "second book." He startled me so soon after its release and without any preemptive discussion, but which soon followed. His focus was squarely on the racial element of the times, the part it played in his life, how that had affected him and most of all, how it affected his hard-working and struggling mother, whom he adored. And who died in 2000 within two months of the unexpected and tragic passing of his much-beloved fiancé, Edith Lawson – mother of his youngest son - of some twenty years. He felt deeply for his fellow Coleman

High athletes, many of whom were comparable athletes, whom he felt did not get a fair shake merely because of race. Of the black townspeople of Greenville who lived under *Jim Crow* and of the Mississippi Delta, with its incendiary and violent racist history – approximate to a dangerous Ku Klux Klan - tarnishing how he was to survive. "You can call it part two," he declared with a certain pretentiousness, begging a response from me of similar rant and enthusiasm by chiming in like fashion, "coming right up!" he was expecting me to say; instead, I gasped at the thought. But I paused momentarily at what he said; I thought another edition could just as quickly be considered a beginning, prequel, or, more likely, a companion to his sporting life biography as memorialized in *Long Taters*. There was still more to tell.

I was unprepared to take this step, or at least right away, considering the heavy lifting required of any discussion about racism, especially the Mississippi kind. His interest was to provide greater detail to the personal encounters and a broader look at the racial element and the injustices, which would best serve in a second publication as a companion. After reading *Long Taters*, which he unhesitatingly declared was a "home run," so he said, it was apparent that I had his complete confidence.

But in July 2013, just four months from turning 69, George quite unexpectedly, if, for that matter, inexplicably, died. It was from diabetes complications, a disorder that beset the family, including his mother, about whom he had once shared with me. I found the news of George's death disquieting, for Boomer was a good friend I had known personally for 17 years. During these times, we would share stories - at times in laughter as he had a sense of humor - mostly to do with baseball, seeking common ground no matter how we were to accomplish that in our otherwise anomalous backgrounds. I knew he had health issues, weight being one of them, that on one occasion placed him in a Greenville hospital for a few days the previous year. He called me from the Medical Center Hospital on East Union Street, formerly the Washington County General Hospital, to chat about plans for a second book but failed to reveal any personal details about why he was there. Nor did I press him. However, I suspected there was a diabetes connection to his eventual passing. He was a proud man who chose not to discuss the matter of his health even with his closest friends, so the sudden fateful outcome surprised me. George's struggle with weight was a personal conflict he had to deal with throughout his baseball career. His well-publicized confrontations with irascible manager Dick Williams, never one to hide his feelings, nor keep them private, especially about George's weight, were legendary. No doubt, the weight issue contributed to his diabetes complications. When I saw him at the November 2006 Red Sox Hall of Fame dinner at the Boston Convention and Exhibition Center that night, where he was honored with induction, he was in a cold sweat. And he seemed in considerable distress, though he remained steadfast and never complained; quite frankly, I was concerned. After the ceremonies, my wife and I, who were at Scott's table, walked him to a waiting limousine provided by the Red Sox and helped him safely into the car that would take him to a nearby Boston hotel. I was incensed that no one of the Red Sox offered to help George, who was distinctly afflicted, including his namesake son, George III, who disappeared early; once more, perhaps symbolic of the shameful aspects of this human tale, heads turned in other directions, away from a faltering Boomer, as he struggled with a visible tottering gait across the convention floor.[1]

On that evening of the 9th, except for Red Sox' HOFr Johnny Pesky, public address announcer Carle Beane, and a handful of staffers, who sought out George during the preliminary cocktail hour leading up to the evening ceremonies, and then former manager Dick Williams who pursued Boomer at the end of the evening to thank him for not publicly embarrassing him for his past transgressions of Scott, no one from Red Sox management, former teammates or any other former players came to his table to congratulate him. ESPN's staff writer Gordon Edes confronted Red Sox president and CEO Larry Lucchino about the matter, who conveniently responded, "I really don't remember that evening very well," recalling he met several people that night but was sorry he had missed George. Lucchino was at a table directly adjacent to George's table.[2]

---

[1] On June 2, 2023, George Scott III, age 54, George "Boomer" Scott's middle son, was involved in an apparent murder-suicide at this writing. He was the assailant of an 8-year-old boy, presumed to be his son, after which he took his own life. His wife (or significant other) had been missing since March of 2019 from their New Bedford, Massachusetts home, and Scott was under investigation as a person of interest in her disappearance.

[2] Edes, Gordon, "Not a happy ending for Boomer," ESPN, July 30, 2013

As it turned out, it was a setback enough to cause me to pause following his death in delivering this exciting and essential part of his story, challenging the boundaries of a reputable shelf life, no doubt, and taking far longer than I had planned. But the message was the same. The truth is this is for George, at his request of me; it was that personal. I desire that he have his just reward, no matter how extraneous the circumstances, knowing that I would fulfill his story of racist memories, and then, in a flash, he was gone.

George Scott bore witness to racial conflict and its aftermath of unspeakable racial hostility among heinous acts of such significance they are remembered and written about today. And which formed the basis for meaningful civil rights legislation highlighted by the Civil Rights Act of 1964. Still, this damage left its mark, manifesting in mental and physical scars he carried throughout his life. These acts of violence, some involving prominent civil rights figures such as Martin Luther King Jr. and Medgar Evers, had occurred in his young life and near where George grew up in Greenville, Mississippi. And in outlying towns, he was personally familiar with essentially having engaged in high school athletic competition there. George was well-acquainted with the Delta landscape and its people, sensitive to the culture and mores of this region of the Delta. Also, he knew the required rules and boundaries of conduct for blacks like him, of Mississippi-style misconduct that left him in its lurch.

Delta citizens, especially blacks, could have hardly imagined such brutal attacks of unspeakable magnitude on human life in any civilized society as they had occurred in and around the Delta in the 1950s and '60s and before, affecting a youthful George Scott growing up there. He was present – a teenager - to observe the injustice of Mississippi's harsh response to the 1961 Freedom Rides, a prominent Civil Rights initiative against *Jim Crow* laws of the South. Their Riders were arrested in Jackson with nothing more than simple due process if that can be said. Local authorities promptly deposited them in the disreputable Parchman Farm, a notorious Mississippi state maximum prison facility in Indianola just outside George's hometown of Greenville. They were transported by the busloads through the summer, amounting to over 300 Freedom Riders assembled there at one time. George witnessed this abomination, watching their conveyance and roadside treatment. His mother made him aware of Mississippi's long history of lynching, such as the infamous "Hanging Bridge" of Shubuta, Mississippi. He was also conscious of the Civil Rights slayings of the '60s, including Medgar Evers. Still, none of these had the same impact or was much closer to his soul than the violent attack of Emmett Till in 1955 when George was 11. Till was a 14-year-old boy, three years George's senior, from Chicago, visiting his cousins. He was tortured and brutally murdered in the nearby Delta town of Drew, Mississippi, for allegedly making a pass at a white woman. Local jurisprudence never reconciled some of the details of that incident, but consensus points to young Till wolf whistling at her, which led to his fate. Scott, a contemporary, never forgot the horror and repugnance he felt for this tragedy nor the open casket photo of Till's mutilated, butchered body he and other blacks of Greenville saw displayed in national newspapers. The *Delta Democrat-Times*, Greenville's local paper, commented little about the murder. Hodding Carter, Jr., the publisher, saw nothing to its advantage in covering this story in depth, fearing it would encourage more racial turbulence. Till's murder aroused the black communities of the South and catalyzed the Civil Rights Movement.

And then there was a sporting life, which was George's ticket to a big-league career and, ultimately, a baseball future. But there were disturbing hurdles along the way here, and racial ones, beginning with a starkly segregated hometown that practiced its implacable opposition to anything or anyone suggesting the social mingling of whites and blacks. Delta towns of the Deep South relied on the still-operative 19th Century Supreme Court ruling of "Separate but Equal" in *Plessy v. Ferguson* in stark furtherance of *Jim Crow* law. The sharp distinction they placed upon black and white athletes of the town forever consigned to play apart on separate designated fields, the blacks being of inferior quality, they said, and on black teams largely unsupported by the city; there was nothing equal about that.

Young George Scott emerged from the racial madness of the Delta to take his chances in professional baseball in the early 1960s with, of all teams, ironically, the Boston Red Sox and the city of Boston, both known for racist propensities. He would soon discover racial bias in his trek through the minors and, predictably, in Boston, with the local media and a skipper in Dick Williams, labeled "resident smartass" in his playing days, who reeked of old school racist behavior.[3] This *Jim Crow* attitude carried over to similar experiences of intolerance with other teams and management that George claimed had racist inclinations. George's encounter with Red Sox historian and public affairs executive Dick Bresciani, who Red Sox fans and the city of Boston viewed as close to sacrosanct in the eyes of the town and the club, and of my encounter with him, stood out. After reading my introductory draft material for *Long Taters*, which I offered to share with him before its publication, Bresciani went on the offensive, seeing a need to confront me about any reference I planned implicating the Red Sox with racism, which I readily dismissed, explaining it was George's story, not mine. To his disappointment, the racial reference remained as I had written it. He was not very happy with that but recognized the fallacy of the argument, hoping I would relent, and instead, he abruptly and ignominiously went silent. In a strange case of irony, he, like George's nemesis Dick Williams, would be honored with George at the 2006 HOF event.

---

[3] Angus, Jeff, "Dick Williams," Society for American Baseball Research; BioProject, 2006; Williams was a protégé of Charlie Dressen, all of 5' 5" and 146 pounds, who managed the 1951-1953 Brooklyn Dodgers, winning two pennants. Dressen was an intense man, known for his high-strung antics when games were on the line, and he passed that on to Williams as his lively bench jockey.

Red Sox Hall of Fame induction ceremonies on November 6, 2006. Left to Right: Dick Williams, Joe Morgan, George Scott, Dick Bresciani and Jerry Remy (courtesy of Boston Red Sox and Julie Cordero)

The Red Sox were a microcosm of a bigger problem in MLB: Institutional racism inflicted upon George Scott that extended well beyond Jackie Robinson's triumph of breaking the color barrier. Robinson may have overcome the hurdle, but he didn't upset the white standard of the intransigence of racial non-acceptance or censoring, which remained intact after Robinson's groundbreaking achievement. And though talking a good game of being a racially tolerant city, and notably defensive when challenged, the undercurrent of racism remained a part of Boston institutions seemingly in lockstep with their town team, the Red Sox, who struggled with shedding the "ism" label. In 2017, Baltimore's Adam Jones was the subject of racial taunting by unruly Fenway fans. Management removed them from the park, but it was an ineffective measure by the team, done half-heartedly, said Jones, claiming that imposing a heavy fine would have been more appropriate and sent the correct message. In April 2018, Yawkey Way, the street contiguous to the park, named after the previous owner, Tom Yawkey, was restored to its original name, Jersey Street. The current owner, John Henry, said he was "haunted" by the racial history of Yawkey's team and appealed to the city for a change. It met with fierce resistance from the Yawkey Foundation, a charitable group funded by the Yawkey family and estate; fearing their name would be tarnished, they strenuously insisted that all previous claims about Yawkey as racially divisive were unreasonable, misleading, and out of context. Ah yes, that mysterious and oft-quoted fallback of a magical phrase, "out of context," applied as a defensive measure to bolster an argument of last resort.

I have memories of George proudly driving me around Greenville and surrounding towns in his red pickup truck when I first arrived in 2006, one of several trips to start my research on the first book. He showed no compunction about driving me through Greenville neighborhoods and, to my surprise, no matter the impropriety, into the backyards of privately owned property, unannounced, to access an abandoned local recreational ball field he once played on. I had visions of being chased by someone with a shotgun as we motored through their yards and across small streams, let alone find ourselves in mud up to the rims with angry residents closing in as we struggled with George's truck. When we arrived on the other side, the landscape was in disrepair and considerably overgrown with a backstop in advanced stages of rusting and collapse and bore little resemblance to any ball field. Little to brag about, but as George reminded me, it's where he began exhibiting an element of pride and skills despite what this represented. Of course, I couldn't imagine what George saw in this long-ago abandoned pasture; to me, it was an inferior ballfield. It symbolized the times and the residuals of segregation in the shadow of *Jim Crow*. But it was being short-sighted; this nothing more than a stubble of a pasture laden with countless rocks and stones, with no outward appearance of a ballfield, was George's baptism into organized sports.

George "Boomer" Scott in his truck taken in Greenville, Mississippi in the spring of 2006 (author's collection)

Backstop of first ballfield where George Scott and friends played baseball informally in Greenville, MS when George was a preteen (author's collection)

In the spring of 2007, George, at the wheel of his Escalade, and I drove about his hometown of Greenville. Without warning, he reached into his jacket pocket, pulling out a 38-caliber pistol in my presence, much to my alarm, grasping it in the palm of his considerable-sized hand. The revolver looked more like a derringer with him holding it. He explained that he required protection from hostile whites and blacks, who would likely take advantage of him in his disabled state. He had difficulty with mobility, needing a cane from injuries he incurred playing professional baseball, and was concerned about his vulnerability; he was profoundly mistrustful, perhaps for a good reason. With no explanation, George suddenly left the roadway with a lurch, using his 3-ton vehicle as a form of four-wheeled support. He drove his Cadillac Escalade onto the sidewalk, parking it directly in front of a Greenville gun shop, prompting the owner, whom he was familiar with, to appear in astonishment at the shop's front entrance. "What are you up to, Boomer," he said as he walked toward George's full-size luxury SUV in the face of an unpleasant situation of George waving his piece menacingly through the open car window as if he planned to use it. His goal was nothing more than gun repairs, innocent enough, but he requested nothing less than full-flared drama.

Despite his age of 11, when the horrifying murder of young Emmett Till, only three years his senior, was committed in the nearby notoriously racist town of Drew, a youthful George Scott Jr. was not unaffected by its impact. Despite local media suppressing what they could, as was their customary ways, knowing that a more significant portion of the black population was in varying levels of illiteracy. And then, three months later, another murder was carried out, this time in Glendora, only sixteen miles from Drew. Elmer Kimbell - a close friend of Till's assailant, J. W. Milam – who had participated in Till's murder, also shot 33-year-old gas station employee Clinton Melton, a father of four. Kimbell killed Melton in cold blood, accusing Melton of pumping more gas than he had requested. These outrageous and chilling stories of the murders had a far-reaching effect on the school children of adjacent towns, including Greenville, especially the black kids, who feared for their lives. Dorsey White, a cousin of Deloris Melton Gresham, daughter of Clinton Melton, remembered their constant fear: "I guess you felt like a rabbit in the forest; you didn't have nobody to run to."[4]

The breadth of George's dysphoria over his town's *Jim Crow* reputation and of surrounding cities to his hometown of Greenville had left its mark. The ravages of *Jim Crow* had dealt a mighty blow to his beloved mother, leaving her impoverished and without help since the death of her husband, struggling with three young children. The racial element was an intrinsic part of George's life growing up in a hostile Mississippi and then confronting the bigotry of Major League Baseball. In addition, there were the dreadful matters of Medgar Evers, Civil Rights activist, visionary, and NAACP organizer, murdered in 1963; Jimmy Travis of nearby Greenwood, shot and seriously wounded, 1963; James Earl Chaney, murdered in 1964 in Philadelphia Mississippi; George Winston Lee, murdered in Belzoni in 1955. Scott listed these names for me to advance the narrative, speaking with unusual solemnity for a man widely described as a "character;" it was apparent this subject ran more profoundly and firmly implanted in his mind than I had ever imagined, or would give him credit for, and thus explained his hastiness to insist on a companion book from me.

George "Boomer" Scott felt the entire thrust and impact of systemic non-acceptance of blacks in MLB, a more subtle manifestation of its kind

---

[4] Giles, Nellie & Richman, Joe, "Clinton Melton: A Man Who was Killed in Mississippi just three months after Emmett Till," NPR, Radio Diaries, August 27, 2020.

that lingered well after Jackie Robinson triumphed over MLB racism in 1947 and followed him through the balance of his career, and of his life until his untimely death in 2013.

I am reminded of what George told a reporter in 1981 while playing baseball in Mexico City of the Mexican League, which is the basis for the title of this book: *"I was born poor, I was born black, and I was born in Mississippi. When you've been through that, you can deal with anything. The only thing I was ever taught was survival."*[5] Ironically, I also have a personal recollection of a more cautionary point of view that was expressed to me, quite earnestly, by a white woman of Greenville who approached me in Greenville's town library where I was doing research several years ago after she discovered I was doing a book on native son George Scott; she expressed to me a warning: *"I hope you don't make this just another story like others have been written trashing the history of our town!"* urging a premise that on the subject of Greenville, there was no basis for shame.

---

[5] Nack, William, "George Scott is Alive and Well and Playing in Mexico City," Sports Illustrated, New York, NY, August 17, 1981.

Chapter 1
Prelude to Poverty

When non-Southerners think of the South, the Delta is what they imagine. It is the South of fiction and fantasy, of forever fields and proper ladies and slow-motion nights. This is the only place left in America with bona fide shacks and mansions side by side, with not enough middle class to blunt the dramatic disparity...nothing happens halfway

Rheta Grimsley Johnson. [6]

The Mississippi Delta of the early to mid-19th century, until the conclusion of the Civil War and passage of the 13th Amendment, was immersed in the practice and propagation of chattel slavery with the full support of abundant cotton plantations smattered across the region and a booming cotton industry consisting of the nation's largest and highly prolific cotton producers.[7] Also known as the Yazoo River Basin or Yazoo-Mississippi Delta, it consists of a rich, fertile alluvial floodplain – some of the most fertile soil in the world - where plantations thrived; it covers 13,355

---

[6] Rheta Grimsley Johnson, "The Delta remains home to the mythical South," The Commercial Appeal, Memphis, TN, July 8, 1990, p. 23.
https://www.newspapers.com/image/773730893/?terms=the%20commercial%20appeal

[7].Slavery in America, History.com editors, "When Did Slavery End," updated May 19, 2022, original published date Nov 12. 2009, The Arena Group.
https://www.history.com/topics/black-history/slavery#

square miles, all or parts of 30 counties, about 200 miles in length and 70 miles wide, ranging between Memphis, Tennessee to Vicksburg, Mississippi. Major rivers that border this area are the Mississippi to its West and the Yazoo, Tallahatchie, and Sunflower Rivers to the East.[8] It was the manifest emergence of an Antebellum South where cotton was king made possible by a great many black slaves – by the thousands, products of the infamous Trans-Atlantic slave trade of which nearly 400 thousand, of some 10.7 million shipped to North America, arrived in America – who toiled in the fields engaged in backbreaking manual labor from dawn to dusk.[9] It was also a period of unmitigated white authority rule and constant suppression of blacks who were subjugated to plantation owner whims and commonplace cruelty; this behavior had not abated until the development of Civil Rights laws of the 1960s.

Land speculation of the Delta flourished in the early to mid-19th century; conspicuous among them was the distinguished Wilkerson family of Virginia and Kentucky origins, venturesome early pioneers of the delta who became prominent buyers and planters of substantial plantation lands. They were prosperous white cotton farmers who migrated to the northwest and central Mississippi Delta regions bordering the Mississippi River and parts

---

[8] Yazoo River Basin, Mississippi Department of Environmental Quality (MDEQ), 515 E. Amite St., Jackson, MS; see also, Mississippi Delta, Wikipedia.
https://www.mdeq.ms.gov/water/surface-water/watershed-management/basin-management-approach/basin-listing/yazoo-river/

[9] 100 Amazing Facts About the Negro: How Many Slaves Landed in the U.S.? by Henry Louis Gates, Jr. The Root. January 6, 2014.
https://www.theroot.com/how-many-slaves-landed-in-the-us-1790873989

of the Southeast, beginning with its patriarch, Peter Wilkerson (1782-1859), born in Virginia during the latter part of the Revolutionary War, who owned a handful of plantations in Mississippi's Bolivar, Grenada, Jackson (Mount Salus) and Washington Counties; he was a land baron with properties not only in Mississippi but also in Raleigh, Union County, Kentucky on the Ohio River. Sometime between 1848 and 1850, when he moved with his third wife to Coahoma County, Peter sold to his son Thomas Jefferson Wilkerson (1807-1868) from a first marriage the *Black Bayou Plantation*. It consisted of 1,700 acres of highly prized and fertile alluvial plain land strategically located near the Choctaw Bend of the Mississippi River. There, he farmed with enslaved black labor until the effects of the Civil War. Reconstruction impacted the black work force, many of whom left the South for better living and working conditions, and freedom at last, seeking greater opportunity in the North and West.

George Washington Wilkerson (1857-1917), son of Thomas Jefferson Wilkerson, who died when George W. was eleven, farmed *Black Bayou Plantation* with his mother and brother until 1900 when the Mississippi Supreme Court decided to establish a new levee, which labor for this was performed mostly by a workforce of sharecroppers, destroying several plantations bordering the Mississippi River, including *Black Bayou*, leaving George Wilkerson without sufficient resources to continue farming, nor was he compensated for his losses. Meanwhile, an enterprising son, the eldest, Jefferson Pinckney (1878-1945), at age 27, married Caroline Mosby Montgomery in 1905, and a partnership was in the making. Caroline grew up on a substantial cotton plantation known as *Loughborough*, while Jeff, as he was known, was raised on *Black Bayou*, only seven or eight miles apart, on the fringe of Winterville in the Delta. Cotton farming and its agrarian lifestyle were deeply rooted in both Jeff and "Carrie" and in 1912, they ambitiously purchased approximately 1,000 acres of prime cotton-producing landscape that once was part of *Loughborough*, known as *Clifton Plantation*. Accordingly, Jefferson Pinckney Wilkerson, at age 34, became a Delta planter like his ancestors before him.[10]

According to his obituary, Jefferson Pinckney Wilkerson ran the Peoples Gin Company, a cotton gin manufacturing business, for the better part of 30 years, complementing his extensive cotton plantation operations, mainly farmed by sharecroppers. Sharecropping, which had its greatest surge in the South following the Civil War, was a type of tenant farming with which it was sometimes compared. It was of no advantage to the cropper who, in exchange for the purported privilege of living and working on plantation land, often had to pay the landlord planter rent and expenses – and, they were often excessive - for materials that were on credit with the planter, and anywhere from 50% to 70% of the cotton crops leaving them in ceaseless debt; basically, it was just another form of slavery but this time an economic one. There was little opportunity for the cropper to escape from his indebtedness to the planter or, overall, make something of himself by owning his own piece of land, which he was often promised but rarely

---

[10] John H. Bryan, "Where We Came From," Chicago, The Coventry Group, 2011

achieved when the planter had complete control of his circumstances, and a foot on the scale; the cropper had no protection nor personal leverage with planter ownership, nor justice with the courts that sided with white ownership. Author Lawrence Goldstone, in his book *Inherently Unequal*, stated that it was a string of Supreme Court decisions, the *"chipping away"* he called it, of the 1875 Civil Rights Act, which the Court declared unconstitutional, squelching the Civil Rights Movement and encouraging the development and wholesale advancement of *Jim Crow* laws lasting for decades. *"All you have to do is look at the rise of Jim Crow and the ability of Southern state governments to segregate, to discriminate, to imprison without trial, to beat to death, to lynch – without anyone ever being brought to justice,"* stressed Goldstone.[11]

Former slave Berry Smith of Forest, Mississippi, expounded on what life was like after the war and what expectations the ex-slaves had of acquiring land based on Federal government and white landowners' promises: *"I hear'd a heap o' talk 'Bout ever' Nigger gittin forty acres an' a mule. Dey had us fooled up 'Bout it, but I never seen nobody git nothin,"*

---

[11] Lawrence Goldstone, "Inherently Unequal: The Betrayal of Equal Rights by the Supreme Court, 1865-1903," Walker & Company, January 1, 2011; See also NPR Staff, "The Supreme Court's Failure to Protect Blacks' Rights," NPR, February 24, 2011.
https://www.si.edu/object/siris_sil_949252
https://www.npr.org/2011/02/24/133960082/the-supreme-courts-failure-to-protect-civil-rights

he blurted out in dismay.[12] And Isaac Stier, the former slave of a large plantation in Natchez, Mississippi, expressed himself this way: *"De slaves spected a heap from freedon dey didn' git. Dey was led to b'lieve dey would have a easy time—go places widout passes—an have plenty o' spendin' money. But dey sho' got fooled. Mos' of 'em didn' fin' deyse'ves no better off. Pussonally, I had a harder time after de war dan I did endurin' slav'ry."*[13]

It was laborious work preceding the era of mechanization that required field hands to do the picking and chopping, except in this case of post-war settlement, white land ownership now depended mostly on the hiring of emancipated black laborers, former slaves, who were now wage laborers, and sharecroppers, to do the work; a consequence of the Civil War and its dismantling of the institution of slavery, the reunification of a divided nation and the effortful challenges of the Reconstruction Era that followed. A new system of labor replacing slavery was in order. However, the nation was not prepared for this, neither by whites nor blacks, and it devolved into aberrant behavior, mostly by whites, who were contemptuous of blacks and not welcoming of the changes.

Journalist Whitelaw Reid, who became editor of the *New York Tribune* in 1868 and who later received appointments of ambassadorships to France

---

[12] Born in Slavery: Slave Narratives from the Federal Writers' Project, 1936-1938, Library of Congress; Digital Collections, 1941.
https://www.loc.gov/collections/slave-narratives-from-the-federal-writers-project-1936-to-1938/about-this-collection/
[13] IBID.

and Great Britain, ventured throughout the "Rebel States" of the Deep South in 1865 -1866 to examine their condition and evaluate effects from the Civil War. His focus was on the cotton plantations of the Mississippi Valley and *"The character of the average plantation negro"*[14]

"With the downfall of the rebellion, there came a change. He would be blind and deaf, who, after a day's stay anywhere in the interior of Mississippi, failed to discern aright the drift of public opinion toward the negro. The boasted confidence in the slave and the generous friendship for the helpless freedman were all gone…the prevailing sentiment with which the negro was regarded as one of blind, baffled, revengeful hatred."[15] Reid found this disposition pervasive throughout the South, having examined Tennessee, Georgia, Alabama, and Louisiana; *"But it was in Mississippi that I found its fullest and freest expression. However, these men may have regarded the negro slave; they hated the negro freeman. However kind they may have been to negro property, they were virulently vindictive against a property that escaped from their control."*[16]

The idea of blacks being on a path of parity with whites was anathema to the latter, who felt that "freedom" had its limitations, according to post-Civil War Mississippi Governor Benjamin G. Humphreys in his November

---

[14] Whitelaw Reid, "After the War: A Southern Tour, May 1, 1865-May 1, 1866," Publishers Moore, Wilstach & Baldwin, p. Preface
https://gutenberg.org/cache/epub/55381/pg55381-images.html
[15] IBID., p. 417-418
[16] IBID.

1865 address to the Mississippi Legislature and Senate. *"The negro is free, whether we like it or not; we must realize that fact now and forever. To be free, however, does not make him a citizen or entitle him to political or social equality with the white man,"* railed Humphreys.[17]

Humphreys made clear the idea of requiring a rigid social caste system, or stratification, between Southern whites and blacks as a consequence of the fallout from the war and not violate the "sanctity" of the races; he was concerned with the mixing of races on a singular level, insisting that blacks should respect their place in society, which was a much lower class, or peasantry. *"And that place – literally – was the cotton field of the South,"* according to historian David Oshinsky.[18]

White Southerners viewed blacks as inferior in every way and held deep resentment toward them after the war viewing them as instruments of the Union and the conflict: *"The white Southerner insisted that slavery, however bad it may have been for the white man, had offered nothing but good to the Negroes,"* wrote Claude H. Nolen in his book *The Negro's*

---

[17] Mississippi, "Message of Gov. Humphreys to the Legislature on Negro Troops – He Holds that the Courts Should be Open to the Negro – His Views of the Freedman's Bureau," The New York Times, Sunday December 3, 1865, p. 3.
https://www.newspapers.com/image/20651603/
[18] David M. Oshinsky, "Worse Than Slavery: Parchman Farm and the Ordeal of Jim Crow Justice," Simon & Schuster, New York, 1996, p. 17; Dan T. Carter, "When the War Was Over: The Failure of Self-Reconstruction in the South, 1865-1867," Baton Rouge: Louisiana State University Press, 1985, p.20

Image in the South.[19] Historian Rayford W. Logan expressed a view that *"So determined were most white Southerners to maintain their own way of life, that they resorted to fraud, intimidation, and murder, in order to re-establish their own control of the state governments,"* adding that *"Basically, however, the new civil war within the Southern states stemmed from an adamant determination to restore white supremacy."*[20]

Following the January 31, 1865, congressional approval of an embattled 13th Amendment to the U. S. Constitution, permanently abolishing the institution of slavery, which was not ratified by the majority of states until December 1865, four million blacks - nearly a third of the population of the South - were freed from slavery by the conclusion of the war. Mississippi, however, did not ratify the amendment until 130 years later, in 1995, but through oversight, negligence, or possibly intentional, failed to make it official. Astonishingly, it wasn't until February 2013 – nearly 150 years after the passage of the 13th Amendment – when Mississippi's Secretary of

---

[19] Claude H. Nolen, "The Negro's Image in the South: The Anatomy of White Supremacy," University of Kentucky Press, 1968, p. 19.
https://www.google.com/books/edition/The_Negro_s_Image_in_the_South/jMQfBgAAQBAJ?hl=en&gbpv=1&pg=PR3&printsec=frontcover

[20] Rayford W. Logan, The Betrayal of the Negro, from Rutherford B. Hayes to Woodrow Wilson, Collier Books, NY; Collier-Macmillan Ltd., New York, April 15, 1965, p. 21.
https://archive.org/details/betrayalofnegrof0000loga

State finally forwarded their 1995 resolution to the Federal Register that it was made official.[21]

In spite of the efforts of the freedmen and, particularly, former slaves to adapt to the idea of freedom and the mobility bestowed to them by the 13th Amendment, many of them struggled with feelings of insecurity of where, or even whether, to go much less how to achieve that. Independence was unlikely; they lacked assets, income, or even a place to live. In the much-celebrated *Slave Narrative Project* of the 1930s undertaken by the Federal government in association with the *Federal Writers' Project,* containing first-person accounts of former slaves, a large percentage of those interviewed favored remaining with their "Marster," or "Marse," as the term was uniformly expressed among the slaves. An official account of the study disclosed that approximately 40 percent alleged moving from their plantations, many of them during the war. *"But most remained where they were, living as tenants or field hands on the same land they had worked all*

---

[21] History Resources, "Ratifying the Thirteenth Amendment, 1866," The Gilder Lehrman Institute of American History; "History: 13th Amendment," History.com Editors, Amanda Onion, Missy Sullivan and Matt Mullen, Jun 9, 2020; Stephanie Condon, "After 148 years, Mississippi finally ratifies 13th Amendment, which banned slavery," CBS News, February 18, 2013. Mississippi voted against ratification in December, 1865, along with Kentucky, New Jersey and Delaware, refusing to endorse the 13th Amendment. The state of Mississippi did not get behind the amendment until 1995, but inexplicably failed to make it official by notifying the U. S. Archivist until February 2013, when it was finally ratified.
https://www.history.com/topics/black-history/thirteenth-amendment

https://www.cbsnews.com/news/after-148-years-mississippi-finally-ratifies-13th-amendment-which-banned-slavery/

along," which was a return to servitude.[22] Some left in high spirits, feeling it was a necessary, if not sensible, thing to do, having been handed their freedom, and traveled to nearby farms to work, but in their eventual confusion to do what they felt was right for themselves and family they soon returned to the plantations where they were the most comfortable and perceived themselves secure. It was, without doubt, a period of great turmoil and disorientation for them.

Ex-slave Charlie Davenport, approaching 100 at the time of his interview, who worked on the Fish Pond Plantation in Natchez, Mississippi, stated that he personally witnessed Abe Lincoln, a visitor to Natchez, declare, *"You don't have to chop cotton no more. You can th'ow dat hoe down an' go fishin' whenever de notion strikes you."* But it was no more than an exaggeration, a false prophecy, implied Davenport. *"I was fool 'nough to b'lieve all dat kin' o' stuff. But to tell de hones' truf, mos' o' us didn' know ourse'fs no better off. Freedom meant us could leave where us'd been born an' bred, but it meant, too, dat us had to scratch for us ownse'fs. Dem what lef' de old plantation seemed so all fired glad to git back dat I made up my min' to stay put. I stayed with my white folks as long as I could."* Another ex-slave, James Lucas. also of Natchez, who worked for "Marster" Jefferson Davis "hisse'f", later President Jefferson Davis of the Confederate States, offered a similar point of view: *"Slaves didn' know*

---

[22] David M. Oshinsky, "Worse Than Slavery: Parchman Farm and the Ordeal of Jim Crow Justice," p. 157

what to 'spec from freedom, but a lot of 'em hoped dey would be fed an' kep' by de gov'ment. Dey all had diffe'nt way o' thinkin' 'bout it. Mos'ly though dey was jus' lak me, dey didn' know jus' zackly what it meant…Folks dat ain' never been free don' rightly know de feel of bein' free," he exclaimed.[23]

It didn't take long, however, for established white Southerners, led by obstreperous white landowners, to put up fierce resistance after the 13th Amendment's passage. Historian Drew Gilpin Faust, in an *American Experience* 2004 interview, cited a statement made by a post-war Virginian, Mary Lee, who viewed Reconstruction with mixed results: *"Political reconstruction is inevitable now, but social reconstruction, we have in our hands and we can prevent,"* interpreted by Faust as despite what Congress will do, there will be an endeavor by white Southerners, in numerous different ways, of introducing guerilla warfare against the domestic citizen in an effort to obstruct societal change.[24]

President Andrew Johnson, successor to Lincoln following Lincoln's assassination, of necessity, not forbearance that he may have preferred, assumed control of the Reconstruction initiative following the war; he was

---

[23] Born in Slavery: Slave Narratives, 1941
[24] Drew Gilpin Faust, "Reconstruction: The Second Civil War; White Southern Responses to Black Emancipation," American Experience, PBS, WGBH, 2004 interviews.
https://www.pbs.org/wgbh/americanexperience/features/reconstruction-white-southern-responses-black-emancipation/

https://americanarchive.org/special_collections/reconstruction-interviews

an advocate of states' rights, including voting laws and the individual Southern states took full advantage, with Johnson showing a blind eye. In October, six months following the Civil War, elections were held, giving rise to former Confederates, including former General Benjamin Humphreys, who, along with his Johnny Reb loyalists, was elected Mississippi governor. In late 1865, on the heels of Governor Humphreys' memorable "Negro problem" speech to his legislature, Mississippi's white legislators took the lead, immediately instituting what was known as *"Mississippi Black Codes."* These were strict, well-defined local and state laws designed to regulate black behavior and were soon after adopted by South Carolina and other Deep South states. They were primarily an initiative to control untoward social manifestations, defined by whites and the black labor force, that was akin to a system of slavery.

It was also a signal for hastening reinforcement and expansion of the *Jim Crow Laws,* which had their beginnings right after the passage of the 13th Amendment. *Jim Crow,* an instrument of white supremacy, remained officially in force for nearly 100 years until 1964, when the *Civil Rights Act* was passed; this was followed by the *Voting Rights Act* in 1965, preventing employment discrimination and affording minority rights to vote.[25] There were many limits imposed by both the *Black Codes* and their sister *Jim Crow laws,* skillfully contrived and all designed in different ways to exploit

---

[25] Legal Highlight: The Civil Rights Act of 1964, Office of the Assistant Secretary for Administration & Management, 200 Constitution Avenue, Washington, D.C.

black labor and the civil rights of former slaves by keeping them confined by state law and regulations to their previous plantations and masters.[26] Such things as the *"Right to arms," "Access to the legal system," "Marriage between races," "Property rights,"* and the all-powerful *"Vagrancy and enticement laws,"* the latter serving to restore ex-slaves to their previous plantations, were all affected by these exploitative, oppressive and very stringent laws.

White Southern legislators earnestly, if not hastily, sought to contrive and construct these new constitutional laws under the direction of new state legislatures, limiting former slaves of their earned freedom. It was a mighty effort to crush any rights conferred to blacks by Northern zealotry, as Southerners saw it, and their "unacceptable" mandates, leading to Reconstruction. In spite of the passage of the 13th amendment, *"The white legislators saw little reason not to continue the tradition of unequal treatment of black persons,"* adding, *"There is such a radical difference in the mental and moral [nature] of the white and black race, that it would be impossible to secure order in a mixed community by the same [law]."* [27] Post-war opposition to Northern control was viewed variously between moderates and Southern purists. However, one thing was clear: deeply

---

[26] Peder Punsalan-Tiegen, P. (2021, May 10). "Mississippi Black Codes, 1865-1866," BlackPast.org; History.com Editors, "Black Codes," Jan 26, 2022; https://www.blackpast.org/african-american-history/events-african-american-history/mississippi-black-codes-1865-1866/

[27] Constitutional Rights Foundation, member of Civics Renewal Network, "The Southern "Black Codes" of 1865-66," Los Angeles, CA. https://www.crf-usa.org/brown-v-board-50th-anniversary/southern-black-codes.html

entrenched in the hearts and minds of Southern whites was a shared feeling of preserving the separateness of races.

Restoring social order was paramount in the eyes of the intransigent white Southerner, and he sought ways, mostly nefarious, to reestablish that. When Federal troops were removed from their post-war watch of the Southern states in 1877, white supremacists exercised their power over the South, along with the resumption of KKK activity, maintaining a body of terrorism and intimidation while the North wrestled with the distraction of financial panic and of the depression of 1873.[28] Eric Foner, a prominent historian of American History, DeWitt Clinton Professor Emeritus of History at Columbia University, and Pulitzer Prize recipient for History personifies the Klan as a rogue group claiming to *"Restore order in what they consider as chaos caused by blacks."* He went on to say the Klan was a *"Homegrown American terrorism"* faction that Southern whites treated with a certain amount of ambivalence. *"Many whites do not approve of this kind of violence, but they will make excuses for it."*[29]

---

[28] Ulysses S. Grant, Article, "Grant, Reconstruction and the KKK," From the Collection: The Presidents, American Experience, 1996-2023 WGBH Educational Foundation.
https://www.pbs.org/wgbh/americanexperience/features/grant-kkk/

[29] Eric Foner, "Reconstruction: The Second Civil War; White Southern Responses to Black Emancipation," American Experience, PBS, WGBH, 2004 interviews.
https://www.pbs.org/wgbh/americanexperience/features/reconstruction-white-southern-responses-black-emancipation/

Professor James C. Cobb, author of the historic work *The Most Southern Place on Earth,* summed it up this way: *"Many of the white 'Insiders' who wrote critically and perceptively about the problem of the Delta struggled on almost a daily basis to reconcile their abhorrence of the racism, poverty, and inequity that pervaded their region with their affinity for its physical appeal, human charm, and the comfortable and intellectually uncomplicated lifestyle it offered them."*[30]

It was always an incremental process; as soon as one state law or code was threatened, they came up with another in a constant revolving effort to maintain white supremacy by overt attempts at suppression of black labor and personal rights that lingered well into the 20th century. As one historian expressed by virtue of the 1964 Civil Rights and 1965 Voting Rights Acts, *"Jim Crow laws were technically off the books, though that has not always guaranteed full integration or adherence to anti-racism laws throughout the United States."*[31]

In 1904, Mississippi Governor James K. Vardaman, known to his followers as the *"White Chief,"* a *"Fire-eater by instinct"* with a swagger in his step, was a left-wing Southern zealot and racist. Shortly after his gubernatorial election, Vardaman began a relentless campaign against the

---

[30] . James C. Cobb, The Most Southern Place on Earth: The Mississippi Delta and the Roots of Regional Identity, Oxford University Press, New York, NY, 1992, p. 322.
[31] Jim Crow Laws, History, The Arena Group, original Feb 28, 2018; updated Jan 11, 2023
https://www.history.com/topics/early-20th-century-us/jim-crow-laws#when-did-jim-crow-laws-end

Southern Negro, calling him an idler and vagrant, incapable of being educated in a civilian manner. This argument conformed with the Black Codes of 1865 and was a latent goal of Vardaman's. It was a waste of money to educate them, he charged, arguing vehemently, often with fists raised and ample body quivering with rage, that *"Black was not White,"* and it should be remembered in that manner. He was applauded by many of the Southern journalists who lauded him for his alleged familiarity with Southern blacks, *"Thoroughly and intimately,"* whom he regarded with unwavering contempt because he had also worked on the plantations and in the cotton fields, purporting that he knew of their unscrupulous character. *"The white man will not and should not share sovereignty and dominion with him,"* vented Vardaman. In his numerous years in-and-out of public office, including governor and senator, he set a tone of racial hatred that deeply sowed the seeds of intolerance of Southern blacks for decades to come.[32]

"[Southerners] have all kinds of ways of drawing lines and resisting the egalitarian impulses of freedom…in every way they can imagine, to change in their society," expressed Drew Gilpin Faust in her 2004 *American Experience* interview.[33] They viewed the 13th Amendment as nothing but an innocuous obstacle, a trivial declaration to be dismissed, but nary a deterrent

---

[32] Emerson Hough, Vardaman of Mississippi, The Columbus Weekly Dispatch, June 1, 1905, p. 5
https://www.newspapers.com/image/465081654/?terms=James%20Vardaman

[33] Drew Gilpin Faust, Reconstruction: The Second Civil War

in their effort to maintain their superiority and elitist leisurely ways over the Southern freedman and former slave.

A personification of such a jaundiced view was expressed by Mississippi governor Theodore Bilbo, a steadfast proponent of racial segregation, who was once asked by Chicago Mayor William Hale "Big Bill" Thompson by telegram to take some of Mississippi's Negroes *"Back home."* Bilbo's response was astonishing: *"If these Negroes have been contaminated with northern social and political dreams of equality, we cannot use them, nor do we want them. The Negro who understands his proper relation to the white man in this country will be gladly received by the people of Mississippi, as we are very much in need of labor."*[34] He much preferred that his state bear hardship than yield to anyone supportive of the Negro. Bilbo had a long and dire tenure in Mississippi's political network, from 1908 to 1947, twice serving as governor and as U. S. Senator; he was a staunch believer in white supremacy, a stalwart member of the Ku Klux Klan, and he had the dubious honor of successfully and very effectively planting the seeds of hate for the blacks of Mississippi, inculcating in them an atmosphere of fear and trepidation; he advocated by *"Any means necessary,"* emphasizing violence, as an instantaneous way to suppress the black vote.[35] On the abrasive matter of southern voting rights, which was

---

[34] David M. Oshinsky, "Worse Than Slavery:" p. 163
[35] Zachary L Wakefield, "The Skeleton in America's Own Cupboard: Mississippi's Theodore G. Bilbo, and the Shaping of Racial Politics, 1946-1948," Dissertation for Doctor of Philosophy to Graduate Faculty of Auburn University, May 8, 2017, p. 149.

his subversive bellwether initiative, Bilbo was manifestly antagonistic, declaring as much in his 1946 run for U. S. Senator. *"For southerners like Bilbo,"* wrote Zachary L. Wakefield in his Doctor of Philosophy thesis, *"The prospect of even allowing one African American to vote posed a dire threat to long-standing traditions of white masculinity and racial superiority."*[36]

In 1954, the U. S. Supreme Court's landmark decision, *Brown v. Board of Education of Topeka*, a unanimous resolution, ruled that racial segregation of public schools was unconstitutional. It was a monumental decision, for it declared the dissolution of the infamous U. S. Supreme Court *Plessy v. Ferguson decision of 1896,* which ruled that *"Separate but Equal"* facilities were constitutional, upholding racial segregation of public facilities such as schools, hotels, theaters, trains, and buses. It wasn't until the following year that the Court took further action on the implementation of their *Brown* decision, known as *Brown II,* by delegating to the local circuit courts the task of desegregating schools "with all deliberate speed."[37] It was an obscure if perhaps enigmatic order, open to interpretation, and perceived by recalcitrant Southern whites as a perfect opportunity to obviate any need to take action, enabled by the Court's neglect, of dismantling their

---

https://etd.auburn.edu/bitstream/handle/10415/5720/Wakefield%20Dissertation%20Submission%202.pdf?sequence=2&isAllowed=n
[36] IBID, p. Introduction
[37] Brown v. Board of Education, Wikipedia, Educational Segregation in the U. S. prior to Brown.
https://en.wikipedia.org/wiki/Brown_v._Board_of_Education

schools. It was also a fortuitous moment for them to pounce into action of their own, and they did, concocting subversionary tactics of intimidation, including ruthless life-threatening vigilantism over blacks, led by the notorious white terrorist group, the Ku Klux Klan. Their membership was mixed with notable public figures like judgeships, chief of police, city lawyers, and heads of public safety among them. *"A third wave [of KKK] arose in the South during the Civil Rights era of the 1950s and '60s. New members, along with some 1920s Kluxers, fought school desegregation and the movement to give blacks equal rights."*[38]

Opposition to *Brown* remained intense in the South well into the 1960s in spite of the Supreme Court decision. There was intense defiance exhibited by numerous Southern political figures, literally within minutes of the Court's decision. Mississippi's James Eastland, a prominent Mississippi Senator, declared that the South would not comport with such a decision. Senator Harry Byrd of Virginia, a powerful force in the U. S. Senate, made the case for *"Massive Resistance,"* arguing fervently that *"If we can organize the Southern States for massive resistance to this order, I think that, in time, the rest of the country will realize that racial integration is not going to be accepted in the South."*[39]

---

[38] Tara McAndrew, The History of the KKK in American Politics, JSTOR Daily, Politics & History, January 25, 2017.
https://daily.jstor.org/history-kkk-american-politics/
[39] LDF: Legal Defense Fund, "The Case That Changed America: Brown V. Board of Education," Washington, D.C., quoting Harry Byrd, 1954.

In spite of *Brown I and II,* very little was being done by the Southern states to implement suitable plans for school integration "to ensure racial balance" in accordance with the Court's 1954 decision. New Kent County, Virginia, was sued for choosing "freedom-of-choice" plans - undermining the court's repudiation of *"Separate but Equal"* - that did not meet the Court's standards outlined in *Brown.* In 1968, in *Green v. School Board of New Kent County*, the Supreme Court took ameliorative steps of putting teeth into the dismantling of segregated schools, *"Root and branch,"* they announced, improving the desired pace for change. This was followed by the Supreme Court's 1971 decision of *Swann v. Charlotte-Mecklenburg Board of Education* that instituted school busing – or *"Forced busing"* as was familiarly known in most cities - of city schools manifesting violent reactions and vigorous resistance to this change. Significant - some violent - uprisings of resistance took place in many of the major cities, none more prominent than in Boston during the busing of the 1970s, especially the neighborhood of South Boston fervently known as *"Southie,"* which was a bastion of blue-collar mostly working-class Irish-Americans, who passionately resisted a culture-mix with Roxbury and Dorchester blacks. The contumacy of these white ethnics was never so paramount than in the display of their revolt manifest against the government's busing order that demonstrated the level of racism in the North.

---

https://www.naacpldf.org/brown-vs-board/southern-manifesto-massive-resistance-brown/#:~:text=Board%20of%20Education%20in%20the,decision%20by%20a%20political%20body."

Jim Crow laws of the South were essentially at an end come 1968. However, segregation efforts were intact and rigorously maintained in some Southern states approaching the 1970s, including Mississippi, largely led by Citizens' Councils, which fought fiercely against the enforcement of school integration. However, it was of a different form in 1964 following the passage of the *Civil Rights Act* in that year. Of the various Citizens' Councils that were formed countrywide, *"Its most permanent impact was in Mississippi,"* according to historian and author Stephanie R. Rolph, Ph.D. and associate professor at Millsaps College, Jackson, Mississippi. In a biography, characterizing Rolph on the essence of her studies on Civil Rights and the Citizens' Council, *"Her work places the Council within a wider network of white supremacy and conservatism that was not unique to the American South,"* as reported by *Women Also Know History* in their Scholar Profile of Professor Rolph.[40]

Council proponent and the Council's developer, Robert *"Tut"* Patterson, fretted that desegregation's impact vastly favored blacks, who significantly outnumbered white citizens of most Mississippi communities that would be cause for the dismantling of segregation in Mississippi's

---

[40]Stephanie R. Rolph, Mississippi History Now: The Citizens' Council, Mississippi Department of Archives & History, Mississippi Historical Society, 2023, article adapted from Stephanie Rolph first book, Resisting Equality: The Citizens' Council, 1954-1989, Louisiana State University Press, 2018. Also, Women Also Know History, Participant Info of Stephanie Rolph, PhD Millsaps College, Jackson, MS.
https://mshistorynow.mdah.ms.gov/issue/the-citizens-council

https://womenalsoknowhistory.com/individual-scholar-page/?pdb=269

public schools. It was a situation he could not - would not - tolerate, and he quickly coalesced local businesses, law enforcement, and elected officials who shared his views to defend their position of maintaining racial separation in a so-called *"Non-violent"* manner against civil rights initiatives that would upset the balance of segregated communities, and of the South, he claimed. He organized the Council into a finely-tuned opposition force to *"Stand together forever firm against communism and mongrelization."*[41] For a considerable while, they were effective in intimidating local businesses economically and black civil rights leaders, under threats of violence, to shut down their vigorous activities. The 1964 *Civil Rights Act*, however, signed by President Lyndon Johnson, was a disruption for them but far from a deterrent. They quickly shifted to the development and implementation of private schools as a means to maintaining segregation by opening a private academy in 1964 for whites-only in Jackson, and others were soon to follow. The lasting effects of the Citizens' Council's measures that were chosen to preserve segregation, especially in Mississippi, are paramount. According to Professor Rolph, the Citizens' Councils' *"Contribution to a new form of segregation through private school support remains a visible component of Mississippi's educational system"* today.[42] They left an indispensable mark on the social and cultural makeup of the state accomplishing, following a somewhat

---

[41] James C. Cobb, The Most Southern Place on Earth, p. 213
[42] Stephanie Rolph, Mississippi History Now: The Citizens' Council.

different road map than what they had originally set out to do - the result, ultimately, being the same - and that was segregation.

Hodding Carter, Pulitzer Prize winner and editor of Greenville, Mississippi's *Delta Democrat-Times* daily newspaper, voiced opposition in 1948 to Northern journalism for their vigorous one-sided attacks on the South, citing bad behavior and their open intolerance of blacks. Carter insisted on a need for balanced opinions pointing out some progress that was being made by the South toward racist behavior, but there was one bias remaining that stood out; he said: *"The Southern white is increasingly overcoming all but one of the emotional biases inherited from 250 mutually blighting years of a master and slave relationship. The one: the white South's insistence upon segregation in the mass."* [43] This stubborn intransigence was no less true in the 1960s than it was in 1948 and even found its way into the 21st century in various forms and forums. Following the Supreme Court's stirring *Brown* decision, Hodding Carter expressed some resistance of his own in responding to Northern impatience of the South's inertness to change. *"No one should expect that a decision of a Supreme Court can soon or conclusively change a whole people's thinking. That must be understood,"* insisted Carter.[44] Pulitzer Prize author and journalist Harry S. Ashmore expressed himself with even greater candor

---

[43] The Press: Jim Crow's Other Side, Time, the Weekly Newsmagazine, New York, NY, Sept 06, 1948, I Vol. 52, No. 10.
[44] Ann Waldron, Hodding Carter: The Reconstruction of a Racist, Algonquin Books of Chapel Hill, 1993, p. 260

about white Southern resistance to change when he declared, *"Southerners will generally treat you politely until they make up their minds to kill you."* [45]

Looking back, the post-Civil War era, from its very closure and ranging into the 20th century, proved immensely frustrating for both the freedman and plantation owner, but in quite different ways: merely that the former slave was in need of a job, and domicile, while the planter was desperate for laborers to harvest their cotton fields, so the idea of a mutual system of sharecropping took hold; but it was anything but mutual, favoring planters, who hoarded the profits of black labor. It was a nefarious system. There was a long-held mythical belief by Southern whites, racially motivated quite by arrangement, that only blacks were capable of growing cotton, and except for a roof over their heads, they expected little in return. As posited in an early 20th century Mississippi agricultural newspaper on the advantages of negro tenant farmers in comparison to the high cost of white northern farm work, suggesting *"They literally believe that 'sufficient unto the day is the evil thereof,' and they do not expect more than a living, and apparently are happy in the thought that they are sure enough to eat and a place to sleep."* Further to that, *"It is also a fact that the climate in which cotton grows most successfully is peculiarly adapted to the African race."* In other words, it is far better for you than for me to be laboring under the hot sun in open fields.

---

[45] Harry S. Ashmore, quoted in Hodding Carter: The Reconstruction of a Racist, Algonquin Books of Chapel Hill, 1993, p. 260.

"Under such conditions, with plenty of negroes to perform this labor, it seems fitting that such work be assigned to them."[46] Remarkably, this hypothesis was perpetuated for a great many years following Reconstruction. As long as there were no mechanical means to harvest cotton, planters depended almost entirely on black manual labor.

Professor James C. Cobb, historian, and author of the historic work *The Most Southern Place on Earth*, pointed out something uniquely different about the Delta's "New South" postbellum elitist planter apart from the forebears of the antebellum period, manifest at the turn of the 20th century. The *"New"* planter was savvier about the economics required of the cotton industry, of profit and loss measures, and well-informed about the type of management style to make their plantations a success. And they were shrewder about what to do with the black freedman to maintain their advantage and, above all, their white superiority. Sharecropping took on a new look of social and legal definitions, enabling the planters to better control their black laborers. Inherent in that was a new social order, *"With a comprehensive and rigidly enforced system of caste further guaranteeing their dominance…reminiscent of the Old South while adhering to an economic philosophy rooted firmly in the New."*[47]

---

[46] J. F. Merry, Mississippi Valley Cotton Lands, Southern Farm Gazette, Starkville MS, Jan 1, 1903, p. 2
https://www.newspapers.com/image/856049764/?terms=mississippi%20valley%20cotton%20lands&match=1

[47] James C. Cobb, "The Most Southern Place on Earth: The Mississippi Delta and the Roots of Regional Identity," Preface, p. ix.

Some of the smaller cotton farms along the southwestern border of the Mississippi River had remained in Wilkerson family hands for generations. *Longwood* area land, however, also in the southwest region of the Delta and in the vicinity of Wilkerson properties - soon to be known as the *Longwood Plantation* - was under new ownership that remained in operation into the mid-20th century. It was here that the subject of this disquisition, the George Scott family, who labored arduously as subordinate farm laborers, would eventually locate themselves, under wretched working and living conditions, on this vastly flat and richly fertile property. George Senior's goal was to leverage his hard work into his own land ownership, but it turned chimerical; planters of the 1930s-40s held fast to control their land, except where the Great Depression of that period eventually played a part in damaging any remaining prosperity they had, and soon planters were selling off to the highest bidder. Cotton prices were seriously impacted, and international markets collapsed.

Backcountry pioneer, land magnate, and planter Benjamin *"Ben"* Smith, one of Washington County's earliest settlers, much like the trailblazers the Wilkerson's with roots in Kentucky, was known for his extensive land holdings in the Delta. He started buying up this land on or about 1829, receiving some of his land that was deeded to him by Peter

Wilkerson circa 1835.[48] For the next 11 years, he purchased over 2,256 acres[49] of highly arable public lands from the federal government in the *Longwood* area, ranging just south of the small rural unincorporated village of Avon, 8 miles north of oxbow-shaped Lake Washington, and 21 miles north of the town of Rolling Fork, the county seat of Sharkey County.[50] Earliest known records point to the town of Anguilla of Sharkey County as George Scott Sr's birthplace.[51]

Smith was among a fortunate number of Southern planters who benefitted from President Andrew Jackson's land seizures of Native American property – amounting to millions of southern acres – emerging as a member of a vaunted ruling class, among a coterie of prominent planters;

---

[48] William D. McCain & Charlotte Capers, editors, "Memoirs of Henry Tillinghast Ireys," Mississippi Department of Archives and History and Mississippi Historical Society, 1954, Chapter 9, p. 346
https://www.lthome.com/genealogy/documents/Memoirs%20of%20Henry%20Tillinghast%20Ireys.php
[49] Bureau of Land Management, General Land Office Records, Benjamin Smith land patents 1831- 1840, Choctaw Meridian, Mississippi, Townships 14-16, Washington County
https://glorecords.blm.gov/results/default.aspx?searchCriteria=type=patent|st=MS|cty=151|ln=Smith|fn=Benjamin|twp_nr=15|twp_dir=N|rng_nr=9|rng_dir=W|sp=true|sw=true|sadv=false
[50] William D. McCain & Charlotte Capers, editors, Memoirs of Henry Tillinghast Ireys, Washington County Historical Society, Jackson, MS, p. 350; Avon Plantation, located just above Longwood Plantation, was under the ownership of the Johnson family, Henry and Edward.
https://www.lthome.com/genealogy/documents/Memoirs%20of%20Henry%20Tillinghast%20Ireys.php
[51] George Scott Sr. Draft Card, Local Board No. 2, Washington County, Feb 16, 1942

Jackson was the protagonist for this; as with his emergence to power so did the planters, such as Smith, acquire a measure of power.

Once described in 1940 by a *Delta Democrat-Times* reporter as *"The hamlet of Longwood,"* it was mostly of flat contour, bordered by stretches of tree stands, and consisting of fertile soil highly suitable for cotton farming.[52] The *Longwood* acreage, only a short distance from the Mississippi River approaching *Longwood Landing*, was to be used almost exclusively for cotton production, and it was managed exploitatively, much like a feudal system, in a manner ascribed by several historians as economic slavery. Smith's extensive land ownership was in contiguous townships but mostly a part of Washington County. [53] But there were other properties he owned besides *Longwood*: two plantations in Claiborne County, Mississippi, situated in the vicinity of Port Gibson, the seat of Claiborne County. He called them *Ever-May*, consisting of 1600 acres "with all the slaves thereon," and *My Mundle Place*, with thirty slaves. Another plantation "in the vicinity thereof" of *Longwood* he called *Hill Place* comprising 140 acres and several slaves. He owned another plantation in

---

[52] Charles S. Kerg, "County's Worst Storm in Decade Hits Early Today," The Delta Democrat Times, November 11, 1940, p. 1.
https://www.newspapers.com/image/20874195/?terms=delta%20democrat%20times&match=1

[53] Bureau of Land Management, General Land Office Records, Benjamin Smith land patents 1831- 1840, Choctaw Meridian, Mississippi, Townships 14-16, Washington County

Washington County he titled *My Black Place*, with 640 acres and 24 slaves "capable of field service," according to Smith's will.[54]

Hugh Sidey of *Time Magazine* commends James C. Cobb of the University of Tennessee, previous to Cobb's 1992 monumental work *"The Most Southern Place on Earth,"* as an eminent scholar of Delta culture. *"He summarizes the melancholy story of the area as 'a scary and fascinating pursuit of the American Dream,'* quotes Sidey, *"by a small group of bright, tough people who, unrestrained by conscience or government, ruthlessly exploited other people and resources even as they cloaked themselves in courtliness,"* admonishes Sidey. It was a near perfect characterization of the Southern planter. It could have been interpreted in multifarious ways as the embodiment of accomplished, self-righteous Southern whites of the Deep South.[55]

Mississippi planters of the Delta were enormously successful business men of affluence, described in the aggregate by Washington County

---

[54] Benjamin "Ben" Smith, Will, July 24, 1846, Ancestry.com, Mississippi, U. S. Wills & Probate, 1780-1982 & Kentucky, U. S. Wills & Probate Records, 1774-1989. https://www.ancestry.com/discoveryui-content/view/3965879:8995?_phsrc=NdM1&_phstart=successSource&gsfn=Benjamin&gsln=Smith&ml_rpos=1&queryId=68b9651fd4b5827b812a7914b1c2a18f
https://www.ancestry.com/search/?name=benjamin_smith&event=1846_louisville-jefferson-kentucky
usa_32672&birth=1785&child=frances_smith&residence=1845_louisville-jefferson-kentucky-usa_32672&spouse=irene_smith

[55] Hugh Sidey, "Hugh Sidey's America: Sad Song of the Delta," Time, the Weekly Newsmagazine, New York, NY, June 24, 1991, Vol. 137, No. 25, pg 18
https://time.com/vault/issue/1991-06-24/page/22/

historian and planter Henry T. Ireys (1837-1923), founder of the Washington County Historical Society, as *"They all, in time, became millionaires."* [56] Traveling North as they often did between May and October, with family and an entourage of slaves in tow, planters were looked upon as royalty; *"the 'pregnant hinges of the knee' were bent to them everywhere,"* wrote Ireys.[57]

They lived opulently in magnificent plantation homes of the Antebellum South; among the many charming and sublime manifestations of these plantations, they were built for entertaining, which was done often, including ornate dinners, elegant parties, and balls, performed in a customary style of unparalleled Southern elite lavishness and splendor. On display in this *"cultured state of society,"* exclaimed H. T. Ireys in his extensive memoirs of Washington County, *"Mrs. Ben Smith of Longwood Plantation had what was considered in that day one of the finest and most costly collections of statuary in the United States."*[58] The Smiths' daughter Fanny was an engaging and delightful young woman, magnetic and quite popular with the young men of the day, and brimming with Southern charm; she was *"A beautiful heiress,"* as described by historian and author Kathleen Jennings. Two steamboats were named for her: the *Fanny Smith*

---

[56] William D. McCain & Charlotte Capers, editors, "Memoirs of Henry Tillinghast Ireys," p. 350
https://www.lthome.com/genealogy/documents/Memoirs%20of%20Henry%20Tillinghast%20Ireys.php
[57] IBID, p. 351
[58] IBID, p. 352

and *Fanny Bullitt,* who traveled the Mississippi River route to Louisville, Kentucky, convenient to the Smith family with major holdings there. [59]Highly educated in the country's finest institutions, planter class children of wealth enjoyed privilege and advantages that the average young person of the South did not; male offspring attended such esteemed universities as Harvard, Yale, and William & Mary while the young women were sent to genteel "finishing" schools, less academic, but more for refinement of their social skills, deportment and matters of decorum. Its culture was agriculturally based, dependent on large numbers of slaves supporting their plantation infrastructure. With over 2,256 acres of alluvial plain farm property, *Longwood* was considered a large plantation. It is estimated that Ben Smith and his successors may have averaged anywhere from 100 to 150 slaves to manage it; with the advent of Reconstruction, they became known as laborers, tenant farmers, and sharecroppers instead of slaves.[60]

---

[59] Kathleen Jennings, Louisville's First Families: A Series of Genealogical Sketches, The Standard Printing Company, Publishers, Louisville, KY, May 1920, p. 29; see also, Henry Tillinghast Ireys: Papers of the Washington County Historical Society, 1910 -1915, Jackson, Mississippi, 1954, Chapter 9, pg. 354.
https://archive.org/details/louisvillesfirst00jenn/page/n8/mode/1up
https://www.lthome.com/genealogy/documents/12%20Chapter%20nine%20-%20Some%20Washington%20County%20genealogy.pdf

[60] National Humanities Center Toolbox Library: Primary Resources in U. S. History & Literature, "The Making of African American Identity: Vol. I, 1500-1865" Enslavement, Plantation; acceptable estimations of the amount of plantation laborers required to service a large-sized cotton farm ranged between 100-500
https://nationalhumanitiescenter.org/pds/maai/enslavement/text3/text3read.htm

The *Longwood Plantation* and Ben Smith's assorted other Delta plantations, of at least another 2,380 acres, were passed down to his wife and daughter, Irene (Williams) Smith and Frances Elizabeth "Fanny" Smith, and eventually their successors, upon Ben Smith's death in August 1846. The properties remained in the family for over 70 years until the early 20th century.[61] Ben Smith's widow, Irene, survived him for 27 years until she passed from *"Cancer of the womb"* in 1873. Their daughter Frances Elizabeth "Fanny" (Smith) Bullitt, who married Alexander C. Bullitt in 1851, died at *Longwood* of typhoid fever in 1855, in her 34th year. She was an only child. Thereafter, in the absence of any direct lineal descendants of Benjamin and spouse Irene Smith, *Longwood* property was to be transferred to their niece, *"Fair and rich"* Irene S. Williams, according to Benjamin's will.[62]

---

[61] Washington County, Courthouse, Index of Deeds, Section 2, Township 15, Range 9. Compliments of Princella (Wilkerson) Nowell of Greenville, MS; see also Benjamin Smith genealogy, KY U. S. Wills and Probate Records, 1774-1989, lists another plantation of his: "My Mundle Place" in Claiborne County, MS. Acreage is unknown.
[62] Kathleen Jennings, Louisville's First Families: A Series of Genealogical Sketches, The Standard Printing Company, Publishers, Louisville, KY, May 1920, p. 29; see also, Benjamin "Ben" Smith Will, July 24, 1846, Ancestry.com, Mississippi, U. S. Wills & Probate, 1780-1982 & Kentucky, U. S. Wills & Probate Records, 1774-1989 https://archive.org/details/louisvillesfirst00jenn/page/n8/mode/1up
https://www.ancestry.com/discoveryui-content/view/3965879:8995?_phsrc=NdM1&_phstart=successSource&gsfn=Benjamin&gsln=Smith&ml_rpos=1&queryId=68b9651fd4b5827b812a7914b1c2a18f
https://www.ancestry.com/search/?name=benjamin_smith&event=1846_louisville-jefferson-kentucky
usa_32672&birth=1785&child=frances_smith&residence=1845_louisville-jefferson-kentucky-usa_32672&spouse=irene_smith

Before the passing of her aunt and receipt of her inheritance, however, Irene S. Williams had married a much older Kentucky gentleman and widower familiar to the family, Alexander C. Bullitt. It was her first marriage, his second. The dynamics of the marriage were, in some measure, difficult to reconcile, with an apparent age difference between them of some 30 years, depending on the trustworthiness of supporting documents. [63] Age difference, however, was a matter of propitiation when examining the history of marriages in the Deep South, especially in the mid to late 19th century, when intermarriage was common. As it was, theirs was an intermarriage. According to historian and author James C. Cobb, *"This pattern of intermarriage was by no means unusual among the Delta's political elite at the end of the nineteenth century"* as a means to maintain solidarity, antebellum qualities, and above all, wealth.[64] Age disparities did not play a significant role among white privilege when measured against the importance of class and the preservation of their elitist way of life; besides

---

[63] A. C. Bullitt birth records, 1860 United States Federal Census, Louisville Ward 3, Jefferson County, Kentucky, lists A. C. Bullitts' age as 50 years, making his DOB 1810; the Kentucky, U. S., Death Records, 1852-1965, list Bullitts' death at age 51, with a birthdate of "abt 1817." Records otherwise point to a birthdate of February 1807.

https://www.ancestry.com/discoveryui-content/view/39469938:7667

https://www.ancestry.com/discoveryui-content/view/54421:1222
[64] James C. Cobb, The Most Southern Place on Earth: The Mississippi Delta and the Roots of Regional Identity, p. 94

wealth, which was of preeminent value, there was honor and, foremost, their intense devotion to racial segregation.

Alexander Clark Bullitt was born to Thomas Washington and Diana Moore (Gwathemy) Bullitt in February 1807 in Louisville, Kentucky. He was a prominent lawyer, journalist, politician, and part owner of the esteemed New Orleans *Times Picayune* newspaper, popularly known as *"The judge,"* or *"A.C."* to his friends and colleagues, and came from a celebrated and very distinguished Louisville Kentucky family; they were early Kentucky pioneers with roots in Virginia and were among Louisville's "first families" as depicted by author Kathleen Jennings in her 1920 biographical narrative of Louisville aristocracy. He was "a man with sound intellect, clear views, statesmanlike qualities, firm, fixed, chivalric qualities of the old Kentucky school," reported *The Picayune* on A. C's character, celebrating *The Picayune's* 50th anniversary year in 1887.

After spouse Fanny's premature passing, leaving A. C. Bullitt, a widower, suffering from grief and chronic melancholy from his personal loss Bullitt, retired from the *Picayune and public life* and escaped to Europe, traveling throughout there for nearly four years. Upon his return from overseas in March 1859, he married Irene S. Williams, who just happened to be the first cousin of his first wife Fanny Smith, with whom he was familiar during his days at *Longwood Plantation*. A. C. and his new wife

Irene shared in the management of *Longwood* with her aunt, Irene Smith, along with the Williams' family businesses, of Washington County.[65]

Longwood became Irene Bullitts' property upon her aunt's death in 1873. In 1876, eight years after A. C. Bullitt's death, Irene married Merritt Williams, an ex-Confederate soldier, and together they oversaw the farm operations and ownership of *Longwood*. [66] Irene was involved in several real estate transactions of *Longwood* properties between 1883-1906, forced land sales due to apparent tax delinquencies and a successful legal action for condemnation of a *"New levee"* through her *Longwood* property, recovering $5,700 (1884), with Fanny Bullitt, her daughter from a previous marriage to Alexander C. Bullitt. Never one to leave any stones unturned where she perceived opportunity, litigant Irene pursued the New Orleans newspaper, *The Times-Picayune*, shortly after her husband Alexander C. Bullitt died in 1868, claiming "interest of her deceased husband's" shared proprietorship of the paper, and requested appointment of a receiver. Her

---

[65] Times Picayune p. 1 & 8, editorial, "The Picayune; Its Semi-Centennial," The Times-Picayune, New Orleans, LA, 25 Jan 1887, p. 1. Also, Times Picayune, 25 Jan 1887, p. 8.
https://www.newspapers.com/image/28301989/?terms=Alexander%20c%20bullitt
https://www.newspapers.com/image/28302108/?terms=Alexander%20c%20bullitt

[66] 1880 Census, Beat 2, 19 July, 1880, Longwood, Washington County; see also Memoirs of Henry Tillinghast Ireys: papers of the Washington County Historical Society, 1910-1915. Jackson, Miss.: Mississippi Dept. of Archives and History and Mississippi Historical Society, 1954.
https://www.ancestry.com/discoveryui-content/view/8919810:6742?tid=&pid=&queryId=1176d32b024e35e1bbf394c6ff5f68d6&_phsrc=eHF1&_phstart=successSource

probe, which it appeared to be, probably amounted to no more than a search mission of false hope by Irene as nothing further can be found on the matter, and the courts likely dismissed it.[67]

Fanny Bullitt, daughter of A. C. and Irene (Williams) Bullitt, was born in 1866. She became Fanny B. Marshall by marriage to Dunbar Marshall of Natchez and owner of the 1000 acre *Forest Plantation*. Her mother Irene died in 1908 at *Longwood*. Daughter Fanny participated in several *Longwood* purchase and sale land transactions until October 1917, when a planter by the name of Thomas "T. H." Bond acquired the *Longwood* property. Bond was the owner of *Longwood* for more than 26 years and was George Scott Sr's employer, who worked there as a sharecropper.[68] Meanwhile Fanny B. Marshall, now in her early 50s, lived a life of privilege, traveling often between properties in Europe, where she resided with her daughter Alexandra, who was married to Italian nobility, and plantation property she shared with husband Dunbar Marshall – whom she married in 1890 - in Natchez, Mississippi.[69] Fanny spent the greater portion of her

---

[67] Newspaper Accounts – Widow [of] Alexander C. Bullitt vs. New Orleans Picayune, New Orleans Republican, 28 May 1870, pg. 1; New Levee at Longwood, Proceedings Board Mississippi Levee Commissioners, The Weekly Democrat Times, 19 Jan 1884, pg. 1; Rights of Way, The Weekly Democrat Times, 28 Jun 1884, pg. 3; Delinquent Tax Sale, The Weekly Democrat Times, 18 Dec 1875, pg. 2

[68] Thomas H. Bond, U. S. Censuses, Department of Commerce – Bureau of the Census, Population Schedules, between 1880 -1950, of Madison (TN), Bolivar (MS), Washington (MS), Sharkey (MS) and Polk (FL) Counties.

[69] Thomas H. Bond, U. S. Censuses, Department of Commerce – Bureau of the Census, Population Schedules, between 1880 -1950, of Madison (TN), Bolivar (MS), Washington (MS), Sharkey (MS) and Polk (FL) Counties.

remaining years in London, England, apart from her husband Dunbar, who remained at Natchez except for occasional visits to Europe until his death in 1930; for all intents, they were estranged. Fanny died in London in 1962 at age 96.[70]

---

[70] Benjamin Smith genealogy, KY U. S. Wills and Probate Records, 1774-1989; Find-A-Grave, Irene Williams Smith, Cave Hill Cemetery, Louisville, KY: FannyElizabeth "Fanny" Smith Bullitt, Find-A-Grave, Louisville, KY, 1850 U. S. Federal Census, Jefferson County, Louisville, KY, and Geneanet Family Tree, also Natchez Daily Courier, May 23, 1851, pg 3; Alexander C. Bullitt, death 6 Jun 1868, The Times-Picayune 08 Jun 1868, Times Picayune 25 Jan 1887; Irene S. Williams, 04 Dec 1908, The Semi-Weekly Times Democrat; 1870 U. S. Federal Census, Jefferson County, Louisville, KY; Fanny S. Bullitt, Merritt Williams, Irene S. Williams, 1880 U. S. Federal Census, Washington County, MS; Fanny B. Marshall, U. S. Passport Applications, 1795-1925.

Chapter 2
Whatever the Terms the Landlord Offered

When a man's home is sacred; when he can protect the virtue of his wife and daughter against the brutal lust of his alleged supervisors; when he can sleep at night without the fear of being visited by the Ku-Klux because he refused to take off his hat while passing an overseer

James R. Grossman .[71]

Author George T. Winston, during his tenure as president of the North Carolina College of Agriculture and Mechanic Arts, in 1901 published an article titled *The Relation of the Whites to the Negroes* in which he explained a very personal view of his own experience on the status and deterioration of black and white relations following the abolition of slavery and Reconstruction. Though not believing it was his intent, it served to fan the fires of what was later to become white resistance, in many odious forms, to the manifestations of black freedoms ushered in by the courts and what occurred between the races upon the conclusion of the Civil War.

"For the first time in our history," said Winston, *"The American Negro is almost friendless. The North, tired of Negro politicians and Negro beggars, is beginning to say: 'We have helped the Negro enough; let him*

---

[71] James R. Grossman, "Land of Hope, Chicago Black Southerners, and the Great Migration, University of Chicago Press, Chicago, 1989, p. 55 https://archive.org/details/landofhope00jame/page/59/mode/1up

now help himself and work out his own salvation.' The South, worn out with strife over the Negro and supporting with difficulty its awful burden of Negro ignorance, inefficiency, and criminality, is beginning to ask whether the race is really capable of development or is a curse and a hindrance in the way of Southern progress and civilization."* [72]

His experience was growing up on a plantation during slavery when *"Scarcely any pleasure was so great to a southern child as playing with Negroes,"* emphasized Winston, who was white.[73] He qualified that viewpoint with colloquial reasoning of the times of keeping blacks and whites on different strata, explaining that slavery had advantages to offer of acceptable social mingling that post-abolition did not: *"Then the two races mingled freely together, not on terms of social equality, but in very extended and constant social intercourse."* He seemed greatly alarmed that that interaction was lost, but qualifying further, in a baseness manner, that *"The Negro is a child race,"* insisted Winston, and more the reason for a need for white leadership, whom he believed was their only redeemer.[74] He spoke of this in a protective manner with feelings of empathy for a down-trodden race truly believing they had no means of self-defense, he declared with compassionate belief. *"It would be a cruelty greater than slavery to leave*

---

[72] George T. Winston, "The Relation of the Whites to the Negroes," JSTOR Early Journal Content, Annals of the American Academy of Political and Social Science, Vol. 18.
https://archive.org/details/jstor-1009885/page/n11/mode/1up
[73] IBID, p. 2
[74] IBID, p. 12

this helpless race, this child race, to work out its own salvation in fierce and hostile competition with the strongest and best developed race on the globe," he pronounced with decided vigor and tendentious behavior.[75]

This was the tumultuous historical backdrop for the young George Scott family trying to eke out a living against numerous odds in the Delta cotton fields in the early part of the 20th-century while, at the same time, confronted by human suffering, economic injustice, the likes of *Jim Crow* at every turn and the iniquitous presence of the Ku Klux Klan. It was also an age of black lynching – still a trend in Mississippi - that was carried out by white mobs who were unopposed. They terrified black communities capriciously, without requital, often by falsifying rape charges, considered the most heinous of crimes set upon Southern white women - idealized as *"Proper,"* well-bred, virtuous, and untouchable - by black male miscreants.

As was true with a vast many of alleged black *"Crimes"* there was no due process, even though many were nothing more than concoctions unsupported by evidence that was drummed up by the white accuser. Historian David Oshinsky described these conditions this way: *"What made mob violence so terrifying in Jim Crow Mississippi was the virtual absence of opposition. Local sheriffs often encouraged it, grand juries never brought indictments, and coroners simply reported "death at the hands of parties*

---

[75] IBID, p. 13

unknown.'"[76] Mississippi far-and-away took the lead of all states in numbers of lynchings from the period of Reconstruction through 1950, at 655, with Georgia at 593 and Louisiana 549. Of the most violative Mississippi counties with the highest number of lynchings were LeFlore and Warren counties, ominously on the perimeter of *Longwood*, where the Scott family took up residence.[77]

Known affectively and more commonly by his journalist peers as "*W.J.*" or "*Jack*" Cash, more formally by Joseph Wilbur Cash, his birth name, whose single-volume controversial treatise *The Mind of the South*, became an American classic, often described the Southerner in terms of Individualism, particularly true in the case of the planter, for whom he placed the greatest emphasis. And yet, despite the Civil War, its devastating impact and effect on the nation, moreover of the South, Cash, who was no stranger to Southern conduct since he grew up there, describes the white Southerner quite differently than one might expect: *"The South, on the contrary, would retain the old primitive feeling and outlook of the frontier. Southerners in 1900 would see the world in much the same terms in which their fathers had seen it in 1830: as, in its last aspect, a simple solution, an aggregation of self-contained and self-sufficient monads, each of whom was*

---

[76] David M. Oshinsky, "Worse Than Slavery: Parchman Farm and the Ordeal of Jim Crow Justice," Simon & Schuster, New York, 1996, p. 105

[77] R. L. Nave, "Report: Miss. No. 2 in Lynchings per capita," Jackson Free Press, Inc., February 11, 2015.
https://www.jacksonfreepress.com/news/2015/feb/11/report-hinds-county-had-most-miss-lynchings/

ultimately and completely responsible for himself."[78] This mindset of individualism, or singleness of lifestyle and purpose, carried into the beginning years of the 20th century, leading to tenant farming. The Southern planter, an aristocrat and a proponent of a rigid caste system, was not about to yield his white sovereignty to anyone, in spite of post-war restructuring mandates, fiercely holding onto his dominance by whatever measure he could arrange, which eventually became entangled in the menacing disciplines of tenant farming.

In rare cases and in some parts of the Deep South post-Reconstruction, blacks achieved certain levels of freedom and autonomy through sharecropping, but ascending this ladder was difficult and dependent on the tolerance level of the planters who owned the land. *"But even for those blacks who did work their way up the ladder, there was a subtler but no less insidious exploitation in this need to be subservient, to know one's place, to differentiate one's self from one's race. They had to be acceptable, nonthreatening, well behaved. They had to compromise their autonomy in order to gain it. Southern agriculture did offer some avenues of progress for 'Good blacks,'"* according to historian Gavin Wright.[79]

---

[78] W. J. Cash – p 111, "The Mind of the South," Vintage Books, A Division of Random House, Inc., New York, original edition by Alfred A. Knopf, Inc., 1941, p. 111.
https://archive.org/details/mindofsouth0000wfca_j0x3/page/426/mode/1up
[79] Gavin Wright, "Old South, New South: revolutions in the southern economy since the Civil War." Basic Books: New York, 1986, p. 106-107.
https://archive.org/details/oldsouthnewsouth00gavi_0/page/107/mode/1up

Before his untimely death by suicide in 1941, the generally known high-strung Cash, who encountered bouts of depression, poignantly explains the contradictions of *"Freedom"* they were to experience confronting a man like George Scott Senior and his family, struggling to find their way, among other blacks like them, who were emerging from the after-effects of Reconstruction and its various incongruities. *"But with the abolition of legal slavery, his [the Negro's] immunity vanished. The economic interest of his former protectors, the master class, now stood the other way about – required that he should be promptly disabused of any illusion that his liberty was real and confirmed in his ancient docility,"* wrote Cash.[80]

Historian and author James C. Cobb was of a similar mind but with a slightly different slant in his *The Most Southern Place on Earth* by his words, *"Behind the seductive and disarming Old South facade of the Delta, the American Dream had been not so much perverted as simply pursued to its ultimate realization in a setting where human and natural resources could be exploited to the fullest with but little regard for social or institutional restraint."*[81]

Racial fear and hatred held sway during the end of the 19th century and into the 20th, and lynching of blacks was epidemic. Blacks had to be on their guard at all times, no matter their circumstances or what footing they may

---

[80] W. J. Cash, "The Mind of the South," p. 113
[81] James C. Cobb, "The Most Southern Place on Earth: The Mississippi Delta and the Roots of Regional Identity," The Oxford University Press, New York, 1992, p 326

have had – or perceived they had - with their employers; no black was immune to this. It was shockingly frightful for Mississippi blacks, where this malicious behavioral pattern lurked – they were terrified - and no less alarmed was the Scott family of Washington County, who lived in constant fear of not knowing when to expect Southern whites capriciously turning on them, without warning or restraints, even though there was social detachment separating them, and carry out their rage, described in some circles as terror lynching; this was common in Mississippi. Dorsey White, cousin to Delores Melton Gresham, whose father died in 1955 from a racially motivated killing, explained that *"We didn't have any protection where the law was concerned,"* he said. *"Any white person could start trouble, and no one would interfere."*[82] The public opinion section of the 1901 *Jackson Daily Clarion-Ledger* contained this posting, presumably made by a farmer or plantation owner, displaying crass indifference, if not outright alienation, toward the welfare of the black laborer, who meant nothing to him personally or even humanly – nothing but an anomaly - except as a means and resource of physical labor: *"It is time to quit burning and lynching negroes, or else there will be difficulty in getting this season's cotton crop picked,"* he said.[83] This same newspaper, showing no accord or

---

[82] Giles, Nellie & Richman, Joe, "Clinton Melton: A Man Who was Killed in Mississippi just 3 months after Emmett Till," NPR, Radio Diaries, August 27, 2020. https://www.npr.org/sections/codeswitch/2020/08/27/906791647/clinton-melton-a-man-who-was-killed-in-mississippi-just-3-months-after-emmett-ti

[83] The Daily Clarion-Ledger Aug 1901, "Public Opinion Piece," The Daily Clarion-Ledger, August 31, 1901, p. 4
https://www.newspapers.com/image/244164155/?terms=Jackson%20clarion%20ledger%20lynching&match=1

empathy, lent its support for the lynching of black males under certain conditions. In this case, a negro male was found in the bedroom of a young white lady, for which he was promptly lynched. According to this newspaper, *"The Clarion-Ledger has always contended that these lynchings will occur as long as the cause for them exists...juries are composed of men who share the same feelings as the lynchers, willing at all times to string up men who attempt to outrage women."* [84] According to W. J. Cash, *"The South had become peculiarly the home of lynching."*[85]

There evolved in the early part of the 20th century a preponderant belief, particularly among the white upper class, who felt the black man was *"Mastered,"* that lynching of blacks, long a problem in Mississippi, was subsiding. Native Southerner and annalist J. W. Cash, however, saw through this and was not as quick as others to support the idea that there was soon-to-be an *"End"* to lynching by the conclusion of 1929. It was a popular belief that was supported by such astute social critics and American journalists as Oswald Garrison Villard, a champion of civil rights and civil liberties, who felt by then, in a manner for him uncharacteristically facile, that the color line was rapidly eroding.[86] Cash demonstrated against these

---

[84] The Clarion-Ledger Mar 1901, Editorial, The Clarion-Ledger, March 28, 1901, p. 4.
https://www.newspapers.com/image/242473508/?terms=%20Jackson%20clarion-ledger%20lynchings&match=1
[85] W. J. Cash, "The Mind of the South," p. 43
[86] Oswald Garrison Villard, Wikipedia, The Free Encyclopedia; John Simkin, 1997-2020 Spartacus Educational Publishers Ltd., www.spartacus-educational.com
https://spartacus-educational.com/USAvillard.htm

views, pointing out that such conclusions were premature and far-and-away too glib for the circumstances. Such political stalwarts as Mississippi's James K. Vardaman, John Sharpe Williams, and South Carolina's Ellison *"Cotton"* Ed Smith, and Coleman L. Blease, each of them noted racists, were still active at the time and, effectively, sought to spew hate and white supremacy at their every turn, advocating lynching in some instances, particularly Blease. As Cash stressed, there was little change in the "emotions" of lynching; *"The number of attempted lynchings still ran very high."*[87]

Particularly during the early part of the 20th century, and in some areas of the Deep South regions and in other states besides Mississippi, lynching was alleged to have been covered up by law enforcement, ascribing them to *"victim suicides." "There is understandable distrust of law enforcement within the Black community because of a long history in the U. S. of public officials using rulings of suicide to cover up lynchings,"* according to historical consultant and researcher Jay Driskell. [88] Cash described blacks as *"open game"* to the whims of the whites and *"all loyal Southerners,"* adding, *"In many districts, particularly in the Deep South, the killing of a Negro by a white man ceased, in practice, even to call for legal inquiry,"* which was accepted practice carrying well into the 1950s.[89] However, even

---

[87] W. J. Cash, "The Mind of the South," p. 301
[88] Jay Driskell, quoted in Mississippi Enterprise-Journal, "Black Man's Hanging Death: Lynching or Suicide?" McComb, Mississippi, May 25, 2021, p. A7.
[89] W. J. Cash, "The Mind of the South," p. 120.

if the legal requirements of inquiry somehow were attained before the Southern courts, responding to a crime, coroners would likely find alternative reasons, such as *"Self-defense"* or *"Justifiable homicide,"* to absolve the white perpetrator of any consequences. The evidence was clear enough that, in spite of the time and a gradual waning of wide-spread-lynching *"Black people knew that they could be attacked and killed for violating any social rule, intentionally or accidentally, as defined by any white person at any time,"* capriciously, according to historians.[90]

The Ku Klux Klan was active, considered a second wave in their history of intimidation and violence, targeting blacks indiscriminately. It was a well-supported movement in the Delta South, *"A significant projection from the past into the present, a meaningful witness of the continuity of Southern sentiment,"* according to W. J. Cash. Perhaps less evident was the part that planters played in this white supremacist effort, always smartly on the periphery, wary of being recognized as the conduit, chary about actual membership. The makeup of the organization was constructed of common whites, *"But its blood,"* said Cash, *"Came from the upper orders."* And among these ranks were the planters, who *"Joined it by the wholesale, and more often than not worked with it when they did not join it,"* wrote Cash. Though the archetype understructure of the Klan, the *"Bony framework,"*

---

[90] Reconstruction In America, "Racial Justice After the Civil War," Equal Justice Initiative, Chapter 4: The Danger of Freedom, Enforcing the Racial Social Order. https://eji.org/report/reconstruction-in-america/

said Cash, was of everyday white farmers and businessmen, *"The people who held it together and coordinated and directed it, were very near to being coextensive with the established leadership of the South."* [91] This cooperativeness between planters and the composition making up the KKK was nothing less than that of a crusader effort for the benefit of preserving the Old South, maintaining white supremacy, and a *"Continuing identity, its will to remain unchanged and defy the way of the Yankee and the world in favor of that one which had so long been its own."*[92]

As the Southern white planter grew richer after the Great War, his obsession with preserving the status quo grew stronger, impacted by the black movement to leave the South and to compete with Northern labor agents who attested to the earning of higher wages in the North – "Yankeedom," scoffed Cash - that became an attraction to Southern blacks. He became *"Distrustful of disorder…which they do not conceive to be directly useful to their own self-interest."*[93]

The ownership of *Longwood Plantation* of Avon, Washington County, and additional properties along the Natchez regions and the Trace to Port Gibson, Mississippi, bordering the Mississippi River, dates to Benjamin Smith, who was one of the earliest settlers to take advantage of fiery Populist President Andrew Jackson's land grab of the 1830s – Jackson's unabashed zeal for seizure of real estate - based on the *"Indian Removal*

---

[91] W. J. Cash, "The Mind of the South," pages 335-336
[92] IBID, page 337
[93] IBID, page 307

Act" of that year, which was passed by a one-vote margin. Mississippi's Choctaw, Natchez, and Chickasaw Tribes were forced to relinquish their lands, and colonizers, like Ben Smith, were quick to supplant them, though by legal means – albeit controversial and popularly viewed as subversionary – with the assistance of the Federal Government. Their forced departure is known, infamously, as the *Trail of Tears*. Thousands of Native Americans lost their lives on their merciless trek, on foot, to Oklahoma.[94] It is believed, actually, that Smith had his eyes on Washington County property even before that, when it was largely under Native American control, and first acquired land there on or about the year 1822, at age 37, according to published genealogical documentation.[95]

---

[94] Politico Magazine, "How Jackson Made a Killing in Real Estate," by Steve Inskeep, Library of Congress, July 4, 2015; also, National Park Service, "Natchez Trace: Early Choctaw History;" National Park Service, "The Trail of Tears and the Forced Relocation of the Cherokee Nation," W. Shorey Coodey to John Howard Payne, n.d.; cited in John Ehle, Trail of Tears: The Rise and Fall of the Cherokee Nation (New York: Doubleday, 1988), 351; Clara Sue Caldwell, "The Effects of Removal on American Indian Tribes," University of North Carolina at Chapel Hill National Humanities Center, Research Triangle Park, North Carolina; "Mississippi Band of Choctaw Indians," Wikipedia, updated March 31, 2023.
https://www.politico.com/magazine/story/2015/07/andrew-jackson-made-a-killing-in-real-estate-119727/
https://www.nps.gov/natr/learn/historyculture/choctaw.htm
https://www.nps.gov/articles/the-trail-of-tears-and-the-forced-relocation-of-the-cherokee-nation-teaching-with-historic-places.htm
https://nationalhumanitiescenter.org/tserve/nattrans/ntecoindian/essays/indianremoval.htm
https://en.wikipedia.org/wiki/Mississippi_Band_of_Choctaw_Indians

[95] U. S. Slave, Slavery in the New World from Africa to the Americas, "Cotton Comes to the Mississippi Delta: Early Delta Settlers," U.S. Slave Blogspot.com, July 3, 2011 http://usslave.blogspot.com/2011/07/cotton-comes-to-mississippi-delta.html

Thomas H. Bond Jr., whose father, Thomas Bond Senior, a former Confederate soldier who was a prominent and well-heeled plantation owner himself in the Nashville, Tennessee region, owning vast amounts of fertile property of considerable value, is found in Bradshaw, Clay County, Arkansas in 1900 at age 28 working as an engineer, an industrial millwright, for a lumber company. He was a boarder with the Francis Williams family of Bradshaw Township. Two days after the 1900 Clay County census was taken, on June 14, T. H. Bond Jr. married charming socialite and *"Brilliant"* elocutionist Bettie Mai Hughes, age 27, of Nashville, Tennessee.[96] Sometime thereafter, Bond and his wife Bettie worked their way 225 miles south along the Mississippi River's eastern edge to Beulah, Bolivar County, Mississippi, where they took up residence, and he was a merchant there in the business of *"General merchandise,"* acquiring plantation property as well in an effort of budding entrepreneurship.[97]

Tragically, Bond's life was abruptly put on pause: his accomplished and very popular societal wife of 13 years, Bettie Mai, died on 1 July 1913; she was a mere 39 years of age. They had no children. [98] Bond worked through his grief while in Bolivar County when a few years later, on March 9, 1916, at age 42, he married Margaret Campbell White, age 32, of Franklin, Tennessee, once again a spouse born to privilege, settling briefly in Beulah, Mississippi. Margaret was the daughter of prominent Tennessee lawyer

---

[96] Nashville Banner, "Society," Nashville Banner, 15 June 1900, p. 5
[97] Thirteenth Census of the United States: 1910 – Population; Beulah, Bolivar County, Beat # 3, enumerated 15 April 1910.
[98] The Tennessean, "Obituary," The Tennessean, 02 July 1913, p. 9

Wiley B. White, who had a distinguished career in politics in Franklin, Williamson County, Tennessee. She was a highly-regarded member of the Franklin High School faculty and lifelong resident of Williamson County, whose friends, according to the local paper, expressed considerable regret for her departure. [99] T. H. Bond Junior and Margaret moved further south from Beulah toward the end of 1916, again along the trajectory of the Mississippi River basin, on Mississippi's eastern side of the river, and for the next four years, began buying up large tracts of rich and fertile farmland in the Longwood-Avon area, contiguous to Lake Washington, much of it originating with the Ben Smith families, and their descendants, following the government's infamous Choctaw-Chickasaw-Natchez tribes land confiscation of the 1830s. They had a network of plantations along this route and often stayed at the Idlewild Plantation at Port Gibson in Claiborne County, neighboring the Natchez Trace.[100]

---

[99] Nashville Banner, "Society," Nashville Banner, 9 March 1916, p. 5; Margaret Campbell White, of Nashville, was a daughter to Wiley B. White, a distinguished Nashville, Tennessee lawyer, Attorney General of the County Circuit, Sheriff of Williamson County, and notable politician. Daughter "Maggie" was a faculty member of the Franklin, Tennessee High School.

[100] Benjamin Smith family genealogy; The Longwood Plantation was first-owned by Benjamin Smith in 1822 until his death in 1846. His wife Irene (Williams) Smith, and daughter Fanny Smith, assumed ownership upon his death; Fanny died in 1855, age 34. There were no other children. When mother Irene (Williams) Smith died in 1872 the family took over the plantations; namely Irene Smith Williams (niece of Ben & Irene) and after that her daughter Fanny Bullitt, whose father was Alexander C. Bullitt, previously married to Fanny Smith. Fanny Bullitt became wife of Dunbar Marshall in 1859, whose Natchez plantation was The Forest. Fanny Bullitt was mostly overseas in her later years and sold the remaining portions of the Longwood Plantation to assorted buyers, including T. H. Bond Jr.

Magnolia "Maggie" Simon, daughter of Edd (or Ed) and Grace "Gracey" (Fesley) Simon, who was to marry George Scott Sr., was born on 30 October 1918, on *Longwood Plantation* that was under the ownership and management of white merchant and prominent planter Thomas H. Bond Jr. Her family, the Simon's, including maternal grandparents James and Laura (Owens) Fesley,[101] who lived next to the Simon family on the plantation working for Bond, as sharecroppers most likely. T. H. Bond Junior was engaged in an extensive cotton business operation in the village of Avon of Washington County.[102] Grandfather James Fesley, whom Magnolia would rely on extensively for her oral history about family, including the slave era, their family background in the face of that, and Reconstruction, was a son of Owen and Margaret Fesley, originally of North Carolina and Alabama, respectively, who most likely were enslaved prior to the Civil War. Owen and Margaret were born circa 1844 and 1846. They raised their family in Madison County, Mississippi, where James, who was their youngest, was born circa October 1869, only four years after the Civil War. The Fesleys, Owen and Margaret, who were Magnolia's great grandparents, lived their lives in Livingston, Madison County, Mississippi, 12 miles southwest of Canton, where *"Slavery was the town's central and defining institution,"* according to historian Nicholas Lemann. During the

---

[101] James and Laura (Owens) Fesley; the surname Fesley, Feasly, Feasley, or Pheasely, varies how the name is reported in censuses and documents, most likely attributable to enumerator error.
[102] U. S. Census – 1920, enumerated April 12, 1920, Department of Commerce – Bureau of the Census

Fesley's habitancy in Madison County, blacks outnumbered whites by three to one, yet they had no preferred social or economic place in the community; it was where *"the whites' economic status and comfort and safety depended on keeping the blacks subjugated."*[103] There is no record of great grandfather Owen's death, as was typical of most Southern blacks' deaths of that era; however, it is likely he died at a young age, sometime between the ninth and tenth censuses of 1870-1880 or between the ages of 26 and 36. Wife Margaret Fesley, age 34 in 1880, was listed as head of the household and residing in Madison County, where she had previously cohabited with husband Owen.[104]

James Fesley was a striking man for his time and culture; he had every appearance of being dignified, determined, rigorously self-disciplined with a sense of purpose judging by a distinguished and uniquely telling photograph of him, most likely taken while in his 20s, which would place this snapshot or *"Cabinet card"* photo, a studio photograph, sometime between 1890-1900.

---

[103] Nicholas Lemann, "The Origins of the Underclass: Free Fall" The Atlantic Online, June 1986
https://www.theatlantic.com/past/docs/politics/poverty/origin1.htm
https://www.theatlantic.com/past/docs/politics/poverty/origin2.htm

[104] Ninth & tenth U. S. Censuses; (1870) Police District 3, Calhoun Station, Madison County, Mississippi, enumerated 22 June 1870; (1880) Madison County, Mississippi, District 3, enumerated 9 June 1880

James Fesley, a cabinet card photo from circa 1890-1900. James was the maternal grandfather of Magnolia Simon Scott, and great grandfather to George Scott, Jr. (courtesy of Janice Brown of the Brown, Greenfield, Henley Ancestry Family Tree)

The era when this photograph was taken aligns with the messaging of that time when Frederick Douglass espoused a need for blacks to take advantage of being photographed as a dignified means toward freedom. Douglass (1817/1818 – 1895), a leading proponent of black imagery, was a social reformer, abolitionist, writer, intellect, and former slave who was the most photographed American of the 19th century at his initiative and who zealously promoted this medium of photojournalism as a tool for black self-empowerment and social advancement. According to author Samantha Hill, in her 2021 article *"How Black People in the 19th Century Used Photography as a Tool for Social Change,"* emphasized that *"To pose for a photograph became an empowering act for African Americans. It served as a way to counteract racist caricatures that distort facial features and mocked black society,"* adding that it was their opportunity *"To demonstrate dignity in the Black experience."*[105]

Douglass furthered this idea by using photography strategically and powerfully not only as a *"Technological weapon"* and resource to alter change for his race but as an important maxim for the ideal of racial progress and *"his purest vessel of truth,"* as described by historian Renee Graham. "Frederick Douglass used photographs to force the nation to begin addressing racism." [106]

It was a compelling message and seems more than likely that James Fesley, himself in pursuit of human dignity, which Douglass strongly espoused, may have picked up on that as his photograph implies and was influenced by Douglass, who was a contemporary having a connection with Mississippi, as well, whose sister Sara was sold into slavery to a planter there in 1832; Douglass became a well-traveled man and orator seeking to spread the principles and truths behind the abolitionist movement, with all

---

[105] Samantha Hill, "How Black People in the 19th century used photography as a tool for social change," The Conversation, February 26, 2021.
https://theconversation.com/how-black-people-in-the-19th-century-used-photography-as-a-tool-for-social-change-154721
[106] Renee Graham, Pop Culture Correspondent for WBUR's Here & Now and the ARTery, "Frederick Douglass Used Photographs to Force the Nation to Begin Addressing Racism," July 21, 2016.
https://www.wbur.org/news/2016/07/21/picturing-frederick-douglass

the earmarks of reaching Fesley in some manner while black photography studios were springing up throughout the country.

Censuses between 1900-1910 reveal that James Fesley was unable to read or write; by the 1920 census, however, at age 51, he could do both, which likely meant he was self-taught, as, at that time, there were no opportunities or encouragement from planters in support of his ambitions. In fact, it was more likely punishment. He also was identified as an *"Employer,"* which meant he was probably a sharecropper with hired hands and had a larger parcel of the plantation property to manage.

Granddaughter Maggie, who quite remarkably progressed as far as the 7th grade, uncommon for black children then, and who was literate, recalled lively – if not somberly - conversations she had with her maternal grandfather, James Fesley, who was born four years following the conclusion of the Civil War and had more than enough to share with his granddaughter. Grandfather Fesley, who was age 49 when Maggie was born, relished sharing these stories with her, emphasizing their benefit to the family, the black communities, and the overall value and importance of their preservation. There was a portentous quality to his messages, said Maggie, as if these stories might be lost to mankind, realizing they could, in reality, be lost if he failed to spend the time to share them; and, Maggie was an eager and willing listener and note-taker. The residual effects of slavery and white supremacy of the South and the Mississippi Delta, in particular, such as *Jim Crow*, still lingered in the minds, hearts, and actions of the black communities; James Fesley was a man of conviction and was not about to surrender the integrity of the Negro story to fortuitous memory, but instead raised it prominently before the eyes of his granddaughter and others who expressed a common interest.[107]

Prior to 1831, some planters manifested attitudes that were, in small measure, relaxed with few restrictions on black education. Planter wives often assumed initiatives, mostly informally, of teaching reading through Christian instruction to their black slave laborers or, as the planters saw it, for them to gain knowledge of the Bible through scripture and to assimilate Christian values. But this soon stopped after enslaved Virginian Nate Turner led a rebellion in August 1831, killing an estimated 55 white people and leading to executions of a similar number of blacks, that led to the renewal of onerous legislation in Virginia, Mississippi, and other southern states, tightening control of black lives *"Including their literacy."*[108]

As a result, the Anti-Literacy Laws of the 19th century prohibited anyone from teaching enslaved and free people of color to read or write without harsh retribution; slave masters feared that black literacy would be a threat to their slavery system, their white Southern "rights" and their established

---

[107] James Fesley, grandfather to Magnolia Simon Scott, was the son of Owen and Margaret Fesley. Owen was born in 1844, Margaret in 1846. There is no record of Owen Fesley after the 1870 census, or wife Margaret, who was 34, after 1880.

[108] Colette Coleman, "How Literacy Became a Powerful Weapon in the Fight to End Slavery," History, A & E Television Networks, January 29, 2021
https://www.history.com/news/nat-turner-rebellion-literacy-slavery

way of life, the latter a driving force of Southern behavior and their unalterable resistance to black freedom.

The abolitionist movement accelerated following Turner's act of insurrection, and soon after, enslaved people discovered ways to read and write, getting around these anti-literacy laws in spite of them. It was really a painstaking, methodical process, such as how Frederick Douglass prevailed with his incessantness through writings and oratory, with others following his lead. Though there was no clear indication that these laws were officially abolished, they were cast aside by the weight of these efforts and initiatives on the part of Douglass, Gerrit Smith, John Brown, and others, including the Emancipation Proclamation of 1863 and the actual conclusion of the Civil War, turning the tide for blacks.

Southern planters and white farmers, however, brazenly resisted these changes at the turn of the century, fearing dangerous consequences, including the loss of black labor, and remained unsupportive. In a small way, Fesley was a beneficiary of these efforts. However, in spite of the successes, croppers, he among them, remained tightly bound to the planters and were dependent on them for nearly everything of importance.

George Scott Senior, who would marry Magnolia Simon and have three children with her, all born on the *Longwood Plantation*, was born to George Scott – among a line of George Scotts - and Mary Ann Butler in Anguilla of Sharkey County, Mississippi, on June 22, 1900.[109] Anguilla is 25 miles southeast of *Longwood*, Avon.

George Sr and Magnolia's first child was Otis Charles, born in September 1936, making Magnolia one month shy of 18 at the time of his birth. The second child and only daughter, Beatrice, was born in 1939, and George Jr. in 1944. There are no records certifying George Sr and Magnolia's marriage, if there was actually anything performed formally or ceremonially, such as a wedding or issuance of an official marriage certificate, but this was not unusual for the plight of the sharecropper. Tenant and cropper farm laborers were considered of a meager lower class, and *"bourgeois properties such as the marriage ceremony were little observed;"* they were deemed mostly of little importance by whites, according to Nicholas Lemann in his *Origins of the Underclass*. The cropper and tenant farmer had no social standing in the plantation community, whose landlords showed them no deference.[110] Hortense Powdermaker, an American anthropologist known for her research of African Americans of rural America, particularly following Roosevelt's *"New Deal"* legislation of 1938 when she spent time surveying Indianola

---

[109] George Scott Sr; it is unclear from the records that George Scott Sr was actually a "senior," as is understood by the Scott family. George's 1942 draft card specifies "(None)" to the draft card questionnaire requesting a middle name.
[110] Nicholas Lemann, "The Origins of the Underclass: Free Fall" June 1986 https://www.theatlantic.com/past/docs/politics/poverty/origin1.htm

https://www.theatlantic.com/past/docs/politics/poverty/origin2.htm

of the Mississippi Delta, pointed out how extraordinarily different sharecropper life was from family life of the rest of the country. Black relationships and their so-called marriages were nothing but common law in the typical sharecropper family, *"easily entered and easily dissolved."* [111] Ruby Lee Daniels, a former black cotton picker who worked on a plantation during the 1940s in Clarksdale, Mississippi, and who was a subject of historian Nicholas Lemann's study on Southern black culture of the 1940s-1960s, spoke in a similar context *"People would get married on a plantation one week, and the next week one of them would be gone."*[112]

Esteemed Ph.D. and American political scientist V. O. (Valdimer Orlando) Key, 1908-1963, who taught at such lofty universities as UCLA, Johns Hopkins, Yale, and Harvard, viewed Deep South agrarian life and its culture, especially that of Mississippi, in a tendentious tone:

"At least in the agrarian economy of the Mississippi sort no great middle class – not even an agrarian middle class – dulls the abruptness of the line between lord and serf. The big houses and the tenant shacks stand as symbols of nether world," exclaimed Key, and *"The tenant and the sharecropper are regarded as lazy, degenerate, shiftless fellows who get*

---

[111] Hortense Powdermaker, "After Freedom," Kahle/Austin Foundation, 1939, p. 68
[112] Nicholas Lemann, p. 32 "The Promised Land," Vintage Books, Division of Random House, New York, p. 32

what they deserve, the sort of people 'that attend revivals and fight and fornicate in the bushes afterwards.'"[113]

Historian W. J. Cash, meanwhile, spoke provocatively, displaying a variance of tone toward the planter and white farmer, whom he described as fomenters of *"Violence, intolerance, aversion and suspicion toward new ideas, an incapacity for analysis, an inclination to act from feeling rather than from thought, an exaggerated individualism and a too narrow concept of social responsibility."* He accused them of being acutely racist with a tendency to *"justify cruelty and injustice."*[114]

The history of the Scott family, as a family unit, originates with planter Thomas H. Bond Jr. and the *Longwood Plantation*; evidence points to their residency there likely beginning circa 1935-1936, when Magnolia was 17 or 18, and George Sr was quite a bit older at 35. They likely married circa 1934-35, although that is not conclusive.

---

[113] V. O. Key, "Southern Politics in State and Nation," Knoxville, University of Tennessee Press, 1984, p. 240-241
https://archive.org/details/southernpolitics0000keyv_a2w6/page/240/mode/1up
[114] W. J. Cash, "The Mind of the South," p. 428-429

Longwood Plantation main house circa 1930s (courtesy of Princella Wilkerson Nowell of Greenville, MS)

They lived in what was customarily known as *"Quarters,"* shack-like conditions, *"Negro cabins"* some called them, *"Nigger house"* as the term was used by the sinister Delta white farmer,[115] or shanties as they were otherwise more bearably known – a step-up from ramshackle slave cabins – consisting of small homes crudely built, usually two rooms a tin roof and front porch, some without glass for windows, nor insulation, and a storage shed nearby for tools and supplies.[116] They lacked running water or electricity, no heat and had only an outside toilet that, at times, was shared by several families. The cabins were arranged in rows or clusters and had the appearance of slave buildings built before the Civil War; not much had changed, nor, importantly, was there any demonstrable call for change; thus, planters remained complacent about sharecropper accommodations, personal conditions, and their meager welfare, whom they perceived as chattel.[117] One newspaper account, marketing the advantages of doing cotton business in the South, made the case of how much more economical it was for the Southern planter to run a cotton farm because of the laissez-faire nature of the "colored tenant" and their peculiarly lowered standards and expectations of themselves, as compared with the Northern black man;

---

[115] Nicholas Lemann, "The Origins of the Underclass: Free Fall"
[116] Nicholas Lemann 4, "The Origins of the Underclass: Free Fall" The Atlantic Online, June 1986
[117] National Park Service, History and Culture of the Mississippi Delta Region, undated
https://www.nps.gov/locations/lowermsdeltaregion/history-and-culture-of-the-mississippi-delta-region.htm

unmistakable words in support of exploitation and the encouragement of unscrupulous behavior, but far from being accurate.[118]

Sharecropper cabin, Coahoma County, Mississippi, by Dorothea Lange, photographer 1937 June-July; Library of Congress, LC-USF34-017481-E; https://www.loc.gov/pictures/item/2017770265/

---

[118] J. F. Merry, Mississippi Valley Cotton Lands: The South A Center of Attraction, Southern Farm Gazette, Starkville, MS, Jan 1, 1903, p. 2

The Delta Leader, a Greenville newspaper, and for many years a beneficiary of robust financial backing and advertising from surrounding planters, regularly promoted a theme of planter benevolence, or noblesse oblige, on behalf of the black farm worker. Planter B. F. Harbert & Co. of Robinsonville, Mississippi, dedicated a single page to a talking point not only promoting their business but defending it: *"A Cotton Plantation Where Good Colored Tenants Like to Live."*[119] An editorial, noted again in *the Delta Leader*, quite disparagingly spoke of the black farmworker this way: *"Farming in Mississippi provides just about the only way out for the black man. Due to the unskilled and illiterate Negro in rural Mississippi, farming to them is a blessing indeed."*[120] George Sr. and his wife Magnolia most likely went into sharecropping on the *Longwood Plantation* and had two of their three children working in the fields from a very young age. It was understood that they would start young, about five years old, or, as one former white farmer explained, *"If they wouldn't put the kids in the field, why, then we'd whup 'em. Then they wouldn't give us any more trouble. We'd tie 'em up and whup 'em with a plow line."*[121]

---

[119] B. F. Harbert, A Cotton Plantation Where Good Colored Tenants Like to Live, The Delta Leader, Robinsonville, MS, December 19, 1943, p. 8
https://www.newspapers.com/image/238463717/?terms=delta%20leader

https://www.newspapers.com/image/238463622/?terms=delta%20leader
[120] Negro Farmer in Mississippi, The Delta Leader, Greenville, MS, December 19, 1943, p. 2
https://www.newspapers.com/image/238463635/?terms=the%20delta%20leader
[121] Nicholas Lemann, "The Origins of the Underclass: Free Fall"

Planting and harvesting of cotton, done largely by the sharecroppers, revolved around the *"Agrarian school calendar,"* which meant that during these times of seeding and harvesting, in the spring and fall, croppers' kids, who were mostly black, were typically absent from school; instead, they were laboring in the fields alongside their families, and would not attend school until the harvesting was done. If there was any chance of school for them, they had to deal with segregated schools with inadequate funding, poor classroom conditions, and unsuitable and limited supplies. Most black children attended no greater than 3-4 years of school before they dropped out. Planters offered them no encouragement – it was the farm or else – and actively disincentivized any effort at learning - including punishments if they did - which of any manner proved a threat to them. *"Black children pick cotton; white children go to school,"* exclaimed Vennie Moore, reminiscing about her days working in the cotton fields of the South and of the inequality between black and white children.[122]

George Scott Senior displayed a certain austere presence about him, a man of ample stature and sturdily built. He was tall, about 6'2" and 185 pounds, muscular, carried himself well, and quite capable of the task of cropper; sedulous in all respects with the bearing and countenance of a

---

[122] Brian Campbell, Laura Hajar interview 1999, Oral History Interview with Vennie Moore, February 24, 1999, Interview K-0439, Oral History Program Collection (#4007) in the Southern Oral History Program Collection, Southern Historical Collection, Wilson Library, University of North Carolina at Chapel Hill. https://docsouth.unc.edu/sohp/K-0439/excerpts/excerpt_6583.html

hardworking man.[123] A third-grade education also burdened him, consistent with most other black children of the day, as mentioned previously, with no opportunity to advance himself. He, like others of his poverty-ridden background, lived under *"An ethic of dependency,"* wrote Historian Nicholas Lemann, and, as a sharecropper, he *"Could never come out ahead…sharecroppers had no money and practically no education, and they counted on the landowner to provide for them – which he did, meagerly."*[124] He was dependent on them for everything, borrowing from the planter for food money and farm supplies, and by the end of the year, when it was time to settle up with the planter, he found himself behind. It was never-ending. Planters insisted on keeping a firm upper hand over their farmworkers in order to protect their coveted interests, controlling the purse strings and movement of their laborers. *"The similarities between sharecropping and welfare are eerie,"* wrote Nicholas Lemann. *"Dependency on 'the man;' more money for having more children; little value placed on education; no home ownership; an informal attitude toward marriage and childbearing."*[125]

---

[123] Draft Card, George Scott Sr. February 16, 1942, U. S. World War II Draft Cards Young Men, 1940-1947, Serial Number 365, Order Number 10.183. https://www.ancestry.com/discoveryui-content/view/268948163:2238?tid=&pid=&queryId=3f656753ce886b285cc523e496a4142a&_phsrc=Mvp1&_phstart=successSource

[124] Nicholas Lemann, "The Origins of the Underclass: Free Fall" The Atlantic Online, June 1986 https://www.theatlantic.com/past/docs/politics/poverty/origin1.htm
[125] IBID

Before George Senior was married to Magnolia Simon in January 1920, we find a young George Scott, age 19, a farmer, in disdainful circumstances as a convict in residence at the Greenville, Washington "County Jail and Crazy House." A mere coincidence? Not the same George Scott? The records of blacks of the South were mostly incomplete or non-existent, so there is no corroborative evidence for this finding that he is the George Scott of interest, and we must work on genealogical assumptions. What does stand out is his age, which matches his birthdate; this is persuasive information, and we find him in Washington County, which helps to put this profile together. Further, it is compelling that you might ask for us to raise the question of how many George Scotts from one specific geographical area who are black, who were born in the same year, 1900, as our subject, are we likely to find with the same profile? And, since we can't find him in any other Mississippi census in that year - but found him in each census before - except being located in the Washington County prison system in Greenville, that has an appearance of being plausible.

Supposing George Scott Senior was that prisoner, and there's evidence pointing to that, he would have been subject to a grueling experience there. Mississippi's county penal system was a mere conduit to the dreaded state penal institution, *Parchman Farm*, notorious for slave-like conditions, including corporal punishment and the ghastly lash that was applied to an extreme. County prisoners were taken to Parchman's substantial cotton farm of some 20,000 acres, covering forty-six square miles; in effect, the convicts were loaned out nearly every day where they labored in the sprawling cotton fields. They were part of an infamous chain gang, always at the risk of being gunned down by the so-called *"Trusty shooters,"* select inmate armed guards who were granted privileges of power, among them incentives of shooting to kill any escapee. A legendary figure known as *"Long-Chain Charlie,"* who was a traveling sergeant of Mississippi's state penitentiary system, was charged with the mandate to round up and escort county prisoners to the notorious state prison of Sunflower County, situated northeast of the major towns of Cleveland and Greenville, and southeast of Clarksdale. *"Long-Chain Charlie"* had much to pick from in his rounds of county jails, with a focus on young inmates who were mostly incarcerated for *"Violations"* of vagrancy, which was an unofficial extension of the infamous Southern Black Codes of post-Civil War days, manifest around questionable minor offenses for which one would be hard-pressed to label as misdemeanors.

Author and Parchman Farm historian David Oshinsky highlights in his book *Worse Than Slavery* notes of a Northern penologist who was visiting Parchman in the 1920s on the matter of inmate guards. Parchman employed an irrational rule of shooting to kill any convict attempting to escape if they were unable to first stop the fleeing prisoner with a shotgun. It was built around a reward system. *"If he failed to stop him, then a guard with the rifle was to shoot to kill him, and if he killed the prisoner, he got a pardon,"* announced the troubled prison administrator.[126]

The Scott family very likely maintained from 20 to 25 acres of land, which was common for the cropper for an average to large size plantation. His role was strictly strenuous manual labor made up of planting seeds by hand, row by row, chopping or thinning the plants, a difficult task, and harvesting, also done manually, requiring hand-picking while stooped over low-slung cotton plants often under a broiling Mississippi sun. *"The conditions for sharecroppers and wage workers of the Delta were brutal,"* wrote Livia Gershon of the JSTOR Daily Newsletters, *"Pay was low, and whole families worked the fields. One census worker noted 10 to 20 people living in two- or three-room homes and women near death from tuberculosis still working in the fields."*[127] Quite possibly, he hired one or two field hands for help with harvesting the crops, including the services of his wife Magnolia - who had the added task of tending to young children - as the 1940 Census lists Scott as an *"Employer,"* distinguishing his farm role as a cropper, over laborer, and making it that much more difficult for any kind of profitable earnings compared to what could be gained by

---

[126] David M. Oshinsky, "Worse Than Slavery," p. 148
[127] Livia Gershon, Automation in the 1940s Cotton Fields, JSTOR Daily Newsletters, March 13, 2017
https://daily.jstor.org/automation-in-the-1940s-cotton-fields/

personal land ownership, as he now had to pay field hands.[128] Planters of the South had no intentions of yielding any part of their farms to what they perceived as alien ownership, especially the black type, to establish any kind of social parity. It was a world of exploitation for them, and they were quite content with that.

There were many historians and scholars who spoke nostalgically of the blue blood of the Old South, and American journalist H. L. Mencken was notable among them. His characterization of a vintage South painted a not uncommon picture of high-quality men of a manner of near unquestionable virtue: *"But in the South,"* he wrote, *"There were men of delicate fancy, urbane instinct and aristocratic manner – in brief, superior men – in brief, gentry."* [129] Mencken's protégé, W. J. Cash, however, saw it differently. A product of the South (1900-1941), Cash saw the South as hedonistic and proponents of the *"savage ideal,"* he so often spoke of, that favored hostility, violence, and deep-seated racism, and it was not limited in time. As Bertram Wyatt-Brown explained in his 1991 *Introduction of The Mind of W. J. Cash*, *"Owing to its succession of frontier stages, the South's leaders, early and late, were chiefly left-handed parvenu – the type whom*

---

[128] U. S. Census 1940, Avon, Longwood, Washington County, Mississippi, enumeration district 76-9; also see Sharecropping, Equal Justice Initiative, November 21, 2018
https://www.ancestry.com/discoveryui-content/view/121600775:2442
https://eji.org/news/history-racial-injustice-sharecropping/
[129] H. L. Mencken (Henry Louis), "Prejudices: Second Series," Octagon Books, New York, NY, 1977, p. 137

William Faulkner characterized in his portrayals of Thomas Sutpen and Flem Snopes."[130]

The catastrophic Mississippi River flood of 1927 that lay waste to Arkansas and Mississippi towns and farmlands, flooding the rich Delta alluvial plain, and exacerbated by the tumult of the stock market crash of 1929 in its wake, wrought havoc on the area - this happening while farmers were still cleaning up from the destruction left by the flood waters of the Mississippi - dealing a smashing blow to the Delta. Landowners were hamstrung in the aftermath and unable to get the credit they needed from banks, which were collapsing, cotton prices crashed, and black labor, the central figures to the success of cotton plantations, was encouraged by these disasters, poverty, and the burdens of *Jim Crow* to move north – leading to a significant wave of black emigration from the South until the full effect of the depression suppressed the initiative - leaving planters in the lurch. But the aftereffects of the flood and stock market disaster not only dismantled whites but permeated Southern blacks as well, whose plight was as refugees.

Hortense Powdermaker, in her extensive ethnographic field study of 1932-1934, came up with certain articles of faith, or a creed of racial relations, she coined it, which were met with nearly unanimous approval by

---

[130] W. J. Cash, quoted from "The Mind of the South," by Bertram Wyatt-Brown, "Introduction of The Mind of W. J. Cash," Vintage Books, New York, 1991, p. xxi (p. 21)

the whites of the region whom she interviewed. As she iterated, a main theme that came out of this study was *"Negroes are all right so long as they stay in their place. Their place is manual work, apart from and below the white person's place...because the whites are so seriously outnumbered, special means must be taken to keep the Negro in his place, and anyone who opposes those means is dangerous."*[131] It was a dominant and unifying theme among the Southern whites essential to their course of conduct with blacks with devout implications. Paradoxically, as much as whites spurned them, Southern planters took an opposite perspective of blacks when it came to serving white landlords, and this was pronounced after the 1927 flood when blacks were at high risk of leaving the Delta. *"Negroes are necessary to the South, and it is desirable that they should stay there and not migrate to the north,"* said Powdermaker in her treatise, codifying a near-unanimous viewpoint of the Southern planter.[132]

In the Delta, nothing was more concerning to planters about losing their tenant and sharecropper farmworkers than a risk of flood, and the 1927 overflow was cataclysmic, leaving thousands of black laborers stranded on the levees of the Delta without work or suitable dwelling.[133]

---

[131] Hortense Powdermaker, "After Freedom," p. 23
[132] IBID
[133] Flood Risk Map of Humphreys County, Mississippi River Flood of 1927 https://www.archives.gov/global-pages/larger-image.html?i=/publications/prologue/2007/spring/images/coast-miss-flood-l.jpg

It is probable that George Scott Senior was in this mix of displaced workers, surely being the case for Magnolia's relations with the Simon and Fesley families who worked the Delta properties of Washington County and were directly impacted by the flood. George Senior, originally of Anguilla, Sharkey County, Mississippi, was situated approximately 25 miles southeast of the *Longwood Plantation*, performing farm work in Humphreys County, 30 miles east of Anguilla. Humphreys County was in the floodplain that was ravaged by the river overflow. He lived with his first wife, Mary (James) Scott, in a more than likely common-law arrangement as was customary for the majority of Delta blacks then. They had been together for three years without children. *"The census information on the marital status of Negroes is especially inaccurate,"* reports historian Nicholas Lemann, *"Since unmarried couples are inclined to report themselves as married, and women who have never married but who have children are inclined to report themselves as widowed."*[134]

It was a chaotic time for both the black laborers and planters beleaguered by the impact and devastation of the floodwaters; each, however, was afflicted differently and possessed dissimilar goals. The farm workers were being held in a manner of servitude and destitute for income, with no means to protect themselves, while planters zealously stood their ground, preventing Northern agents' tampering with refugees, or allowing

---

[134] Nicholas Lemann, "The Promised Land," p. 29; also, U. S. Census 1930, Humphreys County, Beat 1, enumerated 28 April, 1930.

their accessibility, and otherwise being denied their human rights. Refugee camps crudely built were quickly formed, harboring tenant farmers and sharecroppers in the shape of prison camps where no one could go in or out without permission; it was a state of peonage. Planters would *"Hold their labor at the point of a gun for fear they would get away and not return,"* wrote award-winning historian of the American South, Pete Daniel.[135]

Prominent planter, attorney, and politician LeRoy Percy, who practiced law and resided in Greenville, Mississippi, who was a defender of Southern blacks against racism under the banner of noblesse oblige assumed a quite different, less compassionate stance toward them than he was accustomed in the circumstances of the 1927 flood. Contrary to the wishes of his son, Will Percy, who favored a compassionate evacuation of the seventy-five hundred refugees stranded on the levee, LeRoy saw this as a business risk that would pose grave consequences to their gilded *"Way of life,"* that both earnestly desired to protect. LeRoy generally sought a balance between planters and blacks. However, neither father nor son saw fit to consult with the refugees in these circumstances, the overall feeling that Delta blacks, though they should be treated fairly, were incapable of making decisions, and they were an encumbrance to them.

"By the end of the 1920s, most Delta blacks lived in severe economic deprivation, politically and legally powerless to improve their material

---

[135] Pete Daniel, "The Shadow of Slavery: peonage in the South, 1901-1969," Urbana, University of Illinois, 1972, p. 153

circumstances or even protect themselves from violence, coercion, or unlawful incarceration bordering on slavery," according to historian James C. Cobb. [136]

---

[136] James C. Cobb, "The Most Southern Place on Earth," p. 119

Chapter 3
The Blues Come Out of The Fields, Baby

All I can say is that when I was a boy we always was singing in the fields. Not real singing, you know, just hollering. But we made up our songs about things that was happening to us at the time, And I think that's where the blues started.

William Barlow [137]

It is not clear how long George was a county prisoner, or even if he actually was a convict as was posited earlier; however, we find him and his spouse Mary in Humphreys County in 1930 as farm laborers. Sixteen years prior to that, in 1914, when World War I broke out in Europe, there developed a shortage of industrial laborers, and with war preparation revving up industrial workers were in high demand, leading to the beginnings of black emigration from the South.

Between 1910, when the black migration movement first began, and the 1970s, an extraordinary movement, in the form of robust migratory waves of black Americans, approximately six million, described as the Great Migration, otherwise known as the Black Migration, left the South for Northern, Midwest, and Western states to escape the poverty, economic

---

[137] William Barlow "Looking Up at Down: the emergence of blues culture," Temple University, Philadelphia, 1989, p. 18
https://archive.org/details/lookingupatdowne0000barl_t3v3/page/18/mode/1up

hardship and discrimination in the South, manifest by the entrenchment of *Jim Crow* laws and the unjust treatment of sharecroppers and tenant farmers.[138]

Yet, George and Mary indefinably resisted the allure of northern industry, fervent recruiters, and even the promise of higher wages by stubbornly standing their ground and comfort of familiarity in spite of dreadful working conditions, social turmoil, and the effects of the flood they were put to endure. *"The result was in some ways disadvantageous for the blacks left in the South, for the planters and labor-employing farmers set themselves ruthlessly to stem the tide by the traditional Southern methods of violence and coercion,"* wrote W. J. Cash.[139] Planters, terror-stricken at the loss of farmworkers initiated an old arrangement of *"essential peonage,"* a Civil War tactic, bolstered by local sheriffs who were employed for administering restraint of black laborers by widespread use of horseback mounted posse's, including the occasional use of the bullwhip for good measure; it was used for the reassurance of seeing in their black workers good and acceptable behavior, but most of all it was simply used for reinforcing restraint with an element of barbarity.

---

[138] National Archives, African American Heritage: The Great Migration (1910-1970), undated
https://www.archives.gov/research/african-americans/migrations/great-migration
[139] W. J. Cash, "The Mind of the South," Vintage Books, A Division of Random House, Inc., New York, original edition by Alfred A. Knopf, Inc., 1941, p. 305.

These were troublesome times for the planters of the South and even more so for their croppers and tenant farmers, who were not benefitting from the government programs and handouts in the same manner that the planters were; although they were struggling as well but with greater room to maneuver nefariously and prohibitively around their less educated, highly dependent and obligated croppers, mostly by means of coercion. There was the 1927 Mississippi River flood that led to such enormous devastation causing social and financial unrest, especially toward blacks being held in refugee camps without recourse when there were better opportunities for them in northern parts of the country. George Scott Senior and wife Mary, who were believed to be in Humphreys County working the fields and plantations at that time, doubtless victims of the flood, were among the numerous refugees who were being tempted by the outreach of northern labor agents soliciting Southern black labor and from news and advertising filtering down from northern papers with questionable inducements, like the *Chicago Defender*, among several widely read black newspapers, exhorting black labor to leave the South for the North. But there was an ingredient of disillusionment mixed in with the movement, maybe not having quite the altruistic appeal that was being advertised. There were distinct racist issues mounting for blacks in the urban cities. *"White folks in Chicago, as everyone who moved North quickly found out, were not so completely different from white folks in Mississippi as was being advertised."* [140] In

---

[140] Nicholas Lemann, "The Promised Land: The Great Black Migration and How it Changed America," Vintage Books, A Division of Random House, Inc., New York, 1992, p. 41

spite of all the encouragement and exhortation they received to leave the South, northern cities like Chicago began to invoke residential segregation measures, such as massive and yet divided housing projects, to deal with the flow of blacks to the city as their numbers grew. Lemann described it, *"As soon as the flow of migrants became significant, though, white hostility toward blacks surged,"* elaborating further in three parts: *"partly from pure prejudice; partly from fear of the importation of the social ills created by Jim Crow; partly from intense competition in the labor market...a primal white antipathy."* [141] During this first wave of migrating Southern blacks, there was a genuine effort by strong leaders, both North and South, to promote an *"ethic of assimilation,"* according to Lemann, whether that be in white society or the black middle class.[142] However, this effort was to change post World War II when the second major phase of black migration was launched, leading to disorder and significant disorganization among the black population, ushering in poverty, white resistance, segregation, and disfranchisement of blacks.

Commensurate with the great flood in the same year were the first signs of the eventual Great Depression emerging from post-war Europe with the slowing of their economy, culminating in the memorable and crippling stock market crash of 1929, or, commonly known by sharecroppers as, *"the*

---

[141] Nicholas Lemann, "The Origins of the Underclass," The Atlantic Monthly, The Atlantic Online, June 1986
[142] IBID

panic crash." [143] Mississippi senior senator and wealthy planter James "Big Jim" Eastland, a fierce segregationist, advocate of white supremacy, and a force of resistance against later civil rights initiatives and government actions, came to the rescue of planters by infusing millions of dollars into their coffers. No funds, however, were similarly offered to blacks, whom Eastland insisted were "inferior" and undeserving. He stood firmly for the premise that whites and blacks should remain separate but conceded that maybe equal, he declared, according to the U. S. Supreme Court decision of 1896. One has to be skeptical, however, if *equality* with blacks received even his slightest attention, moral backing, or even political support, or if it wasn't just an illusion. The Supreme Court decision was a convenience to him, merely a talking point, but it never received his full embrace.[144]

Although the planter suffered greatly from the market collapse, black destabilization was even greater. W. J. Cash wrote: *"It was the conclusive disaster for the South. Immediate disaster for farmer, planter, tenant, and sharecropper, manifestly – disaster precisely like that in the nineties."* [145] This was 1931, and George Scott Senior was among the mix of sharecroppers and tenant farmers confronted with the exigencies of insolvency. *"The outbreak of the Great Depression in 1929 caused*

---

[143] Nicholas Lemann, "The Promised Land," p. 22
[144] Mike Wallace, "Interview with Senator James Eastland," Harry Ransom Center, The University of Texas, July 28, 1957.
https://hrc.contentdm.oclc.org/digital/collection/p15878coll90/id/22/
[145] W. J. Cash, "The Mind of the South," p. 360.

widespread suffering and despair in black communities across the country as women and men faced staggering rates of unemployment and poverty," wrote Mary Elizabeth B. Murphy of the Oxford University Press. [146] *"Few suffered more than African Americans, who experienced the highest unemployment rate during the 1930s,"* wrote Christopher Klein, history author and freelance writer, on the effects of the Depression on American blacks during this period.[147]

The doleful circumstances of sharecroppers and tenant farmers at this Post-World War I juncture were dreadful, as described unflatteringly by suffragist-activist Beulah Amidon Ratliff, who actually lived for a while in the Delta: *"The life of the Mississippi plantation Negro is toil, ignorance, hopelessness, animal stupidity and bestiality,"* she stated painting a picture of them as ill-bred and boorish, but with an intimation this was not of their own doing. [148]

---

[146] Mary Elizabeth B. Murphy, "African Americans in the Great Depression and New Deal," Oxford Research Encyclopedia, November 19, 2020
https://oxfordre.com/americanhistory/display/10.1093/acrefore/9780199329175.001.0001/acrefore-9780199329175-e-632;jsessionid=6303473D6310CFE48DF03D7DB5D7FA92

[147] Christopher Klein, "Last Hired, First Fired: How the Great Depression Affected African Americans," History, A & E Television Networks, April 18, 2018
https://www.history.com/news/last-hired-first-fired-how-the-great-depression-affected-african-americans#

[148] Beulah Amidon Ratliff, "Mississippi: Heart of Dixie," The Nation 114, May 17, 1922, p. 588

In his 1932 publication *Human Geography of the South* in which he describes the Mississippi Delta as *"Cotton obsessed, Negro obsessed, and flood ridden, it is the deepest South, the heart of Dixie,"* University professor and sociologist Rupert B. Vance described the Delta plantation conditions between whites and blacks as diametric; *"As long as they (white planters) held control, state politics preserved at least the form of dignity and decorum. Conversely, here the Negro is to be found at his lowest levels in America."*[149] There is little to no doubt that George Scott Senior was at his lowest level of personal affliction and anguish among so many of his kind who were struggling like him. We can't be sure he was even with Mary at the time of such chaos, mass confusion, and in the company of the poverty-stricken, but we will learn later that he would soon be on the *Longwood Plantation*, absent wife Mary. Their anguish was palpable as they wandered in large numbers along the rural streets, hoping for reassurance and comfort that was not about to come, leading them into nearby towns and the slums that were forming where farmworkers, out of jobs and soon their possessions, would congregate. *"Everybody was either ruined beyond his wildest previous fears or stood in peril of such ruin,"* wrote Cash about the *"general picture of the South in 1932."*[150]

---

[149] Rupert B. Vance, "Human Geography of the South: A Study in Regional Resources and Human Adequacy," The University of North Carolina Press, 1932, pages 266 & 270.
https://archive.org/details/humangeographyof0000rupe_i7i7/page/266/mode/1up
[150] W. J. Cash, "The Mind of the South," p. 362

In these lean years when profits were slim, planters found it hard to ignore the unrighteous opportunities of deceiving their croppers and tenants, tipping the financial scales in their favor. *"And so he was inevitably subject to the same temptation to grind or cheat his dependents which had beset his father,"* wrote Cash.[151] During this toxic period of adjustment to the stress of the Depression, the common white farmer was struggling to find any footing affecting him financially and socially, and he was beginning to frown upon elitists and blacks, creating in him a sense of and a state of class-consciousness. Cash, who claimed to be closer to the Southern mindset than most others since he grew up there observing and studying it first-hand, wrote: *"the common white had increasing cause in the decade to feel irritation – that there were powerful forces to move him toward the development of class consciousness all along the line."*[152] This would soon have repercussions on race relations, beginning with the 1950s when racial unrest rose dramatically to the surface catalyzed by the Emmett Till murder in 1955, which will be discussed in a later chapter.

When Franklin D. Roosevelt came into presidential power during the Depression, in that same year, 1933, that he took office, he immediately instituted programs and regulations that were officially labeled "The New Deal" in an attempt to quell the economic crisis. A major part of that initiative was the Agricultural Adjustment Act (AAA), which was aimed at

---

[151] IBID, p. 281
[152] IBID, p. 283

limiting crop production and in exchange, offering farmers and planters subsidies to offset the losses. Of course, this impacted the sharecroppers who were not direct recipients of government subsidies: the planters were – nor were these funds that were issued to the planters often shared with the croppers, contrary to what the government expected them to do - and once again unemployment had greatly mushroomed. It was a win-win for the planters. Cobb writes on the subject, *"It was the Delta planters, however, who actually became the prime beneficiaries of these new government initiatives, which not only boosted their incomes through acreage-control payments and price supports but reduced their labor needs and relieved them of their responsibilities as providers as well.*[153] Jim Powell, a Senior Fellow at the Cato Institute, published a report – contrary to widespread and archetypical government propaganda praising the plan - on the harmful effects of Roosevelt's New Deal on Southern blacks, which was cause for prolonged joblessness. The National Recovery Act authorized the president to issue executive orders that included a minimum wage; the regulations for this made it illegal to hire unskilled people who weren't worth the minimum, and Southern blacks lost their jobs.

The AAA Act aimed at cutting farm production forced an increase in food prices, further impacting black workers. Furthermore, New Deal spending had a major political element attached to it: the Roosevelt

---

[153] James C Cobb, "The Most Southern Place on Earth: The Mississippi Delta and the Roots of Regional Identity," p. 253.

Administration had its eye on the next election and not where it was needed most, thus largely distributing funds to both eastern and western sections of the country where he won by tight margins and funneling money away from Southern blacks. As Powell summed it up, *"If FDR's policies weren't conceived with racist intent, they certainly had racist consequences."*[154]

Planters were given a wide range of latitude and undeserved trust in navigating the government's AAA regulations encouraging deception, and any tenant farmer impudent enough to charge a landlord with cheating ran the risk of immediate eviction if not something worse. What's absurd about this is how the planters were themselves cheaters who manipulated the croppers and their tenants under the plan. By the AAA plan's encouragement of cutting back productive farmland and the fallout from that, tenant and cropper displacement, there evolved more day laborers who were exposed to depressed wages. According to economic historian Gavin Wright in his book *Old South, New South,* the AAA administration naively assumed that the plowing of crops *"would come proportionately from the entire plantation acreage, the wage-labor section and the tenants' plots."* But, as he noted, benefits from reductions in tenants' acreage had to be shared while those from wage labor were not. *"The best option from the landlord's standpoint was to take the reduction from the tenants' acreage*

---

[154] Jim Powell, CATO Inst, "Why Did FDR's New Deal Harm Blacks?" The Cato Institute, Washington, DC.
https://www.cato.org/commentary/why-did-fdrs-new-deal-harm-blacks

but report it as coming from the wage-labor section."[155] A win-win for the planter, or one might avow a *"winked-at deception"* manifestly, per James C. Cobb.[156]

At about this time, it was apparent that George Scott Senior was no longer residing with his wife, Mary. There are no records to explain the reason for this separation, and thus, it is left to conjecture. However, Lemann, in his work *The Promised Land*, summing up years of historical scholarship on speculation about sharecropper marriages and comparisons with marriages and family under slavery, stated this, citing author Herbert Gutman: *"the available evidence about the sharecropper family indicates that first marriages of lifelong duration were the exception,"* compared to families under slavery, but the actual structure of the sharecropping family remains *"somewhat mysterious"* and not fully examined.[157] Since, in most cases, records of Delta blacks were scant during this era, some genealogical assumptions come into play. As speculated earlier, based on census, family birth, and death information, it is likely that George Senior and Magnolia were on the *Longwood Plantation* together sometime between 1934 and 1935, working as sharecroppers for white planter Thomas T. H. Bond, whom Magnolia's parents and grandparents had been working for, and

---

[155] Gavin Wright, "Old South, New South: revolutions in the southern economy since the Civil War," New York: Basic Books, 1986, p. 228.
[156] James C. Cobb, "The Most Southern Place on Earth", p. 189.
[157] Nicholas Lemann, "The Promised Land," p. 30. Lemann referenced Author Herbert Gutman on the subject of black families during and post-slavery, from his book "The Black Family in Slavery and Freedom, 1750-1925, Pantheon Books, New York, 1976.

where they were residing, prior to the arrival of George Senior to this property. Their oldest son, Otis, was born there in 1936. George Senior, his wife Magnolia, who was also born and raised in *Longwood* in Avon village, Otis, and daughter Beatrice were verifiably located on the *Longwood Plantation* according to the 1940 census.[158]

The social panoply of the Southern plantation's sharecroppers and tenant farmers, previous to World War II, was, in a word, dysfunctional; croppers, amongst other black farmworker types, were coexisting in a manner of full reliance upon their landlords who had *"set up a system so as to inculcate a state of dependency in the sharecroppers...kind of a permanent dole,"* wrote American psychologist and social scientist John Dollard.[159] Charles Johnson, an American sociologist and lifelong advocate for racial equality, wrote predictively that because sharecroppers lived in such a high degree of social isolation caused extraordinary limitations and deviant behaviors; among them, moral issues, illiteracy, the worst of public education, and violent crime, and such was in greater evidence the closer they got to tangible American society and its values, if that was to happen. It was the more likely they would be confronted with social disorganization

---

[158] U. S. Census 1940, Avon, Longwood, Washington County, Mississippi, enumeration district 76-9
[159] John Dollard, "Caste and Class in a Southern Town," Garden City, NY: Doubleday and Co., 1937, p. 404
http://www.mississippidelta.com/AAv106no2June2004.pdf

https://academic.oup.com/ahr/article-abstract/43/2/428/48380

and ultimately end in failure. *"The very fact,"* he asserted, *"of this cultural difference presents the danger of social disorganization in any sudden attempt to introduce new modes of living and conceptions of values."*[160] His hypothesis of ensuing social disorganization held its ground, as we shall see during phase two of the Great Migration.

Insightful white planters, a highly suspicious breed of the gentleman class, were sensing unrest at the beginning of the pre-war 1940s, accompanied by the eventual erosion of their "way of life" with Southern blacks of the Delta; their main interest was the preservation of the institution of segregation, and they were searching for some kind of equilibrium. Black World War II veterans enjoyed a taste of freedom from their segregationist past and were agitating for further leniencies from intransigent Southern whites. Planters had suffered a considerable loss of black labor that had left the South for the industrial North. In deference, they appealed to Northern black leadership in an effort to appease the migrants to return but were warned that any such thing would have to be conditional; black leaders were asked to submit a list of grievances, which they did extensively. *"Confronted with all this, the whites did nothing,"* wrote Lemann.[161]

---

[160] Charles Johnson, "Shadow of the Plantation," University of Chicago Press, 1934, p. 209.
https://archive.org/details/shadowofplantati0000john_b0b5

[161] Nicholas Lemann, "The Promised Land," p. 48

It was a prelude to mechanized cotton farming accompanied by further destabilization of the work force. Although mechanized equipment for harvesting cotton had its early beginnings in the mid-1940s, it wasn't until the mid to late 1950s, and some operations extending into the 1960s, that cotton crops were, to a great extent harvested mechanically in the South by use of combines, which had a cataclysmic effect on black farm laborers, struggling as they already were, as their services in large part were no longer being needed. In October 1944, on the Hopson plantation in Clarksdale, Mississippi – Clarksdale being the fountainhead of so many significant Delta beginnings rooted in black history - the mechanical cotton picker made its debut, compliments of the *International Harvester* company that perfected its invention, and, as importantly, their ability to mass-produce it. Howell Hopson, the plantation owner, doing some fancy cost-accounting of his own, estimated that *"picking a bale of cotton by machine cost him $5.26, and picking it by hand cost him $39.41. Each machine did the work of fifty people,"* he claimed.[162] *The Wessels*, celebrated farmers of York, Nebraska, historians of farming operations and agriculture, published a historical essay on the efficiencies of cotton harvesting and sharecropping, commenting on the evolution and impact on field hands brought about by mechanized farm equipment; *"It's estimated that each two-row cotton combine replaced about 80 sharecroppers and farm workers."* [163]Lemann writes, *"What the*

---

[162] IBID, p. 5
[163] Bill Ganzel, "Farming in the 1950s & 60s: Cotton Harvesting, the Ganzel Group, Wessels Living History Farm, York, Nebraska, 2007.

mechanical picker did was make obsolete the sharecropper system, which arose in the years after the Civil War as the means by which cotton planters' need for a great deal of cheap labor was satisfied."[164] In April 1944, Richard Hopson, who managed the Hopson Plantation's finances, wrote an ardent letter to the local cotton council pointing out the alarming labor shortages affecting the Delta coupled with an emerging and "serious racial problem" on the horizon manifest by recent racial unrest and the likelihood of it getting much worse; his message to the Delta farmers was one of urgency to make a change, a big change before real trouble began by *"changing as rapidly as possible from the old tenant or sharecropping system of farming to complete mechanized farming,"* requiring smaller amounts of labor bringing equilibrium to the work force and *"make our racial problem easier to handle."*[165]

The success of mechanized cotton pickers led to a further departure of black farmers – or, phase two of the Great Migration of the 1940s - who emigrated to the Northern and Western states and into an entirely new lifestyle: urbanization. Some hung on, and possibly that included George Scott Senior, as day laborers, left to the chopping of cotton that mechanized pickers could not handle, or in rare instances, they took on jobs as salaried employees driving tractors. With the changes, there was, of course, no further need for large numbers of field hands like croppers who were being

---

https://livinghistoryfarm.org/farminginthe50s/machines_15.html
[164] Nicholas Lemann, "The Promised Land," p. 5
[165] IBID, p. 49-50

rapidly discharged by landlords and whose jobs were being supplanted by agricultural mechanization. Cash spoke of the mechanized cotton picker as, *"an ominous machine...it promises to eliminate most or all of the sharecroppers and a great many of the tenants within a short period since it overcomes the last and principal barrier to the mechanization of Southern cotton farming."*[166] This had to ignite a sense of foreboding and feelings of great incertitude in the mind of George Senior as he watched his colleagues uprooting their lives in significant numbers. George Hicks, a black migrant himself, who rose to management levels within the Chicago Housing Authority, saw nothing but hopelessness among the many uneducated migrants who left the South arriving in Chicago, landing on welfare and into the projects of Chicago; he was more deliberate, if not blunt, in his assessment of the true cause of black emigration occurring in such large numbers: *"The cotton-picking machine had thrown them out of work,"* it was that simple exclaimed Hicks, according to Nicholas Lemann in his book, *The Promised Land*.[167]

A greater problem was emerging, or at least was contemplated, by noted historian and prolific non-fiction writer David L. Cohn (1894-1960), who was born and raised in Greenville, Mississippi, in the heart of the Delta. It was said that no one knew the Mississippi Delta and the South more intimately than Cohn. In his most noted and best-known publication, *Where*

---

[166] W. J. Cash, "The Mind of the South," p. 411
[167] Nicholas Lemann, "The Promised Land," p. 275

I Was Born and Raised, written in 1947, Cohn sounded the alarm of an ensuing displacement of some five million farm workers, warning the Northern public of *"an enormous tragedy"* that was about to befall the United States; they were mostly blacks, who were already in different stages of migration, but the long-range effects would prove of even greater consequences as their numbers continued to mount. These were farm labor blacks, unskilled and completely unprepared for urban and industrial life, who were uprooted from the South and would land in Northern whites' backyards unannounced. They also happened to be unprepared for their arrival. *"If tens of thousands of Southern Negroes descend upon communities totally unprepared for them psychologically and industrially, what will the effect be upon race relations in the United States?"* he questioned. He also raised the specter of what the impact would be on migrant Southern blacks: *"Will the victims of farm mechanization become the victims of race conflict?"* A compelling question, he intimated, laced with components of prophesy.[168] Clarksdale, the county seat of Coahoma County, a major part of the cotton belt and where the blues music originated, had shed a large percentage of their black labor. *"It seemed as if the whole black society of Clarksdale and the Mississippi Delta had transferred itself to Chicago,"* wrote Lemann.[169]

---

[168] David L Cohn, "Where I Was Born and Raised," Kahle/Austin Foundation, 1948, p. 330
https://archive.org/details/whereiwasbornrai0000davi/page/330/mode/1up

[169] Nicholas Lemann, "The Promised Land," p. 95

It is difficult to know just what might have been going through *Longwood* planter-owner Thomas H. Bond's mind all during this time as obtrusive dynamics, including unsavory group dynamics, were in force, many of them surely unsettling for him, that was likely to affect his plans and ultimate course of action as he set his sights on the workings and future of his considerable plantation. The civil unrest prevalent in the Delta's Mississippi counties had to be disturbing as there were rumblings of school desegregation about to occur throughout the Southern states, manifestly in Mississippi, that was getting the white South's attention, and not in a good way. Additionally, the New Deal, in spite of it having been introduced 10 years before, was still causing unrest among a multitude of plantation ownership and black laborers playing a part in their mass emigration. And then there was a general awareness of the development and manufacture by the Rust brothers of Memphis of the mechanized cotton picker, actually as early as 1934, but delayed from mass manufacture for a while because of their "social conscience," said "Jack" Cash, of what impact it would have on yeoman white farmers who were heavily invested in traditional farm operations, including a few plantation owners, who, at first, were reluctant to invest in the costly new machinery. Many of the landowner classes put up initial resistance to the government's meddling with cotton farming operations, according to W. J. Cash: *"Planter and yeoman alike were plainly heading for disaster in their stubborn failure to analyze the situation before them, their smug insistence on assigning most of their troubles to a man, (namely, Roosevelt), or a set of men in Washington."* [170]

All of this had to be troubling to *Longwood*'s Thomas Bond, who may have been a man of immutable views and more or less set in his ways; it was not unusual for a refined Southern gentleman planter of his class and generation believe that the preservation of traditional Southern comportment and customs was of paramount importance, above all else. For that matter, and to illustrate this, daughter Eva Mae Bond filled the society pages of the local papers, including a large portraiture photo in Greenville's *Delta Democrat-Times* in the fall of 1937 announcing her impending marriage; it was the embodiment of Southern societal splendor on display in its truest of traditions manifest of the Old South, epitomizing where T. H. Bond may have stood in the political and moral culture of the Delta.[171]

It is doubtful Bond would have flinched at the idea of introducing mechanized cotton pickers – harvester combines - to his extensive cotton operations, however, as he was no stranger to understanding the advantages of heavy equipment and machinery, having once been a partner of a levee

---

[170] W. J. Cash, "The Mind of the South," p. 413
[171] The Delta Democrat Times, Oct 1937 "Society, Clubs and Personals, Engagement Announced, Announcement Party for Miss Bond," The Delta Democrat Times, Greenville, Mississippi, Oct 24, 1937, p. 10.
https://www.newspapers.com/image/33932537/?terms=T%20H%20bond&match=1
https://www.newspapers.com/image/33932656/?terms=T%20H%20bond&match=1
https://www.newspapers.com/image/33932719/?terms=Eva%20mae%20bond&match=1

construction company, known popularly as "levee contractors," in Bolivar County. Surely, he saw the advantages they would generate to managing a cotton farm operation with greater efficiency and lower cost. It is even possible that he was one of the first plantation owners to use one, though mechanization was in the groundbreaking stages.[172] But, importantly, it was also a time when black farm laborers were pulling up stakes and leaving the South in large numbers and at a rattling pace for what, as they were informed by means of goading by labor agents and quite extravagant initiatives and inducements by media types, was "the promised land" of Chicago and other greater northern and western cities; the die was cast. Doubtless, Thomas Bond saw the writing on the wall with their departure and was forced to make decisions he had not confronted before. As Lemann writes, *"The black migration was one of the largest and most rapid mass internal movements of people in history – perhaps the greatest not caused by the immediate threat of execution or starvation."* [173] Lemann points out, *"The invention of the cotton picker was crucial to the great migration by blacks...five million of them moved after 1940, during the time of the mechanization of cotton farming."* If we were to point to any foremost reason for blacks deserting the Southern cotton farms, leaving black America *"half Southern...and less than a quarter rural,"* it would have to

---

[172] The Bolivar County Democrat, pg 5-6 "Minutes of Regular July, 1918, Meeting of the Board of Mississippi Levee Commissioners," Rosedale, Mississippi, July 27, 1918, pages 5-6
[173] Nicholas Lemann, "The Promised Land," p. 6

be mechanized farming, with living in poverty and lack of upward mobility a close second.[174]

T.H. Bond was, all the same, between the ages of 70-71 when much of this widespread restlessness and social disruption was transpiring around him and may have quite simply decided it was a convenient, if not strategic, time to retire, which he did so in the spring of 1944. In fact, there is evidence he may have been an absentee landlord for a while, which was coming into fashion at right about this time. His announcement was made in the fall of 1943, yet we find the family still in the *Longwood* area, Greenville, and at Bond's other plantation, *Idlewild*, until at least May 1944.[175] It is not known how long he may have remained in this working arrangement, bathed in elements of avarice, it seems, if that's what he was doing. Cash's treatise of the Southern mind, of which he was intimately familiar, spoke about absentee landlordism in his book *The Mind of the South*, pointing to a phenomenon of landowning farmers selling their properties to speculators, many of whom lived in other states and counties. In many instances, however, white property owners preferred to hold onto their farms, renting to croppers and tenants instead of selling and extracting what profits they could. *"The growth of absentee landlordism often meant that the tenant saw*

---

[174] IBID
[175] The Delta Democrat Times, 1943-1944 "Mrs. W. D. Stovall Elected President of Longwood Club," The Delta Democrat-Times, Greenville, Mississippi, September 21, 1943, p. 3: "Longwood Culture Club Has Interesting Program," The Delta Democrat-Times, Greenville, Mississippi, May 28, 1944, p. 6

his landlord now only occasionally; often, he saw him not at all, but dealt with him only through an agent," pointing to the erosion of any social value to be gained that was once shared between croppers, tenants, and their plantation ownership.[176]

As difficult as it might have been for plantation owner T. H. Bond by the same measure, it had to have been infinitely unsettling for George Scott Senior and his family. Their lives were a paradox; both were faced with problematic decisions but from quite different perspectives, one who had leverage within which to make crucial decisions while the other, George Senior, who was dependent on the former. For George, it had to be heart-wrenching. Despite the mass exodus of his contemporaries who were seeking better lives for themselves, or at least it's what they were made to believe, for whatever his reasons might have been for staying put at the time, George Scott Senior went against the grain, as was his inclination, choosing to remain behind on *Longwood Plantation*. Croppers had the option of leaving one plantation for another in the hope of bettering themselves, which they called "slipping," and exerting some kind of control over their lives, but it usually made little difference. It still came down to making the more difficult decision of actually leaving family and friends and at least anticipating some small support from landlords that they could not expect by moving away. However, *"The blacks who stayed behind suffered from abject poverty and near starvation,"* wrote Hugh Sidey of *Time Magazine*,

---

[176] W. J. Cash, "The Mind of the South," p. 282

and we can expect that the George Scott Senior family was most likely among them. Sidey drew attention to the words of an alarmed U. S. Attorney General Bobby Kennedy during his 1967 spring visit to the Delta, *"My God,"* Kennedy blurted as he viewed the poverty, *"I didn't know this kind of thing existed. How can a country like this allow it?"*[177]

George Senior and Magnolia's third child, George Charles Scott Jr., who would later rise to fame as a professional ballplayer, was born on March 23, 1944, on the *Longwood Plantation*, in their distressingly cramped cabin, where the extended family resided and worked, approximately 12 miles south of Greenville, the seat of Washington County. Daughter Beatrice, who lived there with her family until about the age of 7, when her mother and siblings moved to Greenville, remembers the cabin more like a shack, describing it in a manner of coping *"in a very small house"* with a couple of rooms, unpainted undried pine clapboards that would shrink in the sun creating drafty conditions, vintage newspapers lining the walls for insulation, no indoor plumbing, and a minimum of furniture that George Senior would have had to pay for with his advance money received from the planter. It lacked window shades, just curtains that provided little privacy, and no pictures on the walls. Her father, George, lacked enough money for family photographs or a camera with which to

---

[177] Hugh Sidey, "Hugh Sidey's America: Sad Song of the Delta," Time, the Weekly Newsmagazine, New York, NY, June 24, 1991, Vol. 137, No. 25, pg 18

take them. Her recollection of living conditions was that it was bleak and well worth dismissing from her mind.[178]

Beatrice, sister of George Scott Jr., and George Scott Jr. (author's collection)

As for staples, notably food, it depended on planters' cash advances, which, in most cases, was deducted at the time of season's-end settlements. Cash advances were often cutoff between working seasons of cotton planting and harvesting, although some landlords would continue them until

---

[178] Beatrice Scott interviews: May 3, 2006 & January 27, 2009

the settlement period when deductions would be made. According to Dorothy Dickins' nutritional study of the Yazoo Mississippi Delta, *"There are a few planters who do not stop advancing supplies the year around but carry all credits and charges on the books until the date of settlement at the end of the year."*[179] Diets of black croppers and tenants *"were much lower in energy value and in the 4 nutritive factors than those of white people,"* and many of them consumed no milk at all for calcium, manifesting in the development of Rickets. Dietary staples were heavy on biscuits, fried pork, and cornbread.[180]

Many planters had allowed their croppers and tenants some land near their cabins to raise their own vegetables and where they could keep livestock, which helped with food supply; however, following the arrival of mechanization, planters conjured underhanded methods of strongarming in an effort to dispense with their croppers whose services were no longer needed; sadly, they plowed under their cropper's and tenant's garden plots and livestock yards in order to grow cotton, as encouragement for them to leave. Disenchantment couldn't have been more widespread among the black croppers and tenants than it was after mechanized cotton pickers surfaced, and their unrest led to their departure, but also further unrest. *"The Delta blacks joined the 5 million Southern rural blacks who fled to the cities*

---

[179] Dorothy Dickins, "A Nutrition Investigation of Negro Tenants in the Yazoo Mississippi Delta," Mississippi Agricultural Experiment Station, A. & M. College, Mississippi, J. R. Ricks, Director, p. 11 footnote
[180] IBID, p. 17

of the South, West and North, bringing to urban culture their broken hearts in a tragic search for a fragment of dignity and security," wrote *Time Magazine's* Sidey.[181]

Magnolia (Simon) (Gilmore) Scott, George Scott Jr's beloved mother, whom he adored and endearingly referred to as "momma" even into his later years, had informed the family of their slavery origins dating to the early 19th Century. Magnolia shared with young George his ancestry with their Fesley family, Owen, and Margaret, George Junior's great-great grandparents, with whom a slave connection is made. Doubtless, there were more slaves in the Fesley family line, the Simons, and most likely the Scott line as well, as this was mid-19th century Mississippi when and where blacks of that era were shown no quarter when it came to their hope for freedom. Family historical written records were scant; oral histories, however, were not, but they were laced with folklore of myth, beliefs, and stories based on assumptions expressed in their own interpretive style. [182] Central Texas journalist Roscoe Harrison reminded black and white audiences, through his presentations and his journalism, that *"black history is kept alive only through generations of storytelling,"*[183] reinforcing what was learned, and

---

[181] Hugh Sidey, "Hugh Sidey's America: Sad Song of the Delta," p. 18

[182] Literacy by Any Means Necessary: The History of Anti-Literacy Laws in the U. S. by Carliss Maddox, January 12, 2022; https://oaklandliteracycoalition.org/literacy-by-any-means-necessary-the-history-of-anti-literacy-laws-in-the-u-s/

[183] Patricia Benoit, Telegram Staff Writer, Temple Daily Telegram, Feb 6, 2022 https://www.tdtnews.com/news/central_texas_news/article_7a3521a0-879b-11ec-9ccc-dfc5dcecb0a7.html

how it was, by the Scott family, and most was in the form of anecdotal evidence, watered down with time.

These stories left their mark on a young George Scott Junior; it was like a millstone about his neck, being born in the Deep South to a legacy of enslavement, *Jim Crow*, racial unrest, segregation, and profound poverty. He would soon realize the extant nature of these dehumanizing conditions while growing up in the nearby town of Greenville and speak often about it, in moments of anguish and occasional tears, mostly from frustration, about how his mother suffered under these egregious terms. It was very painful to him and a dominating force in any decisions he was to make about his own future that was to affect his mother.

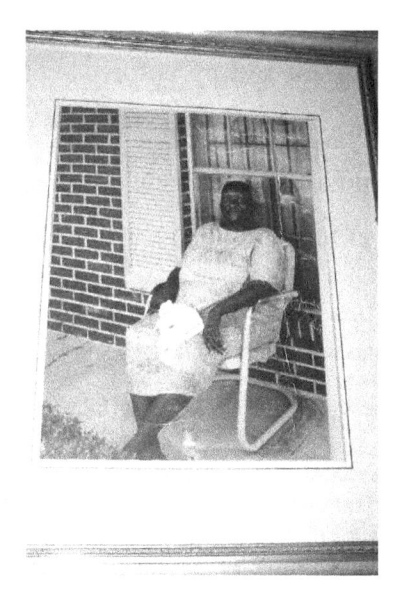

(Courtesy George Scott, Jr.)
Magnolia (Simon) (Gilmore) (Scott) Straw,
mother of George Scott Jr., circa 1990-2000

Of the considerable number of Mississippi's black-American population of the early to mid-20th century, outnumbering whites in most towns by 60%-70%, it just may be that the Delta's blacks, whose noteworthy skill was cotton farming, were marginalized even more than their counterparts of neighboring Mississippi counties. [184] Though hard to imagine anything more difficult than what blacks generally confronted in Mississippi, being a black sharecropper of the Delta may have been worse; it was merely a different kind of slavery, arguably as punishing and unrewarding, with nothing to offer them but a bleak outlook. And of little doubt, this kind of work imposed a heavy toll on George Senior's long-term tolerance, acuity, health, and, by all means, his personal endurance.

They were in a mix of altogether unenlightened, undereducated people, structured into a caste system and by enforcement measures meant to be kept that way by white landowners, who provided them with few opportunities, ruling by political disenfranchisement, with a de-emphasis on education, which was enforced in most cases. For those who chose to

---

[184] - Story Behind the Number: Literacy and Lynchings, NPR, All Things Considered, February 4, 2006.
https://www.npr.org/templates/story/story.php?storyId=5189912
Race and the Economy of the Delta, Race and the Economy of the Delta, Racial and Ethnic Tensions in American Communities: Poverty, Inequality, and Discrimination Volume VII: The Mississippi Delta Report, U. S. Department of Commerce
https://www.usccr.gov/files/pubs/msdelta/ch1.htm
Based on the data presented in tables 1.1 1.9 above, it is clear that the Delta is an economically impoverished region for both blacks and whites. However, the data also reveal that black Delta citizens are the poorest of the poor. In every section of the region a majority, or near majority, of the black residents live in poverty. Such is not the case for a majority of the region's white residents.

abandon the South for what they understood were greener pastures, there was the anomaly of social segregation as their background, which was manifest in the cultural character of the black Southern farmworker; the fallout from this was a more problematic deviant element of social disorganization, a spatial concept defining a subculture and the stunting of human development leading to inevitable delinquency and crime at neighborhood levels. Whereas the first great migration was an effort to assimilate blacks with whites or the black middle class, this ethic broke down during the second migration. *"The preaching of assimilation by both blacks and whites stopped. What followed was a kind of free fall into what sociologists call social disorganization,"* postulates Lemann. [185] To bolster such heinous efforts of entrapment, Southern states organized themselves in the late 19th century by establishing new constitutions that imposed onerous poll taxes and voting literacy tests that unsurprisingly, perhaps also remarkably, withstood decades of Southern politics and state court deliberations. When one method of white suppression was overturned, the state would invent a way to come up with another ad nauseam. Astonishingly, these acts of political and judicial malfeasance held rural blacks hostage for decades until the Civil Rights Movement of the 1960s.

Few things were more gratifying or quieting in the minds of black sharecroppers during these arduous times and stressful moments of *Jim Crow* than the evolution of a uniquely black-inspired anomalous music form

---

[185] Nicholas Lemann, "The Origins of the Underclass," June 1986

called *The Blues*, which had its origins in the Delta cotton fields of the late 19th and early 20th centuries, to become the quintessential foundation of America's popular music: jazz, rhythm and blues, rock, pop, and country music. There was a distinctive correlation between the sharecropping of the Delta and the origination of this *"disturbing monotony"* of music, so expressed by W. C. Handy, called the blues. [186] Handy, it turned out, was honored with the moniker *"Father of the Blues,"* having discovered this form of music he called his "enlightenment" during a trip through Cleveland, Mississippi, which he aptly used as a title for his 1941 autobiography.[187] Lemann writes, *"The black culture associated with sharecropping – including that culture's great art form, the blues – found its purest expression in the Delta. The Delta was the locus of our own century's peculiar institution."*[188]

An early pioneer of blues music, Booker T. White, more often known by the sobriquet *Bukka*, named after prominent black educator, activist, and presidential advisor Booker T. Washington, was an acquaintance and contemporary of George Senior, having met in the juke joints of Greenville

---

[186] W. C. Handy, "Father of the Blues: An Autobiography," Macmillan Company, New York, 1941, p. 77
https://archive.org/details/fatherofbluesaut00wcha_0/page/74/mode/1up
[187] IBID, p.76; also, "The Enlightenment of W. C. Handy," HMdb.org; the historical marker database, Cleveland in Bolivar County, Mississippi
https://archive.org/details/fatherofbluesaut00wcha_0/page/76/mode/1up
https://www.hmdb.org/m.asp?m=90071
[188] Nicholas Lemann "The Promised Land," p. 15

on Nelson Street in the early 1930s.[189] George Senior played the harmonica and was known to engage with Bukka and another harmonica player, George "Bullet" Williams, on Saturday night foregathers in the town and pick-up music joints of adjacent towns, such as Greenwood and Itta Bena, where they would congregate and play their blues music.[190] Bukka White, who spent a brief time as a resident in the infamous state's Parchman Farm prison system between 1937-1939, allegedly for committing a murder, and would later, after his release, bring his new blues music to Chicago, where he made his recordings, had labored on cotton plantations of the Delta. White's flamboyance and passion about the origin of the blues are found in David Evans' manuscript *Big Road Blues,* in which he states: *"That's where the blues start from, back across them fields, you know…It started right behind one of them mules or one of them log houses, one of them log camps or the levee camp. That's where the blues sprung from."* [191] Cobb, in his 1999 tome *Redefining Southern Culture,* referring to Booker T. Washington's celebrated and historical book, *"Up from Slavery,"* explains his own suggested variation to that title, or where he felt the emphasis

---

[189] Bukka White; based on information passed down by Magnolia Scott through her daughter Beatrice, interview January 2009
[190] Beatrice Scott interviews 2009
[191] David Evans, Big Road Blues: tradition and creativity in the folk blues, New York: Da Capo Press, 1987, p. 43

should be, in the context and expression of the blues: *"Instead of 'Up from Slavery' the message of the blues was 'Up from Slavery, but Not Far.'"*[192]

A phenomenon known as *field hollers* was the source for the blues that emerged in the late 19th to early 20th centuries among Southern blacks; bards of a sort they would come up with any topic, mostly rueful or with touches of melancholy, they could put to a tune and ply to lyrics – expressions of alienation, dissatisfaction, separation, man-woman relationships, social injustice – performed in painfully, frequent wailing, in falsetto, and overall distressfully mannered cries that would waft over the cotton fields; this frequently elicited in-kind holler responses from farmworkers of nearby and outer-reach farms as a means of communication to break their sense of isolation. Lawrence Levine wrote, *"The rise of the blues did not call for the invention of wholly new musical forms. The same musical repertory and traditions out of which black spirituals, work songs, and hollers were forged was sufficient to structure the blues as well."* He states further, *"When the blues was created is less important than when it became a dominant musical form among Negroes throughout the country; when it can be taken as expressing the consciousness, the attitudes, the experiences of large numbers of Negroes in America."*[193] And so, it was shaped: the foundation

---

[192] James C. Cobb, "Redefining Southern Culture: Mind & Identity in the Modern South," The University of Georgia Press, Athens, Georgia, 1999, p. 98 https://archive.org/details/redefiningsouthe0975cobb/page/97/mode/1up

[193] Lawrence Levine, Black Culture and Black Consciousness: Afro-American folk thought from slavery to freedom, Oxford, New York, Oxford University Press, 2007, p. 221

for these various black musical cacophonies, rhythms, tones, melodies, and even euphonies evolved into a musical form that we have come to know today as the blues.

"Generally, this music was played at house parties, roadhouses called juke joints, outdoor picnics for dancing, and for tips from onlookers on sidewalks, railroad stations, store porches, and wherever else a crowd might gather," according to professor emeritus of history and southern studies at the University of Mississippi, Charles R. Wilson, who co-edited *Encyclopedia of Southern Culture*, with Dr. William Ferris, scholar and former chairman of the National Endowment for the Humanities. [194] Croppers and farm laborers often found time to assemble at neighboring shacks at the end of a work day, even if only for a short time following a hard day's work, with their assortment of instruments - some homemade - to strum, pick, tap and stomp simple rhythmic musical patterns that met with the full approval of the cotton farmers attending, and who were participating, at these gatherings. George Scott Senior performed with rhythmic, harmonic movement, smoothly known for his skilled accompaniment of fellow hobnobbing musicians. The informality of this was of a folk-blues format, known as *"jug bands, which generally consisted*

---

[194] Wilson, Charles R. & Ferris, William R., "Encyclopedia of Southern Culture," Chapel Hill, University of North Carolina Press, pgs 995-996

of a guitar and harmonica supplemented by other novelty or homemade instruments such as a jug, kazoo, washboard, or one-stringed bass." [195]

The harmonica played a meaningful role in the evolution of the blues from the origins of the loose field hollers to the emergence of blues ballads, and George was very much a part of this, but mainly in an informal way: on the plantations, in juke joints and informal pick-up gigs. As for the harmonica's importance, especially in the early years of the blues, Evans wrote, *"the field holler vocal was combined with one of the common harmonic accompaniment patterns of the blues ballad,"* in the form of narrative folksongs of life events common to blues ballads.[196]

William Barlow saw *"a clear historical connection"* between the insurrectionary spirit and restlessness of the black cotton farmer and the new music of the blues to explain their *"mass exodus out of the cotton belt."*[197] Scholar Joel Williamson, Ph.D. professor of history at the University of North Carolina, known as the "historian's historian," for whom a distinguished professorship was founded, wrote that the blues was *"the cry of the cast-out black, ultimately alone and lonely, after one world was lost and before another was found."*[198] With all the turmoil and angst

---

[195] IBID, p. 996.
[196] David Evans, Big Road Blues: tradition and creativity in the folk blues, New York: Da Capo Press, 1987, p. 44
[197] William Barlow, Looking Up at Down: the emergence of blues culture," p. 6
[198] Joel Williamson, The Crucible of Race: black-white relations in the American South since emancipation, New York; Oxford University Press, 1984, p. 213

being provoked by the blacks of the South at the time, causing them to leave, historian James C. Cobb makes the point about the blues, in deference of that: *"The blues were no more the music of those who had decided to leave than of those who had decided to stay or, perhaps more so, those who were unable to decide."*[199]

A profound point of view, and this was surely the quandary that George Scott Senior doubtless was dealing with as he watched his counterparts in large numbers marching off the cotton fields in their quest, and their zestfulness, for that avowed so-called promised land. It had to raise his distress level to greater heights as the support system with which he was familiar and in which he coalesced was collapsing around him, and as he became one of the few remaining croppers at *Longwood*, it caused him further strain.

For the stragglers, as in George and Magnolia, *"There was anything but stability and promise in their existence,"* wrote Cobb. *"They became part of a forever shifting, essentially rootless farm labor force, more concerned about survival than advancement."*[200] The restlessness and doubt they felt about making difficult choices were inexorably inculcated in the quality of their music, such as the following example of Mississippi blues traveling musician Charley (or Charlie) Patton:

---

[199] James C. Cobb, "The Most Southern Place on Earth," p. 284
[200] IBID

Sometimes I say I need you;

Then again, I don't...

Sometimes I think I'll quit you;

Then again, I won't.[201]

Patton, a mixture of black, white, and native American, often referred to as the Father of the Delta Blues, was a preeminent pioneer of blues music who tired of the sharecropper lifestyle and chose to travel in vagabond fashion along the Mississippi River, vocalizing his torments and misfortunes, in joints, storefronts, and railroad stations, playing among an assemblage of fellow croppers, farm workers, and black town folk and picking up "coins," as his sustenance, tossed at him as a reward for his music.

Despite the advent of their accomplished and soul-searching music, the blues, its entertainment, and the escape it brought to the black plantation farmer, which posed a social solution for many of the black croppers, it fell well short for most blacks as a means of escape from the vicissitudes of their daily lives. They were impoverished people merely existing in a sequestered lifestyle. *"There are, however, certain inescapable characteristics of this agricultural economy: The plantation communities in which Negroes live, in so far as they are areas of highest population concentration for this*

---

[201] David Evans, Big Road Blues: tradition and creativity in the folk blues, p. 19

group, are also likely to be areas of greatest cultural isolation.... measurable in terms of illiteracy, mobility, schooling, tenantry, and like factors," wrote sociologist Charles Johnson.[202]

It was a matter of stagnation, poverty, and high anxiety for the Scott family and a world into which George Scott Junior, later to be known as "Boomer" from his baseball days, was assigned by birth on March 23, 1944, on the *Longwood Plantation*. *"My life really began on an honest-to-goodness godforsaken cotton plantation where I was born, in a place called Longwood in Avon, Mississippi, can you believe it, on a plantation,"* exclaimed George Junior incredulously.[203] *Longwood*, at the time, was owned and operated by Thomas H. Bond, situated about twelve miles south of Greenville, in the heart of the Delta, at the end of a long dusty tree-lined road hung over with Spanish moss, bordering the Mississippi River.

"Dated back to the 1700s, I was told," said Scott. *"There was once slavery there like other plantations around here, and, frankly, from what I understood from my momma, there was little difference in how we were treated, you know, the Jim Crow thing, except we could move about more freely, and my dad earned a wage. Not much momma said, but it was a wage. We were beholden to the white owner; lived on the plantation in a very small house provided, probably one of them slave kind of shacks, all*

---

[202] Charles Johnson, "Shadow of the Plantation," p. 210.
[203] George Scott, Jr, interview Jan 24 2006

five of us, just two rooms: my father, momma, older brother Otis, sister Beatrice and me; I didn't remember it. I was the youngest, too young to remember them times; it was what my momma told us."[204]

---

[204] IBID

Chapter 4
Jim Crow's Alive and Well

Until 1960 – in several ways a turning point – the Southern resistance had been able to persuade itself that the civil rights movement was wholly the result of 'outside agitators,' that Southern Negroes were contented and happy with the 'Southern way of life,' that they preferred segregation, and that left to themselves they would never think of protesting.

C. Vann Woodward [205]

World War II was coming to a close after six years of conflict in European and Pacific theaters. Germany surrendered in May 1945, Japan was soon to follow in September, and soldiers were returning home. Among them were a multitude of Southern blacks, several thousand of them who, having had a taste of some civility - of a minor scale - toward them during the war. However, they were maintained in segregated units and found no changes in Southern *Jim Crow* hostility greeting them upon their return from the tinderbox of war. *"Planters who hoped that a measure of labor stability would return as soon as the war ended were soon disappointed,"* wrote James Cobb. *"Returning black veterans were much less likely to accept shoddy and unfair treatment at the hands of landlords."*[206] The

---

[205] C. Vann Woodward, "The Strange Career of Jim Crow," Oxford; New York: Oxford University Press, 2002, p. 168-169
[206] James C. Cobb, "The Most Southern Place on Earth, p. 203

NAACP founded in 1909 but gaining the greatest traction after the war, dug in in their efforts to push back the white Southern landlords who persisted in their resistance to change and sought some sway from the significant increase in their ranks, growing tenfold, after the war. Bryan Greene, writing for the *Smithsonian Magazine*, made the important point, *"The civil-rights organization would need this war chest, as white Southerners redoubled efforts post-war to preserve their economic, political, and social subordination of their black neighbors...out of the fear that returning African Americans would refuse to work the farms as sharecroppers, and a great many did indeed leave the South altogether."*[207] This led to utter chaos and pernicious initiatives according to author Alexis Clark describing returning black soldiers who were *"facing violent white mobs of those who resented African Americans in uniform and perceived them as a threat to the social order of Jim Crow."*[208]

Meanwhile, George Scott Sr., though registered in Washington County for military service in February 1942, was not drafted. He was age 41 at the time of registration. He possibly received a deferment based on the

---

[207] Bryan Greene, contributing writer, "After Victory in World War II, Black Veterans Continued the Fight for Freedom at Home," Smithsonian Magazine, August 30, 2021. https://www.smithsonianmag.com/history/summer-1946-saw-black-wwii-vets-fight-freedom-home-180978538/

[208] Alexis Clark, "Black Americans who served in WW II Faced Segregation Abroad and at Home," History, History Classics, Original August 5, 2020, Updated August 3, 2023
https://www.history.com/news/black-soldiers-world-war-ii-discrimination

agricultural farm worker's exemption of that year, "essential to the war effort," or possibly because of his age. It is also possible he was exempted because of a health condition of a "growth behind the left ear" noted by the local board registrar and which was listed on the registration card.[209]

It was July 1945, in the midst of a sweltering Delta summer, when heat snaps caused temperatures to rise in excess of ninety degrees, a heat index approaching one hundred or more on certain days. The cotton fields were shimmering in rising heat haze with the appearance of obscure outlined images of miraged field hands laboring in the hot sun while hunched over hoes and corresponding hand tools chopping weeds around cotton plants while thinning them out in the open sun-drenched field, humming and singing their field songs accompanied by a chorus of cicadas. Cotton plants were being readied for harvesting in the fall by early September.

George Sr. had been laboring in the field that day in the intolerable sweltering sun of insufferable conditions working the cotton rows manually with a long-handled hoe, known as the chopper, pulling up and turning over weeds and thinning out new plants that had clustered overabundantly and had to be dug out. From there, he transferred weed debris he had removed by wheelbarrow and carried them on up to his truck for delivery to outer parts of the farm property, dumping it as scrap. Arduous work. It is not clear what happened to George Sr. during this undertaking, whether because of

---

[209] George Scott Sr. Draft Card, Local Board No. 2, Washington County, Feb 16, 1942

the heat, he either experienced a heart seizure, heart attack, or a stroke. However, he was found collapsed lying on the ground beside his truck next to his wheelbarrow full of weed materials he apparently had just transported up the slight incline of a hill. Whatever the cause for his abrupt collapse that was never medically defined or that we are aware of, he apparently never regained consciousness, although the facts surrounding the event, typical for that era of black repudiation and ill-treatment, are unclear. If he did have any chance of survival, the healthcare system for blacks was nearly non-existent, and whether he would be transported in time to a hospital acceptable to medical care for blacks was improbable. *"After the Reconstruction era and up through the end of World War II and beyond (1885-1950), hospitals in Mississippi paid little heed or service to the medical needs of the state's black majority,"* wrote journalist Earnest McBride of the *Jackson Advocate*, a Jackson, Mississippi black-owned weekly newspaper, founded in 1938 as the "strident voice" for African Americans and poor whites. *"With only a few exceptions, seriously ill black patients were usually shunted off to an unkempt and thoroughly segregated 'charity' hospital, a one-or two-room area at the back entrance of the hospital that served as the 'colored' ward."*[210] Social Darwinism, or the tenet that only the most fit will survive, was a long-held belief of Delta whites, particularly in the early 20 century, and being of "the fittest"

---

[210] Earnest McBride, "Life and Death of Mississippi's four Black-Owned Hospitals," The Jackson Advocate, Jackson, Mississippi, February 25, 2022
https://jacksonadvocateonline.com/life-and-death-of-mississippis-four-black-owned-hospitals/

reasoning had a foothold in Mississippi; they embraced the belief that black Mississippians were unfit for survival, which was often the basis for white indifference, if not outright ill will, toward blacks and their healthcare needs. In rare instances, scattered community white hospitals would provide a back entrance for blacks; otherwise, they were required to be transported to the nearest black-owned hospital, which was few in number, for care, regardless of the personal urgency or their level of emergency: *separate but unequal* was the standard of care for them, and it was carried out with practiced efficiency. Black surgeon Dr. Frank McCune, who had his own clinic in Jackson, Mississippi, during the early 20 century, emphasized in his weekly radio broadcasts the premise of whites, which was that *"professional medical treatment for black people was a waste of time and money."* [211] In George Senior's circumstance, had he required the services of a clinic that day, it would have been the *Taborian Hospital* in Mound Bayou, a "truly modern facility" established in 1942 but 59 miles and more than an hour's ride from *Longwood*, which, for any emergency situation at that distance, if that was the case for George Senior, would have been forbidding if there was any hope for survival. Stories are rampant of the numerous incidences of Southern blacks requiring emergency healthcare but being forced to go elsewhere than white hospitals, who ultimately died because of critical minutes lost in such a trip before they could reach a black-owned hospital in time to save them. Whether there was a chance for

---

[211]-IBID

George Senior, which was not known, the outcome for him would have been unpromising at best.

A bereft Maggie, now a widow at age 26 and left with three young children, was confronted with unexpected and crucial decisions about what to do with her family as eviction was staring her in the face. Plantation landlords were not likely to muster any compassion of their own for widows of sharecroppers, whom they considered impotent to the task, especially with children in the equation, nor were they likely to work with women, particularly black women, deeming cropper management solely that of a man's job. Spouses of the male sharecroppers were considered the support mechanism of their husbands, to raise the children and bear primary responsibility for the home, which was really no more than a shack; however, in addition to these duties, she also shared the burden of fieldwork consisting of all the tasks of farm labor, including behind the plow, performing these tasks even when unwell. Foremost, it was expected that *"every member of the family contributed. But expectations fell disproportionately on women,"* signifies *Women & The American Story*, or WAMS, a teaching body for the design of curriculum on the role of women in the course of U. S. history. *"On top of helping to plow fields and pick crops, women were responsible for maintaining the home. Wives cooked, cleaned, gardened, and raised children. The work was constant and exhausting."* [212] The children ranged in age from Otis, the oldest at age 8, Beatrice, age 5, and George Jr., just over a year, hardly what a cotton farm entrepreneur would consider a productive farm labor *work unit* capable of generating the kind of results he would come to expect; in his eyes, they were ineffectual and wholly dispensable. Landlords saw little value in them absent a male counterpart, where they carried the burden of managing children, which they saw as a major distraction. Further, they were women, black women at that, and Southern gentlemen generally viewed them as weak, incapable of the requirements of a male cropper, and on a much lower caste scale than the male. The element of *caste* stood out in their deliberations.

"Momma and our little family had to leave after my father died. The plantation owner had no use for us anymore now that my father was gone. He was the sole breadwinner; everything about us as a family was on his broad back. Momma packed us up and we headed for Greenville about fifteen miles up the road where she felt she had a chance, maybe, to do domestic work for white folk. I don't know if she had any kin nearby to help. No one had her back. Honestly, like being a slave, she was. Momma had no skills except being a good mother to her kids, but that wasn't going to get her no money; no social system like today to support us, and the community

---

[212] Women & the American Story, WAMS, "Sharecropping in a Depression," New York Historical Society
https://wams.nyhistory.org/confidence-and-crises/great-depression/sharecroppers/#resource

wasn't going to help us black peoples anyway. We were poor. She was on her own, and no one who really showed care, except for some black peoples that lived nearby who were almost as poor as we were, and they were struggling like the rest. We hung together as best we could mind you. Other black peoples would show care when they could. We could never look to the city for help."[213] In the early 20 century, *"black women were not permitted to live by the same standards as white women,"* according to author Elise Vallier of the *Transatlantica*[214] White women, however, were relegated to accept a standard of domesticity and live by four important Victorian codes, or cardinal virtues as they were known, which were characterized as the values of being a *true woman*. These cult virtues consisted of piety, purity, submissiveness, and domesticity. Black women, on the other hand, who once were *"not regarded as human or as women but as chattel,"* wrote Vallier, were excluded from this definition of women, and that unfolded in different ways and manifestations ranging into the early part of the 20th century.[215] In essence, they lacked the *true woman* values of white women. *"Most of them indeed had to keep embracing both the domestic sphere and that of work,"* announced Vallier, and this persisted if not formally, at the least informally for many years, and Maggie Scott, without her husband or a male partner, was confronted with fulfilling *"double chores – take care of*

---

[213] George Scott interview: January 3 2006
[214] Elise Vallier 1, "African American Womanhood: A Study of Women's Life Writings," Transatlantica, February, 2017
https://journals.openedition.org/transatlantica/10220
[215] IBID

their homes and children, and work outside," and soon feel overwhelmed.[216] The culture of servitude was manifest, an intrinsic part of the mind and makeup of a young Maggie Scott now confronted with the repudiation of her as a black woman and her lifestyle that once gave her some meaning, though slight, and maybe even a small amount of security. Now, she was suddenly expendable. Although we lack any details about the communications that might have transpired between Maggie and their planter landlord, Thomas Bond, we must assume there was little leniency offered her, empathy, or encouragement, as she left *Longwood Plantation* for Greenville soon after her husband George Senior's passing. There was nothing more for her at *Longwood*: strictly business.

Hodding Carter, the progressive journalist and managing editor of the new *Delta Democrat-Times (DDT)*, and majority owner of the paper, who embraced the cause of black American civil rights, was laying a controversial foundation for himself in 1937-1938 by his views on racial matters; they were troubling to the white Greenville community and altogether the white Southerner. *"Anything that was not ultraconservative enraged the people and was not considered 'normal,'"* stated Don Wetherbee, a former senior management employee of the DDT. *"When the newspaper printed a picture of a black man, it changed the relationship."*[217]

---

[216] IBID
[217] Ann Waldron, interview of Don Wetherbee quoted in "Hodding Carter: The Reconstruction of a Racist," Algonquin Books of Chapel Hill, North Carolina, 1993, p. 81.

In January 1944, Carter wrote a best-seller novel, *Winds of Fear*, on Southern racism, *"balanced and almost clinical in its detachment,"* wrote C. V. Terry of the *New York Times*. Bucklin Moon in *Book Week* wrote that it was *"one of the clearest pictures of the mounting racial tension in the South thus far to appear."[218]* But then he received a kickback from journalist Ben Burns of the black newspaper, the *Chicago Defender*, on his alleged reluctance to go the full measure of defending Southern blacks. *"Louisiana-born Hodding Carter is one of those super-liberal dixie fence-sitters on the race issue,"* wrote Burns. It would plague him throughout his journalistic experience with the DDT. [219] In the summer of 1945, Carter, after a four-and-a-half-year absence, who had left the management of the DDT, spending time in the military, and was into independent writing as well, made the conscious career decision to regain majority ownership of the DDT. And, he did so with gusto, regaining a foothold on the paper's conscience and writing editorials spewing his opinions both local and national. Among them, once again, was the subject of race: *"Pay the Negro good wages for his work, give him the opportunity to demonstrate his own capacity to learn, work, and earn, give him his Constitutional rights and you have solved this distorted so-called race problem,"* he wrote, adding *"Only the demagogue tries to make political capital of social equality and*

---

[218] Ann Waldron, on book reviews by C. V. Terry of NYTBR, Oct. 22, 1944; Bucklin Moon, Book Week, Oct. 22, 1944, quoted in "Hodding Carter: The Reconstruction of a Racist," p. 135.
[219] Ann Waldron, on Ben Burns comment in the Chicago Defender, Oct 28, 1944, "Hodding Carter: The Reconstruction of a Racist," p. 135.

racial marriage." Social equality was a term used by white Southerners who abhorred even the thought of integration.[220] Though Maggie had someone in her corner, by the strength of this conversation, it was bound to fall on deaf ears, as it always did. The Delta white man was no closer to racially integrating than was Mississippi's infamous white supremacist senator Theodore Bilbo, who was running for re-election that year; Carter described him as being *"so soaked in the poisonous slime of his bigotry that he reminds us of nothing so much as a neglected cesspool."*[221] Bilbo responded, after numerous skirmishes with Carter, with a counterattack of his own and in an extraordinary manner, denouncing Carter as a *"disgrace to the white race"* and *"the biggest liar in Mississippi and one of the biggest in the nation."*[222] It didn't require a lot of convincing that there was no love lost there.

Mississippi now had two U. S. Senators in power, James Eastland and Theodore Bilbo, both Democrats and both ardent white supremacists – although Eastland performed his role with more political stealth than did Bilbo, who shamelessly attacked civil rights abetment as an attack on the Southern white's "way of life" – who resisted all efforts to integrate, or even desegregate, admonishing any effort at civil rights legislation. These

---

[220] Ann Waldron, on Hodding Carter DDT editorial, July 24, 1945, "Hodding Carter: The Reconstruction of a Racist," p. 151.
[221] Hodding Carter, "Bilbo's Skinning Party," The Delta Democrat Times, Greenville, Mississippi, May 16, 1946, p. 4
https://www.newspapers.com/image/33995810/?terms=delta%20democrat%20times
[222] James C. Cobb, "The Most Southern Place on Earth," p. 225

attitudes and measures by powerful congressional leaders such as Bilbo and Eastland held sway over any hope that civil rights would emerge for Mississippi blacks until much later and, until then, had Maggie in its grip.

The job of moving was wearying for Maggie, who was still grieving lacking help gathering her belongings. At the same time, she struggled famously with three young kids, one, George Junior, just a toddler, and finding her way north to Greenville, the principal town and seat of Washington County. This was most likely accomplished either by automobile, or more so by public transportation, with the help of her 77-year-old grandfather James Fesley, a reliable, stalwart resource all her young life, who had moved to Greenville himself, or, possibly, some of her siblings aided her had they been still living in the area. As logical as it may have seemed as a suitable resource for anyone's conveyance, a black owning a combustion engine-driven automobile in 1945 – the upshot of a fledgling new industry - if he could afford it in the first place, was a privilege, especially in the South, and particularly in the Delta where blacks had no privileges and were restrained by nearly everything they did that was of their own initiative – not of a white man's - and fell outside the boundaries of *Jim Crow*. *"As manufacturing efficiency rose and consumer prices fell anyone with a decent job could afford a car,"* touted storyteller Lindsay Graham of the *American History Tellers*, explaining the ease with which the common American citizen could reap the benefits of a post-war economy. But this was not meant for everyone, of course, available only to a mere few Southern blacks who were still struggling with *Jim Crow*.[223] The comprehensive study of the American Negro entitled *An American Dilemma*, published in 1944 by Gunnar Myrdal, pointed to the vintage perspective on the affordability of the relatively new phenomenon, the automobile, and how this also had affected Southern blacks who could swing for such a purchase. *"The coming of the cheap automobile has meant for Southern Negroes, who can afford one, a partial emancipation from Jim Crowism,"* he wrote.[224] Thomas Sugrue emphasized that what the auto's development meant to blacks was a means to *"subvert" Jim Crow. "Driving gave Southern blacks a degree of freedom that they did not have on public transportation or in most public places."*[225] Whether he owned an automobile relies on conjecture, but if he did, if there was anyone who would have attempted to break the mold of black resistance by its use and go against *Jim Crow*, it likely would have been grandfather James Fesley, who had all outward appearances, pugnacious at times, of following the precepts of American abolitionist and activist Frederick Douglass.

---

[223] Lindsay Graham, "History of the Lincoln Motor Company," American History Tellers, Wondery, Nov 20, 2018.
https://wondery.com/shows/american-history-tellers/episode/5279-history-of-the-lincoln-motor-company/
https://wondery.com/about/

[224] Thomas J. Sugrue, quoting Gunnar Myrdal from his 1944 work An American Dilemma, "Automobile in American Life and Society; Driving While Black: The Car and Race Relations in Modern America; The Car and Jim Crow."

[225] Thomas Sugrue, The Car and Jim Crow, "Automobile in American Life and Society; Driving While Black: The Car and Race Relations in Modern America; The Car and Jim Crow."

However her move from *Longwood Plantation* was to be achieved, Maggie would settle into temporary quarters – a three-room "shotgun house"[226] in Greenville, 12 miles up the road from rural Avon, on East Clay Street in a poor section, largely comprised of black residents positioned in statutory-like rows of similar "shotguns," they were popularly known, to the south side of the railroad tracks in the south end of town. She was only a few blocks away from her grandparents, the Fesleys, who were on West Starling Street, also on the south end. Maggie was compelled to find work, and she wasted little time finding a job as a cook at the Mayflower Café, a historic seafood restaurant in downtown Greenville at the corner of Roach and Theobald Streets, the latter a main thoroughfare in the town. "*It would have been very hard work,*" said Zelma Kelly, a former resident of Greenville who was familiar with the city and the Scott family.[227] It was about an eight-block walk from her new residence, which she made nearly

---

[226] Shotgun House – also known derisively as the shotgun shack – is an African American house design originating in West Africa, with its passage into the Caribbean, Haiti, and on into New Orleans and the Deep South. They were often found on plantations; but the legacy is they were also plentiful in Deep South towns and cities, especially in the Delta, designed, and used, in a sinister way with African Americans in mind. They were quite small, typically long and narrow, most no more than 12 feet across and from two to four rooms deep without hallways, meaning you had to walk through each room in order to access the next. Some say it's so-named because one can fire a shotgun through the front door with all the shot exiting the back door without ever touching a wall. Though possibly hyperbole, no basis can be found for this description. One black Greenville resident explains the likely origin for this description: "Because we lived under the gun. I mean that's not a stretch," which may actually speak for the languishment of local hysteria symbolizing the horror of the Jim Crow years.

[227] Zelma Kelly interview: September 5, 2008

every day, exclaimed son George Junior. *"I watched her leave the house early in the morning and she wouldn't return home until it was dark, and she was tired,"* said George, emphasizing in angry, contemptuous tones the long hours his mother was obligated to work as sole breadwinner, with few rewards; *"and then she would do maid jobs for white people,"* as a secondary job.[228] Within the year, Maggie relocated to a house a short distance from East Clay, on 111 Gum Street, once more pulling up stakes with three young children. George Junior was now 2 years old, still a toddler, and dependent on child – nearly nonexistent - care while his mother was away at work. Possibly the oldest, Otis, who was 10, would fill in some of the time, although he was enrolled at the nearby all-black Lucy Webb School along with his sister Beatrice, age 7.

Lucy Webb School, elementary school where George Scott Jr. attended, along with brother Otis and sister Beatrice (author's collection)

---

[228] George Scott interview: August 15, 2008

More likely, George Junior was cared for by his maternal grandparents, the Fesleys, who also lived nearby. Or, there was also a new Greenville Day Care facility for young black children that had been founded in 1941 and was situated on the corner of Ohea Street and Railroad Avenue, in the South end, that might have been a resource for Maggie. According to Betty Jo Boyd of Greenville, an advocate of racial reform, her mother, Alice Ruth Hayes, had started this daycare to protect the very young and downcast black children who lacked a personal caretaker, whose parents had no choice but to work without assistance for their children, leaving them at home, making-do with their circumstances and what little resources they had. *"They had a small day care for white children but it was strictly white like everything in those days....my mother was just very anxious to do something about this [inequity],"* said Ms. Boyd, whose mother was anguished at the sight of black children, whose parents were working, fending for themselves while wandering unattended on Greenville's city streets until their parents arrived home; for many this meant late nights. [229] Maggie Scott fit the definition of a mother in need quite well, exhibiting qualifications for such a daycare service while faced with mounting poverty and nary a moment of relief. Of course, there is no information to support that she had ever made such an arrangement, but the logical argument, aside from Maggie receiving assistance from the maternal grandparents, was for her to make use of such a facility; it was of no cost to her although an

---

[229] Betty Jo Boyd interview: September 3, 2023

inconvenience to get there as it was located several blocks away from her residence likely requiring public transportation, at a cost.

"My momma managed to get some work with a white family of means on Washington Street in the center of Greenville; domestic work," said George Junior. "There were several peoples like them all in big houses, owned cotton farms or businesses along the [Mississippi River] levee, white aristocrats they called 'em; peoples of privilege. Momma – she was called Mag or Maggie - cleaned for them, did their dishes, cooked, took out the trash, watched their kids, their dogs, their cats, just about everything you know. Mind you, when you think about it today how was that any different than when we as black peoples was slaves, except she could go home when the day was done? But, momma didn't; after she finished her day with the white family she went to a second job, worked as a cook, at a restaurant in town.

"We lived in a small three-room building peoples called a shotgun house in the south end of town. My momma didn't have no money to buy anything more than that. I wondered how she even managed that. It was the poorest section of our black neighborhood in the poorest part of town; they called it Booker Town. Booker was an old black family I was told had musical roots. One of them took his music, the Blues I guess, all the way to the big cities in New York and Chicago. As for the house we lived in, I don't know how it got called that, a shotgun house. Sounds like a threat, really, that we all knew so well growing up in the Delta. Many of us poor blacks *lived in one. I suppose the white folk gave it its name. They said if you stood at the front door, you could shoot a shotgun through the opening and the bullets would never touch the walls but go out the back door behind it. Of course, the house wouldn't be damaged, they said; just the blacks that lived there. There was a lot of stories like that I heard growing up, of white peoples, the bastards we knew as Ku Klux Klan, going to black homes, ripping peoples from them and shooting them dead, or lynching, for no reason, except they was black. It happened all the time in nearby towns. We was just plain scared wondering if this could happen to us. The Ku Klux Klan gave us a lot to be worried about. They was always around tearing up black peoples' lives, stomping on our very souls,"* said George.[230] The plexus of *Jim Crow* managed to find its way well into the 1960s in numerous Mississippi Delta towns, with its racist standards still firmly in place, particularly in towns where the Citizens' Council, an economic racist initiative built upon white supremacy serving to preserve *Jim Crow*, was hotly active and growing. *Jim Crow* was alive and well in Greenville and surrounding areas of the Delta in 1946. It was a time when young blacks were beginning to stir in their search for equality that they didn't have before the war but wanted now. *"World War II had exposed thousands of young black men from the Delta to places where segregation didn't exist, and having fought for their country, they seemed to feel entitled to things they didn't have in Mississippi,"* wrote Lemann.[231] At the same time there

---

[230] George Scott interview: August 15, 2008
[231] Nicholas Lemann, "The Promised Land", p. 48

were transformations taking place on the Delta cotton farms as planters, some grudgingly, many apprehensively. However, each, with cautious optimism, began to acquire mechanical cotton picker machines, using them as substitutes for black manual labor while sensing the ominous threat of black insurrection and a civil rights crisis in the making. *"Besides, the more far-sighted whites in the Delta had begun to detect a slight crumbling in the citadel of segregation.*[232] School desegregation issues were also emerging by the 1940s, leaving whites ostensibly shaken. *"The school desegregation issue had reached the notice of white planters,"* wrote Lemann, setting that matter of unrest into rapid motion that would become much more volatile as this conflict broke out into widespread conflagrations, especially as the Supreme Court's judgment on the epic civil rights case of *Brown v. Board of Education* was reaching a crescendo and a decision was just around the corner. And another phase of the black migration effort was overtly in full swing. Aaron Henry, an active member of the NAACP, civil rights leader, activist, politician, and a native Mississippian whose parents were sharecroppers, once described the black flight from Mississippi and, correspondingly, the whites' passion to be rid of them on both political and economic grounds, expressed in acerbic terms: *"They wished we'd go back to Africa, but Chicago was close enough."*[233] It was on this occasion, in the summer of 1954, two months after the *Brown* decision, that the Citizens' Council first formed in Mississippi, taking the lead of several Deep South

---

[232] IBID
[233] IBID

states that were soon to follow. Its central structure and the mechanics for this consisted of a grass-roots, hard-core constituency comprised of prominent Mississippi citizens in positions of power who formed secretive vigilante groups to address what they believed was a serious threat to their established and inalterable manner of living. Robert "Tut" Patterson, its founder, had reacted to Mississippi Supreme Court judge Tom P. Brady's seditious May 27 anti-black speech, *"Black Monday,"* made to the Mississippi branch of the Sons of the American Revolution, which was to stir Southern whites into launching a full-out defense against the *Brown* decision. It was just what Patterson was looking for as a catalyst, and it was his call to take action. The Council, under his leadership, was the most effective of several Deep South radical organizations opposing and defending against the high court's decision on desegregation and its enforcement measures.

The Council's central focus and means to success was to attack the desegregation effort by applying "massive resistance" through popular support, keeping schools segregated and black and white students firmly separated, by advancing their theme of "protectors" of the "Southern Way of Life." If there was no other meaningful achievement that can be ascribed to the Citizens' Council in its years of trepidation and subversive initiatives, one legacy stands out from all the rest: the privatization of schools, which has had a lasting effect throughout the country, particularly in Mississippi. Professor Stephanie Rolph, in her adaptive article "Mississippi History Now" from her book *Resisting Equality: The Citizens' Council, 1954-1989*, emphasized, *"Over the course of its existence, its work initiated the private school movement across the South and forged national and international networks of white supremacy that would deeply influence the political and cultural landscape of post-civil rights America."* [234] Previous to the emergence of the Citizens' Council - between 1946 and 1948 - inordinate mistrust was taking hold of the Delta planters and their peers across the South who were disappointed in new U. S. President Harry Truman, who did not share in the South's racial philosophy. The Dixiecrats were formed– a segregationist political party - in 1948, which was a breakaway of states' rights advocates from the national Democrat Party who were primarily active in the South. *"Not surprisingly, the quickened racial consciousness of blacks and white concerns over the potential aggressiveness of returning black servicemen led to escalating racial violence in the wake of the war…black men were being killed at the rate of one per week,"* wrote James C. Cobb. [235] There was a level of brutality and terror not seen in Mississippi since the late 19th and early 20th centuries, grounded in white paranoia, irrational behavior, and utter mistrust. Just a few short miles outside of Greenville, in Leland, where - hosted by the local Rotary Club - an initial portentous speech introducing the Citizens' Council was made and got everyone's attention, including *Delta Democrat-Times*' liberal Pulitzer Prize editor Hodding Carter, whose ire was aroused at not only the idea of

---

[234] Stephanie R. Rolph 1, Associate Professor, Millsaps College, "Mississippi History Now," October 2019; adapted from her book, "Resisting Equality: The Citizens' Council, 1954-1989, Louisiana State University Press, 2018.
[235] James C. Cobb, "The Most Southern Place on Earth," p. 212-213

it but the clandestine manner it was being promulgated. Carter was provoked by the initiative, and he was determined to fight back. And, fight back, he did. In the early spring of 1955, Carter wrote an article for *Look Magazine*, which he titled *"A Wave of Terror Threatens the South."* He felt that, politically, the Councils were vulnerable to "gangsterism," ultimately comparing them to the Ku Klux Klan, which aroused a state of rage across Mississippi whose citizens largely defended the idea of the new Council, maintaining segregation but favoring the philosophy and principles of non-violence espoused by them. Council founder Robert Patterson was furious beyond measure, blasting Carter as an enemy for comparing him to the Klan. While standing outside of a conference room of a meeting being led by Patterson, DDT journalist David Brown overheard Patterson castigating Hodding Carter and his newspaper, the DDT. After the politically charged meeting, Brown confronted Patterson and expressed his discomfiture with the Council leader after Brown had written a DDT article about the Council feeling it was a fair opinion of the nascent organization, which Patterson had openly approved. Patterson, however, in a demonstrative manner, quickly clarified for Brown: *"I wasn't talking about you. I was talking about your boss,"* said Patterson, clearly viewing Carter as an adversary to his initiative.[236] In the latter part of that year, according to an article in *Time Magazine*, appearing before the Memphis Public Affairs Forum, Carter *"denounced the pro-segregationist Citizens' Councils as 'dangerous and unholy unworthy to be called American...a kind of uptown Ku Klux Klan,'"*

---

[236] Ann Waldron, "Hodding Carter: The Reconstruction of a Racist," p. 237.

labeling them as extremists. With that, he and his paper, the *Delta Democrat-Times*, promptly lost a $25,000 printing order contract with the state because of *"political differences,"* said Carter.[237] He assumed a different strategy from the Northerners in advocating a remedy for racial intolerance - a subject for which he won a Pulitzer Prize in 1946 – that was contrary to the constant malicious badgering, as he saw it, from the Yankee North labeling them as *"carping Northern critics."* The Northerners preferred a tactic of wholesale and immediate eradication of the racist South by turning it on its head. He was *"No bourbon & Magnolia reactionary,"* wrote *Time Magazine* in summing up Carter about his forthrightness on racial intolerance. *"We Southerners just don't take to that,"* said Carter, addressing Northern behavior and their need to alter their approach. *"The racial concepts and prejudices which the Southerner holds…cannot be changed by law, by ridicule or by threat. Only reason and education, an old concept of brotherhood…can change them,"* he said.[238] Curiously, Hodding Carter, who was the champion of racial tolerance, favored a gradual desegregation process over the court's hastened "all deliberate speed" approach to the matter, emphasizing that the outcome has been damaged *"by forcing both segregationists and de-segregationists to 'extremes.'"*[239]

---

[237] Time Magazine, "The Press: The Hot Middle," Vol. 65 No. 20, May 16, 1955. https://content.time.com/time/subscriber/article/0,33009,866355,00.html
[238] Time Magazine, "The South: Stop Badgering," Vol. 48 No. 20, Nov. 11, 1946. https://content.time.com/time/subscriber/article/0,33009,854191,00.html
[239] Time Magazine, "The Press: The No. 1 Story," Vol. 65 No. 3, Jan. 17, 1955. https://content.time.com/time/subscriber/article/0,33009,891160,00.html

An integrationist, he was not. *"Desegregation Does Not Mean Integration,"* Carter wrote compellingly for the *New York Times Magazine,* dispelling any ideas that he might be sharing in the North's idolatry and why purposeful integration *"was not in the cards for the Deep South for a long time to come."*[240] Though only 10 at the time, George was made aware by his mother, Maggie, and by older classmates of the overhead threat – as they viewed it – of the scornful Citizens' Councils whom Hodding Carter of their local paper had alleged would likely incite the actions of the Ku Klux Klan, which to them was terrifying. In later years, he was more circumspect about what really happened, speaking from a different frame of reference and not so complimentary as in his younger years.

"The town politicians, the white [Citizens'] Council they called themselves, formed after the government spoke for us on our colored rights, and worked hard to keep us apart and not interfere with their way of living. [They] made us feel it was a privilege that they built a new school for us, and a big outdoor swimming pool made only for blacks, like we was kind of special. I was too young to realize what they was really doing. To me we were getting a brand-new school and a pool. To them, the white folks, we were simply being kept apart like we always was. They had no plans to pay any attention to the new laws."[241] Greenville, like many other Delta towns, built two swimming pools, the Bobby Henry Memorial Pool for whites-

---

[240] Ann Waldron, "Hodding Carter: The Reconstruction of a Racist," p. 294, quoting Hodding Carter's article for The New York Times Magazine of Feb. 11, 1962
[241] George Scott interview: March 3, 2006

only, named for its Congressional Medal of Honor recipient, and, secondarily without any tribute, more like a task, *"an identical pool for the Negro half of the population,"* as it was phrased in passing, in 1950. A photo of the white pool, showing all white children and families attending at its opening, was displayed prominently in the *Delta Democrat Times'* newspaper on October 31, 1951, as part of a discussion on Greenville's community center managed by their new park commission. There were no corresponding photographs or articles of the black pool, as was customary for the times.[242] *"To run any news at all about black folk was considered to be an assault on the established way of life,"* said Hodding Carter III, who made it clear that *Jim Crow* was still firmly in place in Greenville.[243] Coleman High School, an all-black school in Greenville where young George Scott Junior attended – enrolling there in 1957 - was built and dedicated in 1952, right around the time of racial unrest that was growing at an exponential pace, causing a stir and considerable disturbance among the town whites who were sensing they would soon be dealing with school desegregation. The 1954 *Brown* decision, in which the Supreme Court declared school segregation unconstitutional, was looming. The Citizens' Council was on the immediate horizon, although not organized at the time. The Court's *Brown* decision would change all of that posthaste.

---

[242] The Delta Democrat-Times, Oct 31, 1951, "Acquisition of Country Club Property Removed Threat of Polyglot Development," Greenville, Mississippi, October 31, 1951, Section D, p. 37.
[243] Hodding Carter III interview: February 9, 2009

The tension was running high in the state after *Brown*. Governor Hugh White, who stood for segregation, announced a plan to preserve it by introducing an equalization process by which, he alleged, he would improve the quality of black schools, bringing them up to the level of the white schools, but the black leaders balked at the idea quite strenuously as not nearly enough since the Supreme Court had spoken. White planters, operating in an atmosphere of greater financial strengths than most white Southerners, were inspired to act, and they did so dramatically. *"Their response to Governor White's proposal was to close the public school system altogether and set up private schools instead,"* wrote Professor Rolph.[244] Mississippi drew up a constitutional amendment in the fall of that year they called a manifesto threatening to close all public schools if the *Brown* decision was enforced. The Citizens' Council pounced on this initiative, offering their complete support of the idea and the amendment, setting the stage for eventual efforts toward the privatization of schools for whites and the outright closing of public schools, leaving blacks with little to no school systems to rely upon, nor be funded, which seemed not to be particularly troubling to the Council members whose energy was directed at unconditional school segregation, white supremacy and altogether a goal of isolation from Southern blacks.

---

[244] Stephanie R. Rolph, "Mississippi History Now"

In the fall of 1955, *Time Magazine* investigated and made an assessment of desegregation initiatives and published a report on the status of 17 Southern and border states and their records on compliance with the Supreme Court's May 1955 order of enforcement of desegregation in *Brown II*, which the court had noted as moving at a dilatory pace a year after their initial decision, declaring that desegregation must be implemented *"with all deliberate speed."* The magazine rated the states from "A" to "F," with the five Deep South states, including Mississippi, receiving flat-out failing ratings. Mississippi's ranking received little to no commentary except for a blunt: *"No move to desegregate."* Of these five states, only Mississippi and Georgia had taken no action of any kind, nor had they even addressed the matter. In contrast, the other three states at least had something of substance, albeit not always positive, on which to report. These states were intransigent, seeing this as a white Southerner victory and a Court that proffered a message of indifference and was in no rush to impose integration on them any time soon. It was an opportunity for them to hedge and postpone, they thought, and they did just that.[245] Desegregation was on the back shelf and would not see the light of day until 1969-1970. The Citizens' Council became highly successful, gaining strength while *"its work initiated the private school movement across the South and forged national and international networks of white supremacy that would deeply*

---

[245] Time Magazine, National Affairs: Report Card, Time, the Weekly Newsmagazine, New York, NY, September 19, 1955, Vol. LXVI No 12, 3 pgs.
https://content.time.com/time/subscriber/article/0,33009,865193,00.html

influence the political and cultural landscape of post-civil rights America," wrote Professor Rolph.[246] *"Violence against black activists who refused to buckle in the face of Council intimidation could be fatal,"* she added.[247] The Reverend George Lee of Belzoni, Mississippi, NAACP leader of that town, and Humphreys County, who forged a path for black residents to vote, was shot and killed on May 7, 1955. It was believed the crime occurred because of the local pressure and intimidation by the Council, which was active there at the time; Belzoni was home to a White Citizens' Council. Although an investigation disclosed two members of the Belzoni Council as possible offenders, the local prosecutor declined to take action. The sheriff explained that he died in a "car accident." The source of the murder was never identified.

This was the tenor of the social and political climate occurring in the Delta confronting the Scott and other Delta black families, who were very much under the thumb and the strength of the influential Citizens' Council, even though many of the black residents were not conscious of everything that was going on nor were they a party to their meetings or politics. It was business as usual for the town's black population, which was to be removed from the equation.

The Delta planters supported the Citizens' Council in a major way, providing them with greater than 75% of their funding in Mississippi.

---

[246] Stephanie R. Rolph, "Mississippi History Now"
[247] IBID

"Throughout the Delta, Citizens' Council members were well positioned to pursue the organization's policy of inflicting severe economic suffering on, as one council leader put it, 'members of the Negro race who are not cooperating.'"[248] A portrayal of that occurred in August 1955 in nearby Yazoo City, displaying the Council's efficiencies when local black businessmen, who had established themselves as having some clout, made a demand in the name of the local NAACP on the school system for immediate desegregation of all schools. The Council took swift action to circumvent the initiative, shutting it down. They ran petitioners' names in the local paper, and soon, first one and then another, they began losing their jobs or business relationships they might have had with whites and could not find work after that. They rapidly began removing their names from the petition, but it was too little too late; they felt eviscerated, and for the most part, many of them abandoned the town for employment and residency elsewhere. *"It soon became obvious, however, that NAACP leaders had underestimated the amount of economic influence that local whites still enjoyed over members of the black middle class in Mississippi,"* wrote Cobb.[249] *"When I was comin' on 8 or 9, my momma fixed-it for me to pick cotton with my older brother and sister on a nearby plantation on the edge of town. That was how the white farmers got their crops picked and harvested, using the black peoples and their kids; white supremacy goin' on right in our little town, right in front of our eyes. Just us blacks doin' the*

---

[248] James C. Cobb, "The Most Southern Place on Earth, p. 215
[249] IBID

pickin'. And, for us it was all we ever knew to do; the only way we could make any money at that age. Momma shook us awake at 4:00 in the morning so we could catch the bus, a rickety yellow god-awful school bus they probably bought from the town, smaller than the regular school buses, and filthy as hell with torn seats with stains on 'em and red road dust on the windows, but good enough for us black kids they probably figured. The plantation field foremen used to go around town and pick us up in them. 'Come-on you next to nothings' they used to scream at us when they became impatient, we wasn't gettin' on the bus fast enough. Treated like prisoners. They loved to harass us black kids. Had to meet their daily deadlines so everything was urgent to them; we were nothin' but their black trash.

We picked cotton all day from morning sunlight until it began to set, on our hands and knees, just pickin' in the hot sun, sweat running off my brow onto my clean overalls my momma had made for me. Like a dust bowl most days, the ground baked dry and so hot felt like you were breathin' in a blast furnace. White peoples didn't do this; just black peoples. Nothin' worse than suckin' up the heat and dust of those cotton fields until you was chokin' like a dog just swallowed a bone.

'Hey chicken feed,' the foreman yelled, who just didn't like me and [found reason] whenever he could to insult me. I was a big kid for my age and somehow, he felt he could bully me more than the others maybe hoping I would start a fight and get me thrown off the farm.

'You best move your ass kid and get to the next row,' he'd say, 'or I'll move it for you!' He was always a threat; always hate and bitterness in his eyes and his manner like he couldn't stand my smell. Yet I was the best picker of the bunch, my hands bleeding from not wearing gloves so I could pick more and faster, too. I knew if I retaliated it would be all over for me so I stayed quiet. It would shame my momma, make it miserable for her, and go against everything the damn town stood for: Jim Crow racists."[250]

---

[250] George Scott interview: Jan 24, 2006

Chapter 5
Bloodstained Whitewash

Neither God nor lawful man discriminates between races when the taking of life or the breaking of the lesser laws of mankind are involved. Think on that, you people who profess to be Christian or democratic or fair.

Hodding Carter[251]

On April 25, 1953, in the small, obscure town of Benoit, Mississippi, of Bolivar County, and 20 miles north of the Washington County seat of Greenville, a newsworthy and pivotal racial event made its mark there, causing headlines, with pertinent and far-reaching civil rights overtones. A black plantation worker, a sharecropper, Claude Otis Johnson, had approached a Benoit storekeeper, John Thomas, who was also a justice of the peace, to discuss an alleged $37 grocery debt, which the storekeeper had provoked. It led to an argument and a struggle, whereupon Thomas claimed that he pushed Johnson down the store's front steps and then shot him three times. Thomas was quickly exonerated three days later by a fellow J. P. claiming that *"no eyewitnesses [were] found"* and further that Thomas was *"justified in what he did,"* yet four witnesses were just as quickly

---

[251] Hodding Carter (An Editorial), "Bloodstained Whitewash," Delta Democrat-Times, April 29, 1953, p. 1
https://www.newspapers.com/image/23807081/?terms=bloodstained%20whitewash&match=1

discovered as reported by the local *Delta Democrat-Times* the day after, but were given no deference, confidence or credence, in the matter.

Thomas, in the course of his own testimony, described Johnson in a hostile light, with a leading statement, *"this darkie came into the store,"* posturing in a manner of being a threat, and this fact alone – being black - was presumptive grounds for his heinous actions. The case went to a Federal grand jury in September; no indictments were brought against Thomas. At the end of October, the case went to the Bolivar Circuit Court in Rosedale, returning a verdict of "not guilty" in a matter of a 10-minute deliberation.[252]

One witness described the scene as deadly when Thomas accosted Johnson about the outstanding grocery bill, and Johnson said he would take care of it and left the store. Storekeeper Thomas wasted no time, *"I saw Mr. Thomas reach up under the shelf and get a gun."*[253]

Another, on the outside of the store, saw Thomas pursue Johnson, grab him by the belt, pistol-whip him on the side of the head and then shoot him. He then proceeded to dig his knee into the man's stomach, holding him down and shot him twice more for good measure.

---

[252] Alabama Journal, "Mississippi J.P. Freed in Slaying," Alabama Journal, Oct 31, 1953, p. 11
https://www.newspapers.com/image/457081426/?terms=benoit%20justice&match=1
[253] Tom Karsell, "Newspaper Found Some Witnesses To Killing," Delta Democrat-Times, April 28, 1953, p. 2
https://www.newspapers.com/image/23806955/?terms=%22delta%20democrat%20times%22%20

Storekeeper John Thomas was no stranger to criminal proceedings, his own, having been indicted for a homicide in 1934 over a domestic dispute. Thomas was a McComb cop at the time and shot and fatally wounded an unarmed man. He was tried twice, in 1934 and '35, both ending in mistrials, described as "heated" and at a level of contentiousness that one McComb resident remembered the events clearly nearly twenty years afterwards. In 1938 Thomas was involved in another shooting, *"killed a Negro while carrying out his duty as a peace officer"* while a member of the police force in Benoit.[254]

He had a reputation that followed him from McComb to Benoit, and for those who embraced his manner of violence and apparent racism, John Thomas didn't disappoint. For that matter, in 1938, an administratrix action based on the 1934 homicide reached the Supreme Court of Mississippi in an action against the city of McComb for being liable for the homicidal actions of their employee, John Thomas, complaining that *"Thomas was known to the council to be an incompetent, untrustworthy, unsafe, and violent person."* It was dismissed on the grounds that the city was not liable for the actions of its employee regardless of his viciousness or incompetence, using their words *"while engaged in the discharge of a governmental duty."*[255]

---

[254] IBID
[255] Bates v. City of McComb, Supreme Court of Mississippi, Mar 21, 1938, 181 Miss. 336 (Miss. 1938)
https://casetext.com/case/bates-v-city-of-mccomb-et-al

McComb was a flashpoint for civil unrest during the 1960s led by Ku Klux Klan violence and various white supremacist actions amounting to black voter suppression efforts, and they were a lead city in their resistance to the Freedom Summer project.

There was a pronounced hate permeating throughout the Delta, radiating at a fever pitch that was being aimed directly at Greenville's newspaper owner-editor, Hodding Carter of the *Delta Democrat-Times*, who frequently stood up to the uncertain white mob. Carter, for some time, had aroused the Delta whites with his editorials; they did not subscribe to his "fairness" theme between whites and blacks, nor with his views on desegregation. When the judge dismissed the murder charge against Thomas in only three days of the shooting, the Benoit city marshal, W. O. Lester, who was sitting in court next to a DDT reporter when it was announced, openly gloated upon the decision of "justifiable homicide," with an in your face told-you-so comment, *"Go back and tell THAT [decision] to your Mr. Carter,"* he ranted in perfect rancor.[256]

Carter, in a provocative editorial - which he was well-known for - four days after the shooting, and clearly written as a retaliatory response to Benoit city marshal Lester, described the Tuesday hearing as a *"wicked farce ...the damndest job of bloodshed whitewashing that ever sickened us,"* pointing out the absence of eyewitnesses, of which there were actually nine

---

[256] Tom Karsell, "Fellow JP exonerates Thomas of Murder, Charges: 'Justifiable,'" Delta Democrat-Times, April 28, 1953, p. 1

total, including bystanders who saw the shooting, and the only person to testify was *"the killer himself,"* highlighting the *"shameful laxity"* of those in charge, and *"a stench in the nostrils of decent, fair-minded citizens."* Carter elevated the topic to yet another level, the seminal narrative that was a fit for him and the one he was most passionate about: racial justice. With an effort at political comity, Carter applied his masterstrokes of sensibility, reminding Southerners of the battle of race that was being waged with outliers, such as the Northerners – a battle in which he had been personally involved - whose accusations of the South, in their demands for swift justice, stood to prevail, *"for which this slaying and hearing provide bloody material."* He refocused, forcefully, and with a stroke of admonishment: *"Until we in Mississippi look upon the law and crime without relation to the color or faith or nationality of the principals, we have no right to lift our heads and ask for equal treatment in the concert of states or the community of nations."*[257]

There were six notable murders that occurred in Mississippi in the 1950s and innumerable others that remained unaccountable yet of epidemic proportions; five of these occurred in the Delta. They started with the Benoit homicide of Claude Otis Johnson on April 25, 1953. Then Reverend George Lee of Belzoni, Humphreys County, on May 7, 1955. He died only days after receiving a threatening note to drop his name from the voting polls, shot while behind the wheel of his car by a drive-by assailant. On August

---

[257] Hodding Carter, "Bloodstained Whitewash," p. 1

13, 1955, Lamar "Ditney" Smith of Brookhaven, Mississippi, Lincoln County, was shot and killed in front of the Lincoln County Courthouse for *"meddling in politics"* and being considered *"a clear threat to the balance of political power in Lincoln County."* Despite *"dozens"* of witnesses to the shooting, the official report came back that he was *"mysteriously shot and killed."*[258]

On November 27, 1955, again in the town of Belzoni in Humphreys County, Gus Courts, age 65, a Belzoni grocer, activist, and organizer for the Humphreys County chapter of the NAACP, was shot by white gunmen in front of his store with serious wounds to his arm and abdomen and considerable blood loss. In spite of the severity of his injuries, his friends managed to drive him over 60 miles to Mound Bayou, a black town, where, remarkably, he recovered in the all-black *Taborian Hospital* since Belzoni's local hospital was white-only. Belzoni police did little investigation of the crime, instead blaming the black community for the violence and its outcome. What was distinguishing about this assault on Courts was the level of influence of the *White Citizens' Council* lurking behind the events leading up to the shooting. They professed to be non-violent, but their sway and counter-influence activities in response to the recent *Brown* decision inspired brutality. *"The Councils' view of themselves as a cut above the*

---

[258] Donna Ladd, "Buried Truth: Unresolved, Disregarded Lamar Smith Murder Haunts Lincoln County," Mississippi Free Press, August 30, 2021
https://www.mississippifreepress.org/15380/buried-truth-unresolved-disregarded-lamar-smith-murder-haunts-lincoln-county

violent tactics of the Ku Klux Klan gained them the title of 'uptown Klan.'"[259] They hid behind this mantra, tinged with violence, and it was effective, advocating boycotting of black retail establishments and of white businessmen who serviced blacks as a principal means of destroying black initiatives. *"White businessmen would face boycotts and politicians would lose votes if they were believed to be sympathetic to African Americans efforts at integration."*[260] Courts experienced constant pressure to abandon his NAACP activism and to reveal the names of his black associates who supported their initiatives. *"The white business community used all its resources to ruin Courts' store – bankers refused him credit, wholesalers denied him service, his landlord tripled the rent, a local gas station refused to sell him fuel, and whites warned blacks not to shop at his grocery."* Courts was a member of the *"older black leadership"* resistance having begun his activities prior to, and after, the *Brown* decision.[261]

And then there was Clinton Melton of Glendora, who was shot and killed by white supremacist and racist Elmer Kimbell on December 3, 1955, for filling the man's gas tank when he alleged he was only asking for two dollars' worth. Kimbell was a close friend and hunting buddy of J. W.

---

[259] White Citizens' Councils, Article, "The Murder of Emmett Till: White Citizens' Councils," American Experience, aired April 15, 2023; From the Collections: Civil Rights, The African American Experience, 1996-2023 WGBH Educational Foundation
[260] IBID
[261] William P. Hustwit, "Gus Courts: (ca. 1889-1969) Activist," Mississippi Encyclopedia, Center for Study of Southern Culture, Birmingham Southern University, July 10, 2017; updated April 13, 2018
https://mississippiencyclopedia.org/entries/gus-courts/

Milam, confessed killer, along with Roy Bryant, of the infamous Emmett Till murder three- and one-half months before, on August 28. Kimbell had accompanied Milam during the abduction of Emmett Till, according to a subsequent FBI investigation. He called on their defense lawyer, J. W. Kellum, to handle the Melton case, and Kellum did so with the same kind of verve that he gave Milam and Bryant: conducted in the same courthouse, with the same defense counsel, and the same result. Sadly, Melton's wife Beulah, just four days before Kimbell was to testify, lost control of her car, which catapulted into the Black Bayou River, and she died in the crash. There was strong suspicion that someone may have intentionally forced her off the road. Unlike what was expected, however, from the Glendora community was nothing but paradoxically earnest irony: it was a wake-up call, a cautious thread, to sensibility. One chagrined Glendora resident announced following the verdict, *"There's open season on the Negroes now,"* he said. *"They've got no protection, and any peckerwood who wants to can go shoot himself one, and we'll free him. Our situation will get worse and worse."*[262]

Kimbell requested his gun back from the deputy sheriff immediately upon the trial's conclusion so he could enjoy more hunting with his friend J. W. Milam.

---

[262] David Halberstam, "Tallahatchie County Acquits a Peckerwood," The Reporter, University of Minnesota, Minneapolis Minnesota, April 19, 1956
http://users.soc.umn.edu/~samaha/cases/halberstam_peckerwood.html

Nineteen fifty-five, when George Scott was a mere eleven years of age, was considered by most historians as one of the most violent and dangerous periods in the history of Mississippi, notwithstanding the dreadful lynchings of the late 19th century, particularly in the Delta, where numerous murders of blacks occurred, followed by the 1960s, which was its equivalence and the height of the Civil Rights movement. This grievous time of extraordinary turbulence was inspired by the Supreme Court's emotionally charged *Brown* decision of 1954 declaring school segregation as unconstitutional and calling for desegregation, which was a decision in the eyes of the Southerners of such high emotional intensity, which they considered an effrontery of them, and the absolute antithesis of Mississippi whites' way of life, that their wherewithal of choice in seeking a solution was none other than exacting human brutality.

"Of course, we young black kids didn't know any better what was going on in any real detail, but we knew it was bad. Our parents would tell us, or we would hear about it from the kids, but we didn't know everything as this was [a similar experience] in most other towns. Our family didn't even have a newspaper, couldn't afford it. I used to go over to a neighbor's house, the Collins Cleaners on our street, almost every day to read their newspaper. Greenville was more levelheaded, but they certainly did follow Jim Crow. We just didn't fight back. We knew better.

"When I was 10, my momma told us about the government in Washington had approved a Civil Rights law [May 1954] that favored us

with rights we never had before. Turned out it was for school desegregation, but it was a start. I wondered, even as a young boy, how this was going to work in this town, honestly, as the black folks of Greenville were made to live apart from whites. It was supposed to be separate but equal, we had understood, but really, it was just separate here, never equal. We were known as the "colored" peoples; water fountains for coloreds, separate restrooms, movie theatre for coloreds with separate entrances from whites, colored restaurants, colored schools, colored neighborhoods. They even built us a separate-colored pool. When whites did speak to black ladies on the street – and it wasn't very often - they would address them disrespectfully, calling them by their first names; white ladies were always known as "ma'am" or Miss. It was just Mazy, Lucy or Flora when they spoke to black ladies, like they were little kids. Happened in doctors' offices and government buildings, too; always the first name. It was insulting, never respectful. I wondered if the white folk even knew how they were around black peoples half the time, speaking poorly to them, but they didn't seem to behave like they knew they was actually doing anything wrong; it just come easy for them to speak in that manner even if they liked black peoples, they talked to us that way, my momma said. It was what they were used to with us. We never said anything; we didn't want to cause no trouble. We knew our place."[263]

---

[263] George Scott interview: March 23, 2006

Greenville's two swimming pools, built and dedicated in 1950, were distinctly segregated: the Robert T. Henry Memorial pool for whites *"and the colored municipal swimming pool"* known as the Katie Lewis Memorial for blacks, according to the *Delta Democrat-Times*' "News Briefs" in their August 26, 1951 paper. They were identical in size and structure, meticulously meeting the generational definition of the Supreme Court's 1896 *Plessy v. Ferguson* "separate but equal" decision establishing the constitutionality of racial segregation. But when the 1954 *Brown* decision, overturning *Plessy* and reinforced by the Court's *Brown II* in 1955, after staunch resistance by the South for several years until the early 1970s, enforced desegregation of schools and introduced a process for integration, things began to unravel in Greenville; the matter of integrating heretofore separate segregated pools epitomized that. A 1972 *Delta Democrat-Times* editorial brought the effect of their town's integration to light: *"There is little doubt about the reason for declining use of the [whites] Henry pool. Blacks have begun using it since integration, and some whites simply don't want to swim with blacks or don't want their children to swim with blacks. There is no similar problem at the other [all-black Katie Lewis] pool since whites rarely, if ever, use it now and, of course, did not use it during the days of legal segregation."*[264]

---

[264] Editorial page, "Haste Makes Waste," The Delta Democrat-Times, September 22, 1972, p. 4
https://www.newspapers.com/image/22190387/?match=1&terms=Katie%20Lewis%20memorial%20pool

Site of Greenville's Katie Lewis Memorial all-black pool, dismantled circa 1977 (author's collection)

Perhaps no story of Mississippi-style brutality has resounded more strikingly and with such an everlasting and dramatic saga and received such extraordinary national attention than the one surrounding young Emmett Till, who was tortured, maimed and savagely killed in a seed barn of the Sheridan plantation, that was managed by J. L. Milam just west of Drew, Mississippi, on August 28, 1955. It was a peal of thunder – a flashpoint - and a call bell for action inspiring a Civil Rights initiative like none other witnessed before that would have such a lasting impact, though with mixed results along the way but overall, positive repercussions benefitting the civil rights movement.

Emmett Till was a 14-year-old boy, having just turned fourteen the month before when he was murdered. "Bobo," as he was known affectionately by family and his mother, Mamie Till Mobley, had, on August 20, traveled by train from his home city of Chicago to a small northern Mississippi town in Money, Mississippi, to visit family there for a two-week stay.

On the evening of August 24, Emmett, with cousins and family friends, mostly his contemporaries, drove a short distance down to Bryant's Grocery & Meat Market in rural Money, bordering the Tallahatchie River. It was a store used frequently by black sharecroppers who worked on the adjacent plantations. A generally accepted version of events was that Till was alone in the store with Carolyn Bryant for a brief time, during which, as Bryant testified later on in the Tallahatchie Courthouse in Sumner, Till was alleged to have made a lascivious motion toward her, including grabbing her by the waist. Till's cousin, Simeon Wright, who entered the store in "less than a minute" of Till being alone with Bryant, saw no inappropriate behavior.

There is general agreement, though, that when Till and his cousins were outside, and Carolyn Bryant exited the store, apparently going for her gun left in her car, Till let out a loud wolf whistle aimed at her that caused the cousins to react in profound fear as he had broken the longstanding *Jim Crow* law of Southern social conduct between blacks and whites. Dreading the consequences, they quickly left the premises. *"It was a loud wolf whistle, a big-city 'whee wheeeee!'"* said cousin Simeon Wright, *"and it caught us all by surprise."*[265]

Four days later, on August 28, when Roy Bryant returned home from a fishing trip and learned of the incident, he appealed to his half-brother John Leslie Milam - together known and described in derogative terms as Southern "peckerwoods," or white trash – who agreed to help Bryant with anything he was about to do. They went to the house where Emmett Till was staying and took him hostage, drove him to the seed barn in the town of nearby Drew, and proceeded to torture him, including mutilation, and then shot him. Weighted down with a large ginning fan, they dropped Till's body in the Tallahatchie River; his swollen and disfigured body was found later near the shore.

The horror of the Emmett Till killing, how it was done, and its stunning conclusion sent a chill throughout the black communities, feeling that nothing was going to stop the whites now from vanquishing them altogether after what had happened to Till, while both offenders escaped prosecution in the face of certain conviction. It was out-and-out unjust. Deloris Melton Gresham, the daughter of Clinton and Beulah Melton and resident of Drew, Mississippi, remarked about the fear that was engendered after the Till murder, especially among the children, feeling that they could be next. She

---

[265] Amy Held, "Cousin, Who Witnessed Emmett Till Abduction Dies At 74," WNPR, The Two-Way, September 5, 2017
https://www.npr.org/sections/thetwo-way/2017/09/05/548647220/cousin-who-witnessed-emmett-till-abduction-dies-at-74

remembers kids at school talking about what had happened and the horror of that. *"I remember being afraid to go to sleep at night cause I was thinking some white people might come in and do the same thing to my brothers,"* she said. She wasn't alone; there was widespread panic and a sense of anguish amongst all of the blacks of the Delta experiencing extremes of paranoia in such a morbid setting.[266]

It was an open casket with Till's massively mutilated face and body on full display – he was unrecognizable; only his mother could identify him because of a ring he was wearing of his father's. The photograph of him in this state, which was published in *Jet*, the black magazine, was authorized – and actually done at her insistence for civil rights purposes - by Emmett Till's mother, Mamie. It was a dreadful sight that had a lasting and numbing effect on the nation and was the beginning of meaningful civil rights initiatives leading into the 1960s.

"Yes, I remember Emmett Till," said George Scott in a much later interview. *"He was badly beaten and murdered by whites in Drew, a couple of towns over from my hometown [Greenville]. They were all rural towns in those days, out in the country, lots of cotton farms around and long dusty country roads separating them. I played sports in several of them towns,*

---

[266] Nellie Giles & Joe Richman, "Clinton Melton: A Man Who Was Killed In Mississippi Just 3 Months After Emmett Till," WNPR, NPR Public, All Things Considered, August 27, 2020
https://www.npr.org/sections/codeswitch/2020/08/27/906791647/clinton-melton-a-man-who-was-killed-in-mississippi-just-3-months-after-emmett-ti

Mound Bayou, Greenwood, Itta Bena, Indianola that were around Drew and Money, where I heard Till got into trouble with local whites. He was older than me by a couple of years. Came down here from up north, Chicago, to visit relatives in Money. It was all over the northern and black papers, I was told, but we heard it mostly passed down [by] word of mouth. I remember one of the kids had a picture of Till in the casket, but you didn't see no pictures around here. They were in northern papers and magazines. They said he made a pass at a white woman working in a store in Money, but no one could prove it. My God, Money is only an hour's drive from here! He did whistle at her outside the store, though, so they said, and that got everyone upset, especially the woman's husband. I would imagine. He and his brother sought out the boy and just beat him to a pulp. It was awful. He had been tortured, threw his body in the Tallahatchie River nearby. I was horrified; shocked me to realize this brutality happened so close to my home. It's what they did to blacks around here when they stepped out of line, my momma would remind me. Kids around here worried it might happen to them.

My momma was concerned. She reminded me there was no room for error. [She] said, 'You don't go to speak to no white peoples unless you're spoken to, and especially no south'un white woman, or if you do, that's what will happen to you.' We were afraid after this because we felt this could happen to any one of us. It seemed like we blacks was fair game to them.

I don't know why our town of Greenville was so silent about the murder, or at least it seemed that way to us. Maybe it was an embarrassment, I don't know. Not much was said except for gossip we heard around town. I did learn that one of the killer's wives came from Greenville, whether that had anything to do with it. We were not used to talking much anyway about things like this, around whites, when it comes to conflicts between us blacks and white peoples. If we did, they would have accused us of stirring up trouble. No black peoples in Greenville had the right to any opinions. But when we did hear about things it was from the black community; it was a survival situation for us. The local paper ran some stories but seemed to favor the white woman [Bryant], my momma said. It was like any other murder reported in Mississippi in them times, not of a racial kind, just a plain murder. No one condemned it. None of us blacks would ever dare accuse, no man. We sure in hell wouldn't. This happened in 1955, same year as another black man [George Lee] was killed in another town near us in Belzoni only a few months before Till. And then there was Medgar Evers, cut down in Jackson, shot in cold blood near his home, a year after I graduated from high school and started with the Red Sox. He was our hometown champion for civil rights when we really had none. It was awful times for all of us blacks in the Delta then. Seemed like our kind was going to be wiped from the face of the earth, if not certainly from Mississippi, at the rate they were being killed. It was like a fire was raging inside them, and we felt it all around us."[267]

Delta Democrat-Times editor and publisher Hodding Carter became enraged at the conduct of "two groups," he called them the NAACP and the friends of the two white men, Bryant and Milam. *"Among the latter apparently can be counted Sheriff H. C. Strider,"* reported Carter on September 6, 1955, in his article *Lynching Post-Facto*. He roundly accused the NAACP of *"seeking another excuse to apply the torch of worldwide scorn to Mississippi"* when, as he pointed out, there was previously *"honest indignation."* Carter referenced the Chicago funeral of Emmett Till, where Till's body was put on full display, blaming the NAACP for its dramatization. It was nothing but *"macabre exhibitionism, the wild statements and hysterical overtones...seemed too well staged not to have been premeditated,"* Carter fumed, for the *"express purpose"* of arousing hatred and reversing attitudes. *"They could make prospective Mississippi jurors so angry at these blanket indictments,"* he declared, *"Mississippi could go down in further ignominy as a snakepit where justice cannot prevail for each race alike,"* and that would suit the NAACP just fine, he was to remark.[268]

---

[267] George Scott interview: February 16, 2008
[268] Hodding Carter, "Lynching Post-Facto," Delta Democrat-Times, September 6, 1955, p. 14
https://www.newspapers.com/image/12930629/?terms=%22Emmett%20Till%22%20&match=1

Civil rights tour guide Jaynes Diming of the Emmett Till Memorial Commission explains that current-day Mississippi is not so welcoming of commemorative initiatives, testimonials or dedications when Till's name is invoked in the name of racial violence history there. *"Telling his story in the Mississippi Delta remains fraught,"* exclaimed NPR's *All Things Considered* Reporter Debbie Elliott in a 2019 visit to the Delta.[269]

The son of one of the defense attorneys in the Emmett Till court case, John Whitten, a former prosecutor himself, is outright contentious in his own accusatory rhetoric, stating, *"Fella came down here and got [himself] in trouble – overstepped his bounds to a degree some folks thought…and they cured him of his problems."* He emphatically takes the position that there is no need or reason to commemorate Till's murder.[270]

The assault on blacks was of epidemic proportions in the Delta, with a rash of murders, many of which were never reported or their stories told, leaving murders unsolved and a criminal justice system that was corrupt and in tatters. Yet, some stories actually did make the news, which spurred the civil rights movement into action; they were a primary determinant and stimulus for civil rights leaders, among them Martin Luther King, who took up the scepter most dramatically at the end of 1955 until his death by

---

[269] Debbie Elliott, "'Why Don't Y'all Let That Die?' Telling The Emmett Till Story In Mississippi," NPR Public, All Things Considered, August 28, 2019 https://www.npr.org/2019/08/28/755024458/why-don-t-y-all-let-that-die-telling-the-emmett-till-story-in-mississippi
[270] IBID

assassination in April 1968. King would often inspire Civil Rights marches down the Delta's U. S. Route 61, the Blues Highway, or Great River Road as it was also known, from Memphis through Greenville down to New Orleans.

In a span of sixteen months, between February 1963 and June 1964, there were seven more prominent racial slayings occurring at the height of the civil rights movement. There were others, but many of these went unreported, which was commonplace in many of the outlying small rural Mississippi towns, which largely stuck close to their rigid views of white supremacy and intolerance of blacks. But these particular murders stood out as they were connected, directly or indirectly, to the era of the Civil Rights Movement. Hodding Carter summed it up, expressing considerable frustration and disapproval, at the conclusion of the Clinton Melton trial, even more senseless than the Emmett Till case, declared Carter. *"So, another 'not guilty' verdict was written at Sumner [courthouse] this week. And it served to cement the opinion of the world that no matter how strong the evidence nor how flagrant is the apparent crime, a white man can not be convicted in Mississippi for killing a Negro,"* wrote Carter on March 16, 1956.[271]

---

[271] Hodding Carter 4, IBID, "Sumner Revisited," Delta Democrat-Times, March 16, 1956
https://www.newspapers.com/image/23664988/?terms=Sumner%20revisited&match=1

"And then there were those three civil rights workers – one of them was from Meridian, where I played some ball," said George Scott. *"They came down to Mississippi to help with signing up black voters and got killed across the state from us. Up to this point the towns' white Citizens' Councils had a powerful grip; gave appearances they were adjusting to prior civil rights decisions, but they weren't. They were opposed to us voting, period, my momma said. In fact, they were against just about everything that meant black down here."*[272]

He was alluding to the June 21, 1964, death of black activist James Earl Chaney, who was killed along with co-activists Andrew Goodman and Michael Schwerner, who were both white and Jewish, outside of the town of Philadelphia, Mississippi, northeast of the capital city of Jackson. They were participating as volunteers with the Congress on Racial Equality (CORE), a civil rights organization, in what was known as *Freedom Summer*. Also known as the Freedom Summer Project or the Mississippi Summer Project, it was launched in June of that year in Mississippi in an attempt to register as many black voters as possible in the state, which infuriated the white residents, particularly a still-active White Citizens' Council, and re-activated the violent resistance of the Ku Klux Klan, members of the state and local law enforcement. *"Despite all of this progress, the South remained segregated, especially when it came to polls,*

---

[272] George Scott interview: January 23, 2006

where African Americans faced violence and intimidation when they attempted to exercise their constitutional right to vote."[273]

It was an important time and at the peak of the Civil Rights Movement, but the effort of messing with Mississippi's voting contrivances against blacks and their political process touched a central nerve in various Mississippi factions, sparking a level of open hostility and violence that led to the deaths of the three men, who disappeared upon release from a Philadelphia, Mississippi jail after being arrested for an alleged "speeding" violation, and were found dead three days later. At the time of the murders, the state of Mississippi made little effort to prosecute, and it wasn't until 41 years from the day of the crime that the mastermind of the murders, Edgar Ray Killen, a KKK member and white supremacist, was eventually convicted of "manslaughter" and sentenced to sixty years. Seventeen others who participated in the murders received varying sentences, but none of them found guilty would serve more than six years in prison.

The Philadelphia civil rights murders galvanized the nation and served as a stimulant for the landmark Civil Rights Act passed on July 2, 1964, the most sweeping civil rights legislation since Reconstruction.

---

[273] History.com Editors, contributing editors: Amanda Onion, Missy Sullivan, Matt Mullen and Christian Zapata, "Freedom Summer," History.com, Original publication, October 29, 2009; Updated April 16, 2021
https://www.history.com/topics/black-history/freedom-summer

On February 28, 1963, in Greenwood, a Delta town, Jimmy Travis, a native Mississippian from Jackson, assisted in black voter registration while working for the Student Nonviolent Coordinating Committee (SNCC), which was situated in Greenwood, and was shot for his efforts. It was a drive-by shooting leading to a bullet being lodged in his neck. But he survived the injury and remained undeterred in his efforts to continue his activism against segregation and racial discrimination.

On June 12, 1963, Medgar Evers, age 37, a distinguished member and field secretary of the Mississippi state NAACP, was tragically slain in his own driveway in Jackson by white supremacist and member of the Jackson White Citizens' Council, Byron De La Beckwith. Evers advocated his black supporters the importance of registering to vote, traveling the state for the cause, and also investigating nine racial murders and significant numbers of maltreatment cases involving black victims across the state, including those of Emmett Till and Clinton Melton.

On May 2, 1964, two black 19-year-old hitchhikers, Charles Eddie Moore and Henry Hezekiah Dee, of Meadville, Mississippi, were approached by two Ku Klux Klansmen, members of the White Knights, who abducted them and took them to the nearby Homochitta National Forest. There, they were joined by several other White Knights who participated in brutalizing the two men. Following that, they were taken to Louisiana 75 miles away and were tossed into the Mississippi River while still alive, chained to a Jeep engine. Klansmen James Ford Seale and

Charles Marcus Edwards were arrested and turned over to state authorities and inexplicably released on a dismissal raised by their attorney. Forty-three years later, Seale was rearrested on federal charges, convicted and sentenced to three life terms on August 24, 2007, for his part in the murders.

Amongst the tumult and commotion of the times, in the mid-1950s and early 1960s, young George Scott and his family were favored by their living in Greenville, which was an oasis among the racial strife of the Mississippi Delta. But there was no mistaking what the town was made of: the element of *Jim Crow* was a fixture in the town, no more dissimilar than any of the neighboring Delta towns. Their public schools were segregated and separated from grade school up, and their community was racially divided. *"Everybody knew their place,"* said George. Basically, a caste system with rules and standards – those for the whites and those for the blacks. But George could feel some satisfaction, though it was guarded, in such a moderate town as Greenville, unlike those who were obliged to deal with the violence in towns around them.

George had begun to make a name for himself in the town sports arena, especially at all-black Coleman High School, but there were always headwinds to deal with. *"In 1955, I was named the Most Valuable Player on the Little League Team. I was eleven and had taken to baseball like a locust to a wheat field; I just loved the game, but we were a segregated league couldn't play with no whites. The fields were bad; the town never helped us that way like they did for the white kids who had wonderful Little*

League fields to play on with dugouts, fences and scoreboards. Tax help and donations, I understood, the white kids had. But we had none of that; no tax money was ever meant for blacks. I learned to field baseballs on rocky diamonds full of stones, very little grass, dust bowls for the most part, and no uniforms to speak of. Baseballs were hard to come by. [They] turned to a dark color from all the use and the stitching would come loose, became misshapen, but we played with them anyway. We made sure when we hit 'em into the woods, we didn't lose 'em, or the game was over. Many of us were poor and we certainly gave every appearance of that.

I'd go down to the railroad tracks a few streets over from my house with my friend, E. T., who could play baseball with the best of them. I called him E. T., but his name was Edward. He was like Hank Aaron, stood up straight when he was batting and just hit line drives all day. Ooh-ee, but he could hit. There were five or six guys like him in town that could have made the big leagues, except they were black and no one paid no attention to them, nor heard about them in the papers, unless they got lucky like me. E.T. and me scrounged for sticks lying nearby or cut bats out of hickory limbs alongside the tracks and hit stones with them in all directions for hours. We were like Willie Mays and Aaron, or Monte [Irvin], calling the shots when we were playing our games: line drive to right or a high pop-up to the infield, or a home run over the wall. Once every so often, a white hard-ass cop come by and shooed us off, screaming that no goddamn no-good-colored kids was going to play there, and if we showed up there again, they'd haul us off. I knew of no reason for their outrage except they hated blacks. They were looking for us to give them trouble, give them a reason to hurt us, but we never did cause no trouble. I remembered what my momma said. But that didn't stop us from going back to the tracks when we felt no more troubles would come of it.

There was a time in Greenville when us black kids had to be off the streets by 5:00 p.m., or they would find a reason to haul us off to the clink, or some such thing, or do something worse that we never wanted to see. It was nothing formal, mind you like it was written anywhere that this was the honest-to-goodness official town rule police could go by, but we knew if we were caught after 5:00, it was an excuse for them to do some harm. They were all white cops. They seemed to want to make the rules like in the old days of Jim Crow. A few of them had a real ugly streak and threatened us harm anyway, sometimes grabbing kids for the weakest of excuses and shoving them around just for spite; and they would get away with it, and they knew it. We knew if we complained to our parents, they would complain to the town, which would do them or us no good and even make things worse for us. Even though our town was known for neutrality, there really was no justice unless we stayed in the "normal zone" of behavior. So, we kept silent and accepted what was coming. Momma would say they used to do *lynchings of our kind for no reason than we was black, and what would prevent them from doing it now! It was always her memory.*[274]

After Little League, I didn't play no organized baseball until my junior year in high school. They didn't do anything for us black kids in the town, no organized leagues like the white kids had, like Babe Ruth, Pony, Dixie Leagues. There was no money for us. The town gave it [the money] to the white kids. We were used to handouts from black peoples around town to supply us with bats, gloves and balls so we could play town ball or semipro, some called it; basically, donations, if you'd call it that. Nothing organized like the white kids had. I had no money, so used a paper bag for my glove."[275]

In 1959, when George was in his freshman year at Coleman High School, he and his family encountered a troublesome period; they were on the brink of poverty and slipping into complete penury. Maggie, his mother, appealed to the children, who at that time was George Jr. at 15, and sister Beatrice, age 20, to help with the family income. The oldest son Otis, who did live in Greenville, was now 22, married, and in the U. S. Navy, so he was preoccupied with military service, as well as with a young family himself. It was up to the three of them, 41-year-old mother Maggie, young

---

[274] Sunset Towns: were meant to exclude non-whites from remaining in their towns after sunset. The town of Greenville was not a sunset community, so it is expected that George and his friends, by virtue of being black, were randomly being harassed with threat of harm by the local police who made the effort to get them off the streets expeditiously; in Greenville, that usually meant by 5:00 PM

[275] George Scott interview: January 23, 2006

George and Beatrice, to keep the family going, which meant that George had to drop out of school, which, in fact, he did. His high school coaches, however, made up of Coleman's football coach and athletic director, Davis Weathersby and basketball coach, Andrew Jackson, arranged with the help of the school and local businesses to assist with finding employment and establishing a part-time work schedule for young Scott to keep the family afloat, and keep him in school.

Andrew Jackson, Coleman High School basketball coach, with George Scott (author's collection)

Andrew Jackson and George Scott (author's collection)

"I was helped by the Collins Cleaners and John Provenza of the Pepsi Cola Company to keep me in school and be given the opportunity to play sports that eventually lifted my mother out of poverty," said George. "She was really struggling and in tears some nights. I never would have played pro sports if this hadn't have happened."[276]

"He was dedicated to his mother, and he never forgot where his roots were. He was just a dedicated family man," said Provenza. "He was very dependable and a really hard worker. He was a hustler," speaking commendably of George. "There's no doubt in my mind he would have been in the National Football League if he hadn't gone into baseball," said

---

[276] George Scott interview: February 16, 2008

Provenza. John Provenza was a fifty-percent owner of the Pepsi Cola Bottling Company of Greenville, handling the production part of the business, and actually hired George to help him and his family with their money issues.[277]

As much as Provenza extolled George's numerous virtues and athletic talents, of which he was keenly aware, and followed him in the local news if or when George was written about or when he was rarely spotlighted in the local paper - and that required some luck to even be recognized by reporters or their editors - his response to an interview question of whether he had actually seen him play organized sports was forthright - *"No, I never did."*[278] This was riveting but not so astonishing, considering the times and the political climate of the Delta. The White Citizens' Council was gaining momentum in the Delta towns, including Greenville, making life miserable for white businessmen like Provenza, who were caught showing any favor toward blacks; they would undermine them and eventually shut their businesses down. To make things more alarming, the Mississippi legislature legitimized the Citizens' Council to a greater and more official degree in 1956, establishing the State Sovereignty Commission that funded the Councils and formed a network to covertly track the activities of blacks and whites. *"White businessmen would face boycotts, and politicians would lose*

---

[277] John Provenza interview: February 17, 2008
[278] IBID

votes if they were believed to be sympathetic to African Americans' efforts at integration."[279]

It was little wonder John Provenza and his Pepsi Cola Bottling Company were at considerable risk if he had made any overtures toward blacks or openly nodded approval of them, whether they were businessmen or residents. It was far too great a risk for him to take. But neither was he deterred, supporting local blacks and their Greenville schools, where he felt he could, in other ways, by funding their activities privately, doing so clandestinely or in smaller ways so as not to draw attention to himself.

John Provenza (author's collection)

---

[279] White Citizens' Councils, Article, "The Murder of Emmett Till: White Citizens' Councils," American Experience, aired April 15, 2023; From the Collections: Civil Rights, The African American Experience, 1996-2023 WGBH Educational Foundation
https://www.pbs.org/wgbh/americanexperience/features/emmett-citizens-council/

Provenza was up against the hardcore effects of the Citizens' Council and surrounding business communities, albeit without a stronghold in Greenville because of the town's urbane and more cultivated social structure, but he was nevertheless vulnerable; the Council's strength in Greenville was tempered, however, because of Pulitzer recipient DD-T editor "Big" Hodding Carter, who because of his national influence and reputation kept the Council at bay beyond the reach of *"The lash of organized intolerance."*[280]

Just the same, and in spite of Carter's vigorous opposition to the Council, he found himself reluctantly conceding to its formation and presence in Greenville, remarking in astonishment at the surprising makeup of the town leadership that was demonstrating their support of the Council; in author *Ann Waldron's* words, *"the names of the town's worthies."*[281]

Sharply at odds with Provenza, as well as being his counterpart in neighboring Belzoni, was the manager of Belzoni's Coca-Cola bottling plant, who epitomized the kind of support the emerging Citizens' Council was receiving from the Delta's white racists, with this very bleak viewpoint: *"Integration leads to intermarriage; then there won't be any whites left or nigras left; there'd be a race of mulattoes. If my daughter starts going to*

---

[280] Neil R. McMillen, "The Citizen's Council: organized resistance to the second reconstruction, 1954-64," Urbana: University of Illinois Press, 1994, p. 255
https://archive.org/details/citizenscouncilo0000mcmi/mode/1up

[281] Ann Waldron, "The Reconstruction of a Racist," Algonquin Books of Chapel Hill, Chapel Hill, NC, 1993

school with nigras now, by the time she gets to college, she won't think anything of dating one of 'em. The nigra's life consists of sex, eating, and drinking...This town is 70 percent nigra; if the nigra voted, there'd be nigra candidates in office."[282]

John Provenza was a good friend and active supporter of Coleman High's football Coach, Davis Weathersby, who was George Scott's high school coach. Upon Provenza's death, Weathersby, who was black, participated in his funeral as a pallbearer, eventful even for Greenville; it was an unprecedented gesture for a Southern white man to ask a black man to partake in any way at their funeral, let alone to have the honor of being their pallbearer. It was a striking moment for Greenville and its residents, black and white, who doubtless were paying closer than the usual attention to this groundbreaking measure and to realize that some of the historic bigotry was softening.

---

[282] James C. Cobb, "The Most Southern Place On Earth," Oxford University Press, New York, 1992, p. 216

Davis Weathersby (author's collection)

Davis Weathersby and George Scott (author's collection)

Chapter 6
The Tryout

Globe reporter Clif Keane subsequently wrote that someone up in the back of the grandstand hollered, "Get those niggers off the field!" near the conclusion of the "tryouts." The voice was never identified. Many speculated it belonged to either [Eddie] Collins or Tom Yawkey, and decades later, Keane asserted it was Yawkey's voice.

Jerry M. Gutlon[283]

When George Scott Junior was a youngster, somewhere between age 8 and 10, he would walk several city blocks from his home to the north side of town to a state-of-the-art minor league ballpark, Sportsman's Park, to watch the local club, the Greenville Bucks of the Class C Cotton States League. It was a park that not only fielded the minor league teams but also the major league barnstorming teams in the offseason who would come through the Southern towns, including Greenville. Such major league baseball stalwarts as Roy Campanella, Monte Irvin, and Bob Feller were known to play there at one time or another, and the House of David ballclubs did as well into the early 1950s. Eddie "Pop" Popowski of the Red Sox organization, who was very close to young George Scott, George's mentor,

---

[283] Jerry M. Gutlon, "It was never about the babe," Skyhorse Publishing, New York, NY, 2009, p. 96

and who himself was once a member of the House of David semipro barnstorming baseball teams, played there.

"I used to walk cross-town to a baseball stadium in the north end they called Sportsman's Park where a pro team, the Greenville Bucks, played when they were in town," exclaimed George in a stout manner, remembering the complexities of his being there. *"If my momma knew about it, she'd be angry, but she worked most of the time and didn't always know where I was. It was a long walk but had its rewards. We black kids could never see the game, or most of it anyway, because the whites didn't allow blacks in the park. They were dead serious about that and got real angry if we tried. If we were lucky, we'd find a crack in the fence or a hole and see some of the action that way, but we were taking a chance if the whites caught us. We couldn't sit on the fence or even look over it, or we'd be hauled off by the scruff of our necks and maybe even put in the local jail. I got to know one of the Bucks' players, Luther Tucker, not personally, mind you, but I knew about him. He was a big left-handed hitter, a catcher, and could knock baseballs out of the park. I chased them down, kept what I could when no one was looking so we had something to play with. We were supposed to return them to the ballpark peoples, and we'd get a small payment for returning it. The kids I used to play with knew I had my sights on Tucker and began to call me "Tuck." Then, in school, it took on a new name: "Pee-tuck." I don't recall the reason for this, but it stuck. My old school friends call me that today.*

One time when I was at the park was memorable for me and a reminder who I am and what I am, and by all means, where I come from: You see, we couldn't actually see the game. So, my friends, like my best friend E. T. [Eddie], would let me know when Tucker was coming up. They'd see him through a knot hole or crack in the wooden fence, and I'd station myself outside the right field wall. Soon, that's what he did: hit a home run, clearing the right field fence, and I was fast on my feet after that ball. I wasn't the only one chasing it down, but I was the first to get to it. I called back to E. T. that I had the ball. I yelled back and put it into the pocket of my large overalls with the big pockets. That may have been a mistake. Thought I was safe, but man, was I wrong.

'Hey, kid! You with the god-damned baseball! You better bring it back to the [announcers] stand, do you hear!' this white guy was screaming at me, seeing me pocket the ball. He was breaking into a run [in my direction], and I knew I was in real trouble, baby. I was black, and he was white! What more would I have to say? I'm from the South! I had committed myself to stealing the ball of a white man's game by stuffing the ball into my trousers, and the only thing I knew at that turn was to run. He was furious, calling on other men [to join the chase], improving his odds he was going to catch me. I could hear the hatred and anger in their voices, and [the rage] in their footsteps close behind me; and the sweat, oh man, did I sweat. And I was running, man, I was just running, scared to death.

'You no good damn nigger kid, y'all come back here! Do ya hear!' he was screaming. *I know if I was caught, I was in a heap of trouble. I was sure my life was over, and maybe it was not so far-fetched; running so fast it was like I was skipping over hot sand, my feet was hardly touching the ground. I was terrified [remembering stories] of other black kids and what happened to some of them in other towns, not so much in Greenville. But there was always a first time. By whatever luck I had in me, I escaped [all of them]. And I had the ball!"* he shouted in contented laughter for thwarting whites and priding himself on a job well done.[284]

In 1961, the White Citizens' Council was in full swing, having penetrated the mindset of the Southern whites who largely adopted their hard-core principles and avowed doctrines in their response to the 1954 *Brown* decision, and there was word filtering down that there would be northern interference descending on Mississippi as an enforcement measure to prod Southern whites into ending racial segregation in the Southern states that, up until then, had ignored the rulings of the Federal government, including the Supreme Court's rulings of *Morgan v. Virginia* and *Boynton v. Virginia* declaring that segregated public buses were unconstitutional. In 1955, the Interstate Commerce Commission ruled in *Keys v. Carolina Coach Company*, condemning the longstanding 1896 Supreme Court decision of *Separate but Equal* in *Plessy v. Ferguson*. This led to a process of numerous other decisions overturning segregation laws and rulings

---

[284] George Scott interview: September 13, 2006

amidst the powerful Supreme Court's *Brown v. Board of Education* decision, which declared segregation of public schools unconstitutional. These were, however, mostly being ignored by Southern states, in particular Alabama, South Carolina and Mississippi of the Deep South, which, because of their intransigence, led ultimately to the formation of The Freedom Riders from the North launching protests in May 1961.

They were an interracial group of students and civil rights activists, nearly 450 of them, amounting to more than 60 Freedom Rides, organized by the Congress of Racial Equality (CORE), that went down to key Southern states by bus – emphasizing by their makeup that all colors were entitled to ride public transportation on interstate transportation routes, including use of their related facilities like restrooms and waiting rooms-crisscrossing the South to protest against racial discrimination. They were physically assaulted in several locations, but especially in parts of Alabama, such as Anniston, Birmingham and Montgomery, where the local Ku Klux Klan had "welcoming" parties, and in parts of Mississippi, including the Delta. In spite of the brutality of these attacks, amounting to significant injuries, the Riders moved on, seeking recruits, departing Montgomery and traveling to Jackson, Mississippi, where a new defensive strategy was devised: "fill the jails." And that's what they did, arriving in Jackson throughout the summer where the Riders were immediately cuffed, put into buses and transferred 130 miles north to the infamous maximum security Parchman Farm state penitentiary of the Yazoo Delta 60 miles north of Greenville, where they were brutalized again.

Mississippi's governor, Ross Barnett, a staunch white supremacist, segregationist and White Citizens' Council supporter, and a Dixiecrat, had a game plan of his own to quell what he saw as an unbridled insurrection that had to be stopped. He was *"out to 'teach 'em a lesson'"* and *"break the back"* of their movement *"by doing 'real-time in a real prison' like Parchman,"* where he felt the Mississippi jailer guards would break their spirit and ultimately their willpower.[285]

The White Citizens' Council had a bona fide stake in this where they staunchly stood for preserving the rule of segregation in the Delta and keeping close ties with Governor Barnett, who became a benefactor to their cause. Taking advantage of the chaos and disturbance created by the Freedom Riders, which, adding fuel to the fire, was a northern-formed organization, the Council pushed back on the basis that this was nothing but northern "interference" in matters that they could handle themselves and insisted they could do it in better ways. *"Nothing, however, has been as much of a godsend to the Council as the continued forays of the Freedom Riders,"* wrote Hodding Carter III, who took over as managing editor of the Delta Democrat-Times, on November 12, 1961. *"Even while their exploits were focusing national attention on segregation in interstate facilities in the South, Council leaders were singling out the 'friction riders' as a convenient symbol of 'outside interference.' The success with which*

---

[285] The Pop History Dig, Civil Rights History, "Buses Are A' Comin,'" Freedom Riders: 1961, First Posting: 27 April 2008; Last Update: 26 October 2019 https://pophistorydig.com/topics/tag/parchman-prison-freedom-riders/

officials in the capital city of Jackson kept the segregation lid on while maintaining law and order as hundreds of Freedom Riders poured into the city was made-to-order propaganda for the Council, which has always promised that segregation could be preserved without violence."[286]

The founding father of the Freedom Rides, James Farmer, who was also co-founder of the Congress of Racial Equality (CORE) and participated in the rides, had this to say about his imminent ride into Mississippi, one of the two most violent Southern states the Freedom Riders were to encounter: *"If Alabama had been purgatory, Mississippi would be hell,"* he exclaimed, with perfect knowledge what he was about to experience, as outlined in his autobiography *Lay Bare the Heart*.[287]

Young George Scott, who had just turned 17 at the time, witnessed some of this with the transfer of the Freedom Riders from Jackson, where they were arrested, to the notorious Parchman Farm. *"Me and some friends got a ride out to the highway up in Indianola where the buses were coming through. We were curious. They sometimes stopped on the road, and we saw them out on the side of the road. They were being shoved around. Had to*

---

[286] Hodding Carter III and Citizens' Councils of America, "Citadel of the Citizens' Council," (1961); Clippings. 75, p. 24
https://egrove.olemiss.edu/cgi/viewcontent.cgi?article=1074&context=citizens_clip
[287] James Farmer, "Lay Bare The Heart," New York: Arbor House, 1985, p. 2
https://archive.org/details/laybareheartauto0000farm_0/mode/1up

wonder what it was going to be like for them once they got to Parchman," said George.[288]

Desegregation and its social ramifications were still smoldering in Mississippi schools in the 1960s, such an action having been shunned by the state's delaying tactics, with the help of the White Citizens' Council, since the U. S. Supreme Court decisions of *Brown v. Board of Education* in 1954 and 1955 – *Brown I and II* - the latter decision in the form of an implementation order by the court in the name of "all deliberate speed." It wasn't until January 1970, fifteen years later, that the Supreme Court took further enforcement action, insisting on a February date, but the U. S. Justice Department postponed the action until September 1970 when the mandate was *"to have every Southern system totally integrated."* Among the Mississippi schools affected by this was Coleman High, George Scott's High School of six years, since the 7th grade. It was customary for the black students of Greenville to enter Coleman High right out of elementary school. But, as with other Mississippi public schools slated for integration, white resistance was at a heightened level in Washington County, and they fled the public school system seeking private school solutions, which was abetted and largely facilitated by the White Citizens' Council.[289]

---

[288] George Scott interview: 9/13/2006
[289] Unattributed, "Public School Desegregation goes into effect across state," The Delta Democrat-Times, January 5, 1970, p. 1
https://www.newspapers.com/image/24175275/?terms=Coleman%20high%20school

All-black Coleman High School was suddenly and irrevocably dispossessed of its very being and summarily converted to an integrated junior high. Whatever could be stripped of its past was done, including the dismantling of its magnificent trophy case of local and state championships across all disciplines, from their powerhouse athletic teams to academic performance, graduating countless students in fields of medicine, law, education, philosophy, music, and the list just goes on.

Coleman Middle School, known previously as Coleman High School, photographed by author 2006 (Author's Collection)

Coleman High School converted to a middle school circa 1970 (Author's Collection)

In 2012, Dr. L. Jordan Jackson, who was a 1962 graduate of Coleman High School – a classmate of George Scott – wrote a commemorative narrative on the school and the town, *Triggering the Memories*, in which she wrote a testimonial on the school's greatness. Included in that discourse of fond remembrances as well as indignation was this: *"I can speak for the entire class of 1962 – it will never be destroyed in our memories."* Further to that, she spoke about the trophies, as did George Scott speak of this frequently and with bitterness, and some of his teammates who were interviewed in preparation for this publication. *"The whites tried to blot out the history of the athletic department after doing a number job on the* school. To me, Coleman High School should have remained Coleman High School, and the Greenville High School (an all-white school) should have been changed to a middle school, and I bet not one trophy would have been lost or destroyed…The destruction of black civilization has repeated itself just as it tried to blot out the history of Africa," she declared in obvious frustration.[290] And as for her town of Greenville, she announced: *"I feel that we as black students were cheated out of recognitions in the community…the history of Coleman High School no longer exists as far as the whites are concerned."*[291] Among individuals of Coleman High that Dr. Jackson felt obliged to point out was George Scott. *"No one in the class of 1962 climbed the ladder in sports as successfully as George Scott,"* she exclaims.[292]

"They just disappeared," cried out George Scott, speaking painfully and disparagingly about Coleman High's trophies and how they simply vanished, never to be seen again. It was an incredible display of impudence by those who were assigned the duty of dismantling and realigning public schools, nor was there ever an explanation or apology by anyone. George's frustration more than fits the theme of Dr. Jackson's narrative as published in 2012, which was the cancellation of Greenville's black community to the extent that would be possible. Symbolic of that was eliminating all of the marvelous trophies the black students earned through their individual and team achievements. There was no sentiment extended to Greenville's black

---

[290] Dr. L. Jordan Jackson, "Triggering the Memories," Xlibris Publishing, Bloomington, IN, 2012, p. 93
[291] IBID, p. 92
[292] IBID, p. 98

community, nor a feeling of respect, during the dismantling of the venerable Coleman High School; it was like they were tearing down a cow barn, voiced some of the black community members and former athletes, who felt degraded.

In 1962, George Scott's senior year at all-black Coleman High School in Greenville, major league baseball clubs were taking notice of the young power hitter and slick fielder who displayed all the markings of a future professional ballplayer. Among the teams showing interest were the St. Louis Cardinals, who had a racial legacy but made the first steps to recruit and sign the 6' 2" shortstop with the powerful bat; however, there were unfortunate headwinds encircling and threatening his chances with them.

The Tiger Baseball Team
MR. ELBERT FOULES, Coach
GEORGE SCOTT
ROBERT JONES
E. T. DAVIS, Captains

Coleman High 1962 baseball team. George Scott kneeling, 4th from left (courtesy of Andrew Jackson)

Coleman High School ballpark where George Scott played 1961-1962 –
(Compliments Princella Wilkerson Nowell)

St. Louis, a fiercely racist city and ballclub of the 1950s – the only major city to specify separate seating for blacks and whites - was one of three cities in the National League where no black player wanted to play: Philadelphia, Cincinnati and St. Louis.[293] *"St. Louis had been the only major league with this discriminatory rule,"* according to Mark Tomasik of *RetroSimba*, which was not only segregated seating for both the St. Louis Cardinals and Browns, but the relegation of black seating consigning black fans to the bleachers and pavilion, which was limited viewing, located essentially at the outer reaches of the ballpark; this practice was finally ended, however, in 1944 having been influenced by Branch Rickey, who was the Cardinals' general manager previous to his departure in 1942 for the Brooklyn

---

[293] Howard Bryant, "Shut Out," Routledge, New York, 2002, p. 71

Dodgers, where he became president, general manager and part owner, and who would later break the color barrier by signing Jackie Robinson.[294]

It was an immutable truth that St. Louis's major league ballclubs of the early to mid-20th century subscribed to the old racist standard of keeping doors closed to blacks; it was also manifestly true that this attitude was ingrained into the culture and character of the city, much to their great pleasure. And the Cardinals perpetuated the maxim by signing white men of southern origin – from *"upper south states,"* according to *Society for American Baseball Research's* (SABR) Scott Powers in his biographical article of the St. Louis Cardinals, and by association with its city.[295]

They were a hardened bunch of tough-minded ballplayers of the 1930s, including administrative personnel and scouts from blue-collar backgrounds. They would do about anything within acceptable baseball rules – and, sometimes, of questionable tactics - to win and eventually were labeled the "Gas House Gang" for their aggressive style. What did not go unnoticed was that they were all white in keeping with the staunch tradition of St. Louis baseball and city standards. They were led by playing manager Frankie Frisch, who oversaw a large contingency of Southerners and South

---

[294] Retrosimba, Mark Tomasik, "Cardinals History Beyond the Box Score," May 1, 2019
https://retrosimba.com/2019/05/01/how-cardinals-browns-discriminated-against-black-fans/

[295] Scott Powers, "The St. Louis Cardinals of the Sixties and Their Effect on Black/White Relations in St. Louis," Society for American Baseball Research (SABR), Phoenix, Arizona, p. 1
https://sabr.org/sites/default/files/powers_2005.PDF

Westerners throughout his tenure, such as the Dean brothers - Dizzy and Daffy - Bill Delancey, Pepper Martin, Spud Davis, Pat Crawford, Taylor Douthit, Lew Riggs, Jim Winford, Flint Rhem, Jim Lindsey, Burgess Whitehead, and a handful of Texas players in the mix.

But the Cardinals' baseball club was rapidly, and even more than that, astonishingly, being transformed into an integrated team by an enlightened August A. "Gussie" Busch, Jr., who assumed ownership of the Cardinals in 1953. Busch saw more than just integration needs but economic opportunity in the city and region. There was common ground; both blacks and whites drank beer, and Busch saw this as an opportunity for The Brewery to bring them together. They were becoming a commodity. Tim McCarver, a former Cardinals' catcher who later went into the announcer's booth, said of The Brewery: *"The Brewery, using its power to force change...was one of the most important but least mentioned aspects of the Cardinals' story,"* said McCarver. *"Without that pressure, he said, there would have been no incentive for Southern businesses to relax and ultimately eliminate the segregated order."*[296]

But there were remnants of racism among the old guard on the St. Louis ballclub, not unusual when considering the depths of their racism persisting as late as the mid-nineteen fifties. When 18-year-old George Scott was playing ball for his Coleman High School ball team, he was making noise

---

[296] Howard Bryant, "Shut Out," Tim McCarver quoted, p. 72

with his play around several local all-black high schools and Jackson colleges, notably Jackson State, which was also showing interest in his football and basketball skills, with the hope and expectations that he might give a nod to college. At the same time, his name was being bandied about major league clubs, which were beginning to take an interest in him by paying attention to their scouts, who were making noises of their own while touting their Southern-most discovery.

Amid these was ex-major leaguer George Crowe, an ex-Negro Leaguer who once played with the New York Black Yankees and Philadelphia Stars and who also played 9 seasons of pro baseball in the white major leagues between the Braves (Boston and Milwaukee), Cincinnati and the St. Louis Cardinals, and became a St. Louis Cardinals' scout at the end of 1961. Crowe was among the early arrivals of black players entering major league baseball after Jackie Robinson, landing, ironically, in the city of Boston's backyard in 1952 – with Lou Perini's National League Braves. It was paradoxical where Tom Yawkey's cross-town American League team, the Red Sox, remained firmly entrenched in a so-called "gentleman's agreement" arrangement, an informal handshake among owners, in which he had participated at the outset, to resist the entry of black ballplayers into the major leagues: ironically they were of the same city, but two major league clubs who couldn't be more different about racial points of view.

There was no official written baseball policy excluding blacks, but it was not needed as major league owners had reached that agreement – a firm handshake - in the early years of the game to resist their entry. There was nothing in writing. Among these pioneers was, famously, Thomas Yawkey of the Boston Red Sox. In December 1942, large locals of several major unions descended upon the major league's winter meetings in Chicago to protest to the executives there and baseball's commissioner Kenesaw Mountain Landis, who held a racial bias, that racial discrimination of major league baseball was unacceptable and demanded that they integrate. One executive, Chicago Cubs owner Phil Wrigley, broke ranks with the other owners, professing he was in favor of integration, but it went nowhere. Wrigley was admonished by the other owners. He went back to the unions, stating that *"there are men in high places who don't want to see it,"* he said to them, and there is a firm *"gentlemen's agreement"* in place.[297] In 1946, there was a meeting of the baseball steering committee of which Boston's Tom Yawkey was a member, sticking with the theme that too many blacks attending baseball games would discourage whites from attending, bringing harm to the national pastime, and thus expanding on what they had decided in 1942 about integration.[298]

Recognizing his potential, the Cardinals' George Crowe spent considerable periods of time with young George Scott, cultivating his skills while visiting Greenville often, working on his batting style that favored

---

[297] Peter Dreier, "Before Jackie Robinson: Baseball's Civil Rights Movement," Society for American Baseball Research (SABR)
https://sabr.org/journal/article/before-jackie-robinson-baseballs-civil-rights-movement/
[298] Howard Bryant, "Shut Out," p. 24

opening his hands, which led to frequent power to the right side of the diamond, but not the left side. Being a right-handed batter, Crowe knew to be successful in the major leagues, Scott had to pull the ball to the left side as well and be able to hit to all fields, and that's what he taught him to do. Crowe got him hitting with better range and substantial power in all fields. Realizing that his young protégé was ready for his "showing" to St. Louis's head scout, Walter Shannon – although, much to his chagrin that as a black scout he was considered "incapable" of making his own decisions about a prospect - which was the routine he was obliged to follow where he had no financial authority; he announced this to Scott's first-year high school baseball coach Elbert Foules, who had some experience himself having played for Negro League teams between the Memphis Red Sox and Birmingham Black Barons.

The St. Louis scouts who went down to Greenville were Cardinals' Director of Scouting and Player Personnel Walter Shannon and William "Buddy" Lewis, an eleven-year Washington Nationals veteran with a lifetime .297 batting average; both were white. In spite of a Cardinals team in the throes of racial change, there were remnants of St. Louis old-style racism in both of them, especially in the case of Buddy Lewis, who was a native Tennessean. Importantly, at the time, *"The Cardinals became committed to the idea of racial acceptance,"* with the emerging personalities of players Bill White, Curt Flood, and future Hall of Famer Bob Gibson, mirroring the club's transfiguration and new commitments, according to Howard Bryant in his narrative *Shut Out*.[299] Apparently, the message didn't catch up with the two scouts who came down to see young Scott; they displayed a certain level of intolerance that immediately got Crowe's attention, recognizing that they were unwilling to listen to him. He was good enough for the minor leagues, declared the scouts of Scotty, but felt he wasn't pulling the ball enough to make it in the Bigs in spite of powering several balls of major league home run caliber. Crowe was clearly frustrated with the two scouts who demonstrated an attitude of indifference to anything he had to say about Scott and their sullying of him that quickly led to their repudiation of him on that day. Crowe knew George was a good bet at making the big leagues and felt the two scouts were being disingenuous by not taking his advice. As it occurred, Scott's dismissal was a leading reason why George Crowe left his role with the Cardinals a short time after the tryout, convinced the Cardinals were still harboring racial bias.

As Scotty put it, *"I would have been a member of the St. Louis Cardinals club if George Crowe had any authority to sign me, and he rightfully should have. That's where I was going, no question about it, until he got derailed by the club because of those scouts who came down to Greenville to see me. George Crowe was very upset and told me so, feeling it was racial and he should have had a hand in this decision. I thought so, too. He apparently*

---

[299] Howard Bryant, "Shut out," p. 72

didn't have any control over the money part of it and couldn't deal with prospects like me because of his color."[300]

George Scott signing Red Sox contract with Coleman High coach Elbert Foules & Red Sox scout Ed Scott (author's collection)

---

[300] George Scott interview: October 14, 2006

There were a number of other teams looking at George Scott, among them the Los Angeles Angels, Pittsburgh Pirates, Chicago White Sox, Houston's Astros, and the Boston Red Sox, who ultimately signed the young slugger. But no discussion of the Red Sox, their insular city, or of their benefactor Tom Yawkey, is worthy of discussion, nor can it be entirely appreciated without first drawing attention to its history, beginning with the mockery of a bogus tryout of three black ballplayers at Fenway Park in the spring of 1945, seventeen years before the arrival of Scott, and how this assumes relevance to the George Scott story, and of other contemporary black players who were just like him.

Thomas Yawkey was a complicated man by most accounts. In 1933, at the prior urging of a friend, future Hall of Famer Ty Cobb – whom Yawkey idolized - then of the Detroit Tigers, Yawkey, having just turned 30, bought a woeful Boston Red Sox team in the spring of 1933 from Bob Quinn who had owned the team between 1923 and 1932. Quinn was suffering from the ravages of the Great Depression and was struggling financially. *"I haven't got the money to continue,"* he said and handed the club and Fenway Park over to young Yawkey – for 1.2 million dollars, a bargain nevertheless - who was awash in a fortune and living the life of privilege and wealth bequeathed to him by the Yawkey family.[301] *"He's a strange man,"* said

---

[301] Glenn Stout & Richard Johnson, "Red Sox Century: A Definitive History of Baseball's Most Storied Franchise," Houghton Mifflin Co., Boston-New York, 2000, p. 175

his adopted daughter Julia to a reporter in the early 1970s when asked about her father, opening a pathway for more questions that were never allowed to be asked of her, let alone were they ever answered.[302] Though benevolent in so many ways, especially to his players, and he was a charitable man, his private side was quite another story. He suffered from intemperance for many years, experiencing bouts of rage when he drank to excess. This unseemly behavior that was cloaked in alcoholism was one of the underlying hallmarks of his style and a long-standing criterion for his preferred choices made in the hiring of his minions – drinking buddies - designated to run the ballclub; among these were Eddie Collins, Joe Cronin and Mike "Pinky" Higgins. According to a South Carolina wildlife biologist, Phil Wilkinson, who worked for Yawkey, *"He [Yawkey] told me that when he drank, his personality changed...to be unpleasantly aggressive."*[303] *"He had many acquaintances, but few friends...a stranger to his adoptive daughter...and [he] blocked the integration of baseball,"* writes authors Glenn Stout and Richard Johnson in their epic account of the Red Sox in their book *Red Sox Century*.[304] The seat of Red Sox racism actually began with Eddie Collins, an original member of the Baseball Hall of Fame, and, in effect, also Thomas Yawkey, who, with Collins, formed a

---

[302] IBID, p. 234

[303] Bill Nowlin, "Tom Yawkey: Patriarch of the Boston Red Sox," University of Nebraska Press, Lincoln, Nebraska, 2018, p. 31

[304] Glenn Stout & Richard Johnson, "Red Sox Century," Houghton Mifflin, Boston, 2000, p. 176

duo at the outset: one an active racist and the other an embodiment of fraternal complicity supporting segregation.

A fellow by the name of Isadore Muchnick, who was a Jewish politician, member of the Boston City Council from 1942 to 1947 and the Boston School Committee from 1948 to 1953, became a friend of baseball's Jackie Robinson two years before Robinson's ultimate arrival with the Brooklyn Dodgers and the historic breaking of baseball's color barrier. Robinson was aware of Red Sox owner Tom Yawkey's intransigence in integrating baseball and the so-called gentlemen's agreement, or pact that he had entered into with his counterparts a few years before. Robinson, who had little patience and a fiery personality, was not just upset with Yawkey and his Red Sox ballclub, but in a much bigger way, with *"the converging myths of the Red Sox and the city,"* according to Howard Bryant in his narrative, *Shut Out.*[305]

The standard refrain of major league owners for why they didn't have black ballplayers on their rosters was the lame excuse they couldn't find quality black players, to begin with, and this was a regular alibi by the Red Sox as the reason for not having them; but as times changed and World War II was about to end new attitudes were brewing, especially among blacks who had served in the war. They took the position that if they were capable of fighting for their country and laying down their lives for it, then by all

---

[305] Howard Bryant, "Shut Out," p.6

means, why weren't they entitled to equal treatment at home? It was a once and for all effort to divest the infamous *Jim Crow* manifestation so ingrained in the national ideology. Black sportswriters like Wendell Smith of the *Pittsburgh Courier* and Sam Lacy of the *Chicago Defender* took the lead in their reporting of black sports achievements by infiltrating white newspapers and publications with their positive messages to gain whites' attention. A local Boston-area black reporter, Maybray "Doc" Kountze, did the same writing more locally for the *Boston Chronicle* and *Boston Guardian*; he was more pointed, however, taking umbrage with major league baseball in 1935 by confronting the secretaries of the Boston Braves and Red Sox challenging them with questions on the color barrier and whether they were aware of the breadth of black talent in the country that was ready for the major leagues. Both were sympathetic to the cause, but Secretary Phil Troy of the Red Sox was skeptical. He was aware, in spite of Yawkey's only two years of ownership, that by his manner, he *"would not be the one to move forward on such a prickly issue,"* wrote Howard Bryant.[306]

Muchnick took up the scepter in 1945 and exerted pressure on the Red Sox, especially bearing down on the elusive Eddie Collins, a smart and shifty kind of fellow, a graduate of the Ivy League's Columbia University, future major league baseball Hall of Famer, Tom Yawkey's confidant and proxy "owner," and Red Sox operations manager, who had a long-standing

---

[306] IBID, p. 26

reputation for intolerance of blacks. Certainly, that was glaring in 1945 when Collins did everything but stand on his head to avoid a tryout with three black Negro Leaguers and by his conduct at Fenway on the day of the tryout. As Bryant points out, *"Eddie Collins was a known insider and a bigot. He played his entire career in a segregated game and saw no reason to change."*[307]

Muchnick persisted in outflanking Collins, forcing him into a tryout with Jackie Robinson of the Negro League's Kansas City Monarchs, Sam Jethroe of the Cleveland Buckeyes, and Marvin Williams of the Philadelphia Stars, by threatening the Red Sox that he would not approve a permit for them to play on Sundays unless Collins agreed to a tryout with the black players. It would have been an extraordinary financial consequence to the Red Sox, and Collins had to concede, but it was purely an accommodation, for he had no plans to change; instead, his intent was to charm, as he often did in his typical polished manner to disarm those he disagreed with, but he had no plans to relent to Muchnick or any others, of a mindset of bringing blacks into baseball, let alone into major league baseball. Of course, Muchnick was accused of insincerity and playing politics to gain black votes in his district as his primary reason, but regardless of the political flack, it was understood that Isadore Muchnick was a progressive thinker and genuinely supportive of the black ballplayer;

---

[307] IBID, p. 28

"Activism was a trademark for Izzy Muchnick from almost the very beginning" involving not only his wife, Ann but also his children in public service.[308]

April 16, 1945, was nothing but a sham, insisted Jackie Robinson, a "farce," declared Sam Jethroe, a lack of sincerity, according to Marvin Williams. There has been a myriad of stories about the infamous Red Sox tryout of 1945 and what had been shouted from deep in the upper recesses of the grandstand of Fenway Park, during which it was alleged to have been said, "get those niggers off the field!" Some who were allegedly there claimed they never heard anything. So, we are left to speculate about not only who was behind these words but whether they were even said. According to *Boston Globe* reporter Clif Keane, who was there, Keane said he was sure it was Yawkey who launched the verbal volley, but in later years he wasn't as certain. But, at the outset, being personally familiar with Yawkey, he believed strongly those words came from him. Some others believe it was Eddie Collins who displayed a distaste for even holding the tryout, having been cornered into begrudgingly agreeing to it, and who famously disappeared soon after he had met the threesome before the start of the tryout; it was Collins who had the full authority to sign prospects, and it was he who dismissed himself from the on-field proceedings. *"Interestingly enough,"* wrote Stout and Johnson, in their epic 2000-year treatise, *Red Sox Century*, *"doorways in the upper grandstand lead directly*

---

[308] IBID, p. 33

to the club's offices," raising an inference that it could have been Eddie Collins who made the offensive remark; he had slipped away from the playing field before the tryout had begun since Cronin and others were still around the playing field when the remark was made. Or, as some suggested that day, it just as likely could have been Yawkey.[309]

According to Sam Jethroe in a 1996 interview held in his hometown of Erie, Pennsylvania, one of the three black players who participated in the tryout at Fenway, acknowledged that he heard someone yelling what sounded to be ranting, repugnant in its tone, from the inner stands, but he did not make out what was said, nor did he seem to care or place any importance in it. *"Through the years I never discussed what I heard on that day, except to friends, but I do remember hearing someone back in the stands, yes. I didn't hear what was said. Jackie [Robinson] seemed upset, but I honestly didn't pay much attention. Jackie could be upset at just about anything. It was the kind of thing that we expected in those days."*[310] In 1950, five years from the "tryout," Jethroe signed with the Boston Braves

---

[309] Glenn Stout and Richard Johnson, "Red Sox Century," p. 242
[310] Sam Jethroe interview: September 10, 1996 – what Jethroe expressed to sportswriter Steve Fainaru in 1991 as reflected in his August Boston Globe article of that year, "Blacks at Fenway," when he said "If that was said, I didn't hear it," was of a different slant than what he said to the author of this publication five years later; the difference, in the author's version, was that he heard a strident outcry from the stands at the end of that day, which sounded incensed, but he was not aware of the actual words expressed, only that it sounded angry. So, except for the credulity we place in sports writer Clif Keane, who did claim he heard the actual words that were expressed that day, it will always constitute a cryptic aspect of Red Sox history.
https://www.newspapers.com/image/439435663/

and was the National League Rookie of the Year in his first season. According to witnesses, Red Sox manager Joe Cronin had his back to the field throughout the tryout, so there were no Red Sox personnel who had hiring authority and were paying attention to the activities on the field that day, affirming the bogus intent.

Sam Jethroe signing autographs with author in Erie, PA, 1996" (author's collection)

Sam Jethroe in Cleveland Buckeyes uniform, circa 1943-1948 (author's collection)

According to Howard Bryant, alluding to the significance of the notorious event held that day in April 1945, he said: *"In fact, instead of becoming a flashpoint for change, the Robinson tryout would for years be known as one of the least known pieces of both Red Sox history and the Robinson legend."* Of further significance, *"the follow-up reporting was largely nonexistent,"* said Bryant. A footnote by Bryant points out that Clif Keane, who alleges he heard Tom Yawkey's voice, likely did do a writeup on the matter, but either it got lost in the *"quirks of a newsroom"* or, merely the *"Globe's potential unwillingness"* to put this into print. Considering the fierce reluctance of the *Globe* in previous years, or even thereafter, to denigrate Tom Yawkey and his operatives, there are strong implications that it was the latter.[311]

Ex-Negro Leaguer Willie Grace, a Mississippian like Jethroe, who played for the Negro American League champion Cleveland Buckeyes of 1945 and 1947, along with teammate Sam Jethroe, who also retired along with Jethroe in the same town, Erie, Pennsylvania, said: *"Sam [Jethroe] said it was a complete farce...he remembers someone yelling from the stands, sounded angry but couldn't make out what was said...they never wanted to sign any of them!"* Grace, who is a member of the Ohio Baseball Hall of Fame and later became an articulate occasional contributor for Erie's local sports television and talk shows and regional shows, has memories of his 1945 encounters with one Jackie Robinson, who was playing for the

---

[311] Howard Bryant, "Shut Out," p. 41

Kansas City Monarchs. *"He was a fiery kind of guy,"* said Grace, *"who could be needled and often would erupt in anger."* Grace recounted one incident during that year when several of the players, knowing they would provoke Robinson, hid his bats on him. *"Sure enough, he exploded, racing around the field raising his finger at players; he was pretty angry,"* exclaimed Grace in laughter, fondly remembering that day. They could arouse him easily, said Grace, and he was prone to take the bait.[312] This unbridled behavior pattern boiled up on many occasions during Robinson's tenure in the major leagues, including his stints at public affairs, sports and NAACP dinners or with reporters, however the subject of race may have come up. At a Lynn, Massachusetts NAACP dinner in 1967, Robinson said, *"Baseball is fine, but the people who run it are not…a Negro star does not get anywhere near the side benefits, the endorsements, that a white star does,"* mentioning such superstars as Larry Doby who had been locked out of baseball while *"trying to get a job for years,"* since his retirement, said Robinson. *"Baseball is still in the 19th century, and I couldn't care less about it,"* said Robinson.[313]

But one baseball man stood out in Robinson's mind as the most prejudiced in the game, and that was Thomas Yawkey. Asked by a reporter during a close pennant race in '67, in which the Red Sox were a contender,

---

[312] Willie Grace interview: September 11, 1996
[313] Ray Fitzgerald, "Baseball Still White Man's Game – Robinson," The Boston Globe, Boston, Massachusetts, may 17, 1967, p. 1 & 65
https://www.newspapers.com/image/434057963/?terms=Boston%20globe

who Robinson liked to win the pennant scramble, he made a brusque remark: *"Anyway, because of Boston owner Tom Yawkey, I'd like to see them lose,"* he said *"because he is probably one of the most bigoted guys in organized baseball,"* said Robinson forcefully in a moment of personal enmity. [314]

Willie Grace, Sam Jethroe's teammate on Cleveland Buckeyes Negro League team (author's collection)

---

[314] United press international, "Jackie Robinson Likes Twins, Dislikes Yawkey," The Boston Globe, Boston, Massachusetts, September 21, 1967, p. 1 & 52
https://www.newspapers.com/image/433889638/

No one of the Red Sox followed up with either of the players despite their good showing. Black reporter Doc Kountze, who held such high hopes for reconciliation of the races by that tryout, expressing the view that all in Boston were *"keenly anticipating the end of the Color Ban at Fenway Park and Braves Field,"* felt shattered at the outcome and disappointed with Tom Yawkey, asserting that he *"failed his big chance."* He concluded his remarks in exasperation: *"I could see this happening in Mississippi, but not in Massachusetts."* Doc Kountze was immersed in disillusionment; he was clearly a man who was ahead of his time.[315]

In spite of the discord that came from that infamous tryout, the Red Sox persisted in their racist stance by rejecting a megastar in the making, Willie Mays, who would become a future Hall of Famer and one of the all-time great baseball luminaries, who was rejected by Red Sox second-year general manager Joe Cronin. *"Joe Cronin was no friend of integration...[he] clearly possessed no great desire to hire blacks,"* said Howard Bryant, although through the years, he managed his politics quite well by leaving impressions that he was, at the least, a "conflicted" soul he was prone to announce time and again responding to the integration question, which he often dangled for the media.[316] A combination of Red Sox scouts, Larry Woodall, a known racist himself and whom it is believed purposely never saw Mays play, and George Digby, who was more than

---

[315] Howard Bryant, "Shut Out," quoting Maybray "Doc" Kountze, p. 33
[316] Howard Bryant, "Shut Out," p. 45

enthusiastic by what he saw in Mays and shared his enthusiasm with Cronin. Cronin, however, turned down Digby and, without as much as an all-knowing wink, accepted Woodall's ambivalence straightaway, along the lines of his own complacence – and Collins' and Yawkey's - of not altering their resistive position on blacks. Woodall, who had little to no tolerance of blacks, complained of game rain-outs explaining his busy scouting schedule and his reason why he had no time for Willie Mays in this fallacious fashion: *"I'm not going to waste my time waiting on a bunch of niggers," said Woodall.*[317]

In 1948, Bob Scranton, a traveling secretary for the white Birmingham Barons of the Double-A Southern Association, out of Birmingham, Alabama - who years later became part owner of the Barons - did some "bird-dogging" as an assistant scout for Red Sox scouts George Digby and Milt Bolling in the Deep South and the Southern league circuit. The Barons were a Boston affiliate between 1948 and 1952. In 1948 young Willie Mays, age 17, during his early years nicknamed the "Say Hey Kid," joined the Birmingham Black Barons of the Negro League; both the white and black Barons teams shared Birmingham's Rickwood Field, the oldest professional baseball park in the United States. The white Barons team and the Black Barons had a working relationship, which was that the black team would give the nod to the white team and the parent Red Sox if they had anybody worth considering for the major leagues. The black team's playing manager,

---

[317] IBID, p. 1

Piper Davis, in accordance with that agreement, notified the Red Sox about Mays in 1949. As it was, instead of Willie Mays, the Red Sox signed Piper Davis, their first black player, to a Scranton Eastern League contract at the end of the 1949 season. Interestingly, a 1949 *Boston Globe* article made a point that although the Scranton club was a Red Sox affiliate, it was *"allowed to act independently when it comes to signing or letting go players,"* as if to emphasize that the parent club did not have a hand in it.[318]

Pure deceitfulness was the way in which this went down, led by Joe Cronin, as the Red Sox had no plans to keep Piper Davis on the payroll. In spite of Davis being the top hitter and fielder on the 1950 team, he played only 15 games with Scranton and was suddenly released by the team for so-called "economic" reasons. Money was never an issue for Tom Yawkey, who was well known around major league baseball and by Piper Davis, so he was left to interpretation and assumptions. The reason for his dismissal was racist dogma. Davis was bitter as he knew better. *"Tom Yawkey had as much money as anyone on the East Coast…I wonder why it all had to happen, why we had to have so much hate,"* he ranted, realizing he could have expected a good future with baseball except for the likes of Tom Yawkey or his counterparts, who were still recalcitrant about change.[319] In later years, Mays would bitterly explain how he felt about the Red Sox,

---

[318] Unattributed, "Piper Davis First Negro Star to Join Sox Farm Team," The Boston Globe, 15 Aug 1949, p. 11
https://www.newspapers.com/image/433619617/?terms=piper%20davis%20negro&match=1

[319] Howard Bryant, "Shut Out," p. 47

along similar lines to the feelings expressed by Jackie Robinson: *"To be honest, I really thought I was going to Boston...they had a guy come down to look at me. They had a good team with [Mel] Parnell and [Vern] Stephens and, of course, Ted [Williams]. But for that, Yawkey. Everyone knew he was a racist. He didn't want me [for that reason]."*[320]

Bob Scranton was positioned square in the center of the social-cultural milieu that was manifest in the infamous Mays – Red Sox segregation affair, which assumed a life of its own in later years. *"We're not interested in him, and I'd rather not discuss it,"* announced scout Larry Woodall, who was assigned the duty to scout Mays, according to Scranton, who heard about the Red Sox sentiments on Mays from Birmingham Barons' General Manager Eddie Glennon after a two-hour closed-door meeting with Woodall, that included Black Barons manager Piper Davis. As Scranton put it, *"Glennon was disgusted, just rolled his eyes,"* and later learned it was all about race. *"They [Red Sox and Birmingham Barons] had a deal going in those days, under the cover and everything else...when the high roller [Woodall] from Boston came down and turned the deal down, it teed off Eddie Glennon. I knew George [Digby, Red Sox scout who was high on Willie Mays] was mad."* Glennon *"knew that it was the big guy in Boston, Joe Cronin, who turned the deal down...we knew what it was about."* It was *"slippery Joe [Cronin],"* said Scranton who complained that Cronin talked a good game for the press and public, but when not in the public eye he was

---

[320] IBID, p. 46

"another man," said Scranton based on his dealings with Birmingham's General Manager Eddie Glennon. It was another of Cronin's characteristics built on duplicity.[321]

It was inglorious to many how the Red Sox could be so remiss in not picking up so much black talent after the war when other teams were making such productive headway. Bryant explains it was simple: they stuck to their commitment stealthily and with such efficiency *"that integration forces could never pin down any member of the team's hierarchy to explain how so many gifted players – starting with Robinson and Mays – were slipping through the net of what was the richest team in baseball."*[322] It would be a trademark that would define Yawkey in later years by remaining in the shadow of his racist practices and ceding the tough questions and storylines to his loyal lieutenants, who performed their roles with precision. One historian indulges in the thought and makes an allegation that Yawkey *"was able to continue his racist practices unopposed because he successfully diverted public attention to his involvement in community organizations,"* asserts Jordan Blumberg Long in his article *Racism and America's National Pastime: The Sad History of the Boston Red Sox.*[323]

---

[321] Bob Scranton interview: February 12, 2007
[322] Howard Bryant, "Shut Out," p. 2
[323] Jordan Blumberg Long, "Racism and America's National Pastime: The Sad History of the Boston Red Sox," Wordpress.com, August 15, 2002
https://jordanblumberglong.wordpress.com/2012/08/15/racism-and-americas-national-pastime-the-sad-history-of-the-boston-red-sox/

It turned out that in the six years between 1945 and 1951, three black ballplayers – Jackie Robinson, Sam Jethroe, and Willie Mays – each were rejected as prospects by the Red Sox as not meeting the team's standards, or, as Yawkey, Cronin and Collins had often declared, as a generalization, *"We wanted a ballplayer,"* went on to win *Rookie of the Year* awards, and, between them, numerous other baseball achievements and awards during their long and distinguished major league careers; in the case of Willie Mays, 23 years, Jackie Robinson, 11 years, and Sam Jethroe 12. Two of them, Willie Mays and Jackie Robinson, became Hall of Famers.[324]

Of the litany of messaging and pronouncements over the years reminiscing what actually took place, or what was even said, as alleged – or not said – on that fateful day in the spring of 1945 that, by some, was called a "tryout," has ranged from a bold denial of any racial transgressions on the part of the Red Sox, pointing to Will McDonough and his shameless attempt at a defense of the Red Sox by mitigating them as a racist organization, twisting the facts of that day - namely that neither Yawkey or Joe Cronin were even at the event, he asserted - to a key witness, reporter Clif Keane, who stuck to his story putting a voice – Tom Yawkey's - to the matter. Keane was backed up by another well-regarded Boston reporter,

---

[324] Glenn Stout, "Tryout and Fallout: Race, Jackie Robinson and the Red Sox," originally published in the Massachusetts Historical Review, volume 6, 2004, 2020 https://glennstout.com/tryout-and-fallout-race-jackie-robinson-and-the-red-sox/;
also, Glenn Stout, contributing author, "Tom Yawkey, Race, and the Smoking Gun II," Boston Baseball, Sep 10, 2017
http://verbplow.blogspot.com/search?q=yawkey+smoking+gun

Clark Booth, who stood by Keane's story, saying that Yawkey was the transgressor. Booth reasoned in his support of Keane's testimony, which was predicated on his interview with author Howard Bryant, *"Without Clif Keane, no one is ever talking about that tryout with Jackie Robinson. He put a voice to it...That sentence 'get those niggers off the field' is the scarlet 'A' on the Red Sox brow...Clif brought that out."*[325]

What seems not to have been addressed that would lend further credibility to the story is how personally close Clif Keane actually was to Tom Yawkey. Despite a business relationship demanding certain required levels of ethical behavior and decorum, they were amiable; they had established a rapport. Keane knew the personal side to Yawkey – a shy, reclusive man and an alcoholic - better than most and was closer to the Red Sox magnate – *"the last of the breed of wealthy owners known in the press of the day as 'sportsmen'"* – than others.[326] Distinguished author David Halberstam captured this unusual relationship in his book, *Summer of '49*, when in 1975 Keane persuaded a hesitant Yawkey to meet with him and Cincinnati's manager Sparky Anderson after game one of the Red Sox-Reds World Series. After the meeting, Yawkey was thrilled, exuding happiness like a youngster. *"Clif,"* he kept saying when he left, *"that was grand – just grand. What fun! What a grand fellow!"* exclaimed Yawkey, overjoyed with the personal exchange he had with Anderson facilitated by Keane.

---

[325] Howard Bryant, "Shut Out," quoting reporter Clark Booth, p. 113
[326] David Halberstam, "Summer of '49," W. Morrow: New York, 1989, p. 134 https://archive.org/details/summerof490000halb_m8t6

Keane was close enough to Yawkey that he felt obliged to address the situation further with him but left it to a soliloquy: *"'Come on, Tom,' Keane wanted to say... 'Why can't you just be a real person, go out and talk to the baseball people all around you, be human, be natural? They'd all like you, you know.'"* It seems that Clif Keane was protective of a sensitive and shy Tom Yawkey, shielding him where it made sense from his foibles and demons, but he wasn't about to be a cover for him either. [327] Looking back at the 1945 tryout, if there was anyone who should have been familiar with the voice of Thomas Yawkey, it would have been his friend Clif Keane; this is persuasive.

Of the three baseball operations figures on the team, Yawkey's "deputies," namely Higgins, Collins and Cronin, each of them segregationists in their own right, the wiliest of them and the most inscrutable was Cronin. *"It was under Joe Cronin that the Red Sox were exposed as a racist franchise,"* wrote Howard Bryant.[328] *"He felt no moral fire to alter the social fabric, but over the years would be politically savvy enough to sound conflicted in the press over the integration issue,"* said Bryant.[329] Two black sports writers, Sam Lacy and Wendell Smith, were exerting pressure on Yawkey's club after hearing feedback that this was a racist team. Both had their fill of Eddie Collins, who ducked and dodged

---

[327] IBID, p. 135   https://archive.org/details/summerof490000halb_m8t6
[328] Howard Bryant, "Shut Out," p. 43
[329] IBID, p. 45

them on the subject of race and then his successor, Joe Cronin, made his appearance into the Red Sox fold. *"The result,"* said Bryant - *"active denial of discrimination while the Red Sox remained a segregated club - was the same."*[330] Cronin was calculating, manipulative, and a man of manifestly duplicitous character, especially as it involved racial matters. Ted Williams, who frequently clashed with Cronin during his formative baseball years, described Cronin in his autobiography as *"a big, good-looking Irishman who could just swoon you. He could suave those writers to death."*[331]

The following account of Red Sox farm director Billy Evans' disputatious firing, entwined with the likes of a duplicitous Joe Cronin and his boss, Tom Yawkey, is based on author Peter Golenbock's interpretation of the information from the notes of sports journalist Harold Kaese's private diary postings, which are based on his recollection of his off-the-record interviews with Billy Evans, the manuscript for which he dated October 7, 1945, over five years from the controversial 1940 firing. According to Golenbock, these personal notes of Kaese are part of the Boston Public Library's *Boston Tradition in Sports Archive* collection. It is noted that the date of September 6, 1941, cited as the date for Evans' firing, as noted in Golenbock's *Red Sox Nation* publication, appears to be inaccurate, and the

---

[330] IBID, p. 47
[331] Mark L. Armour, "Joe Cronin: A Life in Baseball," University of Nebraska, Lincoln, Nebraska, 2010, p. 125

likely firing was a year earlier according to newspaper accounts, actually occurring on October 8, 1940. Billy Evans died in 1956.[332]

In a discussion like this, the matter of Red Sox farm director Billy Evans stands out. An example of this double-dealing was on display in 1939-1940 when Joe Cronin was a player-manager for the Red Sox and who had set the tone for their racial instability in later years. Esteemed baseball man Billy Evans – "prestigious," said one baseball journalist - and a notable American League umpire of the early 20th century, beginning in the Deadball era, that got him elected to the Baseball Hall of Fame posthumously in 1973, signed with Tom Yawkey's Boston Red Sox in 1936 to form and run his farm system. Evans was a brilliant judge of baseball talent and a superb administrator and by 1940, after a mere four years in the job, had built a nexus of Red Sox minor league ballclubs that was eye-catching. As part of his acquisitions was the purchase of the Louisville club of the American Association, which had as its star player Harold "Pee Wee" Reese, who, himself, would rise to baseball's Hall of Fame. Evans saw the value of Reese, and since the Red Sox's current shortstop, Joe Cronin, was nearing the end of his playing career, or at least that's what he thought, Reese, Evans felt, was a perfect candidate to supplant him. *"What Evans hadn't anticipated,"* however, said baseball author Peter Golenbock, *"was Joe*

---

[332] Peter Golenbock, "Red Sox Nation: An Unexpurgated History of the Boston Red Sox," Triumph Books, Chicago, Illinois, 1992, p. 101-104; Sports journalist Harold Kaese, who died in 1975, was a distinguished sports writer, and, along with esteemed sports writer Red Smith, a posthumous recipient of the J. G. Taylor Spink award by the Baseball Writers' Association of America in 1976.

Cronin's fierce fight to protect his job and Tom Yawkey's fierce loyalty in protecting Cronin." In other words, it was Tom Yawkey's cronyism that he became famous for in all of its grandeur, along with Cronin's scheming ways to manipulate Yawkey, on display in Cronin's effort to protect himself at the sacrifice of the team.[333] *"But Cronin was still playing,"* said former Red Sox player Tony Lupien in his interview with Golenbock, *"so all of a sudden Cronin cut Billy's legs off by selling Pee Wee Reese to Brooklyn…Joe didn't want to play third base,"* said Lupien, for the sake of the team, which he could have done to accommodate Reese.[334] Lupien ran into Evans after this fiasco, and according to Lupien, he was livid. *"He said, 'How the hell can you run a farm system if you made a deal for an outstanding guy, and then you give him away?'"*[335]

According to Lupien, Evans had begged Cronin to come down and see Reese, who was performing sensationally; he appealed to Cronin to send down a scout in his place. Cronin responded with disinterest and pugnacity, *"I'm not interested in Reese,"* he said in a manner similar to how he rejected Willie Mays later on.[336] Cronin's actions in humiliating Evans and selling off a great prospect like Reese were indicative of things to come with him, particularly when dealing with black Red Sox hopefuls in the '40s and '50s

---

[333] Peter Golenbock, Red Sox Nation, p. 102
[334] Peter Golenbock, "Red Sox Nation," interview of Tony Lupien, p. 102
[335] IBID, p. 103
[336] IBID, p. 104

that ended with the repudiation of a handful of good black prospects, including future Hall of Famers Jackie Robinson and Willie Mays.

Billy Evans was very upset about the fiasco instigated by Cronin and the loss of Reese, and he was particularly angry with Joe Cronin for undermining him, using Yawkey as his pawn. The matter continued to simmer until the end of September, or possibly early October 1940, when, according to Evans, Yawkey phoned him at Evans' Cleveland home to inform him he was letting him go *"in the best interest of the Red Sox."*[337] Evans said Yawkey was clearly drunk when he called him, that the firing was based on Cronin's discussions with Yawkey, who goaded Yawkey into firing him, and it was all about the Pee Wee Reese matter, which Evans garnered from his discussion with Tom Yawkey. Yawkey, who felt tormented about the phone call, later said in a more sober moment that he could have been more pleasant with Evans. According to the record, Yawkey attempted to rescind the firing, but for the sake of preserving his own dignity, Evans dismissed the offer. Having failed at that, Yawkey insisted that Evans take his 1941 "boosted" salary – inclusive of a pay raise - of $17,500, which he had just announced to him a mere few days before the firing, which can only mean it was likely someone other than Yawkey who inspired the firing, and that was Cronin said Evans. The contradiction

---

[337] Peter Golenbock, Red Sox Nation, from the notes of sportswriter Harold Kaese dated October 7, 1945, from an off-the-record interview Kaese had with Billy Evans, p. 103

in this was glaring. *"All is not hotsy totsy in the Red Sox family,"* wrote *Evansville Press* sports writer Dick Anderson, *"so Cronin asked that Evans be fired."*[338] Speculation about the "resignation" was all the buzz coming as *"a real surprise,"* said Scranton's team owner Eddie Kirschner, who was with Evans on or about October 7 during the 1940 World Series in Detroit.[339] The entire episode was a public mystery, especially to the baseball world, which found it baffling, except to Billy Evans, Joe Cronin and Tom Yawkey. It was apparent that Yawkey himself was bewildered over the affair, thinking it a mess, but in the habit of his carte blanche acceptance of what his baseball operations lieutenants, like Cronin, had to say – and, who most likely was snookered by Cronin – gave in to Cronin during a weak moment and discharged Billy Evans, in a rare moment of uncharacteristic belligerence.

"Cronin," who was the prime scourge in all of this according to Evans in his explanation to Kaese, *"is too impetuous. He has too many likes and dislikes and makes up his mind too fast. Yawkey is also impulsive, and Collins is nervous and impulsive. The Red Sox need a stabilizer. Cronin*

---

[338] Dick Anderson, "Firing of Billy Evans May Make a Difference Here," The Evansville Press, Oct 17, 1940, p. 20 https://www.newspapers.com/image/763253403/
[339] Unattributed/multimedia, "Billy Evans Out Boston Sox Post," The Standard Sentinel, Hazleton PA, October 10, 1940, p. 12
https://www.newspapers.com/image/351542590/

lacks patience. Yawkey wants results in a hurry. He's too impressionable"[340]

Evans concluded his interview with Kaese with the words, *"I was successful, and they fired me."*[341]

Joe Cronin had a reputation of self-preservation, often at the expense of others, a legacy that seemed to follow him with the reporters after the Billy Evans intrigue. They didn't trust him, and that emerged once again when Boston sold slugger and future Hall of Famer Jimmie Foxx, popular with the fans and a sports writer's favorite, to the National League's Chicago Cubs in June 1942. The reporters laid the blame squarely on Cronin for Foxx's sudden departure, dismissing Cronin's reasons that Foxx had lost several steps, including his alleged fear of the pitched ball after a beaning he received by a Negro Leaguer several months before in a barnstorming game. Foxx was not appreciative of his dismissal or the way in which it was done and made some public noise speculating with reporters as to why his previous manager, Connie Mack of the Philadelphia Athletics, was a successful skipper while Cronin was not. *"One manager knew what he was doing; the other didn't,"* said Foxx, who didn't mix well with Cronin; he was a foremost Cronin critic of disparate personalities and, like others before him, a man Cronin felt he could do without. One reporter *"went so*

---

[340] Peter Golenbock, "Red Sox Nation," p. 104
[341] IBID

far as to say Cronin dropped Foxx because he feared Foxx was a threat to his job."[342] It had all the suspicions of the Pee Wee Reese matter that involved Billy Evans' firing. Although that charge was never proven, nor is there evidence it was even pursued, it was nonetheless a sentiment that was widespread among the reporters; they remained unconvinced that Cronin somehow was not behind the man's removal - which they viewed as nothing less than contemptible - from the team and the city judging by his reputation from previous dealings. However, several years later, the *Globe's* senior sports writer Harold Kaese brought this into focus: *"Many Red Sox players have left the Sox thinking that [Eddie] Collins was responsible for their going [Lefty Grove and Jimmie Foxx] when actually Cronin was the man who discarded them."*[343]

The Boston sports reporters' insights into the Red Sox skipper and their corresponding "trust" factor based on the doings of Joe Cronin rekindled again at the end of 1946 during an intensely controversial confab among reporters, emerging during the Sox' World Series engagement with St. Louis, involving blockbuster trade talk of two superstars, the Red Sox's Ted Williams and New York Yankees' Joe DiMaggio. The *Globe's* intrepid sports writer Harold Kaese, who had been involved in Cronin controversies before and with whom there was a frosty relationship, brought up the matter

---

[342] IBID, p. 143
[343] Harold Kaese, The Boston Globe, "35,000 Fans May Settle Controversy Between Cronin and Yawkey," Oct 9, 1946, p. 9
https://www.newspapers.com/image/434098533/?terms=%22Harold%20Kaese%22%20&match=1

that was billowing around Boston, titling it, with a touch of sarcasm, *"which way blows the wind today?"* when a rumor was surfacing about a possible trade. Ted Williams got wind of it and complained loudly that he had no desire to transition to New York. Meanwhile, neither did Tom Yawkey favor it, who coveted his star outfielder, though he was feeling pressure from Cronin, the kind that few but Joe Cronin was capable of wielding and known for, who had made up his mind that the Red Sox slugger had to go, calling Williams *"temperamentally unchangeable."* It seems that Cronin had attempted to impose a batting style on Williams, such as bunting and hitting to left field against "screwy defenses," but Williams would not abide him, which provoked Cronin, who was easily angered and was inclined to retaliate, trading him was the intended outcome. But it never happened with all parties, including Yawkey, objecting to the line of questioning but never eliciting a denial. However, it was pointed out that since there was never a denial made about the story, it likely had credibility. Both Cronin and Collins backpedaled in an effort to explain the "rumor" that it was a "National League Scheme" designed to unsettle the team.

It can be safely said that sports reporter Harold Kaese, a distinguished athlete himself highlighted by his squash skills and notable achievements in the sport, and who knew something about sports comportment, was not a fan of Joe Cronin and did not generally show him favor, especially in mid to later years; in fact, he was highly suspicious of him and of his moral character and spent time during the mid-1940s ferreting out stories about the shifty Joe Cronin highlighted by the Billy Evans – Pee Wee Reese story.

According to Howard Bryant, Cronin wielded enormous power in the Red Sox organization fueled by Tom Yawkey. He believed that both whites and blacks, the latter if not inferior, were better off and more likely to flourish in segregated societies. *"These feelings were revealed both by Cronin himself and, more importantly, by the complexion of the players he chose to play for the Red Sox,"* wrote Bryant. *"Still, he would claim otherwise,"* exhibiting a clear double standard.[344]

"The wind blows from the front office, and it says that Joe Cronin and Tom Yawkey disagree on the trading of Ted Williams...they have differed over other players, but usually Cronin has had his way," wrote Harold Kaese[345] What Cronin did not accomplish in his frequent dealings with Yawkey was his attempt during the war years to bring back Ben Chapman, who played for them in 1937-38, as a player and coach. *"Yawkey would not stand for it,"* according to Kaese. Chapman had a reputation for racist bigotry that was magnified while a manager for the Philadelphia Phillies, taunting Jackie Robinson after he joined the Brooklyn Dodgers.[346]

---

[344] Howard Bryant, "Shut Out," p. 8
[345] Harold Kaese, "35,000 Fans May Settle Controversy Between Cronin and Yawkey," The Boston Daily Globe," October 9, 1946, p. 9
[346] IBID; ironically, Tom Yawkey, who was attempting to build depth to his team in 1936 acquiring slugger Jimmie Foxx in the mix of new players, tried to acquire Ben Chapman - and did so in 1937 - who was dealing with antisemitic accusations made against him by a New York fan that reached a crescendo, yet he stood firmly against acquisition of the rabble-rouser against Joe Cronin's wishes, who wanted the controversial player back on the team, a few short years later in the early '40s.

Cronin had his likes and dislikes, conspicuously highlighted by Kaese based on his interview with Red Sox farm director Billy Evans, and these rigid traits were at the forefront of his personality. A simple characterization of Cronin was raised by *Globe* reporter Roger Birtwell just prior to the opening day of the 1946 Red Sox-Cardinals World Series when reporters inquired about pitching selections for the Series. The managers, Eddie Dyer of St. Louis and Joe Cronin of Boston, couldn't have been more different. Dyer was forthright; Cronin was not. *"Dyer was open, Cronin withdrawn and cagey,"* basically unapproachable, and at a level of mistrust intimated Birtwell.[347]

---

[347] Roger Birtwell, Boston Globe, "Cards to Start Pollett; Cronin to use 'One of Three Pitchers.'" The Boston Globe, Oct 5, 1946, p. 1
https://www.newspapers.com/image/434082585/

Chapter 7
The Great Wall of Boston

McDonough never contacted me again after the incident, never acknowledged receipt of the documents in regard to the tryout, and never wrote about the issue again. After the story appeared, I wrote Globe sports editor Don Skwar and asked that a correction appear in the paper. Skwar contacted me a few days later and, despite the fact that McDonough's story contained errors verified by the newspaper's own reporting, told me simply, "We don't think that is necessary." The author then responded by writing a "letter to the editor" to the Globe. The Globe edited the letter without my input, made it appear to defend Tom Yawkey, and excised all references to McDonough's factual errors.

Glenn Stout[348]

When the Red Sox purchased the Minneapolis Millers, a Double-A minor league team, in 1957, the story was that they picked up black ballplayer Pumpsie Green, by default, as part of the business deal, claimed the NAACP after Green's sensational and very controversial 1959 spring training demotion, about which the NAACP strenuously objected. In fact, the official MLB record was that the Red Sox signed Pumpsie in February

---

[348] Glenn Stout, "Tryout & Fallout: Race, Jackie Robinson and the Red Sox," originally published in the Massachusetts Historical Review, vol. 6, 2004; footnote Lxxxiv, Will McDonough
https://glennstout.com/tryout-and-fallout-race-jackie-robinson-and-the-red-sox/

1956 from Stockton of the Class-C California League, after which he was assigned to Boston's Albany Senators of the Eastern League. Dick O'Connell, a business executive for the Red Sox at the time – one of the few on the team to take these matters seriously, beyond backroom bravado and a generally laissez-faire attitude, and do the necessary homework to defend the team - came to the team's rescue disputing the NAACP's argument proving Green was indeed purchased directly by the Red Sox in 1956 from Oakland, a minor league club, which, for the moment, defused the clatter and acrimony instigated by the black player's demotion.

Previous to that, in 1953, the Red Sox signed a black six-foot-three specimen of a ballplayer, very athletic and a catcher, who was Earl Wilson, out of Louisiana, whom the Red Sox converted to a pitcher. He had all the tools: he was big, strong, and exhibited good hurler mechanics – except for occasional wildness he would learn to harness – with a major league fastball. He would have been the Sox's first black roster player, but he was drafted by the Marines and missed the '57-'58 seasons. Instead, he arrived on the Red Sox major league club in the spring of 1959, one week after the arrival of the Red Sox's first official black major leaguer, Pumpsie Green, who, along with Wilson, was from the Double-A Minneapolis minor league club.

Prominent black reporter Sam Lacy of the Baltimore *Afro-American*, who pushed hard for baseball integration and was frequently disappointed at the lack of progress, had special words for Tom Yawkey, whom he didn't trust, right around this time when Green and Earl Wilson were seeking promotion to the big club. This was after Joe Cronin, the Sox' general manager, who was delegated considerable responsibility and control of the team by Yawkey, announced affirmatively that the team was anything but racist. *"The Red Sox care nothing about a man's color,"* he said. *"They only want good ballplayers,"* and he would harp on this numerous times, especially as the critics and their attacks grew exponentially, and he was feeling the heat from the NAACP, Massachusetts Commission Against Discrimination, and other similar activist groups.[349] Lacy made clear the extent of his mistrust: "The Red Sox will never have a colored player as long as Tom Yawkey is owner," ranted Lacy if anyone in Boston was willing to listen.[350] Of course, this was a hyperbolized opinion as both Wilson and Green were about to step onto the major league club's turf, having been called up. What Lacy did have right, however, was that the Red Sox would never hire a black player while Pinky Higgins, Eddie Collins or Joe Cronin was running the club, and this manifestation would prove to have consequences for both Wilson and Green while they were earnestly trying to make the team.

The timing was not favorable for the two young black ballplayers. Tom Yawkey was going through a burn-out after twenty-one seasons of mediocre baseball, attributable, some say, to himself, with big spending and showing

---

[349] Howard Bryant, "Shut Out: A Story of Race and Baseball in Boston," Routledge, New York, NY, 2002, p. 48
[350] IBID

nothing for it. He spent much of his time on his South Carolina plantation, showing indifference to his Red Sox club. In the breach, Yawkey's general manager Joe Cronin stepped up in October 1954 and hired Yawkey's drinking and hunting buddy, Mike "Pinky" Higgins, who had been managing the Triple-A Louisville club, and the man's racist incarnations were soon on fertile footing. *"What Yawkey did best was drink...so he brought in his boys, and while the club was losing, Yawkey tuned out. He let them – one particular man named Pinky Higgins – run the show,"* wrote Howard Bryant. And, backed with the loyalty of Yawkey, run it he did nearly into the ground.[351]

Higgins was in a slow burn himself at the outset and immediately took a stand soon after he assumed managerial control of the team by announcing to reporter Al Hirshberg, *"There will never be any niggers on this team as long as I have anything to say about it."*[352] By then, the Red Sox had both Wilson and Green in their system. For the next four-and-one-half years, until July 1959, Higgins ran the club but was replaced on July 3, 1959, by Billy Jurges of the Washington Senators, which came as a big surprise to Tom Yawkey, who was distressed at the move made by his general manager Bucky Harris, another Washington Senators alumnus. In fact, *"Yawkey personally phoned Mike Higgins in Baltimore yesterday [July 3],"* wrote

---

[351] IBID, p. 3
[352] IBID

Boston Globe reporter Jerry Nason, and told him, *"Fly to Boston and see me. We want you [back] in our organization."*[353]

Clearly, Yawkey had an affinity for Higgins. Jurges, who was out of his element as manager, had lost control of the team rather quickly and was openly critical of ownership, leading to his dismissal in June 1960. Yawkey immediately got behind old friend Pinky Higgins and reappointed him as field manager. *Boston Globe* reporter Harold Kaese wrote a scathing satirical piece on the rehiring, *"Sox Save Money by Naming Higgins; Only Fans Unhappy,"* in which he tore into an evidently complacent Red Sox team that seemed content with losing. *"Now the Red Sox can finish in the second division, and everyone can be comfortable – except possibly a few unreasonable fans who take winning too seriously… Rehiring Higgins raises a question: do the Red Sox know what they are doing? They fired a fellow because he was not getting good results, even with Jackie Jensen and Sammy White. Now they rehire him [Higgins], implying that (1) he has acquired new skills, or that (2) they were wrong the first time."*[354]

In September 1960, Yawkey inscrutably made a startling move elevating his drinking buddy and racist, Mike Higgins, to a new prestigious and powerful position on the Red Sox: he was assigned a dual role, with a

---

[353] Jerry Nason, "Yawkey Gets New Manager: Writer Breaks News to Owner," The Boston Daily Globe, July 29, 1959, p. 13
https://www.newspapers.com/image/433692619/

[354] Harold Kaese, "Sox Save Money by Naming Higgins; Only Fans Unhappy," The Boston Globe, June 13, 1960, p. 23-24
https://www.newspapers.com/image/433307479/?terms=Boston%20Globe

three-year contract as field manager and appointment to a front office position of general manager replacing Bucky Harris, his nemesis, who was fired. Yawkey was inexplicably doing nothing more than continuing to feed the problem with this apathetic maneuver. *Boston Globe* reporter Harold Kaese called it *"the beheading at Jersey Street."* It had all the ramifications of a coup. Boston Globe's Clif Keane's September 30 article headlined the maneuver, *"Free Hand to Run Sox Given Higgins."* Newly appointed business manager and executive vice president Dick O'Connell, who would eventually find himself in the top general manager slot himself in 1965, spoke freely about Higgins' new assignment, which was extensive. *"O'Connell put the conference pretty much in the hands of Higgins, who is going to run the club on the field along with making the trades,"* wrote Keane.[355]

Boston Globe reporter Hy Hurwitz added some embellishment: *"Manager Mike Higgins remains in his position but with full authority over all player deals and to a certain extent a general manager without portfolio."* O'Connell, according to Hurwitz, offered a further explanation about Higgins' broad authority, *"Mike will tell us what he wants, and we'll try and get it for him. He'll have the last word on deals,"* said O'Connell.[356]

---

[355] Clif Keane, "Free Hand to Run Sox Given Higgins," The Boston Globe, September 28, 1960, p. 53 https://www.newspapers.com/image/433788431/

[356] Hy Hurwitz, "Sox Fire Bucky Harris; O'Connell Vice President," The Boston Globe, September 28, 1960, p. 1 & 41 https://www.newspapers.com/image/433784272/?terms=Hy%20hurwitz%20Boston%20Globe%20&match=1

There seemed little doubt where Yawkey stood in the matter and of the message he was sending to major league baseball and local fandom, which had been losing confidence in Higgins.

Bucky Harris, the general manager until Higgins' appointment, was instrumental in developing and elevating both Pumpsie Green and Earl Wilson to the major league roster in 1959. Furthermore, on June 10, 1960, Harris made a momentous decision to initiate the first Red Sox trade for a black major league ballplayer, Baltimore's Willie Tasby. This trade was actually made two days before Higgins' return to the Red Sox as their manager; some labeled it his 49-week leave of absence from the helm. It didn't take him long; Higgins was seething at the trade. Once again, he displayed his intolerance for hiring or maintaining any black players on his team, and now, with the full authority he had over operations, he was destined to preserve Yawkey's "gentleman's agreement," which was entirely alright with him, and apparently also with Yawkey. In fact, Tom Yawkey himself had been exhibiting signs of restless displeasure with Bucky Harris that quickly led to Harris' departure and, to his relief, brought his pal Mike Higgins back into the fold. Harris was having no qualms about promoting blacks off their farm, and, though Yawkey was not openly forthcoming, which was his nature in racial matters - if not his methodology - he discreetly left this all to his henchman Higgins, who showed no hesitancy to express himself, especially on racial matters. It was no surprise to anyone that Tasby had departed the Red Sox and Boston at the end of the 1960 season now that Higgins had assumed control.

Harris and Higgins were no friends, disagreeing on many decisions, but the one that was the most troublesome was when Harris brought up Pumpsie Green to the Red Sox parent club in 1959. On September 28, 1960, *Globe* reporter Clif Keane furthered the story on Higgins and Green, *"Bucky Says His Split With Higgins Began Over Pumpsie in Spring of '59,"* based on his interview with Harris. Green had batted over .320 with Minneapolis the previous year and, was named the MVP in the American Association, and was a good candidate for a Red Sox club that had been languishing near or in the cellar. But Higgins would have none of it. He complained loudly, according to Harris, *"Well, I don't want the fans in Boston booing Don Buddin. If Green is around, they will,"* spouted Higgins. An incredibly lame argument and rooted likely in other more nefarious considerations, apart from building a good baseball team. *"But I've got a spot for Green on the team,"* insisted Harris in response. *"That, according to Harris, was the beginning of trouble – or lack of cooperation between them,"* wrote Keane.[357]

Harris, who was new in his job of GM, had actually acceded to Higgins' demands of demoting Green, *"presumably with Yawkey's approval,"* revealing the power Higgins possessed in the organization, wrote Stout and Johnson.[358] Green was summarily dumped back to Minneapolis despite his

---

[357] Clif Keane, "Harris' Side of Story: Bucky Says His Split With Higgins Began Over Pumpsie in Spring of '59," The Boston Globe, September 28, 1960, p. 41 https://www.newspapers.com/image/433786083/

[358] Glenn Stout & Richard A. Johnson, "Red Sox Century: The Definitive History of Baseball's Most Storied Franchise," Houghton Mifflin Company, Boston, 2000, p. 291

strong spring performance, and Harris would ultimately pay the price for his entanglement with Yawkey's crony and hobnobber Mike "Pinky" Higgins. In spite of the fan reaction and media frenzy that seemed to engross the city over the decision, Higgins spoke without apologies and expressed no regret, boldly announcing to Boston media that the decision was all his, with the statement, *"It was my own decision when it became obvious that Pumpsie was not ready for the major leagues."*[359] He remarked that he was actually doing Green a favor. The NAACP and the Ministerial Association, however, did not agree with him announcing plans to take further action.

This led to an April 21 meeting called by the Massachusetts Commission Against Discrimination (M.C.A.D.) on behalf of three agencies: the local NAACP, The Ministerial Alliance, and the American Veterans Committee. None of the Red Sox front office, except Dick O'Connell, attended. But O'Connell had done his homework and was persuasive in his defense of the team, reporting that the team had seven blacks in their minor league system and one black employed at Fenway Park. The MCAD exonerated the Red Sox by extracting a promise from them that they would make every effort to end segregation, which in itself was an admission, in the form of a "good faith" letter requested of them, and the matter of race was once again placed on the shelf.

---

[359] Editorial, The Boston Globe, April 11, 1959, p. 1 & 5
https://www.newspapers.com/image/433696741/;
Unattributed, "Boston NAACP Blasts Red Sox for Sending Player to Minors," The Star Press, Muncie Star, Muncie, Indiana, April 12, 1959, p. 18

What the Red Sox were not mindful of, nor heeding the warnings, was how they were creating an *"unflattering portrait"* for themselves, according to Howard Bryant. The black players who had joined other teams began to focus on the Red Sox, which was well supported by the black media, *"that the Red Sox were no longer just another team, but the living symbol of racism in baseball. It was this environment that Pumpsie Green reported to Red Sox camp in 1959."*[360]

The Red Sox were feeling the pressure of civil rights initiatives that had their beginnings with the infamous 1945 tryout of Robinson, Jethroe and Williams. And, now, it was the matter of a young, uninitiated black ballplayer, Elijah Pumpsie Green, placed reluctantly in the spotlight, who only wanted to play baseball and suppress any noise associated with racism, which was in the forefront again fourteen years later. According to historian Jules Tygiel, who authored *Baseball's Great Experiment: Jackie Robinson and His Legacy*, quoting Green, *"To me, baseball was a tough enough game to play itself. I can't think about racial things and try to get a jump on a curve ball."*[361] It was enough to inspire the Red Sox to explore the resolution of their integration issues, overcome their long history of racism, and recognize that the world was rapidly changing and fast leaving them behind. O'Connell, who was out ahead of a hitherto management with an aversion to change was already exploring the operations with minor league

---

[360] Howard Bryant, "Shut Out," p. 8
[361] Jules Tygiel, "Baseball's Great Experiment: Jackie Robinson and His Legacy," Oxford University Press, New York, 1983, p. 332

director Neil Mahoney, taking the lead in this initiative. Between them, they were looking to rebuild the team starting from scratch, including an eventual effort with player development, which was a sore spot for years because of integration implications. O'Connell was resourceful and found ways to navigate the bureaucracy. *"He did the work of a soldier while the generals told war stories and tossed back scotch."*[362]

Relying on his new-found influence with the front office and his aversion to the MCAD's disdain for the club, Dick O'Connell, concerned about the underrepresentation of black players, navigated a move for one that, inexplicably seemed to get by Higgins, who had just assumed his new duties. He picked up Billy Harrell in November 1960. Harrell was a fringe player in a limited role in '61, with only 38 plate appearances, and was sent down to Seattle, Boston's Triple-A club, in 1962. He later played a mentoring role with both George Scott and Reggie Smith in 1965 in a brief stint at Pittsfield.

In keeping with that initiative at the end of April 1961 – two years from the MCAD infamous encounter - the Red Sox took a colossal step and hired not one, but two black scouts, Edward Scott – who discovered Henry Aaron - of Mobile, Alabama, and Spencer "Babe" Davis of Winston-Salem, North Carolina; in Red Sox lingo it was simply unheard of. This was inspired by Red Sox former scout and public relations director, Milt Bolling, whose

---

[362] Stout & Johnson, "Red Sox Century," p. 298

collaboration with O'Connell got the ball rolling. They were expected to cover the South, which other Red Sox scouts always treated as "off limits." No question, the hiring effort was based on overcoming, if not mitigating, the constant criticism of civil rights leaders and organizations and the past comments and legacies of executive-level front office types such as Joe Cronin, Eddie Collins and Mike Higgins, and *Boston Globe's Yawkey* crony Will McDonough who was a fierce defender of Tom Yawkey and Joe Cronin. Meanwhile *Boston Globe* sportswriter Clif Keane announced that this action was done *"in a moment of brilliance."*

Ed Scott, a native of Mobile, Alabama, who was not related to young George Scott of Greenville, Mississippi, had broad-based geographic responsibility to navigate in his quest, if not mission, for primarily black talent, including the Deep South states of Alabama, Mississippi, Louisiana, Georgia and South Carolina, as well as Arkansas, Florida and Texas, spanning considerable miles of long and lonely dusty roads. He was frustrated after several months of coming up empty, but finally, in the spring of 1962, a year from his scouting start with the Red Sox, Scott got a lead from a group of Alabamans he was sitting with near his home in Mobile, sharing small talk, who were expounding on a young black kid in Greenville Mississippi who was tearing the cover off the baseball, they exclaimed. It got his immediate attention, and he soon planned a trip to Mississippi and the Delta town of Greenville.

Farm director Neil Mahoney rose to his farm director position linked to the drama of the September 1960 catharsis of Red Sox executive-level hiring and firing, which also brought O'Connell and hard-drinking, small-minded Mike Higgins to the front office. It was, along with senior scout Milt Bolling's advocacy, instrumental in bringing about Red Sox black scouts into the organization. But Mahoney had cautioned Ed Scott upon his hire of the dangers of being too eager too soon, running the risk of prejudging without being sure of a prospect, which established some hesitancy in Scott's mind. He was leery of what Mahoney would say in his noticeable rush to tie down George Scott. Word had leaked, however, up to the parent club and reached Mahoney that they had a prospect from Mississippi, the table being set, leading to smoother communications between Mahoney and his first-year scout Ed Scott about his namesake, George. He explained in an interview the nervous exchange he had with Mahoney, who he thought would push back vigorously against the rookie scout: *"Mr. Neil,"* said Scott, *"If this kid [George Scott] doesn't make the big leagues, then you can take my paycheck, or fire me. I really felt that strong he would be a good one. He said to me, 'If you think you have something there, then go ahead with it.'"*[363]

---

[363] Ed Scott interview: August 6, 2006

L to R, Ed Scott, Felix Maldonado, Eddie Popowski (author's collection)

Word was, however, that young George Scott had the tools, and he was well worth a hard look. The Red Sox were unaware that the St. Louis Cardinals had taken a lead in the pursuit of George Scott, and the Redbirds were already sizing him up. Ed Scott's arrival, however, couldn't have been better timed as the Cardinals had already gone soft on him, and other clubs, such as the Los Angeles Angels, Chicago White Sox, Pittsburgh and Houston, who were interested, were slow to react. Meanwhile, Ed Scott, contemplating George as possibly being his first official signing, seized the opportunity to pick up the pieces left behind by the Cardinals by quickly establishing a relationship with mother Maggie Scott, helping her out when he could, posturing himself with the family, and working assiduously with young George to ensure he had all the right qualities, and was ready, for success. But there wasn't a lot of time with major league clubs on their heels, and even the St. Louis Cardinals had reconsidered their biased stance and were back in the pursuit, calling Scott's high school coach, Elbert Foules, the day after the signing only to learn they were a day too late. The Red Sox had signed him. Persistence paid dividends for Ed Scott, who, with senior scout Milt Bolling, sat on Coleman High School's steps on May 28, 1962, the day of George's graduation, waiting to capture the young high school athlete who had just left the stage, with a diploma in hand. *"The morning after Scott was signed by the Red Sox,"* said Foules, *"the Cards called me long distance, but by then, the die was cast."*[364]

Jim Crow sentiment was still smoldering in and around Greenville, Mississippi, when Ed Scott was actively scouting young George Scott. On the day before the signing, he met with Red Sox senior scout Milt Bolling, who was white, to strategize plans for the next day. They chose to do this in a parked car as the best location for a black and white to be together in Greenville, as found anywhere else, but this type of seclusion would draw too much adverse attention. But the strategy failed them as soon they were approached by a white Greenville cop who was not pleased with what he was seeing – a black and white together - which was against customary or

---

[364] Roger Birtwell, "Sidearm Pitcher Saved Scott for Sox," The Boston Globe, May 23, 1966, p. 28
https://www.newspapers.com/image/433691776/?terms=Roger%20birtwell&match=1

acceptable behavior. But it amounted to nothing along with a suitable explanation, level heads prevailing, and the city's finest went on his way.

Head Red Sox scout George Digby, of course, had a hand in George's contract negotiated by Ed Scott and senior scout Milt Bolling, who needed Digby's approval. Black scouts, as few as there were, had no financial authority to transact any deals, as was true with George Crowe of the St. Louis Cardinals, a conspicuous reason why George Scott did not sign with them. In this case, Ed Scott was a rookie scout, but he was also black, which had its repercussions based on team history, so it was up to Milt Bolling, who took the lead negotiating the deal and Digby to approve any money transactions. It was thirteen months after Ed Scott was hired by the Red Sox when he signed George Scott and made his first signing.

Head scout George Digby, though he was from Louisiana, a Deep South state, had not done any appreciable scouting of black ballplayers there. It was definitely off limits to scouts for many years until Ed Scott was hired to initiate the practice of searching for black baseball talent, fertile ground for a Red Sox team that had avoided signing black players, particularly from the South. Digby had the savvy, however, and familiarity with protocols that were necessary to navigate the political and cultural territory of scouting black ballplayers and getting around *Jim Crow*, which he shared with Ed Scott, pointing out to him that southern blacks were accustomed to hosting visitors in their homes when their guests applied the right social initiatives accomplished with aplomb. *"I taught Ed Scott how to go in a [black's] house and stay with 'em when he couldn't get into hotels. [They] couldn't get into the motels. In those days, blacks couldn't get into either restaurants or hotels in the South,"* said Digby.[365]

There was another side to Digby, however, that emerged during an interview with him that subtly betrayed a bias that was framed, if not nurtured, by a racist Red Sox front office with which he was associated for many years. During his first swing into Greenville to see the young Coleman High School shortstop, he became alarmed by the number of blacks in the town and being the only white, as if surrounded, attending an all-black sporting event, feeling he might be in danger. *"Well, he played in a little town. It was an all-black community up in somewhere in Mississippi,"* said Digby. *"I can't think of the name of it. It was an all-black community. They played there. I remember driving up in my car to see him play and I saw all these buses coming along with black people in it. I went to the coach and talked to him, and [with concern] I said to the coach, 'Is my car going to be safe out there?' He said, 'Oh yeah, you won't have to worry about it.' And it was safe. And that's when I first saw him play at shortstop."*[366]

It was later said that Digby was overheard complaining about the Tommy Harper racial matter in 1985 when Harper complained about the Elks Lodge, a local segregated Florida entertainment spot that catered to white Red Sox players to the exclusion of their black players. It led to a

---

[365] George Digby interview: January 18, 2007
[366] George Digby interview: January 20, 2007

lawsuit by Harper, followed by his firing by the team for retaliating against the Red Sox organization. Digby, it was said, questioned the entire disturbance this brought to the club and city and laid the blame on Harper, labeling him a "troublemaker." It may not have been provoked by any racial intent by Digby, but it was a common reference of the local journalists, such as the *Globe's* Will McDonough, when black ballplayers expressed their personal opinions against the hometown team, insisting on being heard. Though Digby never exhibited any racist manifestations, highlighted by the Willie Mays matter of 1950 when he desperately wanted to sign him, there were nonetheless troubling racial overtones in the statement.

George Digby and Ted Williams (courtesy of George Digby)

All was not charming, however, for rookie major league scout Ed Scott during his 1961 initiation with a Red Sox team that, for segregation reasons, only two years before, was engaged in an intense encounter with the Massachusetts Commission Against Discrimination (M.C.A.D.) and the prominent local NAACP, who were alleging racial discrimination. His introduction to its racist remnants that stirred the city occurred during a gathering of Red Sox scouts at an empty Fenway Park while at a meeting of the scouts when he was confronted by a fellow Red Sox scout sitting nearby. *"I think he was a [Red Sox] scout out of Pennsylvania,"* said Scott. *"I was standing up. There wasn't nobody in the stands or anything like that but us scouts. Another scout was sitting with him, and I was standing up, and he looked around at me [fiercely and shouted loudly] to 'sit down, everybody sees you!'"* Scott exclaimed angrily as if it was just being said for the first time, remembering that day and the racial implications that were contained in such a rancorous remark.[367]

And the discrimination continued into the early '60s at Red Sox rookie camp in Ocala, Florida, when scouts were expected to be there with the newly signed players. During Ed Scott's first rookie camp farm director Neil Mahoney pulled him off to the side to break the news that where he slept and ate his meals had to be separate from the white personnel, and that included players. Mahoney, according to Scott, claimed the team had already made hotel reservations, which was at a white-only facility, and

---

[367] Ed Scott interview: August 3, 2006

since Scott was new and the reservations had been previously made – and he was black – they weren't going to change them but would help him find alternative arrangements. *"I thought,"* said a rankled Scott, *"you know, they didn't have to have [the Red Sox] stay there, you know."* Not much had changed.[368]

Tom Yawkey was arguably a complicated man, a mixture of benevolence through his charitability, then again, a less than approbative side that would come to plague him: he showed an indifference to affairs that should have concerned him, that were demanding his full attention and requiring his leadership and that was a matter of racism in nearly every part of his organization, which he famously ignored, finding, instead, the occasional diversion of receding into the comfort of his Mt. Pleasant Plantation, South Carolina retreat.

Looking back at a defining moment, at a 1951 Boston Baseball Writers dinner attended by Sam Jethroe, who had just won the National League Rookie of the Year award, who sat next to Red Sox' general manager Eddie Collins, a racial bigot, at the dinner, included in their small talk was a statement by Collins praising Jethroe for his success with the Boston Braves. What Jethroe, one of the three black ballplayers who participated in the 1945 Red Sox tryout, said to Collins could just as easily have been said to Yawkey, had he been there: *"You had your chance, Mr. Collins. You had*

---

[368] IBID

your chance," which was as much an indictment of Yawkey, according to Jethroe, as it was of Collins for not taking a leadership role by seizing the moment and the opportunity made for them to alter the team's moral compass and character to one of inclusion.[369] Yawkey could have been the hero on that day. Instead, that opportunity evaporated and was left open for Brooklyn's Branch Rickey, who grabbed the baton two years later when he signed Jackie Robinson. Robinson proceeded to win the National League Rookie of the Year award in 1947, in his first year in the major leagues, and he was enshrined in the National Baseball Hall of Fame in 1962.

Tom Yawkey's biographer, Bill Nowlin, has provided an interesting perspective on the plausibility of whether Yawkey was personally racist, devoting an entire chapter and an epilogue to its discussion in his laudable book, *Tom Yawkey: Patriarch of the Boston Red Sox,* based on numerous interviews of people who knew or were close to Yawkey. He poses a rhetorical question: *"But does the fact that his team was the last to desegregate prove that Yawkey was a racist?* And, answering his own question, *"It proves that – for whatever reason – he didn't take the lead...We know that several of his fellow owners made explicitly racist statements; Yawkey never did."*[370] Later on, he states, *"The Red Sox were the last team to integrate, and therein lies the best case for Yawkey's being*

---

[369] Howard Bryant, "Shut Out," p. 33; also, Sam Jethroe interview: September 10, 1996
[370] Bill Nowlin, "Tom Yawkey: Patriarch of the Boston Red Sox," University of Nebraska Press, Lincoln, Nebraska, 2018, p. 421

considered a racist," but yet points out it is *"built on circumstantial evidence."*[371]

Nowlin also brings up the matter of Mike "Pinky" Higgins, Yawkey's drinking buddy, who was unmistakably racist and had been quoted with racist remarks, pointing out, *"there is no indication he was called to task by his boss...the issue wasn't going to go away, but that realization still didn't prompt him to act,"* wrote Nowlin. Yawkey was stubborn and often would say he would handle his ballclub in whatever manner he chose and would not be influenced by outsiders. As Nowlin rationalizes, *"To the extent he took such a stance regarding matters of race, it doesn't necessarily evidence racism, but it does countenance it."*[372]

Interviews by Bill Nowlin with Bill Gutfarb of the Yawkey Foundation and Dick Johnson of the Sports Museum of New England, and co-author of *Red Sox Century*, pointed out the likelihood that Tom Yawkey never made *"a racially disparaging remark [outwardly],"* said Gutfarb, or that, *"Any suggestions of personal racism attributed to Yawkey were 'completely second-hand,'"* said Johnson.

Phil Wilkinson, who had worked for Tom Yawkey for ten years, expressed the view that Yawkey may have been a product of the times: *"I think that he had that [matter of his era of] growing up with the situation*

---

[371] IBID, p. 423
[372] IBID, p. 422

where whites were considered to be a little more advanced than blacks were in this part of the world. That rubbed off on him somewhat, but he never acted like he believed that." [373]

As Nowlin points out, Yawkey was also a believer in the precept of "the buck stops here" business approach, which he accepted philosophically on other issues, as his duty throughout his watch with the Red Sox and from which he never equivocated. *"Because he was the sole owner of the team, the buck stopped at his desk,"* said Nowlin. *"He had the power to see that the team was integrated."*[374]

It is entirely plausible that any personal or direct evidence of racism by Yawkey is not manifest, as baseball historian and author Bill Nowlin seems to emphasize. What does stand out, however, is Yawkey's years of complicity, unmistakably in evidence when he had numerous opportunities to make a difference, but he didn't, with the appearance of choosing not to. As Sam Jethroe pointed out to GM Eddie Collins years ago, *"You [The Red Sox] had a chance."*

But there are other disclosures that raise persuasive arguments that Yawkey's bias on integration was more detectable, if not pronounced, than what others are traditionally reporting. As has been stated in numerous publications on the endless stories of Thomas Yawkey and the subject of

---

[373] IBID, p. 426
[374] IBID, p. 111

racism, he was deftly skilled – if, at times instinctually - at leaving business decisions to his Red Sox cronies, whom Yawkey carefully selected to comport with his beliefs and personality, such as Collins, Cronin and Higgins, thus distancing himself as often as he could from the public spotlight. He also had a remarkable way of being insulated enough that he was, mysteriously, not approached or challenged very often by the local media – and, therefore, avoided the hard questions - who treated him as a person with a certain inviolability and was to be considered "off limits" by the Boston press. And they certainly lived up to that charge.

One of the standard-bearers of this line of thinking was *Boston Globe* columnist Will McDonough, who was a stalwart Red Sox apologist who could see nothing wrong in Tom Yawkey or Joe Cronin, and therefore nothing flawed about the Red Sox, in spite of their inalienable shameless resistance to integration and failure to support minority ballplayers. He was the patron saint of that sentiment. McDonough clung to the notion that the sole reason the Red Sox failed to integrate was that their top farm teams, Louisville and Birmingham, were situated in the south; in fact, they allegedly were anxious to pursue black players, McDonough argues, but they *"were hamstrung by societal limitations… In fact, there is only proof of the contrary,"* wrote Howard Bryant.[375]

---

[375] Howard Bryant, "Shut Out," p. 68

Will McDonough was a tough street-wise Irish kid from South Boston, "Southie" as it was affectionately – and politically - known in the region, who was combative by nature, and it showed in his columns, especially when he spoke about Tom Yawkey's alleged racism, which was infrequent as he didn't believe Yawkey was a racist, thus wasting his time to put print to paper. His rants were nothing more than a contrived effort to quash stories or their sources, whether by the public, authors or even fellow reporters, of Red Sox racism, and particularly attacks on one Thomas Yawkey.

Two of the most preeminent and fiercely competitive sports journalists of the 1970s, Peter Gammons and Will McDonough, both of the *Boston Globe*, who became rivals, received more Boston-area adulation than other sports journalists. They couldn't have been more different, Gammons the suburban kid, a Groton School "preppy" and University of North Carolina Chapel Hill graduate, while McDonough was the tough guy from the streets who earned his dues the hard way, a Northeastern University product that, at the time, was considered somewhat of an inferior education to such esteemed colleges as the Ivies of Harvard and MIT. The pinprick in all of this rivalry was *"class differences;"* According to Howard Bryant, *"McDonough and Gammons would exemplify nothing more than the historical struggle between the Irish and the Yankees,"* a political and cultural struggle for generations in the city of Boston.[376]

---

[376] IBID, p. 103

While they saw things differently in most cases, one thing that Gammons and McDonough seemed to agree on was the race story in Boston, but for entirely different reasons: *"Peter Gammons did not seem to own much of a personal or moral passion for the race question, while McDonough simply did not believe that race in Boston was a story at all,"* wrote Bryant.[377] *"More than any other reporter in the city, it would be McDonough who would deny the existence of race as a legitimate factor in assessing the club...Gammons was different,"* said Bryant. *"Race was not a journalistic topic that particularly energized him, but he would never doubt the existence of a serious racial chasm inside the Red Sox organization."*[378]

McDonough's power-of-the-pen opinions and his bias carried considerable weight in the Boston arena, always tainted by his political insider role as a member of the Boston majority, the Irish Catholic, that could not be ignored; In effect, he wielded an inordinate influence and was amidst the *"political power brokers"* of the city.[379] *"When he circled the wagons on you, you were finished,"* said award-winning journalist Clark Booth. *"I never saw someone who could be so unforgiving of a person. And he was a giant, so you didn't want to get on the wrong side of him."*[380]

---

[377] IBID, p. 105
[378] IBID, p. 101
[379] IBID, p. 109
[380] IBID, quoting Clark Booth, p. 104

One who did was Glenn Stout, baseball historian and co-author of the epic narrative *Red Sox Century*, who encountered a red-hot McDonough who exploded at Stout, calling him by phone to rant about how inaccurate the book was about the 1945 tryout and other racial subjects on the Red Sox. He wildly asserted that Joe Cronin and Clif Keane were not even there on that day, though this was blatantly inaccurate, scoffing at the idea the Red Sox played any part in racism and further raging that *"The only problem the Red Sox ever had with blacks was finding blacks who could play, alright?"* McDonough huffed in his usual condescending manner. Afterward, in his weekly column, perhaps uncharacteristically feeling some vulnerability on the subject, McDonough pursued the issue further by going to Red Sox CEO John Harrington to attack Stout's *Red Sox Century* for the public's benefit. It was apparent, according to Stout, that Harrington, like McDonough, had not read the book. Harrington, however, fell upon old and quite stale Red Sox arguments exhibiting *"the same level of ignorance and denial that had dogged the ballclub ever since that April morning so long ago."* Harrington blindly defended Yawkey, charging that the Red Sox did not sign Robinson *"because their top farm clubs were in Louisville and New Orleans."*[381] Stout summarized the unfortunate event with McDonough and Harrington

---

[381] Glenn Stout, "Tryout and Fallout: Race, Jackie Robinson and the Red Sox," originally published in the Massachusetts Historical Review, volume 6, 2004, 2020 https://glennstout.com/tryout-and-fallout-race-jackie-robinson-and-the-red-sox/

with these words: *"The team, its fans, and the city that hosts them have chosen to distort or overlook history as if they could make it disappear."*[382]

Importantly, an implicative Sports Illustrated feature article of June 28, 1965, *"The Great Wall of Boston,"* by staff writer Jack Mann, brings the subject of race and Tom Yawkey into a better frame of reference and also considers a better focus on the argument of whether racism was evident in him. Mann, unlike most reporters and journalists, especially those in Boston, was willing to courageously broach the question of race with Yawkey directly, eliciting interesting - maybe even troubling - answers. Mann confronted Yawkey with the idea that to win, you needed the best players and of the teams that rose to the top, they were infiltrated with black players, yet the Red Sox lagged behind. Mann pointed to how easy it was to place blame on Mike "Pinky" Higgins, whose racism stood out like a beacon in the night and was well advertised, becoming the so-called "bona fide" racist element behind the Red Sox' failures. However, as Mann emphasized, *"Higgins, who did not become field manager until 1955 and did not take a desk job in the front office until late 1962, could hardly have been the Caucasian in the woodpile."*[383]

---

[382] IBID

[383] Glenn Stout, "Tom Yawkey, Race, and the Smoking Gun II," Verb Plow, Boston Baseball September 2017
http://verbplow.blogspot.com/search?q=yawkey+smoking+gun

Yawkey went defensive with Mann and intimated, *"They blame me,"* he said. But in a next breath spoke of blacks stereotypically as being *"clannish,"* of like kind, and once the story got around, they all decided to go elsewhere, accepting no-fault himself but, instead, blaming the ballplayers.[384]

Yawkey's concluding remark to Mann was revealing: *"We scouted them right along, but we didn't want one because he was a Negro. We wanted a ballplayer,"* argued Yawkey. Yet blacks were filling ballclubs ever since Jackie Robinson signed in 1947 and winning awards, but the Red Sox neither put a black player they had signed on the field or traded for one until Pumpsie Green arrived in 1959. And, of course, they ignored the opportunity to sign one of the greatest athletes and baseball men of all time, future Hall of Famer Willie Mays, who surely qualified as "a ballplayer" in the tactless words of Thomas Yawkey.[385]

One of the preeminent and most enlightened authors of the day, David Halberstam, a standard-bearer for distinguished journalism, an eclectic thinker of diverse worldly matters, and prize-winner of journalistic awards including the 1964 *Pulitzer prize for International Reporting*, who momentarily turned to sports writing as a diversion with a certain focus on Red Sox narratives, being *"Outside of the city's parochial walls,"* spoke of

---

[384] IBID
[385] IBID

Thomas Yawkey by defining him as *"clearly a racist,"* according to Howard Bryant, and a man *"who accepted the social order and embraced its benefits."*[386]

This panoply of Red Sox racism and the men behind it formed a cornerstone for what George Scott might have expected as he signed with the Red Sox in 1962, knowing of the fiasco of Pumpsie Green only three short years before and that Mike Higgins was still the general manager of this ballclub. He knew going in that playing for the Red Sox could be troublesome, but he also felt they were ripe for making changes – and, he was right - whereupon he took a chance with them. He felt he had the talent to break through and was encouraged by Red Sox black scout Ed Scott to follow his instincts, especially knowing that he had inside information and viewpoints and was a man he felt he could trust. But what he didn't know, and as yet had been warned, was the climate of the city itself and how to personally navigate that, which became dispiriting. Later on, in Boston, it came into better focus after he had met and formed a friendship with the Celtics' superstar Bill Russell, who was contemptuous of the city of Boston; Russell cautioned George: *"Bill Russell told me what to expect as a black guy living in Boston. He told me that this is basically a racist city, but not to get carried away too much about what people say,"* said Scott. *"One day,*

---

[386] Howard Bryant, "Shut Out," p. 135

they'll be on your bandwagon, and 24 hours later, they'd be off it. He was right. It's just that kind of town."[387]

George pointed out his reasons for signing with Boston, explaining: *"[It] was because I knew that Boston did not have no blacks. I knew that they were looking for good black ballplayers, and I felt if I could go there [to the Boston Red Sox], I could go through their organization pretty fast if I showed 'em I could play, and that's exactly what happened."* His passion for rapidly ascending the Red Sox ladder had one inalienable focus: his mother, who was living in poverty, and for whom he was determined to deliver a promise, and that was to set Maggie free from a miserable and long-standing impoverished way of life. It was a matter of deep-seated anguish for George, and he was not about to abandon his quest for justice until he reached his goal. He would set aside in his mind the risks of playing in Boston, which would require adjustments, but he made them before in the Delta, and if he could do so and survive in *Jim Crow* Greenville, he could do the same in Boston, he reasoned.[388]

The quaint little town of Olean, Cattaraugus County, New York, hosted eighteen-year-old George Scott and his Olean Oilers teammates of the Class D New York Penn League. The Oilers were affiliated with the Red Sox playing at 4000-seat Bradner Stadium, in which Jackie Robinson had once

---

[387] Larry Whiteside, "Sox Children of the '60s Look Back: The Black Athlete in Boston," The Boston Globe, July 29, 1979, p. 80
https://www.newspapers.com/image/437079904/
[388] George Scott interview: January 12, 2006

played with the Brooklyn Dodgers in 1947. From there, he went to Wellsville, New York, another small northern town that didn't pose any racial problem.

L to R Bob Guindon, Hal Holland and George Scott, Olean New York (author's collection)

"I had never been away from home, and I missed my family," said George Scott, *"but in some strange way, it was pleasing to be in a northern town, in upstate New York, in the minors where I started with the Red Sox in 1962, and away from the hatred and violence of the Delta. It just was. Those peoples in New York had no mind to attack us blacks playing there, but then there were few of us in those days; Boston still had a mind not to*

go with black ballplayers; that's what I saw. There wasn't many of us in camp."[389]

However, in 1964, he was promoted to Winston-Salem's Red Sox in North Carolina of the Carolina League – a High-A league and a faster-paced, more competitive brand of baseball laced with players who were in preparation and leveraging themselves for the major leagues; however, it was also a league rife with racism, among the fans as well as some of the ballplayers and teams. It was young George's first experience with a racist element since he began his minor league venture, but it was an intense one that turned out to be very personal.

"I had graduated to Winston-Salem of the Carolina League, A-ball at the time, in 1964 after spending two short years in the NY Penn League. I had no trouble when I was in New York, but I had plenty of it with fans and teammates when I was in the Carolinas. Oh man, did I ever. They was a hotbed of racism down there, as much as I had seen in the Delta. They didn't take kindly to no blacks. But then again, we were in the South. I wasn't happy with some of the reporters down there. 'Another Negro' player was coming to Winston Salem, one newspaperman wrote announcing my arrival there; that bothered me as if we were different than the rest. As if we were

---

[389] IBID

some kinds of disease or something terrible about us that set us apart," said Scott.[390]

The seat of North Carolina racism that was apparent in the Carolina League appeared to be centered in the greater Raleigh area, with several incidents of racism at the surrounding parks of Wilson, Durham, Rocky Mount, Kinston and especially Raleigh. On one occasion in Raleigh, George Scott was confronted by several Raleigh players who had brought a live black cat to the ballpark, holding it up in front of the visitor's dugout where George was sitting, screaming obscenities while comparing the cat to Scott's sister, Beatrice, drawing laughter from the crowd; but not from George. The city of Winston-Salem, which had the major college of Wake Forest among Winston-Salem State, Carolina University, and some smaller colleges making it more cosmopolitan, were not as likely to participate in racist behavior, but there was racist subtlety amongst some of the sports reporters, defining black players not by their athleticism but by their color, such as "another Negro" attributed to George Scott, or, "A Negro," or a "Negro infielder." Clearly an attempt to set them apart from white players, which was an old Southern habit of racist folderol.

"Even some of the guys on your own ball club [were racist]," said manager Bill Slack – *"they were from the South, right? That's the way they were brought up – George, he'd be playing third base. When we got past*

---

[390] IBID

Raleigh – Raleigh was sort of bad enough because the stands were right on the field, and so was Rocky Mount and Wilson, North Carolina. First time I'd go over to Rocky Mount, they'd have that one section right back of third base, there, and, oh God, I mean, they were calling him everything, and I'm saying, 'What's the matter with these people? That's bad; what are they doing? They'd say [to me], 'Well, that's the South.' They were calling him 'jungle bunny' and 'nigger' and 'black boy' and Sambo.' I couldn't understand it coming from Canada," declared a very irritated Slack as if he was reliving a memory.[391]

While the team was traveling through Carolina, Scott's team set out to humor the young ballplayer, or at least that's what they thought, by dressing up in Ku Klux Klan white-sheeted costumes and surprising him in the motel where they were staying. There were several team members forming a small crowd, which added to the threat, who wore the intimidating garb that, by their numbers, had all the elements, if not actual presence, of serious provocation that frightened George with nascent memories of his southern upbringing. He wasted little time after *"jumping about ten feet in the air,"* said his coach Bill Slack - who discussed the incident with the ballplayers - after which George dashed for the motel bathroom where he locked himself in. He was called downstairs to the room to see if he could convince George that it was only a stunt and to help extricate the petrified ballplayer. Slack said at first, it seemed funny to him, being nothing but a prank, but when

---

[391] Bill Slack interview: June 8, 2009

George couldn't be pried from the restroom Slack soon realized how sobering a matter it was.

"So, I knock on the door, and I said, 'George, this is the skipper, your manager, Bill.' He said, 'No, I'm staying in here. They ain't gonna get me.' I said, 'What do you mean? George, everything's alright, open the door.' Finally, we got him to open the door," said Slack. But as Slack said, being a Canadian, he never experienced or imagined the racial unrest quite like George Scott was familiar with in the Deep South, and how such an apparent joke – though Scott was hardly amused - turned out to be such a serious racial manifestation that he never could have imagined. It presented a cause for pause for him and a deeper sensitivity to young black athletes joining his team, of which there were not many. Winston-Salem had only a small handful of black players. [392]

Ball clubs arranged with black residents to take black ballplayers into their homes – many of them class citizens, such as doctors and lawyers – because blacks were not welcome in the hotels unless they were specifically designated black hotels. The players were shuttled to the ballparks by bus and picked up after the games. George was stunned at the level of racial hatred in these towns that well exceeded anything he had seen like that in his hometown of Greenville.

---

[392] IBID

George's boyhood and close friend Edward Davis, whom George called "E. T." was, among some of his former high school athletes, an exceptional ballplayer – as good as himself, said George - who deserved a chance at major league baseball, and he brought it up with the Red Sox management. They decided to give Davis a tryout and agreed with George that Davis had talent, assigning him to the Greenville Red Sox of the Western Carolina League. *"His style was like Hank Aaron,"* said George, *"just stood up straight in the batter's box and hardly an effort just kept swatting line drives all over the place!"*[393] But it was all downhill from there: the experience and memory of it were anything but pleasant, according to E. T. Davis. *"Blacks were not welcome there [in the Carolinas],"* said Davis. *"The [racial] atmosphere there, you could cut it with a knife!"* What was most shocking to Davis was how he was ignored by the team's management and the media, and with each game Davis was pushed closer to the end of the bench, and no one was talking to him. George later attempted to line Davis up with the Cincinnati ball club, but Davis objected, saying, *"I told George, 'I don't want this hurt again, man. I don't want to get hurt like that again.'"*[394]

---

[393] George Scott interview: January 12, 2006
[394] E. T. Davis interview: April 20, 2006

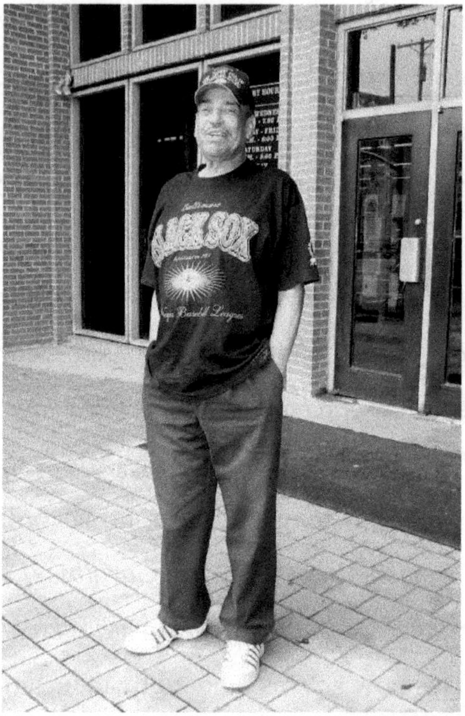

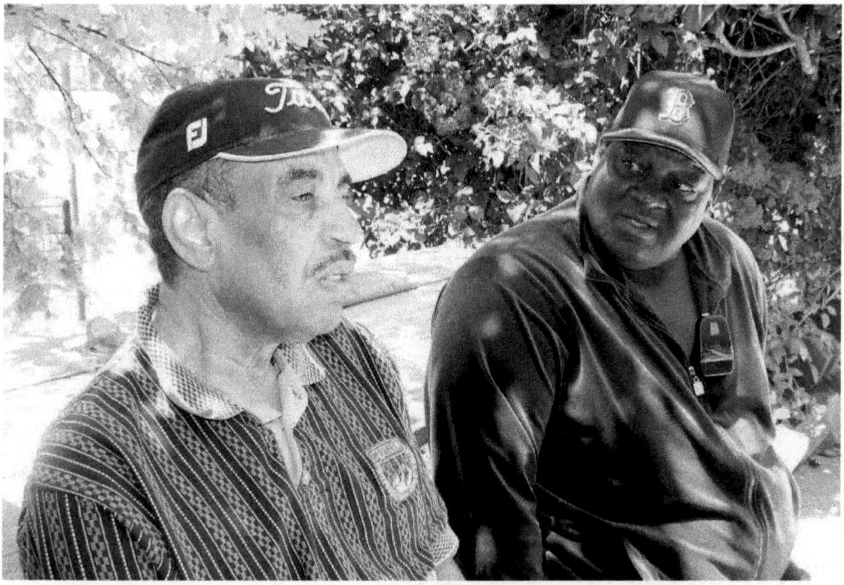

E. T. Davis, George Scott's best boyhood friend (author's collection)

Many black ballplayers of the '60s, a tough time in the heyday of the civil rights movement, when racial bitterness was proliferating, found unendurable the racial intensity permeating the southern minor league towns that regularly exhibited "unwelcome" signs to any black ballplayer performing there, and who often found themselves dropping out of baseball. This was the case of E. T. Davis, who had had enough of the abuse and packed up for home. But there were some tough-minded blacks, all of them, who hung on in the face of it; that described George Scott. He was resilient and constantly alert to situations, especially racial challenges that posed a threat. *"He avoided the street pitfalls that got Joe Foy into trouble and a quick ticket out of town…I'd been born and raised in the South, and I'd had tough times before,"* said Scott. *"He married Lucky Pena of Falmouth,*

Mass., [January 1968] a Cape Cod native who knew her way around, and if there were problems, they dealt with them,"[395] wrote black reporter Larry Whiteside.

It got him some personal mileage that others like Red Sox teammate Reggie Smith couldn't achieve by reason of their combative styles, which Boston reporters found offensive and patronizing, especially by the old guard, like McDonough, whereas George humored them and got some laughs, but usually at his own expense, in whichever manner he conjured appeasing them; "the clown" says historian Howard Bryant, always the clown, which Red Sox future Hall of Famer Jim Rice fiercely opposed feeling they were encouraging others to view them as nothing more than objects of derision, or simpletons, a long-standing tradition practiced by some black athletes in order to gain favor when it was felt they could not achieve acceptance by any other means. It was a circumstance well understood by Southern blacks who used this measure, bringing deference to themselves in order to placate their white farmers and planters and counteracting their acts of contempt. *"I knew,"* said Scott, *"that sometimes, by playing dumb with the media, we blacks could get away with things. Guys like Reggie [Smith] could never do that and he paid a price. The media was tough on guys like him. They wouldn't accept a black guy standing up [to the media]."* [396]

---

[395] Larry Whiteside, "Sox Children of the '60s Look Back," p. 80
[396] George Scott interview: January 16, 2007

"A guy like George Scott had learned to accept it [racism] because he was from the South and probably thought that was the way of life there," said Reggie Smith, who was being interviewed by *Boston Globe* reporter Larry Whiteside. *"Quite possibly, he couldn't understand why I didn't feel that way. I wasn't used to being treated that way. It took time, but I learned to handle it…I really don't believe Boston was ready to accept an outspoken black at that time, particularly since I was somehow looked upon as being possibly 'their' Jackie Robinson or Willie Mays."*[397]

---

[397] Larry Whiteside, "Sox Children of the '60s Look Back," p. 80

Chapter 8
Boston, The Little Rock of the North

There is actually more [racial and religious hatred] in the North than in the South...I am ashamed of the discrimination which the Negro Suffers in the South...But [we don't] pretend that it doesn't exist. That pretense is assiduously practiced in the North.

Hodding Carter Jr[398]

Young George Scott, now 21, reached the zenith of his minor league baseball experience when he was promoted in 1965 from Winston-Salem to the newly established Pittsfield Red Sox of the Double-A Eastern League, two steps below the major leagues. Pittsfield, the "Shire City," was nestled in the Berkshires of Western Massachusetts, a far cry from the racial hostility of Winston-Salem and the Carolina League, which, if it weren't for his determination to succeed, would have dismantled George and his ambitions. Pittsfield was an old Yankee town, modest in its size and moderate political makeup, with no particular aspersions built into it that would make black ballplayers like George not feel welcome. One of the great moments in George's life, and his baseball experience transgressing into the major leagues, was meeting up with diminutive Eddie Popowski, all 5' 4" of him, who was the manager of the newly-formed Pittsfield Red

---

[398] Time Magazine, Editorial, "The Press: With a Capital L," August 22, 1949 https://content.time.com/time/subscriber/article/0,33009,800621,00.html

Sox. He became an important role model for the young ballplayer from Mississippi who thrived under "Pop's" leadership, his sense of humor, and unparalleled skills in dealing with young ballplayers. If he recognized potential, as he did with Scott, he wasted no time tutoring the youngster to shape him into a major league prospect if the skills were there. *"If it wasn't for 'Pop,' I doubt if I would have played in the major leagues,"* said George respectfully. *"He taught me how to play…and if [he knew] you could play, he really made you work."*[399]

There was something special about "Pop," said George, that endeared him to his players. "Trust" was the byword when describing this bantam of a man. He had earned it – trust - from all of his ballplayers. George thrived on it as Pop was like a father to him that the young ballplayer never had, teaching him invaluable lessons about fielding, hitting and life. *"I had my best year ever in baseball playing for Pop,"* said Scott. *"He was a great man. He never showed any racism or prejudice with any of the black ballplayers…it is a thing where, as a black ballplayer playing for white coaches, you would not get well-liked anyway. I did not get close to anybody but Pop. I was never nobody's friend. He was like a father to me. He taught us a lot of baseball. He loved me, man. He loved George Scott…I loved the man so much."*[400]

---

[399] George Scott interview: May 20, 2006
[400] IBID

Under Popowski's tutelage, coupled with his heightened baseball skills and prowess, George Scott swept himself into the hearts and minds of the Pittsfield crowd with a mind-bending season that is still talked about. With one swing of his prodigious bat, George single-handedly led his team to victory and a league championship with a home run that won the game and the title. That home run also gave him the home run title, earned him the prestigious Triple Crown, and later the Most Valuable Player award, finishing the season with the best batting average, RBIs, total bases, base hits, doubles, at-bats and tied for games played. Popowski took honors of his own by being named the Eastern League's Manager of the Year. George was causing the parent club to take notice and regard him as a possible contender for the third base slot that heretofore was considered a shoo-in for the Red Sox Triple-A club's Joe Foy, who was also an MVP. After only three and a half seasons of minor league ball, Scott was poised for at least a spring trial with the major league team, promising himself with perfect confidence that he would surprise the Red Sox management, making it hard for them to send him down.

George Scott, 1965 Eastern League MVP and Triple Crown winner (courtesy of George Scott)

His timing couldn't have been any better; long-time Tom Yawkey crony and drinking buddy Mike "Pinky" Higgins – an avowed racist - who was the general manager between 1962 and 1965 and who resisted the influx of black ballplayers swearing he would never accept a black player on his team, was, quizzically, fired by Yawkey on September 16, 1965. On the same day, he replaced him with an unknown business manager Dick O'Connell, who was neither a Yawkey crony nor a drinking pal with no roots in the South. He was given free rein, and since he was under no higher authority, such as Eddie Collins, Joe Cronin or Higgins, who refused to accept black players, Yawkey had turned ambivalent toward the team, having lost patience with the city for refusing to build him a new ballpark, O'Connell found himself in the driver's seat. George Scott was one of the first moves he made, bringing him up to the parent club following his appointment.

There was no racial element to Dick O'Connell; he was pure business – which would years later curiously get him into trouble with Jean Yawkey, who had ownership of the team following Tom Yawkey's death – and began for the first time the task of seriously finding, signing, developing and, above all, integrating black players for the parent club. It was not an easy transition for him, however, in his attempt to amalgamate the team or with the new black Red Sox ballplayers, including George Scott, who still had to deal with a racist city – Boston – that displayed little to no patience, or tolerance, for black athletes outside of the boundaries of stadiums or the arenas they played in, to include contiguous white residential areas. In other words, it was alright to be entertained by them, but that's where the line was drawn. *"The city was run by the Irish, just the way it had been since the turn of the century,"* wrote Bill Reynolds, long-time columnist for the *Providence Journal* and member of their sports department. *"And to the Boston Irish, politics was serious. It was the way they controlled everything, the lesson they had once so painfully learned from the Brahmins, back when they had run Boston with an iron fist, and the signs, both visible and buried in the psyche, were 'No Irish Need Apply.' The Irish had learned the lesson well. They controlled the city's government. They controlled the city jobs. They controlled the schools. And they weren't going to willingly give that up, for to give that up was to give up power...The Irish ran Boston the way they did because they could. It was their club, and they made the rules."*[401]

Roxbury was the epicenter of the Boston-area black culture, and parts of Dorchester, Hyde Park and Mattapan in the 1960s-1970s, but they lacked leverage with the city. *"African-Americans had no clout in Boston,"* said Reynolds. *"There were none on the city council. There were none on the school committee. And their neighborhoods were mostly out of sight, to the point that it was possible to come into Boston, see a show in the theater district, go to the Garden to see the Bruins, go out to eat, go to a club in the Back Bay, go to Fenway, hang around the colleges, do just about anything there was to do and see very few black people. Certainly, Fenway was like*

---

[401] Bill Reynolds, " '78: The Boston Red Sox, a historic game, and a divided city," New American Library; Penguin Group, New York, NY, 2009, p. 59

that, where you saw more black faces on the field than you did in the stands, and that wasn't a whole lot either."[402]

The circumstances of black and white division in and around Boston may have been best described by George Scott, who, for the first few years following his arrival in the city and with the Red Sox, kept a low profile in Roxbury, where he took up residence for a while before marrying Falmouth's Malvina "Lucky" Pena in 1968 and transitioning to Cape Cod, where his new wife had her roots. Bill Reynolds made the comment: *"George Scott had been right: Fenway Park and Roxbury truly were worlds apart."*[403]

As much as George Scott had eagerly awaited a better and more serene society in a cosmopolitan city like Boston than what he had experienced in a troubled South, ironically, it proved to be anything but a smooth transition for him, if, in some ways, it was worse; for as much as he had hoped for a more civil northern atmosphere he found, instead, a city immersed in racial turmoil not dissimilar to what he was familiar with in southern cities. In fact, some labeled Boston *"the Little Rock of the North,"* tracing back to the violence of 1957 in Little Rock, Arkansas, associated with

---

[402] IBID
[403] IBID

desegregation efforts when nine black students attempted to gain access to Little Rock's Central High School and were turned away.[404]

Like the South, which reacted forcefully, and in some parts of Mississippi, violently, to the 1954 *Brown* decision, calling for desegregation of schools, that was met with resistance led by a *White Citizens' Council* that was formed in Indianola, Mississippi that year, so also, fifteen hundred miles north, in the city of Boston, there was a similar reaction with immediate and heavy opposition to the government's order that was perceived as threatening the city's status quo. Pulitzer prize recipient and a leading Mississippi citizen Hodding Carter, who regularly pushed back at Northern outsiders who foisted their propaganda on the South, made an observation about a racist North that if it was not profound, was certainly very close to being accurate: *"There is actually more [racial and religious hatred] in the North than in the South...we never had a Bund or a Christian Front in the South...the North has almost a monopoly on neurotics...dipsomaniacs, abnormal sex delinquents, divorced couples, Communists, crime-comic readers, [and] gin-rummy addicts"*[405]

In fact, according to American historian C. Vann Woodward, winner of the Pulitzer Prize for History, in his treatise, *The Strange Career of Jim Crow*, cited the sharp distinctions between the North and South in their

---

[404] Ronald Formisano, "Boston Against Busing," The University of North Carolina Press, Chapel Hill, NC, 1991, p. 1
[405] Time magazine, Editorial, The Press: with a capital L, Aug 22, 1949 https://content.time.com/time/subscriber/article/0,33009,800621,00.html

desegregation efforts in response to the Supreme Court's October 1969 ruling that school segregation must be ended *"at once."* Woodward emphasized that Southern schools had made great progress with desegregation between 1970 and 1971, yet the North lagged well behind. *"The schools of the South were now more desegregated than those of the North, where less than 30 percent of the black children were in majority white schools. Boston, for example, found its public school system was more tightly segregated than that of any Southern city of importance below Washington,"* wrote Woodward. He added, *"Segregation in the North was no less real for being de facto instead of de jure, but it is different in origin and more difficult to counter. Like that of the South, it was the consequence of race prejudice, but it was the prejudice of individuals, not the act of the state or local government, that was responsible for residential segregation, which gave rise to the segregated schools."*[406]

The manifestation of the school busing era emerged in Boston in 1963 and was enforced by a Federal Court order in 1974 when the local National Association for the Advancement of Colored People (NAACP) made demands on the school board and city for better schools for blacks. Louise Day Hicks, a lawyer and politician, and a member of the Boston school board, including chairwoman of the school committee between 1963 and 1970, gained national notoriety for her opposition to initiatives of the

---

[406] C. Vann Woodward, "The Strange Career of Jim Crow," Oxford University Press, New York, NY, 1955, p. 212 & 213
https://archive.org/details/strangecareerofj0000wood_m0h2/page/212/mode/1up

NAACP – which were mainly for the improvement of educational facilities available to black students - including a steadfast resistance to the desegregation of Boston public schools, and especially court-ordered busing. Although Hicks was identified as the establisher of this movement, in fact, these antithetical policies preceded her. *"But, consistent majorities on the school committee, with or without Hicks, pursued essentially the same policies for a dozen years,"* wrote historian and Ph.D. Ronald Formisano in his epic narrative *Boston Against Busing*.[407]

As early as 1961, Boston's blacks, with the guidance of the local NAACP chapter had its start by pushing hard against the Boston School Committee for remediation of the public school problem and their quest for virtuous educational systems for black children. But it met with constant resistance led by *"antibusing's Mother Superior,"* a moniker so assigned by historian Formisano to Louise Day Hicks, who took the lead in this fight. *"The Boston School committee, dominated by Irish politicians and highly sensitive to aroused local groups, adamantly resisted demands for school reform…Boston and Mrs. Hicks became symbols as early as 1963 of the 'white back-lash' that was perhaps the most significant northern white response to the civil rights movement."*[408]

There was something strangely inimical about the city of Boston; it embodied a pattern of resistance, cronyism and adversarial relationships

---

[407] Ronald Formisano, "Boston Against Busing,"
University of North Carolina Press, Chapel Hill,
1991, p. 2
[408] IBID, p. 2 & 10

rooted in Irish, or Gaelic, society clinging to ethnic proclivities that would soon reveal outwardly its blistering hostility toward the city's blacks with the advent of busing in the 1970s. As Formisano pointed out, *"shocking images of racial bigotry and violence emerged from Boston, that graceful, cosmopolitan city known for the excellence of its educational, cultural, and scientific institutions, a city once called 'the Athens of America.'"*

The Irish Catholics were largely in control of the city and, historically, at odds with the black population of Boston. *"Blacks and Irish Catholics often have continued to regard one another with hostility across cultural barriers that are composed in part of perceptions and stereotypes, but also real differences, both cultural and material,"* wrote Professor Formisano, adding, *"They were not inclined to give away anything to the black civil rights leaders who seemed to be seeking leverage by assuming for their group a special moral status based on white guilt."* Thus, said Formisano when the NAACP appealed to the Boston school committee for concessions *"the committee balked at most black demands."* [409]

"In 1974, the tough, mostly Irish, working-class neighborhood of South Boston became as much a symbol of white racism as Selma, Alabama had been in 1964," pronounced Formisano.[410]

---

[409] IBID, p. 11
[410] IBID, p. 1

Boston maintained a parochial demeanor about itself that was impervious to outside ethnic interests. *"Boston, with its jagged notions of race and deeply segregated neighborhoods, was by its own complex design a racial powder keg. The city was woven into ethnic conclaves that were tight and inflexible,"* wrote Howard Bryant.[411] One of Boston's all-time greatest signature black athletes, NBA great Bill Russell, who ironically donned the Celtic green – steeped in Irish origins - of the champion Boston Celtics, but who disliked the racial climate of the city and its image and felt miserable performing in it, held deep contentious feelings about the city, which he would often share with fellow athletes and teammates, including George Scott upon his arrival to the city in 1966. *"It was that Boston possessed an insularity that was by definition exclusionary,"* wrote Howard Bryant. *"In Boston, Russell thought, you had to be an insider. If you were white, you had to be Irish. If you were Irish, you had to subscribe to the proper strain of Catholicism. Then you had to belong to the right clubs, attend the right schools, and know the right people."* It was a difficult city for anyone who didn't fit these requisites, he felt, particularly if you were black. He once wrote, *"I had never been in a city more involved with finding new ways to dismiss, ignore or look down on other people."*[412]

Russell viewed Boston's blacks as bafflingly passive. They were little seen around the city except in menial jobs, rarely found in executive

---

[411] Howard Bryant, "Shut Out," p. 55
[412] IBID

positions or in boardrooms. They seemed to be acceptive of their impassive status, which infuriated Russell. He once referred to the city as a *"flea market of racism.'"*[413]

"Boston's neighborhoods commonly swelled with a localist pride that made their residents highly conscious of turf," said Formisano.[414] He added about the Boston Irish element and their influence of *"Enjoying several advantages over other immigrant groups, they seldom practiced politics as a way of maximizing the public good, but rather, in nonideological fashion as a means to upward mobility by gaining status and patronage, and distributing jobs, favors, and contracts to kin and friends. Their ethic was personalist, particularist, and competitive."*[415]

Though his eyes were fixed on baseball in 1966 and in just making the major league roster with a Red Sox club, George Scott was quickly made aware of Boston's racial element by members of their pro basketball club, the Celtics, with whom he formed friendships and would informally practice, including with superstar Bill Russell. Scott was a highly talented basketball player and all-around athlete who, just four years before, led his Coleman High Basketball team to a state championship. UCLA's John Wooden, a future Naismith Memorial Basketball Hall of Famer, enshrined

---

[413] IBID, p. 56
[414] Ronald Formisano, "Boston Against Busing," p. 7
[415] IBID, p. 10; also, U.S. Commission on Civil Rights, "Desegregating the Boston Public Schools: A Crisis in Civic Responsibility." Washington, D.C: GPO, 1976, p. xix https://archive.org/details/ERIC_ED115706/page/n17/mode/2up

in two categories: as both a player and coach, who Scott remembers coming down to Greenville, said that Wooden claimed he was a shooter in the caliber of future Hall of Famer Pete Maravich. The word got around when he arrived in Boston, and George soon linked with the Celtics' Jones boys, K. C. and Sam, who invited him to the Garden, where they trained. He would go there on off days and do some shooting and take part in a few scrimmages. He didn't recall that either K. C. or Sam Jones talked a lot about the racial situation, but Bill Russell did. *"I remember Bill Russell complaining a lot about Boston,"* said Scott. *"He said there was a lot of prejudice here and to watch my butt. Sam [Jones] and K. C. [Jones] were from the South and used to the abuse, and were not as upset with it as Bill [Russell] was."*[416] In a 1979 interview with The *Boston Globe's* Larry Whiteside, who was the *Globe's* lone black sports journalist, Scott expanded on his relationship and communications with the Celtics' star, with whom he had formed a friendship: *"Bill Russell had told me what to expect as a black...in Boston. He told me that this is basically a racist city but not to get carried away too much about what people say...he was right."*[417]

Athletes of the 1950s-1960s like the "Jones Boys," Sam and K. C. of the Boston Celtics, the Red Sox' Pumpsie Green, later on Luis Tiant, and even George Scott, who found their way around the city's racial politics and

---

[416] George Scott interview: July 22, 2006
[417] Larry Whiteside, "Sox' Children of the '60s Look Back," Boston Sunday Globe, July 29, 1979, p. 8

were *"more tolerant of Boston's quirks and personality,"* wrote Howard Bryant, than the explosive more confrontational nature of blacks like Bill Russell and Reggie Smith, and in that same bracket Earl Wilson and Tommy Harper. *"There was a certain black personality that could thrive in those days and one that would likely endure hardship,"* wrote Bryant.[418]

Bryant expanded on this, citing the opinion of Author and baseball historian Glenn Stout, who co-wrote the epic Red Sox story in *Red Sox Century*: *"There was a certain subjugation that had to take place for the black athlete in Boston to exist well. The players who could do this would have fewer problems in Boston and were not apt to view the city with such permanent disdain."*[419]

As young as he was – age 22 – when he first encountered the mostly white-dominated city of Boston and its beloved team, the Red Sox, George Scott adroitly navigated the city and its racist vicissitudes relying on his savvy gained from living in the Deep South, managing to avoid the effects of the city's racist shortcomings whereas several of his black teammates could not find it in them to emulate Scott, such as Reggie Smith, who was from California and who became greatly distressed, and intolerant, of what was going on there with both the city and the team, and didn't hesitate to share his feelings with them head-on, without restraint. This, of course, led to further trouble for him from his lack of endearment toward the city, he is

---

[418] Howard Bryant, "Shut Out," p. 86
[419] IBID

perceived as a maverick and a black one at that. As Whiteside penned about Smith's teammate Scott, *"As a Southerner, Scott handled Boston better than most black athletes."*[420] Explaining the challenges he met with finding apartments in the Boston suburbs and the redlining that was going on there with local real estate, George emphasized the importance of being resilient in perfect Southern fashion, if merely to display a certain level of tolerance, which was a trait he had learned in the Delta when confronted by whites. *"I'd been born and raised in the South, and I'd had tough times before,"* said Scott. *"But I also realized that to get anything, you had to run into the right kind of person who would accept you regardless of the color of your skin."*[421]

The Boston suburbs proved difficult for Boston's black professional athletes to find suitable residential real estate opportunities – where there was realty red-lining in force - or find neighborhoods that appealed to them and where they would be accepted because of a pervasive racist element that had settled into Boston's surrounding towns and cities, partly due to the Irish factor many of whom had left the big city for the suburbs because of the influx of blacks and the soon-to-be anticipated desegregation enforcement and looming busing laws. The conflict materialized as the "burbs," in a burgeoning "whites" growth pattern, along with an expanding Irish component, began to take on a new look and, with that look, a resistive

---

[420] Larry Whiteside, "Sox Children of the '60s Look Back," Boston Sunday Globe, July 29, 1979, p. 80
[421] IBID

persona to the social discord from which they had fled. *"[White] neighborhoods commonly swelled with a localist pride that made their residents highly conscious of turf...pockets of ethnicity, class, and the like. These small worlds often reacted with instinctive hostility to any outsiders,"* wrote Professor Formisano. They carried with them an ethnicity-awareness, said Formisano, an "ideological ethnicity," leading to an intolerance toward desegregation. *"The ethnics of the 'urban villages' of the North often felt most vulnerable to blacks in the latter's efforts to break out of the ghetto, and for the urban ethnics, theirs was foremost a vulnerability of place. It was their schools and their blocks into which blacks would be coming."*[422]

Professor Formisano posited that the uniqueness of what had transpired in the latter part of the nineteenth century was foundational for the city of Boston and its suburbs, even so much as affecting racial bias and the imbalance between Boston and the suburbs. *"In the long view, the answer runs back partly to the halting of Boston's annexation of the near suburbs in the 1870s, a pivotal event that brought Boston into the mid-twentieth century as one of the smallest cities in the nation in relation to its metropolitan area. This legacy, together with the nation's exemption of suburbs from participating in solutions to racial problems (culminating in Milliken v. Bradley), made any school desegregation plan applied only to Boston highly biased in terms of class,"* wrote Formisano.[423]

---

[422] Ronald Formisano, Boston Against Busing, p. 7.
[423] IBID, p. 225-226

With the influx of a black population after World War II, there became an expanding ghetto in the city, while, simultaneously, *"whites migrated to the suburbs so that by 1970 Boston's population of some 600,000 was ringed by a 'suburban noose' consisting of over a million and a half persons, more than 98 percent white in racial composition....Jobs, as well as population, flowed out to the suburbs...the central city population, but especially the public school constituency, was in general less affluent than the suburban, in part because of the extensive Catholic parochial school system, which also tended to siphon off families with greater resources or higher aspirations and concern for the quality of education."*[424]

There were several voices in and around Boston who took umbrage with what they called "suburban liberals" who were found living in their "safe sanctuaries" outside Boston, who took to criticizing Bostonians they called 'racists' and 'bigots.' Among them was Dick Sinnot, a local Boston journalist, who said: *"And they go home to their Newtons, their Wellesleys, their Marbleheads, their Braintrees – their rinso white communities – where a select few minority kids come out and spend six hours in their schools but are forbidden to live there."*[425]

The gladiator of anti-busing fame, Louise Day Hicks, of staunch Boston Irish influence, stood defiant in her scorn of suburban critics who, as she deemed it complained a great deal about Boston-Irish misconduct and

---

[424] IBID, p. 226-227
[425] IBID, 1974 interview with journalist Dick Sinnot, p. 189-190

racism yet did nothing themselves to assist with the problem – except complain. She viewed them as an *"arrogant gentry who would dictate to Bostonians,"* according to Professor Formisano.[426] Journalist Bill Reynolds, quoting Hicks in her stance against the suburbs, and position on busing, pointed out how Boston schools were being victimized for the failures of the city: *"Boston schools are a scapegoat,"* she said, *"for those who have failed to solve the housing, economic, and social problems of the black citizen. If the suburbs are so interested in solving the problems of the Negro, why don't they build subsidized housing for them?"*[427]

During Governor Francis Sargent's leadership in 1972, *"The suburbs, he never tired of pointing out, refused low-cost housing for the poor and erected barriers against blacks becoming their neighbors while insisting that Bostonians bus their children into black neighborhoods."*[428]

Outlying suburban towns of Somerville and Winchester, which were confronted with the busing question and parity of whites and blacks, took up Boston-style protesting and the dissemination of racist slogans throughout their towns. Winchester – *"where, it is said, affluent Irishmen go between retirement and death"* – put up stiff resistance, which *"only reinforced the Boston antibusers' notion that they were being picked on and their belief that the desire to avoid blacks was widespread in all sectors of*

---

[426] IBID, p. 56
[427] Bill Reynolds, "'78: The Boston Red Sox," p. 65
[428] Formisano, "Boston Against Busing," p. 56

white society. Militants sometimes told reporters: 'Sure we're racists – isn't everybody?'" Conceivably, a mea culpa statement embodying the Boston problem and what was confronting Boston's pro athletes en masse.[429]

It wasn't just about race in Boston during the turmoil, however, but also social class, which had deep roots wafting back to the Brahmin class of the nineteenth century that held deep resentment for the Irish, but also the conflict between blacks and the white Boston Irish, both of whom were surfacing socially and, with mixed success, politically, seeking status in the city. *"As early as the mid-1850s, blacks and the Irish were fighting for a foothold in society's pecking order. A century and a quarter later, the same two groups, still poor, would fight each other over school integration,"* stated Howard Bryant.[430]

Amidst this unrest intertwined in a city ringed with high tension and soon-to-be desegregation initiatives compounding that, young George Scott, about to turn 22, made his spring training debut in Winter Haven with the Red Sox, having been promoted to the major league club after his '65 celebratory performance in Pittsfield. He was eager to prove himself in the face of a heretofore racially troubled team. It wouldn't be easy with an old-school style manager like William Jennings Bryan "Billy" Herman, who played during baseball's heyday of the '30s and 40s fraught with visceral bench jockeys and on-field rabble-rousers mixed with remnants of early 20th

---

[429] IBID, p. 179
[430] Howard Bryant, "Shut Out," p. 17

century cranks, fiends, and rooters. There was nothing sacred at that time; anything went, including an intense and unwavering repudiation of black ballplayers. It would have been no surprise for Herman to favor the old theme of black rejection being a product of an early era, but it was not evident in his seven years with the Red Sox, coaching between 1960-1964 and managing them from 1964-1966; he was, however, glaringly impatient with young ballplayers and that was especially true of Rico Petrocelli, for whom sportswriter Al Hirshberg described Herman's aversion toward the young shortstop as "almost pathological." Americo (Rico) Petrocelli was one of only two kids on the 1965 team, the other being Tony Conigliaro, both who had star potential, but Rico, the Brooklyn kid, was insecure, and Herman feasted on him. Described by Peter Golenbock, who was a featured baseball writer in his epic book *Red Sox Nation*, Rico was a *"sensitive, skittish rookie…insecure and needed continual assurance that he had the talent to stay on the team*," though he hit 40 home runs one year, and was in the running for MVP in the course of three years.[431]

Tony Conigliaro, a Boston-based kid and a mere 20 years of age, who, according to George Scott, was a close friend both having played on the Wellsville, NY team, was a superstar in the making before a tragic baseball beaning accident and resultant injury took him down in 1967; he was of the new generational breed of rebellious youth that sprung from the protest era of the Vietnam War of the 1960s; he was also volatile by nature, an

---

[431] Peter Golenbock, "Red Sox Nation," p. 277

anathema to the older set of baseball men, like Herman and Dick Williams, the latter who played on the 1964 team. *"His [Conigliaro's] ability and temper continued to march hand-in-hand,"* said Golenbock.[432]

He disapproved of the way rookies were being handled by veterans, treating them with aloofness, like Herman, Dick Stuart and Dick Williams. Conigliaro wasted little time in confronting bit-player Williams, who had called him "bush," harkening back to his bench-jockeying days because of a near-miss line drive hit by the rookie. Conigliaro, angered at Williams' insult and aiming to confront him, the next day tossed a ball at Williams' head, blatantly returning the insult of "bush" to Williams that enraged the veteran and no doubt set the tone for their tempestuous relationship later on. Had it not been for the commanding presence of Dick Stuart standing between them, who intercepted the charging Williams, the outcome could have been baneful for both and, though news-worthy, not the kind of news beneficial to the team. The incident, in the long run, may have been insignificant, but it personified what to expect once Dick Williams became a Red Sox field boss - particularly for George Scott - which occurred at the end of 1966, relieving Billy Herman of a shabby managerial performance, losing 182 games in three seasons. Herman and some of his veterans, including, of significance, future Red Sox manager, virulent bench jockey and quick-tempered tough guy Dick Williams, did not take well to the impudence of the young ballplayers, whom they felt lacked such a privilege

---

[432] IBID, p. 275

of "voice" or opinion until they proved themselves. This applied even more so to Boston athletes like the Celtics' Bill Russell and prominent athletes from other major league cities. *"In Boston, as well as most other sports towns, the concept of black assertiveness was not particularly welcome, much of it for the basic reason that most sports fans take a certain ownership over the local athlete,"* according to Howard Bryant.[433]

It was springtime in Winter Haven and warm weather was beginning to settle into the area, and northern snowbirds were beginning to stir for some major league baseball along with expectations of seeing new talent. Scotty's firsthand experience with major league level baseball was dealing with Mike "Pinky" Higgins' personal friend and manager, Billy Herman, a future Hall of Famer in his own right – into his eighth season overall with Boston – along with his indifference and laissez-faire approach to the game, a usual game "plan" theretofore, but which was quite the opposite of a high-energized and youth-favorite, Eddie Popowski. Scott was introduced to the club and facility, where it was explained to him the accepted protocol for uniforms, bats and balls, calisthenic scheduling, fielding and hitting practice, and where he would be assigned in the locker room next to other black players.

He stared for a moment, heart skipped a beat, overwhelmed in a startled manner by the reality of being where he found himself, where he stood, in

---

[433] Howard Bryant, "Shut Out," p. 82

an actual major league spring camp, and then sensibility returned, reaching across the aisle into the locker opposite from him, the one he was assigned, next to Joe Foy and some other black players – which was a Red Sox protocol - he picked up the shoebox that held the new cleats he was about to wear; it displayed his name, George Scott, inscribed next to the supplier's name, John T Riddell, manufacturer of Finer Athletic Equipment. They were nothing like he had imagined, or at least so he thought, as he was on a definite high. Oh, he might have had similar spikes he had been issued coming up through the minors, but they were not of the same caliber, he convinced himself, even though the clubs resorted to using the same quality of equipment. These were the majors, the Red Sox parent club, nothing but class, he thought, and somehow, they took on a much different meaning than before; a feeling of high esteem. He had finally made it. Damn, but they were nice, he thought, shiny black patina and a fresh smell of leather reminiscent of harnesses and saddle ware, recalling his experiences with some of the local towns' constabulary scrutinizing them as they rode on horseback through the black districts exploring the opportunity or, more like an excuse, to take remedial action if they perceived black kids were not following white rules. He began to handle the new cleats, coddling them as if they were fine jewelry. He pulled them from the box and slipped them onto his size 12 feet. They fit well, according to the dimensions he gave in advance to the team, so he laced them up and really felt strangely good about himself all of a sudden.

"I wasn't used to having new things being black and living in the Delta where blacks enjoyed no privilege[s]; the white kids received all the town's favors. There was no plain sense to it, but we survived it. In my day, we made do with [well-worn] Army surplus shoes and bought, or in some fashion managed to borrow, laces to keep the shoes together so we could play. It's just the way it was then; we had no money. My momma was poor," exclaimed George. [434]

According to Howard Bryant, the Red Sox had signed George Scott *"as an amateur free agent in 1962, one of just a handful of black players the club had signed in its history. The Red Sox integration began in earnest with the signing of George Scott, who was signed by none other than Ed Scott, who had discovered Henry Aaron eleven years earlier."* [435]

"Scott, like most black players, was well aware of the team's notorious reputation when it came to dealing with blacks, and his early years in the minor leagues were characterized by his heightened sensitivity to slight and the surprising relationship he forged in Winston-Salem with Eddie Popowski, the long-time Red Sox minor-league manager." [436]

"It was 1966, and I was just out of high school, really, a couple of years. I was just a bald-faced rookie with only a slight chance to win a spot with a major league club; can you imagine the Boston Red Sox of all teams? Can

---

[434] George Scott interview: January 18, 2006
[435] Howard Bryant, "A Life of Henry Aaron," p. 433
[436] IBID, p. 434

you believe it? I knew they had a poor history with blacks like me, but it was a chance; I had to take it despite them. I was among a handful of new black players, and some older ones from other teams the Red Sox brought in, being profiled to prove my worth, and perhaps even fail; [there was] strong rumor about that, however, that was to work out [for me]. I knew the Red Sox complained they didn't hire no black players because they couldn't find one of quality, and there was every damn good possibility it would happen again. I knew that was wrong. But I also knew the club was feeling pressure from the colored peoples association and the local black community to make things right in the city and with the club, so I signed with them knowing I had a dang near even chance I could make the team. If I did well enough in spring training, maybe the Boston crowd would stand behind me, I thought, remembering what happened in their city over Pumpsie Green a few years before when the team shamed him after having such a great spring. Even the fans were upset with the team. Honestly, I really didn't feel the fans would accept me as a man, you know, a black man; that wasn't going to happen from what I heard about how they looked upon blacks there. But they might at least favor me as an athlete, and that's all I ever wanted at the time. Dammit, I felt I could handle any slights on my color. I did it at home with no-good racists, the likes of Jim Crow all around me, then I could do it here. No, nobody of a northern racist was going to be any uglier than my experience in the Delta. I heard that Boston people liked their athletes, no matter what color they were, as long as they kept themselves on the playing field and not on their streets or in their suburbs.

They were kind of fickle that way, racist more like it, I suppose. That's what Bill Russell [of the Boston Celtics] told me, and he was right. But I just wanted to make the team, play wherever I could, and do whatever it took to make money enough to get my momma out of poverty. I wanted to build her a house. That was my goal. How she lived and was being treated pained me something awful, like being cut to the quick. I would deal with the city in the best manner I could. I couldn't deal with the manner that she was living."[437]

He talked about his earliest experiences at the beginning of Winter Haven and what he encountered in those first few days, which were not welcoming and, of course, not put into print:

"I was nervous looking around at other fresh new rookies, like me, black and white, and a few veterans, trying to make the club, who were ready to take the field for the first time as major leaguers, and who, I knew, were going to whip my ass if they could. But so wasn't I going to [whip their asses].

I mumbled a 'hello' to one of the white rookies standing next to his locker, who didn't seem interested [in talking]. I was nervous trying to find something to say, just to be friendly, to be cool. I didn't expect much in return, and that's what I got: nothin' more than nothin'. He acted like he knew this team found fault with blacks and he was right pleased about it.

---

[437] George Scott interview: January 2009

He was from Alabama, and that explained it. 'How long do you think they'll keep you, boy?' he said with a snotty look. He grunted and then left for the field. I followed behind him. Seems like that's all we did in our town: follow behind the whites, and now I was doing it again. He didn't amount to nothin' and wasn't in camp very long.

As for the black rookies around there, it seemed odd to see them in Winter Haven competing for jobs, knowing this was a team that's reputation was to show them no favor. I had to wonder if there was any truth to this arrangement or whether it would just be another Jackie Robinson workout by the Red Sox, which I heard was nothin' but a sham: make a good showing but turn their backs when the time was right. That's what I heard anyway, what they did. They led him to believe he had a shot at making the team; they humiliated him. I heard that Sam Jethroe, another black that worked out with them on the same day as Robinson, never got over his resentment. What was funny was that Jethroe went across town to the Braves, the other major league team in town, and they could see their way of accepting him. Explained a lot what I was dealing with there in Boston."[438]

---

[438] IBID

On the big league roster. Rookie George Scott looks over the bats he'd use against American League pitchers (courtesy of Boston Herald)

Without Higgins, who had been the omnipresent anchor around their necks, Dick O'Connell, without restraints and with an opportunity to alter the character of a team once held hostage by a man who preferred the status quo, began his youth movement, including the assimilation of black ballplayers promoted from their farm system, and through trade. One had to wonder what Higgins, the consummate racist who kept the team under his thumb for the better part of ten years, had on his mind during this Red Sox reorganization effort that suddenly and dramatically included an influx of blacks that was directly opposite his professed beliefs. Similarly, the fan base also had to wonder how his friend, Tom Yawkey, with whom they shared an affinity, was managing these untoward events that seemed less than normal business transactions amounting to previously being relieved of his field duties for performance, rehired in 1960, and, in 1962 being elevated by Yawkey to a dual role of field manager and general manager. It seemed farcical that Higgins was to be promoted to such a prominent role when more likely he should have been relieved of all duties. *Boston Globe* sports journalist Harold Kaese, reacting to the puzzling move made by Yawkey, wrote a satirical piece in which he questioned: *"Do the Red Sox know what they are doing?"* Furthering his sardonic message, he said, *"Rehiring Mike Higgins to manage the Red Sox, after what amounted to a 49-week leave of absence, was a good move. Now the Red Sox can finish in the second division, and everyone can be comfortable – except possibly a few unreasonable fans who take winning seriously. Red Sox players are generally delighted. In his previous 4 ½ years as their manager, they found him good-natured, solid, unexcitable, solid, methodical, solid, and easy to lose for.*"[439] Higgins was close to Yawkey, who once said, *"toughest thing I've ever done"* was to fire Higgins.

Once again, in October 1962, at the conclusion of the baseball season, for a second time, Higgins was relieved of his field manager role, which had been nothing to marvel about, but this time, he was inexplicably promoted to full-time general manager of the Red Sox with Johnny Pesky appointed as field manager for the '63 season. Yawkey, who favored cronyism and keeping his friends "happy," explained, *"This is a natural follow-up to the organizational change announced today. Mike will be given a free hand in making trades as outlined the other day."*[440]

Pesky's performance was underwhelming for the next two seasons, and he had lost the respect of his players, which had everything to do with Higgins, who was not supportive, a big first baseman and quick wit Dick Stuart, and eventually their future Hall of Famer Carl Yastrzemski who didn't like some of the field changes Pesky was making. Higgins embarrassed Pesky, a Boston legend, with two games to go in the season by replacing him with Billy Herman, a close friend of Higgins' whose main interest was golf, and that was the conversation he preferred with his players and the media, and who promptly managed to lose a woeful 100 games in

---

[439] Harold Kaese, "Sox Save Money by Naming Higgins; Only Fans Unhappy," Boston Globe, June 13, 1960 p. 23
[440] Jack Barry, "Sox Sign Higgins 3 Years," Boston Globe, Sep 30, 1960, p. 29 https://www.newspapers.com/image/433797782/

1965. Attendance, at an implausible low - the club's lowest since 1945 - forced the attention of Yawkey who was confronted with hard decisions he was not comfortable with nor did he appreciate making. On September 16, Tom Yawkey reluctantly took steps to fire his good friend and drinking pal, Mike Pinky Higgins, which was astonishingly done during a no-hit game being pitched by the team's Dave Morehead. The timing could have been far better for a victorious Morehead as Higgins' firing was a significant distraction receiving major attention, stealing the headlines from Morehead. It was a mutual agreement; Higgins approached the Red Sox owner asserting that he was not popular in Boston and he would be better off with a new GM; Yawkey took the bait, *"and got tangled up with Dave Morehead's no-hitter. It's been that kind of year for the Red Sox all around,"* wrote Will McDonough.[441]

"Mr. Yawkey is very sad and upset [about Higgins' firing]," said Vice President Dick O'Connell. *"Mike was a very close and dear friend [of Higgins]. It hurt Mr. Yawkey deeply to make the decision." "One thing is certain,"* said McDonough, *"Mr. Yawkey [really] didn't want to fire Higgins."*[442]

This backdrop of Red Sox turbulence under Higgins and their cultivation of racism slowed dramatically with Higgins' firing in '65 - who,

---

[441] Will McDonough, "Sox Brass Undecided on Higgins' Successor," Boston Globe, Sep 18, 1965, p. 5
[442] IBID

ironically, was released by his drinking pal, Tom Yawkey, because he was "unable to control his drinking" - opening the portal for the new man, Dick O'Connell, to walk through without restraint and develop a team, including access to black players, that was long overdue. Boston's fan base had lost their patience with Red Sox management, glaringly with Higgins, whose decision to dismiss Pumpsie Green still festered, and to a lesser extent with Yawkey, who seemed ambivalent about his team. *"It received little attention then,"* remarked Howard Bryant, alluding to a Boston press that was all too familiar with the status quo, *"but it would soon become a decision of major impact, the best move the Red Sox made in a generation."*[443]

The table was set for their new general manager and Vice President, Dick O'Connell, the consummate professional and a determined competitor and the first non-player of Yawkey's regime to assume a major role. He had already been working behind the scenes with the Sox' minor league director of player personnel, Neil Mahoney, to rebuild the team before he was to realize he was about to ascend into higher places in the organization and in a position to make those unfettered decisions. He took immediate action favoring youth; included in that initiative was a sizable effort to infuse black talent onto the team from their farm system and through trade. Joe Foy, a black player coming off an MVP season at Triple-A Toronto and *The Sporting News' minor league player of the year*, was high on the recruitment

---

[443] Howard Bryant, "Shut Out," p. 64

list for replacing veteran third baseman Frank Malzone, who had been released by the team that November. Of even greater importance, O'Connell called up two rookies who would make an impact in major league baseball: Reggie Smith, a seven-time All-Star, Gold Glover, with a lifetime .287 batting average and 314 home runs among his credits; and, then there was the "Boomer," George Scott, the tag "Boomer" having been assigned to him early in his career by his friend and teammate Joe Foy because of his colossal and resounding home run blasts, who assembled a major league lifetime record of 271 home runs, eight Gold Gloves, and was a three-time All-Star. Newspaper columnist and author Leigh Montville described him as *"the Red Sox first certified African-American star"* in his 2013 obituary commemoration of the former baseball star.[444]

Future Hall of Famer and teammate Carl Yastrzemski paid homage to Scott, as noted in sports journalist Nick Cafardo's book *Boston Red Sox: Yesterday and Today*, with the comment, *"In my 23 years in baseball, I have never seen a better defensive player. I have never seen a player with the instincts of Scotty."* Having come from a man who spent so many years in the company of outstanding ballplayers and who was a seven-time Gold Glover himself, it was the ultimate tribute.[445]

---

[444] Leigh Montville, "Remembering Baseball's George Scott," July 30, 2013 https://www.wbur.org/onlyagame/2013/07/30/george-scott-mlb-obit
[445] Nick Cafardo, "Boston Red Sox: Yesterday and Today," (Akron: West Side Publishing, 2007)

O'Connell avowed that *"I don't care what color a player is as long as he can play...if he is any good, I want to sign him."*[446] Living up to his word, he signed several more black players, utility players whom he signed in 1965, including Lenny Green, George Smith and Joe Christopher. The latter two players were traded for by O'Connell, along with a solid fast-throwing right-handed pitcher - a Latino - Jose Santiago, who O'Connell purchased in October 1965 from the Kansas City Athletics. Santiago would play an important role in the 1967 American League Champion *Impossible Dream* Red Sox; it turned out to be a savvy move by O'Connell. In June 1966, he acquired reliever John Wyatt and lightning-speed versatile all-around player Jose Tartabull, both from Kansas City, who also played a significant role on the '67 team. The Red Sox team, beginning in 1966, consisted of the largest assemblage of blacks in their history, compliments of one Dick O'Connell. As baseball historian Glenn Stout put it, *"While those [promissory] words had long been mouthed by Boston's front office, O'Connell meant it and backed it up with action."*[447]

---

[446] Glenn Stout and Richard Johnson, "Red Sox Century," p. 312-313
[447] IBID, p. 313

Instructions on hitting from one of baseball's all-time best. George Scott, the student, and Ted Williams, about to be inducted into the National Baseball Hall of Fame (courtesy of Boston Public Library)

Spring 1966, Winter Haven – George Scott hustles to first as Tommy McCraw of the White Sox takes the throw (courtesy of Boston Red Sox)

And, of course, until June of that year, there was Earl Wilson, had it not been for the controversial trade of the veteran pitcher to Detroit, who

O'Connell later profoundly regretted having traded, feeling it was a definite mistake – his error of being swayed, when he had promised himself there would be no racial bias on his team - in spite of the pressure he had received about dumping him over the Cloud Nine matter, which will be discussed. It turned out that 30-year-old outfielder Don Demeter, a mediocre player whom the Sox picked up in the trade and who was at the end of his career, was not looking forward to his new surroundings, and it soon began to show. *The Boston Globe's* Clif Keane, who interviewed Demeter prior to his arrival in Boston, titled his article about the man who was key to replacing Earl Wilson: *"Demeter Doesn't Rate Fenway as Favorite Park for Hitting,"* and made other disparaging remarks and slights about the situation, displaying little affinity for Boston and hardly endearing himself to the team or the Boston fans.[448] *"That trade will win the pennant for Detroit,"* exclaimed Jose Santiago, notably a critic of the transaction. And that's precisely what happened in 1968 when Detroit won it all.[449]

Wilson, it turned out, went on to win 64 games for the Tigers in five seasons, including 22 wins in 1967, and made an appearance in Detroit's triumphant 1968 World Series. Demeter was largely a non-contributor; he only played portions of two years with Boston, with a mere 224 plate appearances and a meager 7 home runs, which was expected to be his forte,

---

[448] Clif Keane, "Demeter Doesn't Rate Fenway As Favorite Park for Hitting," Boston Globe, June 17, 1966, p. 50
[449] Ray Fitzgerald, "Four New Red Sox To Make Debuts Tonight," The Boston Globe, June 15, 1966, p. 63
https://www.newspapers.com/image/433833157/?terms=Joe%20Christopher

and left for Cleveland – his last year in baseball – during the Red Sox' '67 championship season. It turned out to be a bit of an embarrassment for the team and for O'Connell when Demeter was projected to be part of the so-called "power alley." Future Hall of Famer Brooks Robinson of the Orioles and his teammates playfully shared some opinions prior to a Baltimore-Red Sox game mocking the *"Wilson-Don Demeter deal."* Robinson, however, in a moment of seriousness, said, *"At the time, I thought it was a good trade…I figured the Red Sox were getting a player who would hit 30 to 35 homers for them because I thought Demeter would be out there every day."*[450]

The writing was on the wall. On June 4, Demeter, along with error-prone Tony Horton, a Yawkey favorite, was traded to Cleveland for pitcher Gary Bell. The Wilson trade was taking on the appearance of a travesty for the Red Sox, with Wilson winning ballgames for Detroit as a starter and looking every bit the power pitcher while Demeter was fading fast. Even the Boston press was taking notice of the paradox of these events and, occasionally, raising the troubled specter of what might have happened in Boston had Earl Wilson not been black. Adding to this, there was even some irony playing a part in this unusual story, for in 1967, Demeter – who was a member of the Red Sox by virtue of the '66 trade with the Tigers – in short order left Boston in the trade with the Cleveland Indians; two months later at the end

---

[450] Ray Fitzgerald, "Slumping Scott Fans Self Out of Job," The Boston Globe, May 27, 1967, p. 5
https://www.newspapers.com/image/433999498/?terms=don%20demeter&match=1

of August Detroit then struck a deal with Cleveland, recalling Demeter, by *"shoring up their bench for the American League stretch drive,"* by adding Demeter again to their roster – the same Detroit roster that Earl Wilson now occupied.[451] However, by a quirk of fate, Demeter never made it back to the Tigers, or even major league baseball, as there was discovered *"a disturbance in his coronary artery,"* and the deal was off.[452]

Upon the Red Sox' trade of Demeter to Cleveland for Gary Bell, *The Boston Globe's* sports reporter Harold Kaese went into satiric mode with the comment, *"Thus, it took the Sox a [whole] year to replace Earl Wilson and cost them also, Demeter, Horton and Joe Christopher."*[453]

---

[451] Unattributed, "Demeter Joins Tigers' Bench," United Press International, The Boston Globe, Sep 1, 1967 p. 22
https://www.newspapers.com/image/433884650/?terms=earl%20Wilson%20don%20demeter&match=1

[452] Unattributed, "Demeter Trade to Tigers Off," Associated Press, The Boston Globe, Sep 6, 1967, p. 30
https://www.newspapers.com/image/433921014/?terms=don%20demeter&match=1

[453] Harold Kaese, "Williams Frank In All Dealings," The Boston Globe, June 5, 1967, p. 23
https://www.newspapers.com/image/433985173/?terms=don%20demeter&match=1

Chapter 9
Post Jackie Robinson – Baseball's Non-acceptance

There were other problems that us blacks and Earl [Wilson] had to deal with with the Red Sox. They [the team] had barbecues and family functions, and only the white players and their wives were invited. Earl Wilson was not going to accept this, and he challenged the team management. He knew he was through, but he stood up to them anyway.

George Scott[454]

The task before O'Connell, and for the emerging contingency of new black players in their organization, was made more difficult when the Red Sox decided to make a change in their spring training venue, moving from an acquiescent more liberal Scottsdale, Arizona that was more accepting of blacks and other minorities – but, even there it was not until 1953, a year before the U. S. Supreme Court's *Brown* decision, when the Arizona Superior Court declared school segregation unconstitutional, that racial tolerance gained some ground, with fewer constraints - to a deeply racist Winter Haven, Florida. In short order, there were problems. The Red Sox 1965 MVP, as voted by the Boston chapter of the Baseball Writers' Association, and 1965 American League Earned Runs co-leader, Earl Wilson, was refused service at the Cloud Nine, a Winter Haven lounge-bar.

---

[454] George Scott interview: May 20, 2006

In fact, to complicate the situation by heaping further insult and frustration on Wilson, he was refused service a second time that same night at another Winter Haven bar. He was 31 and a solid pitcher, also a senior member of the Red Sox – known, respectfully, by his teammates as "The King" - having pitched a no-hitter in 1962, and deserved better than this. Earl was the second black to make the Red Sox major league roster in 1959, only a few short weeks after Pumpsie Green, Wilson's arrival having been delayed because of his military service obligations in 1957-1958. He had signed with the Red Sox (May 11, 1953) before Green (February 8, 1956) and was only their second black to actually sign with the team, following Piper Davis; Davis signed with the Sox in 1949, but because of unscrupulous measures inculcated by the Red Sox interrupting Piper's baseball career, never made the major league roster, though he was well qualified.

O'Connell was frustrated about the incident and, being a new and inexperienced general manager gave the appearance he had more concerns with its impact on the club and his own plans than with Wilson. In fact, he tried to make light of it, injecting humor as a ploy to create a distraction or even to dismiss the matter, though he was not of the personality type to pull off a joke such as that, remarking that the bartender who refused Wilson service was ironically from Massachusetts, but it was done in poor taste and fell flat. Although not clear, the message was that the Red Sox upper brass, which likely included O'Connell, issued a "silence" order, which manager Billy Herman followed with perfect assiduity by informing Wilson to "forget the incident." Supposedly, Mike Higgins had a say in the matter, according to Wilson in later years, though Higgins had been fired as general manager in September 1965, unless possibly he was hanging around for a while after his dismissal from the team where he was close to Tom Yawkey, though that, too, was unlikely, as Higgins had signed on as a scout with the Houston Astros in October 1965. *"When it happened, I was told by Pinky Higgins not to create any bad feelings. In other words, don't say a thing. That, of course, is not in my makeup,"* said Wilson, whose personal disapproval of Higgins was so intense that nothing could convince him otherwise – thirteen years from the incident – that anyone other than Higgins was likely to have made such a disparaging remark.[455] The culprit who did confront him, however, at that time was manager Billy Herman, who, it was well publicized, was assiduously following the company line in delivering the wretched news. He insulted Wilson and told him to inform the meddling press that "it never happened" and to just forget about it.

Wilson harbored deep resentment for Higgins, who took management's lead in 1959 to quash his and Pumpsie Green's ambitions with the parent Red Sox. But it wasn't limited to just Pinky Higgins, but also the team wrote Howard Bryant: *"He was humiliated from the start. A Boston scouting report on Wilson leaked out that was not only crushing to Wilson but also revealed the bigoted train of thought that ran through the organization. It referred to Wilson as a 'well-mannered colored boy. Not too black. Handles*

---

[455] Larry Whiteside, "Sox Children of the '60s Look Back," The Boston Globe, Jul 29 1979, p. 80

himself as a gentleman.'"[456] In fact, there was more to that report according to Peter Golenbock: the scout, who was Tom Downey, added that Wilson was *"pleasant to talk to...[made a] very good appearance,"* and instead of the word Bryant used, which was *"handles"* himself as a gentleman, according to Golenbock the word[s] the scout allegedly, actually used was *"conducts"* himself as a gentleman, which carried more of a behavioral tone, or behaving in a controlled manner, expected of blacks of the South, terms that were commonly used in the plantation days.[457]

When manager Billy Jurges, who was never a good fit, suddenly resigned after making inflammatory remarks to the media about Red Sox management – or, more likely, he was fired – leaving the team in June 1960, Yawkey immediately reinstated his buddy Mike Higgins as manager, for a second time, a mere 49 weeks following his first firing. Higgins dispatched Wilson back to the minors for the 1961 season, reinforcing a climate of repudiation for black players as long as Mike Higgins was at the helm as field manager. But once again, there was unrest on the Red Sox; Higgins, in his "quest" for more of the same - status quo, led the team to mediocrity for which he was accustomed with two losing seasons, finishing 6th and 8th, and he was steadily losing favor with the Red Sox fans, who were vocal about him, remembering Pumpsie Green, with attendance dropping. Meanwhile, Earl Wilson, who had been in Higgins' doghouse in Triple-A

---

[456] Howard Bryant, "Shut Out," p. 77
[457] Peter Golenbock, "Red Sox Nation," p. 225

Seattle, purportedly due to "wildness," was recalled in 1962 and shortly demonstrated his competence on June 26, pitching a solid no-hit game – the first American League no-hitter by a black pitcher - with a home run of his own in the 2-0 contest, convincing Fenway's fans that, maybe for a change at last, they had a certain winner here; and maybe the racial element would be put to rest.

Wilson had the tools but labored for several years in the minor leagues.

"It never bothered me what people said in the stands in Boston," said Wilson. *"What I heard in the South was so much worse. I just wonder why it took me so long (six years) to get there. I was ready long before that."* [458]

"Team owners trembled when players upset the prevalent traditions in the southern towns during spring training," wrote author Peter Golenbock. *"Going up against Jim Crow brings negative publicity to the team since the local white supremacists tend to blame the club, not the traditions of inequality, for the bad publicity."* [459]

"Black players were accepted as players [only]," said Wilson, which George Scott would also claim in his later years when talking about the favoritism shown by Tom Yawkey to the white players, especially Carl Yastrzemski. *"But management,"* said Wilson, *"didn't want guys who*

---

[458] IBID
[459] Peter Golenbock, "Red Sox Nation," p. 229

created waves. No team had more than one or two of us [blacks] in those days, anyway."[460]

He followed the company line initially, which was management's request of him that he remain silent but his anger eventually got the best of him. *Boston Herald* sportswriter Larry Claflin, who later on would be implicated in a racist event of his own involving George Scott, nudged Wilson about the Cloud Nine story but was told by Wilson, consistent with his orders by management, to remain silent. It eventually leaked out anyway, and upon being confronted by other sportswriters, Wilson, knowing he would be "cooked" by the team but feeling degraded, blurted out the story.

Another reporter who picked up on the story laid the blame at the feet of Wilson, inexplicably ignoring the racial bias element but emphasizing that in addition to Wilson, Red Sox pitchers Dave Morehead and Dennis Bennett had gone to the bar with the intent of carousing, which should have been off limits, so said the reporter, never mentioning the racial matter. Manager Billy Herman picked up on the theme with his own comments that remained consistent with the Red Sox propaganda. *"There have been some pretty good ballplayers who have been drinkers,"* said Herman, which was his lame and strikingly accusatory response to the matter, adding fuel to the fire.[461] On June 13, Boston acquired two new black players, John Wyatt and

---

[460] Larry Whiteside, "Sox Children of the '60s," p. 80
[461] Peter Golenbock, "Red Sox Nation," p. 230

333

Jose Tartabull. Wilson, who roomed with Lenny Green, also a black player, and Green amused themselves by joking that there were too many black players on the club and someone had to be traded. It didn't take long that someone turned out to be Earl Wilson who received a call from manager Herman the next morning announcing he had indeed been traded, which was to Detroit for Don Demeter.

"Wilson added that he may have sounded very militant at the time, but he was not standing up for a cause but merely for himself... 'we didn't live with the white ball players in Arizona, but we didn't have any problems in the town (Scottsdale). I was told by the Red Sox the same was true in Winter Haven. I only had to live there three or four days to find out differently.'"
[462]

Reggie Smith was another matter at another level of fervency. He was baseball's counterpart to basketball's Bill Russell, in some ways a replication of Boston's great center, both of whom were from California, and both who were intense, explosive and cocky, which never set well in Boston, especially if you were black; it seemed befitting of anger they both steadily mounted against the debauched city's Irish, whom they rigorously complained about, was a match for Boston's version of the "galoots," who are described scornfully in the famous screen drama, *The Last Angry Man*. "Outside of Bill Russell, no black player would endure a more pronounced

---

[462] Larry Whiteside, "Sox Children of the '60s," p. 80

conflict with Boston than Reggie Smith," wrote Howard Bryant. *"Smith would smolder about Boston, a city that for him represented the worst of class and racial struggles."*[463]

Black sports reporter and award-winning journalist Lawrence "Larry" Whiteside, whose sports reporting career, at age 21, began in Iowa in 1959 writing part-time for the *Des Moines Register* and the *Tribune* while a student at Drake University, became a full-time sports writer with the *Kansas City Kansan* that same year. He later moved to Milwaukee – where George Scott would find contrasts in the Milwaukee town of both fulfillment and affliction – covering the Braves baseball team and outsized Civil Rights issues for *The Milwaukee Journal* in 1968; in 1973, he moved to Boston to confront more racist challenges there, including busing, with both the city and their major league team the Red Sox, as the only countrywide black journalist covering major league baseball for a major daily newspaper, *The Boston Globe*. A scholar of the Negro Leagues, he would become a factor in reporting on black athletes, including George Scott, who played for both the Red Sox and Milwaukee Brewers teams, shadowing each other's careers starting with Scott's arrival in Milwaukee in 1971.

"Earl Wilson, Pumpsie Green, Joe Foy. They were black ballplayers who came along in a time of change and turmoil. The '60s were hard times

---

[463] Howard Bryant, "Shut Out," p. 88.

for black athletes, particularly in Boston, where the word 'Negro' was still a novelty," wrote Whiteside in his epic 1979 treatise of a *Globe* series on the black athlete in Boston.[464]

The matter of racial non-acceptance in baseball and other sports, and the proclivity for that, remained an issue long after the baseball color line was overcome in 1947 with the signing of Jackie Robinson. In spite of the historic *Brown* decision of 1954 and *Brown II* in the following year, there was an implacable resistance to change despite Jackie Robinson's and Branch Rickey's triumph of '47, and it shook them both to the core, for society, especially in the South, but also in the North, was intransigent; and, this is what Reggie Smith, Earl Wilson, George Scott, and other black ballplayers were feeling but expressed about it in different ways and various levels of intensity.

Reflecting on the origins of this phenomenon we have come to know as *non-acceptance*, post-Jackie Robinson, we see a Branch Rickey in 1947, after Robinson had played his first full season in major league baseball with the Brooklyn Dodgers, dealing with a troublesome matter in the South that left him feeling bereft and broken. In November of that year, as baseball writer and successful author Lee Lowenfish explained in his award-winning book *Branch Rickey: Baseball's Ferocious Gentleman*, *"Rickey provided another example of his genuine concern about racial fairness when he tried*

---

[464] Larry Whiteside, "'Sox Children of the '60s," p. 80

to mediate a dispute between his alma mater Ohio Wesleyan University, and Rollins College in Orlando, Florida." Ohio Wesleyan had a black player on their football team that Rollins College, whom they were to play the day after Thanksgiving, declined to play as long as their black player, Kenneth Woodward, a star player, would not accompany the team to their Florida campus. Florida's segregation laws were tightly fixed and unforgiving. Rollins decided to cancel the game rather than incite the community.[465]

"Branch Rickey sighed sadly at the outcome. He had tried to bring reason and his sense of fair play to the college controversy, but he realized that only in professional baseball did he have the ability to influence racial change in a progressive manner," yet even that sense of optimism was tainted.[466] In spite of the Supreme Court's *Brown* decision and Jackie Robinson's arrival in 1947, *"gradualism"* would play a large part in baseball for the next forty-five, or more, years, as was evident with Reggie Smith, George Scott, Earl Wilson and several of their black teammates, extending into the late 1980s with Tommy Harper, and George Scott's repudiation in later years by the Red Sox and Major League Baseball when he tried to come back as a coach or instructor, and was repugnantly discarded.

---

[465] Lee Lowenfish, "Branch Rickey: Baseball's Ferocious Gentleman," University of Nebraska, Lincoln, Nebraska, 2007, p. 439-440
[466] IBID

Author Henry D. Fetter, award-winning author, baseball historian, and Independent Scholar, raised questions in a 2011 paper about the impact of Jackie Robinson's 1947 entry into baseball and the breaking of the color barrier, which touched upon the *non-acceptance* theory, saying, *"The broader social significance of Jackie Robinson's breaking major league baseball's color line remains subject to debate...this heroic narrative has, however, met with resistance from those who have questioned the actual impact of 'baseball's great experiment' on American race relations in general."* [467]

Quoting historian Joram Warmund in his and co-writer Joseph Dorinson's 1998 book *Jackie Robinson: Race, Sports, and the American Dream,* Fetter added emphasis to his argument on Robinson's breakthrough and its all-embracing ineffectiveness in broad-based race relations: *"baseball supposedly was one of the great definers and influencers of American values. Yet, it did not have the spillover effect one might have expected; certainly not in the immediate future [...] even if 'baseball' was progressive, its influence was either not that great, or it was of a more subtle and long-range nature."* [468]

---

[467] Henry D. Fetter, "Racial Fault Lines in 'Baseball's Great Experiment:' Black Perceptions, White Reactions," Transatlantica, Open Edition Journals, February, 2011 https://journals.openedition.org/transatlantica/5462

[468] IBID, quoting Joram Warmund & Joseph Dorinson; "Jackie Robinson: Race, Sports and the American Dream," Armonk, N. Y., M. E. Sharpe, 1998, p. 3-12 https://journals.openedition.org/transatlantica/5462

Similarly, American historian and University of Pennsylvania professor Thomas Sugrue possessed doubts about the impact of Robinson's entry into major league baseball. *"But Robinson's breakthrough, however celebrated, was largely symbolic. It would take much more than a handful of black sports heroes to transform race relations in postwar America,"* wrote Sugrue.[469]

Mounting editorializing along with sports historians, researchers and their writings supported the view that Robinson's 1947 entry lacked the positive effect on race relations being pursued, but rather a view that was antithetical to some others who claimed that it did; in effect, for the skeptics, it was a matter of lingering non-acceptance as they saw it; in other words, the color barrier may have been broken, as with Robinson, but not the mindset of racial intolerance. Assembling these assorted viewpoints, Henry Fetter summarized his own thoughts on the subject in this way: *"When it came to racial integration, baseball had arguably moved ahead of the curve of American public opinion—but its meaning for the larger society was not as boldly progressive, or transformative, as it is usually made out to be. The story of "Baseball's Great Experiment" reveals cautious gradualism, ingrained suspicion (among both whites and blacks) and enduring conflict as well as the more celebratory, and more often celebrated, chronicle of*

---

[469] Thomas Sugrue, "Sweet Land of Liberty: The Forgotten Struggle for Civil Rights in the North," Random House Trade Paperbacks, Oct 13, 2009, p. 121

Jackie Robinson's victory for racial justice and the highest values of the American Creed."[470]

Author and historian Thomas Sugrue emphasized the contradictions of race relations after 1947 when Jackie Robinson made his major league debut, and, in some circles, it was felt that racism was finally overcome. Yet, as Sugrue painted the portrait of an unsettled aftermath, it was largely overlooked *"how deeply entrenched racial hostility remained in the North."* The problem then was with the North and white society there, which was to drag on for decades. *"Most players – four out of five by the best estimate – supported integration,"* he remarked, *"but white fans regularly heckled the rookie [Robinson], and in an infamous incident, members of the Philadelphia Phillies catcalled the rookie as 'nigger.'"*[471]

Reggie Smith, who joined the team full-time in 1967, having made a token appearance in '66, regaled in knowing that the Red Sox had a solid club in '67, a championship team that nearly won it all against a powerful St. Louis roster. But there was another side to him that he couldn't accept, such as when he was injured and the team management became intolerant of him. *"They had such great expectations for me. But when I got hurt, nobody wanted to believe me,"* said Smith, having been confronted with the age-old and decades of attitude and accusation, often advanced by the press,

---

[470] Henry D. Fetter, "Racial Fault Lines in 'Baseball's Great Experiment" https://journals.openedition.org/transatlantica/5462
[471] Thomas J. Sugrue, "Sweet Land of Liberty," p. 121

that was common to 20th-century baseball, and that was the allegation of "dogging." White managers and coaches, who held little regard for their black players and were desirous of getting the most from them, even when injured, would often and openly ascribe the defamatory charge to black players whom they felt were "dogging it" – or, in today's parlance, we may think of it as race-based norms, or, in a stretch could be considered a form of "race-norming" - there was no "injury management," such as sports medicine, in effect in those days, except for traditional athletic trainers who were politically tied to the team. *"I know I went out on a limb on a lot of things I said and did,"* said Smith. *"But they were things I believed in and things I still firmly believe in."*[472]

With similarities to what had been happening in baseball for so many years regarding injuries and their treatment, depending on skin color, the National Football League (NFL) was met with comparable complaints years later, though these complaints actually contained "teeth" and had to be dealt with as opposed to what was occurring with black ballplayers of the early to late 20th century, whose grievances about their treatment were readily and summarily dismissed.

A lawsuit was filed in 2020 by two former black NFL players alleging that the NFL "explicitly and deliberately" discriminated against black ex-pro athletes in the qualification process for payouts for head trauma

---

[472] Larry Whiteside, "'Sox Children of the '60s," p. 80

determined to have occurred while playing, diminishing the effect of a black's brain injuries, and labeling it as "Race-Norming." At the risk of mischaracterization, race-norming evolved from the imprecise reasoning that black athletes were assumed to begin their athletic career at a lesser level of cognitive function than white players and, therefore, entitled to less of a so-called payout for concussive brain injuries, such as dementia. It can be argued that the attributes of this demeaning practice are similar in many respects to what was occurring in professional baseball; a similar reasoning applied, that black ballplayers were thought of as cognitively inferior, fundamental to the argument of race-norming, and their stereotypical character – thought of as a so-called "lazy" race, with a lower baseline of cognitive abilities, and unqualified for management roles – required different standards of treatment, so thought white management. There were a handful of white managers and coaches of an earlier era who demonstrated low tolerance of their black players, accusing them of "dogging it" when they were injured, and who distinguished the nature and quality of injuries as having a difference between white and black players.

But the character of the practice has similarities that also fit black baseball players, alleged to have been thought of as cognitively inferior, who were often accused of "dogging," as the term was used, because of injury; it was a common refrain during the early to mid-20th century among older managers and coaches who lived through the era, and who distinguished the nature and quality of injuries between white and black players. Though written in the context of the NFL's alleged practices, it may have a baseball side to it, as well – *"Black Americans are systematically undertreated for pain relative to white Americans,"* according to a study of the *Proceedings of the National Academy of Sciences of the United States of America (PNAS)*, published in 2016.[473] It was an *"Afterlife of Slavery,"* according to authors Tracie Canada and Chelsey R. Carter in their article *The NFL's Racist 'Race Norming' Is an Afterlife of Slavery*. How true that appears to be, and that's a story for a later chapter.[474]

The Red Sox were floundering in 1966 under manager Billy Herman and would finish in 9th place, just barely ahead of the cellar-dweller Yankees. Boston actually had one more loss than New York, but two more wins kept them in 9th. Herman's team lost 100 games in 1965. Nothing to cheer about. Scotty had fallen into a batting slump in the late spring of '66 after an imposing start to his major league career, leaving him frustrated if not confused, and the Boston press, adjusting to a gaggle of black ballplayers never before seen in Boston in these numbers, was doing him no favors. They never had to deal with a talented first-string black ballplayer such as George, and with some, there was an attitude of racial intolerance

---

[473] Researchers Kelly M. Hoffman, Sophie Trawalter, Jordan R. Axt, and M> Norman Oliver, editor Susan T. Fiske of Princeton University, "Racial Bias in Pain Assessment and Treatment Recommendations, and False Beliefs about Biological differences Between Blacks and Whites, PNAS, April 4, 2016.
https://www.pnas.org/doi/abs/10.1073/pnas.1516047113
[474] Tracie Canada and Chelsey R. Carter, "The NFL's Racist 'Race Norming' Is an Afterlife of Slavery," Scientific American, Division of Springer Nature America, Inc., July 8, 2021
https://www.scientificamerican.com/article/the-nfls-racist-race-norming-is-an-afterlife-of-slavery/

that would creep into the picture. Scott had been on a roll from the first day he had made his appearance in a Red Sox uniform at Fenway, clouting a triple off of seasoned Baltimore pitcher Moe Drabowsky on April 12, and showed positive signs of fielding prowess and flash the likes of which Boston fans had not seen before, throwing out the savvy and fleet-footed veteran Luis Aparicio on a bunt attempt clearly showing some savvy of his own. By mid-May, he had hit 10 home runs, and they were all jaw-dropping monster shots, leading some to think they had another Sultan of Swat - as it was being advertised among sports critics and fans - in the making.

George Scott was struck in the ankle by Baltimore's Steve Barber in his first major league game. Scott later hit a triple off Moe Drabowsky, his first major league hit (courtesy of Boston Herald)

On April 25 Boston opened in New York, beating them 8-5, Scott going 3-for-4 nearly hitting for the cycle. The Yankees saved themselves some embarrassment by intentionally walking the young slugger – an unheard-of deferential treatment for a rookie so early in his career – and, astonishingly, they did it again deliberately walking the young slugger the next day; they feared his bat. April 26 was memorable for George – and, for baseball – matched against Yankee southpaw and future Hall of Famer, crafty Whitey Ford. The rookie slugged a colossal wallop off Ford that sailed into the left field upper deck of Yankee Stadium, one of the longest home runs ever hit off of him, exclaimed the reluctant Yankee pitcher, and one of the longest struck at venerable Yankee Stadium, estimated between 500 and 505 feet.

It was a colossal wallop struck with such concussive force that it seemed as if to jolt the partisan Yankee fans, whose collective gaze was riveted on the high-flying missile that appeared headed for outer space.

"That rates in my top three [of longest home runs hit off of me]," said Ford after the game. Scott said the homer was his *"biggest thrill because everyone knows how tough a pitcher he [Ford] is."*[475] *"I'll never forget it,"* exclaimed former teammate Rico Petrocelli, who was walking to the on-deck circle at the time and heard the concussive blow. *"It was the longest home run I've ever seen...when he hit that ball, it was such a loud crack...it seemed like it [would] never come down."*[476] *"That's the home run that*

---

[475] Syndicated article, Valley News, April 27, 1966, p. 9
[476] Rico Petrocelli interview: October 17, 2008.

never was talked about, and it is never talked about today," lamented a latter-day George Scott in his 2006 interview. *"They always come up with other guys [when the longest home run is discussed],"* grumbled the former slugger. *"It would have gone out [of the stadium] if it went more to the right."*[477] There were a few local regional newspapers that covered the "titanic homer," as described by one reporter, but the New York press squelched it as if it was an insult to their celebrated superstar, and that's the way it came off post-game when Ford was attempting to avoid the frantic New York press who were looking for a story just to preserve his dignity, until *New York Times'* esteemed sports journalist and Pulitzer Prize recipient Arthur Daley got ahold of the story some ten weeks later and made it a feature article in his July 7, 1966 column. According to Daley, it was *"territory hitherto explored only by Jimmie Foxx,"* referring to a memorable blast once hit by the future Hall of Famer that landed in approximately the same spot as Scott's blast. To their discredit, the Boston press never saw fit to feature it or otherwise elaborate on the story beyond their usual linear game-day sports reporting, treating it ineffectually.[478]

Had it been Carl Yastrzemski who hit that home run, a personal favorite of owner Tom Yawkey who controversially sought cronyism with the ballplayer, which George Scott had once affirmed about their relationship, the Boston press – more the sycophants than critics - may have approached

---

[477] George Scott interview: January 21, 2006
[478] Arthur Daley, "Great Scott!" Sports of the Times, NY Times, July 7, 1966, p. 58

the story differently. There was a personal alliance between Yaz and Yawkey, which Yawkey promoted, but Yaz was emboldened, according to Scott. Furthermore, he approached blacks and whites differently in the clubhouse, said Scott. According to Yawkey biographer Bill Nowlin, who interviewed several Red Sox ballplayers from those teams, Yawkey's clubhouse visits were impartial, and to the extent he spoke to everyone, it was. Red Sox infielder John Kennedy said, *"I think he got a bad rap from some people who said that when he went in [to the clubhouse], he only talked to Yaz...he might eventually get to Yaz, but he would stop and talk to everybody on the way."*[479] However, according to George, it was the quality of those conversations; there was a distinct favoritism with Yastrzemski, and team strategy was discussed between them, which had the effect of undermining the manager that Dick Williams fiercely resented. Though he would stop briefly for a pat on the back of other players, Yastrzemski was clearly his focus like a father to a son.

Former teammate Joe Lahoud, who was interviewed by baseball historian Peter Golenbock, had this to say about the Yawkey-Yastrzemski alliance: *"The manager was secondary. A lot of that was brought on by Tom Yawkey. Yawkey loved Carl Yastrzemski. He was like his son. He would come down, and they would sit, and Mr. Yawkey would have his arm around him, and Carl would always go up to Yawkey's office. Some of the players*

---

[479] Bill Nowlin, Tom Yawkey, p. 282-283

resented that."[480] Had the Boston scribes caught on to this, as they should have, and some did, as it became more habitual and more of a pattern in the '67 championship year and in later years, they may have come across differently with their criticisms; however, as they were accustomed, when they did speak about the cronyism that appeared to be linked with Yastrzemski, they spoke speciously about it apart from the featured story that it deserved to be. *"He [Yawkey] didn't show the same kind of interest in blacks that he did the white players like Yaz [Yastrzemski] or [Jim] Lonborg, and those types,"* said Scott. *"He fawned over Yaz. He was always around him in the locker room, and it was noticed by the press and the players. Some in the Boston papers reported on it, but the press really didn't make much of it. Reggie [Smith] was upset as only Reggie could be. It was sad as he was such a great player and had a cannon for an arm, but he was traded a few years later; he couldn't take the discrimination. He really didn't like what was going on with the Red Sox, Yawkey or the city."*[481]

When Dick Williams was let go by Tom Yawkey in September of 1969, Williams' wife Norma was critical, complaining that it was the Sox' superstar Yastrzemski who created this debacle, which is the way she saw it and could see little that was praiseworthy of Mr. Yawkey either. Speaking to a Salem, Massachusetts news reporter, which was later reported in the *Boston Globe*, *"without any display of ill will,"* according to the reporter,

---

[480] Peter Golenbock, Red Sox Nation, p. 336
[481] George Scott interview: Feb 14, 2008

she blamed a lingering *"country club atmosphere"* that cost her husband his job and pointed the finger directly at Yaz, who was part of the so-called country club, when it was a country club, of the early to mid-1960s. *"But Yastrzemski is a real favorite with Mr. Yawkey she continued. And he takes advantage of every opportunity to promote himself with the owner. Yastrzemski is for Yastrzemski and no one else,"* she exclaimed.... *"he effectively went about undermining the manager and helped speed his firing."*[482]

Dick Williams later said in his book, *No More Mr. Nice Guy*, who was not at the interview, that according to his wife Norma she was misquoted. *"One newspaper printed quotes from Norma about Yaz stabbing me, but those quotes were false,"* said Williams.[483]

Clark Booth, a veteran Boston journalist, wrote a scathing critique of *"certain [Red Sox] roster malcontents"* over the years, listing Carl Yastrzemski in the mix, accusing him of so-called *"'back-stairs visits'* to

---

[482] The Boston Globe, "Mrs. Williams Blames Yaz," September 26, 1969 , p. 47 https://www.newspapers.com/image/435177027/?match=1&terms=Mrs.%20Williams%20blames%20yaz

[483] Dick Williams & Bill Plaschke, "No More Mr. Nice Guy," Harcourt Brace Jovanovich, San Diego, New York, 1990, p. 117

the owners' inner sanctum," continuing to say, *"But Yawkey should never have listened to them. He was dead wrong."*[484]

As time passed, Scotty infrequently received the kind of praiseworthy notice that he should have received from the Boston press but rather stories laced with more culpable aspects, derisive or fanciful conversation bordering frivolity, a form of *"subjugation,"* according to baseball historian Glenn Stout; or, the object of "clowning."

On May 4 in Detroit, Scott stroked two more home runs, both of them crushed, one measured at 415 feet, the second a titanic monster shot that nearly cleared Tiger Stadium in the left centerfield upper-deck section of the ballpark of a magnitude approaching the blast he had hit off of Whitey Ford. He was on a roll, and it was being noticed. It got the attention of Detroit's pitcher Hank Aguirre who witnessed Scott's prodigious blasts in Tiger Stadium and made the observation, somewhat patronizingly, that *"he [Scott] could be the best Negro player ever to come into the league."* It was probably well-intended but came off hermetically patronizing at best; more like old racial lines were still in evidence with that statement merely defining the times.[485]

---

[484] Clark Booth, "When it comes to mutinous behavior, the roll call of Red Sox player vendettas against managers allows for no comparison," Dorchester Reporter, August 23, 2012
https://www.dotnews.com/columns/2012/when-it-comes-mutinous-behavior-roll-call-red-sox-player-vende

[485] Larry Claflin, "Big or Small, A. L. Parks Look Easy to Bosox Bombshell Scott," The Sporting News, May 21, 1966, p. 18

Another home run for the big rookie first baseman, George Scott (courtesy of Boston Public Library)

The Red Sox and their newfound slugger left Detroit for Minnesota and a four-game series with the Twins, who had a stable of quality pitching to challenge the young home run specialist who seemed to have no weakness, comprised of a future Hall of Famer, a Cy Young award winner, and others with several All-Star appearances to their credit. He didn't disappoint the partisan fans and the sports reporters and journalists, who came out to see this young phenom crushing three home runs, a double and a triple.

May 13, 1966, Anaheim Stadium – Tony Conigliaro (left), the American League's 1965 home run leader, and George Scott, the rookie sensation who had already hit 10 homers, peer over the new Anaheim Stadium, home of the California Angels. Scott hit his 11th homer there on May 14. (courtesy of Boston Public Library)

Although marveling at his rookie's breakout displays of solid baseball performance that included flashy work in the field that would soon prove to be his trademark, manager Billy Herman's team was wallowing in last place at 7-17 on May 11 with Red Sox pitching falling apart, in spite of Scott's accomplishments. Being pursued by a zealous press looking for a hot story, Herman's somber mood while searching for appeasement and something good to say about his team led him to discuss any possible weaknesses of his young phenom, which is what the sportswriters were looking for; it seemed, arguably, to be a moment of betrayal as Herman began to speculate in all seriousness what might upset his boy wonder suggesting that moving the ball around the strike zone, or making him chase bad pitches could be the magic bullet for getting him out; and, of course, this revelation was quickly dispersed countrywide by the press. Pitching coach Sal "The Barber" Maglie, no slouch for the knock-down pitch he was known for, even suggested the infamous beanball could be the ultimate solution. Whether coincidence or simply happenstance, this is what followed upon the Red Sox's arrival to California and a four-game series with the Angels. It had all the appearances of a bona fide reaction to what Herman and Maglie had to say to stop Scott. Pitchers, who quickly picked up on the messaging of Herman and Maglie, were throwing steady breaking balls and off-speed pitches outside of the strike zone that broke the young slugger's timing, causing him to reach for bad deliveries and look worse.

He was clearly frustrated after whiffing 12 times during a stretch of ten games, reaching a crescendo on May 22 when, in front of a hometown Fenway crowd, he was called out on strikes by umpire Bill Haller, who Scott felt was making rather atypical if not outright peculiar calls on him before this game. He had made a half-swing at a pitched ball, which Haller at first said was not a strike, yelling, "No, you didn't [go through the swing, for a strike]," according to George, but then in a delayed tactic, embarrassing the rookie who was already heading to first, changed his mind, boldly yelling "Yes, you did!" calling him out with a flare of the theatrical accentuating his embarrassment. It angered the young ballplayer - not only because of the call but how it was done - who immediately slammed his helmet and bat on the ground and was promptly ejected - his first-ever ejection – by the 5th-year umpire. Haller said later that he made the call himself without help from the flashy rookie first base umpire, Emmett Ashford, who, at the time, was the first and only black umpire in the major leagues. There were those who questioned Haller's decision not to appeal to Ashford when the call was a close one and where Ashford was in a better position to see if Scott had gone through with the swing. In fairness it would have been the better decision and, in fact, was a prescribed major league rule later on for dealing with tough calls, which it clearly was. George said that Haller seemed to be picking on him in other games as well, suggesting bias or possibly something worse. This would happen again more than once, highlighted in 1971 with umpire Bill Kunkel who made calls on Scott that were outrageously outside of the strike zone – visible to everyone - that had all the merits of being personal.

It's possible that where Emmett Ashford was a new guy in the umpiring fraternity – and the first black umpire – had something to do with Haller's decision not to call on him. Ashford, an articulate man, reflected in later years after his retirement on the challenges confronting a black umpire and, left to the reader for interpretation, what may have entered into why Haller made the choice that he did with George Scott. He pointed out the "breakthrough" by Jackie Robinson and what it meant: *"But we're talking about two entirely different things. It's one thing for a man to be accepted as a player [like Jackie Robinson], accepting him as an equal on the field. It's very different to accept a black man as a man of authority, as the man overseeing everything and [being] in control. My race was always there...always a factor."*[486]

Upon his retirement, which was mandatory at age 55 for umpires in major league baseball – some say it was forced – in April 1971, Ashford was appointed public relations adviser to baseball commissioner Bowie Kuhn to *"make public appearances for baseball and in other ways make use of his 'unique personality and unique talent.'"*[487] Kuhn's intent was for Ashford to not only talk about baseball but help ameliorate baseball's black-white issues much like Jessie Owens' role in 1968.

On June 14, the unpopular trade of Earl Wilson to Detroit came down in exchange for on-again, off-again outfielder Don Demeter, who could also play first base, which was on Billy Herman's mind while his current first baseman, Scott, was mired in a batting slump. *"Wilson is still not convinced*

---

[486] Jim Hackleman, "Emmett Ashford: Against the Odds," Honolulu Star-Bulletin, Aug 9, 1972, p. 39
https://www.newspapers.com/image/271347335/?terms=%22Emmett%20ashford%22%20&match=1
[487] David Blanchett, "Sports Line," The Tustin News, Orange County, California, Apr 15, 1971, p. 12

that his famous incident at the Cloud Nine Lounge in Winter Haven," said *Globe* reporter Larry Whiteside, *"where in the spring training of 1966 he was refused service, and the subsequent national publicity and embarrassment the Red Sox had to endure because of it, didn't lead directly to his being traded."*[488] Boston fans were not at all pleased about the trade, raising justifiable questions about whether this was trending along the lines of the Pumpsie Green episode of 1959, in which a well-qualified player who had shined in spring training, who just happened to be black, was mysteriously sent down to the minors. To them, there seemed to be a far more insidious reason behind the trade with the sudden and inexplicable departure of Wilson, a bona fide major league pitcher who four years before pitched a no-hitter, than was being explained by the Red Sox, whose pitching was the worst of the ten American League clubs. Why give up an established major league pitcher, they asked, when pitching was their Achilles heel? Billy Herman, who had to reluctantly deal with Wilson in other matters that involved Red Sox family functions excluding black players and their families, was frustrated with the uncomfortable situation and with Wilson openly accusing him of being *"a drinker and a troublemaker,"* displaying no remorse by sending his talented and promising black ace to Detroit.[489]

---

[488] Larry Whiteside, "'Sox Children of the '60s," p. 80
[489] Howard Bryant, Shut Out, p. 80

Manager Herman was about to bench his heralded rookie, George Scott, much to the displeasure of the Fenway fans, who became confused, aroused and quite vocal about it, and it made headlines in the Boston papers. Once again, here was a popular young player, a performer who just happened to be black, with whom the Red Sox were mucking around with their recollections of the mishandling of previous black players like Earl Wilson and Pumpsie Green. It actually had a name for it: they called it *"The George Scott Case,"* as reported in a July 25 *Boston Globe* feature article.[490]

In a July 19 article, Clif Keane wrote: *"George Scott, who quite likely has more all-around baseball talent than any Red Sox player since the days of Babe Ruth, needs help."*[491] Keane, a complicated fellow in his own right who was a manifest racial bigot himself, described by many as cut from an older generation of racist sports personalities, and a veteran *Boston Globe* sports reporter, wrote an emotional article entitled *"Benched Scott Feels Low, Pleads for Help."* In it was an appeal it seemed to everyone, *"from his manager, the coaching staff, the ball players, and the press,"* but especially noted was an appeal being made to Scotty's manager, Billy Herman, who appeared to be avoiding any kind of remedial measures that would benefit the discouraged rookie, other than benching him.[492] George was young, a

---

[490] Unattributed, "Scott changes stance, feels slump over," Boston Globe, July 25 1966, p. 17
https://www.newspapers.com/image/433814628/?terms=George%20Scott&match=1
[491] Clif Keane, "benched Scott Feels Low, Pleads for Help, Boston Globe, July 19, 1966, p. 21
[492] IBID

mere 22, and very sensitive, as noted by Keane, describing him as not knowing *"a great deal about human nature, since he comes from a part of the country where they don't acquire it: Greenville, Miss.,"* which, if any conclusions can be drawn from that rather reckless statement, it may have been that he personified his own bias. [493]

Speculation was brewing whether George was being treated fairly by the club; here again, whether there was something unsavory going on as he complained that his teammates and Red Sox management were showing disloyalty toward him, as if *"nobody wants me around here,"* he exclaimed, recounting previous years when such managers as Eddie Popowski would take him aside and rebuild his confidence, which was an important feature of his personality bolstering his composure and self-esteem.[494] He thrived on it. But this time, he was seeing none of that. *"I got a kind of funny feeling, really, that I'm not too well accepted,"* said Scott, which, in later years, he explained may have been an element of a racist moment, which he largely blamed on the press.[495] Keane summarized the predicament with Scott by explaining that this was the *Globe's* best effort to help him but suggested that a more meaningful effort to solve the problem would be better if it came from the team. *"And now,"* said Keane, *"Captain Carl [Yastrzemski], you*

---

[493] Clif Keane, "Puzzled Scott Asks Sox, Press for Help," The Boston Globe, July 19, 1966, p. 35
https://www.newspapers.com/image/433838613/?terms=Clif%20Keane&match=1
[494] Clif Keane, "Benched Scott Feels Low," p. 21.
[495] Clif Keane, "Puzzled Scott Asks Sox, Press for Help," p. 36

can take over from there on the team end of it. Or, maybe Billy Herman would like to," shifting the blame to the manager who was in a much better position to help the young and confused rookie…that is, if Herman was even remotely willing to help, which was questionable.[496]

In a later interview, Scott blamed the Boston press as the main culprit for his being underrated. He felt steadfast, because of their attitude of not crediting him when he thought it was due, but yet were the "first ones" to seize on and embellish his mistakes and momentary lapses when he was not doing well. To him, they were an unhealthy mix of glaring omissions and censure. *"I don't know why, but I think I do,"* said an anguished Scott, remembering his days in Boston dealing with the media, pointing out that some of them may have been racially intolerant. *"Well, they weren't used to me,"* said Scott of the Boston Press, who, for the first time, had to deal with a black Red Sox starter. He elaborated further: *"In fact, that could have been said for any of the black players I played with on that team. The Boston newspaper guys didn't know what to do with us [blacks]."* He was nothing but an anomaly to them in the eyes of the Boston press.[497]

Manager Herman was not of that ilk, however, placing the blame for Scott's slump squarely on Scott and that it was up to George to straighten himself out, not the role of the manager or the team, he insisted. In fact, indecorously, he was quick to openly accuse Scott of not listening to advice,

---

[496] IBID
[497] George Scott interview: March 23, 2006

even though there was no indication or proof that any such guidance was being offered. According to young Scott, no one was coming to his aid or would even talk to him, especially Herman. *"They didn't work with me,"* said Scott.[498]

The Red Sox had a long history of neglect of player prospects and inadequate player development, which the parent club astonishingly blamed on their scouts, alleging they were not getting good prospects, while the scouts countered with the argument they had done their job yet the organization had no suitable plan for their prospects' handling and development. It was an old front office chorus going back to the days of Eddie Collins, Joe Cronin and Tom Yawkey, who, defensively, placed any blame about prospects – particularly when it was about blacks – on the scouts, alleging, in the matter of black athletes, that they altogether failed to find any of quality. The scouts, on the other hand, resented the accusation: *"We signed players other clubs wanted, but they were not developed and handled properly,"* they said. *Boston Globe* reporter Harold Kaese took the front office to task, stating, *"If he [Scott] isn't a prospect, a million of us do not know a potential star from a mountain goat...A rookie like Scott deserves the most careful handling, the most expert instruction, the most patient encouragement."*[499]

---

[498] George Scott interview: March 23, 2006
[499] Harold Kaese, "Herman on Spot In Scott's Case," Boston Globe, July 20, 1966, p. 43 https://www.newspapers.com/image/433843064/?terms=%22harold%20kaese%22%20&match=1

A case in point, among several young Red Sox pitchers of the '60s, was Jerry Stephenson, who threw hard and was destined for great things, but he never got there. In an interview, Stephenson said, *"Strange things happened to our young pitchers,"* which reflects a certain indifference on the part of the team in developing or even rescuing prospects. Stephenson was prone to wildness and looked to ex-major leaguer Mel Parnell, known by Red Sox fans and baseball pundits as *"the Yankee killer"* for his apparent mastery of the Bombers, who was doing some managing and coaching for the Red Sox in the minor leagues. Parnell informed the young pitcher that the brass, rather bluntly, told him to *"just let you throw"* and *"it was all the instruction he was to get."* Said Stephenson, *"I needed a lot of help, and I never did get it...thinking about that, maybe that's one reason the young pitchers never did come around."*[500] There were many teams that took the same tact with their young pitchers, particularly black pitchers, during the late '50s and early '60s, among them one of the finest black pitchers of all time and future Hall of Famer, St. Louis Cardinals' great Bob Gibson. There were strains of racism in the organization, one standout being Solly Hemus, who was never convinced that Gibson had the intelligence to be a good pitcher. *"Blacks lacked the intelligence or discipline to play that position"* was the stereotypical attitude about black pitchers in the major leagues, according to Peter Golenbock. *"'Just throw it over the plate, Gibson, if you can' was the extent of Hemus' teaching of Gibson."*[501]

---

[500] Peter Golenbock, Red Sox Nation, p. 331
[501] IBID, p. 72

Red Sox scout Ed Scott reinforced that opinion of a somewhat laissez-faire, or hands-off, attitude by the team about young Red Sox prospects that was soon to catch up to his young discovery, George Scott. *"George had all the raw talent for success but they [Red Sox management] didn't seem to support him, left him alone when he was struggling. Not like Eddie Popowski did when he was in the minors,"* said the scout.[502]

"Having been called the probable successor to Babe Ruth, the critical eye of baseball's enormous following is on Scott and his handling by the Red Sox and [Billy] Herman," remarked *Globe* reporter Harold Kaese, who realized that, once again, they may have had a Pumpsie Green matter on their hands and Red Sox fans, who had taken to the young rookie, were even angrier pointing fingers right at Herman and the Red Sox front office pleading with them to do something, and not send him down.[503]

Herman had another losing season once again, finishing next-to-last in the American League, a mere one-half game better than the last-place New York Yankees. On a Thursday, September 8, sixteen games short of the end of the season, Billy Herman was fired by the Red Sox, which was officially announced on the following day. Haywood Sullivan, the team's vice president in charge of player personnel, made the announcement to the team while executive vice president Dick O'Connell was informing the Boston press. *Boston Globe* reporter Harold Kaese, who was highly critical of

---

[502] Ed Scott interview: March 3, 2007
[503] Harold Kaese, "Herman on Spot," Boston Globe, July 20, 1966, p. 43

Herman in his treatment of George Scott, spoke of Herman's firing in the context of his lack of the *"pedagogic drive"* to instruct and lead a team, especially young players, which only seven weeks before there was rookie Scott who was struggling for leadership, and who was a case in point. Sullivan alluded to the importance of dealing with youth and improving the club's reputation in that stead: *"We want a younger man to go with our building program,"* he said.[504]

A younger man they got in 37-year-old Dick Williams of their Triple-A Toronto affiliate on September 28. Williams was known as a hard-nosed, very tough, no-nonsense type of leader, with a winning record as manager of Toronto. *"Most of the players are going to do the least amount of work they can do unless you stay on them,"* said Williams. *"When I took over the ballclub, I felt it was very important that I establish who was boss."*[505]

One who was clearly not a slacker, but a man who would work assiduously in his quest to be the best, to be a champion, was George Scott. Refining his baseball skills and playing winning baseball would present numerous challenges for the young slugger now that a manager of the type of Dick Williams was in the mix. Senior *Boston Globe* sports writer Will McDonough once described Williams as a man of complex moods and personality to match with a quick and explosive temper. He would appear

---

[504] Bob Sales, "Herman Fired As Sox Pilot," The Boston Globe, September 10, 1966, p. 1 & 13 https://www.newspapers.com/image/433899668/
[505] Dick Williams, quoted by Pete Golenbock, author of Red Sox Nation, from Williams' and Bill Paschke's book "No More Mr. Nice Guy," pages 291-292

to George as an anomaly unlike any baseball manager or coach he had ever seen, becoming almost pathological and penetrating George's deepest emotions and sensitivities. A close friend and teammate, Joe Lahoud, said of Scott, *"Nobody worked harder than George Scott. He was outspoken but supersensitive."*[506] Lahoud was particularly sensitive to Williams' handling – or mishandling - of Scott feeling he failed the leadership test with him. *"George needed all the moral support he could get because he was never that sure of himself,"* said Lahoud. *"He knew he could hit taters, and he knew he could play first base, but he didn't know if he could do everything that was expected of him."*[507] Once again, an old-school manager type who showed little to no deference toward the new-age young ballplayer other than what they were hired for and could do on the field. Although there were wide differences between Herman and Williams, they had this in common.

"The country club disappeared," wrote best-selling author and baseball historian, among other sports, Peter Golenbock. *"He [Dick Williams] was a bastard every day, giving no ground, accepting nothing less than perfection, and railing at the players and in the press when he didn't get it."*[508]

---

[506] Peter Golenbock, "Red Sox Nation," p. 321; quoting Joe Lahoud.
[507] IBID.
[508] IBID, p. 296

Chapter 10
Dick Williams

He [Dick Williams] fought with umpires as though he hated them. His goal was to Inspire his players. He wanted everyone – including the umpires – to know the Red Sox were serious about winning. When he was thrown out of a game at Fenway Park, the Fans leapt to their feet to cheer him.

Peter Golenbock[509]

Howard Bryant, whose forthright and touted narrative, *Shut Out*, about Boston's historical and widely popular baseball club, the Red Sox, the hometown city of its heritage, and the matter of racism that enveloped both, just may have rewarded Dick Williams with more than enough credit than he might have deserved; to be sure Williams was a highly successful, technically sound and accomplished baseball manager amassing 1571 career wins (1451 losses) over 22 seasons, and was rewarded with an induction into the esteemed National Baseball Hall of Fame by the Veterans Committee, on July 27, 2008. But Dick Williams, the field manager of men, had another side: he was an exceedingly complex man; hard-nosed, testy, tempestuous and highly driven – a man possessed, said the *Globe's* Will McDonough, even Williams was to admit - much like the controversial and

---
[509] Peter Golenbock, "Red Sox Nation: An Unexpurgated History of the Boston Red Sox," Triumph Books, 1992, Chicago, Illinois, p. 296

fiery Brooklyn Dodgers' bench jockey that he once was; he was not often understood by his players, or even management for that matter, such as in Tom Yawkey of the Red Sox who became annoyed at Williams' unorthodox style of field managing, despite Williams having turned Yawkey's laissez faire "country club" ball team entirely around in 1967 – his first year as a manager - to win the American League Division title and nearly win the World Series, had it not been for a black future Hall of Fame pitcher named Bob Gibson, who carried the National League's St. Louis Cardinals team to victory over the upstart Red Sox club; the irony, if not amusement, being that a championship-starved Tom Yawkey could not rise above a club loaded with talented black ballplayers: among them Bob Gibson, and an assortment of black and Latino position players, all-stars all of them, who not only won the 1967 World Series but would rise to Hall of Fame prominence.

It was often said by baseball pundits and sports writers that Dick Williams was a man who did not distinguish between his players and that he treated them all the same: miserably. In fact, he said it himself; his only goal was to win, at all cost, and no one ballplayer would stand in the way of that, even future Hall of Famer Carl Yastrzemski. *"Fair enough"* was the oft journalistic response to these legendary words, perhaps as an assuagement or compromise. But there was another side to him that few acknowledged - including the sports writers, especially Boston's - or at least who were reluctant to own up to, except for what was known by several of the seasoned black players by their association with Williams, and that was that he landed more heavily on his black players, who were charter members of his notorious "doghouse." Elston Howard, who was picked up by the Red Sox from the Yankees in '67, was upset with Williams, whom, he alleged, slighted him by ignoring him for weeks at a time, and who failed to take advantage of using Howard's mentoring qualities for the benefit of new-age younger players, like George Scott, who said about Howard, *"I don't know, Elston Howard was a great pick-up for the Red Sox, but Dick Williams seemed to ignore him most of the time; didn't use him much. He made some great plays for us. I think he could have been used better [for the benefit of the team]."*[510] Newly-acquired Elston "Ellie" Howard took an immediate liking to George, the young slick fielder who was already being compared to future Hall of Famer and three-time Gold Glover Gil Hodges. Howard was touting Scott to the New York press and to whoever would listen during a clubhouse rant after a game with the Yankees about the young first baseman's skills: *"Meet the Great Scott,"* said Howard, *"Better get to know him. He's going to be around for a long time. This man's got a pair of hands going to be put in the Hall of Fame before he's through."*[511] Sadly, his manager, Dick Williams, rarely elevated any discussion about Scott with a mind of openly celebrating his emerging star unless it was to criticize him or, in his sharp-tongued manner, attack him with sarcasm; instead, he was Williams' unwitting fall guy for most that was wrong with the Red Sox, his

---

[510] George Scott interview: August 10, 2008
[511] Milton Gross, "Hodges Had Nothing on Scott," The Boston Globe, August 31, 1967, quoting article by Milton Gross syndicated sports columnist for the New York Post, p. 50. https://www.newspapers.com/image/434081709/

steadfast critic, sometime weight trainer and bariatric clinician. *"'The name of the game, as far as I'm concerned, is 'win.' I don't believe that popularity counts as much as winning games,"* said Williams in the old Brooklyn Dodgers style of what constitutes winning baseball and where he got his legs in his baseball indoctrination.[512]

According to the *Globe's* Alan Sheehan's assessment of why Williams lost his job in 1969, *"Williams couldn't be blamed for Lonborg and Santiago, but many critics blamed him for not making it easier for Foy and Scott,"* both black players. [513]

Catcher Jerry Moses, who played for the Red Sox during the tumultuous Dick Williams years of 1968-1969, had another spin: *"'We won in 1967. We didn't win in '68 or '69. Whose fault was that? You can blame it on Lonnie getting hurt, Santiago or Conig getting hurt, or 'I didn't motivate the players.' Or maybe it's a trade they didn't make. Most likely, it was a combination of all three. I do not believe Dick Williams allowed anyone to undermine him,"* said Moses showing no sympathy for the former skipper but, to the contrary, expressing concurrence with Yaz – though it was not a unanimous opinion among teammates - in the relationship established between Yastrzemski and team owner Yawkey; it was his view that the

---

[512] Alan H. Sheehan, "Williams' Baseball Credo was 'Win.'" The Boston Globe, Sep 23, 1969, p. 49.
https://www.newspapers.com/image/435171402/?terms=dick%20williams&match=1
[513] IBID

manager had an obligation of loyalty to the man paying him. *"'Dick, because of his personal attitude, undermined himself.'"*[514]

Claiming Dick Williams treated them "all the same," however – because that's what it looked like to the average sports fan, and even more what they read in the papers, that was regularly proffered by the newsies - is a bit of a sidestep, if not a lame excuse, often used by journalists in describing Dick Williams without taking the extra journalistic steps, or the inkling to do so. Acclaimed sports journalist Howard Bryant, in his book *Shut Out*, seemed to follow that line of reasoning with his comment, perhaps in a moment of dalliance, *"and if he took a no-nonsense approach with the players, he was also 'fair' in his seeming disdain for all of his players instead of embracing the country club attitude of the previous regime, where the rules were different based on a player's batting average."*[515] Rico Petrocelli, however, was of the opinion that Williams was patently picking on George Scott more than the others that, questionably, was neither necessary nor deserved. In other words, it was *not* all the same when it came to George or some of his black teammates, who were often in his doghouse. It was true he made no exceptions to his hard-line or tactics, but he did, however, make one exception, and it was George Scott, whom he looked at like it was pathological by design; it was that extreme. He seemed to relish any

---

[514] Peter Golenbock, Red Sox Nation, quoting Jerry Moses, p. 328
[515] Howard Bryant, Shut Out, p. 86-87

opportunities to humiliate him in the media, as if wielding a weapon around George as his tactic to get the best from him, according to Petrocelli.

Red Sox teammate Jerry Moses, who was also a good friend, both of them from Mississippi, pulled Scott aside at the end of the '68 season, noticing how tormented he was at the hands of Dick Williams. *"He won't play me,"* exclaimed George, *"The guy just won't play me."* Confused by the tirade knowing that Scott had made more than 400 plate appearances that year, Moses challenged him about that, querying his rationality. *"Yeah, but he doesn't have any confidence in me. He won't put me out there and leave me alone,"* ranted the Red Sox slugger, who obviously had lost his confidence.[516] And that was the rub. This confusing effort of what he meant by his indignation was being expressed in the broader context of George's dealings with Dick Williams, whose irreverent treatment of the young first-sacker, the implication being that Scott was unreservedly sensitive, may have been more beneficial every so often by applying more compassionate or conciliatory overtures than the hard-lined one size fits all approach favored by his manager.

---

[516] 516 Peter Golenbock, Red Sox Nation, quoting Jerry Moses, p. 321

Spring 1967, Winter Haven - Dick Williams giving pointers on playing first base to pupil George Scott, in his first year of eight Gold Gloves (courtesy of Boston Herald)

It all began on September 28, 1966, when new Red Sox roguish manager Dick Williams, emerged as the new guy at the helm, quite unlike anyone or anything neither Boston fans nor the local press had ever seen before, and it was to be the beginning of a stormy relationship between their accomplished second-year first baseman, George Scott, and the new skipper. Williams brought with him a preordained bias of installing his minor league champion Toronto club's first baseman, Tony Horton, in the Sox' first-sacker position, in spite of Scott's respectable '66 performance at the position that earned him several awards during the season, when he was named to the American League All-Star team, and, at the end, winning the Red Sox Rookie of the Year title sharing the distinction with third baseman Joe Foy, and nearly winning the American League Rookie of the Year title. Williams wanted Horton's bat, which ultimately proved nowhere near the power or scope of a George Scott, but he was being touted by Williams as a solid ballplayer, yet just a "good fielder," which, it turned out, was anything but true. Horton was a one-dimensional player who couldn't field, whereas Williams knew that Scott was much more versatile, yet the messages he was sending about the situation to sports writers and to Scott were that the position was Horton's to lose. It was insulting to George. *Boston Globe* sports writer Will McDonough had once summed up Williams as a man of complex moods and personality with a quick and explosive temper. He was to be an anomaly to George Scott throughout his Boston experience and even afterward when he had to contend with him as an All-Star manager whose player selections in 1973 and '74 left Scott off the roster, in spite of having All-Star credentials with the bat and recognized unanimously as the best first baseman in the American League; in essence, he was snubbed.

In Dick Williams' autobiography, *No More Mr. Nice Guy*, written in collaboration with sports journalist Bill Plaschke in 1990, he wrote about his experiences in 1965-1966 as a manager with the Red Sox Triple-A Toronto ballclub, his intense desire to win at all cost and the rage he felt for ballplayers that appeared indifferent and lackluster about the game. If he sensed this in a player, *"I'd damn near kill him,"* complained a pugnacious Williams. *"Losses, dressed up in mistakes and nonchalance, made me a deadly weapon."*[517] Williams' intensity about winning and losing and why he was such a fierce competitor was wrapped around an inbred "hate factor," which he brought with him from his Brooklyn Dodgers and bench jockeying days. He reasoned that athletes give 100 percent because they *"hate something,"* not because they actually want something. If what it took to win was instilling a level of hate into the equation of baseball, in the Dick Williams way, then that's what he inculcated in his players, in whichever manner it had to be executed, as long as it was to achieve the "best" on-field performance from them. Those who appeared complacent or nonchalant in how they managed themselves and were tolerant of losing, for them he gave another reason for them to hate, and it was him, Dick Williams.[518]

---

[517] Dick Williams and Bill Plaschke, "No More Mr. Nice Guy," p. 77.
[518] IBID, p. 78

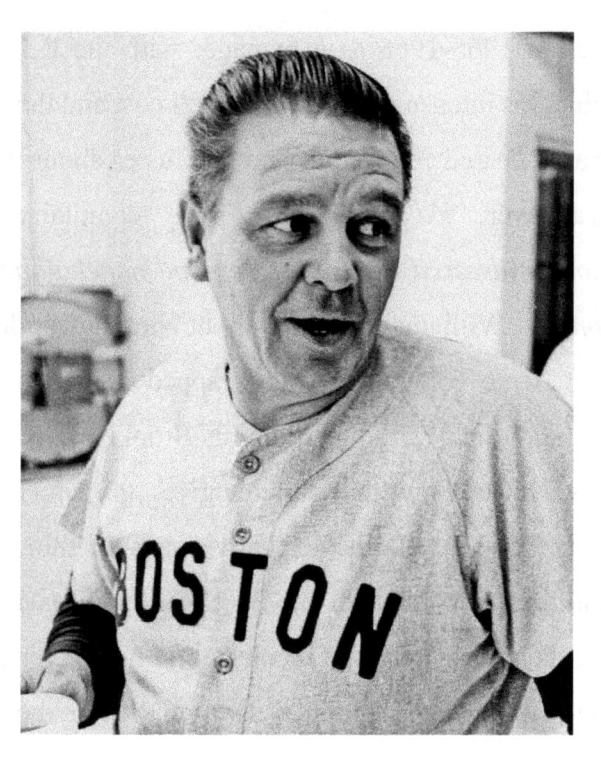

Red Sox manager Dick Williams, who George Scott claims nearly drove him out of baseball (courtesy of Boston Red Sox)

    This was the philosophy that the new manager brought to his team in 1967, nothing but hardball, forceful and uncompromising, and what young George Scott was about to encounter in his next three years with Boston. As hard as he was on the team, he was especially tough on his young first baseman. For reasons not always clear to his teammates, Scott was the object of Williams' derisiveness, bordering on racial implications, some teammates and reporters cautiously reasoned: he became a poster child for the scorned in the face of acerbic behavior and from time-to-time truculent leadership. An unaware George Scott was about to see his life change dramatically from his days under a compassionate manager like Eddie Popowski, who, by his compassion, had as much to do with George's elevation to the major league level and Billy Herman, for that matter who, to a fault, exhibited indifference and had much less to say to his players than Williams. The hate element self-described by Williams would play a part in his approach to his players, with a laser focus on George Scott.

There was probably little that annoyed Dick Williams any more than an overweight ballplayer, and it was he who drew up the rules – not the trainer - on what constituted a "proper" weight level for each of his players. His focus was on Joe Foy and George Scott, both black players, who Williams felt often did not meet up to his homespun playing weight and conditioning directives, for which he kept a weight chart with the threat that if they failed to comply with his requirements, they would be removed from the lineup, and remain that way until they lost the weight. He lived up to his word. *"[George] Scott and I spent the year engaging in – how should I put this? – guerrilla warfare. In his second season as the Sox' regular first baseman, he'd come straight to the big leagues from Double-A Pittsfield, so I'd never managed him in the minor leagues. Good thing because we'd have killed each other. Scott was a likable guy with a weight problem – in both his belly and his head. I once said, 'talking to him is like talking to a block of cement.' Everybody thought I was joking, and even Yaz told somebody it was a rather cruel joke. But it was no joke. I meant it,"* alleged the irascible and former

Red Sox chief, doubling down on his less-than-perfect behavior.[519] In spite of his unapologetic swagger and ready dismissal of the insulting remark, insisting on its appropriateness in the circumstances, and his openness about it as justified, it was indeed a cruel joke, for, without reservation, it was both intended for and expressed to the local press, which would have repercussions both locally and nationally, and most certainly among his teammates.

Distinguished journalist and gentleman Bud Collins, who had a sterling sportscasting and sports writing career for which he was rewarded with induction into the *National Sportscasters and Sportswriters Association Hall of Fame*, took umbrage with his remarks and their ineptitude, and the fact they were made in the very early stages of his new managerial role. *"Williams is off to a dangerous start,"* exclaimed the mild-mannered journalist. *"Clearly Williams is not playing fair…he has become a case for the Anti-Defamation League in giving opinions in the three critical areas: his own players, the umpires, the league president. This cannot be tolerated. And apparently, it won't be, according to Haywood Sullivan, general manager of the Red Sox. 'Maybe they won't fine him this time, but he won't be saying things like that anymore,' states Sullivan."*[520]

---

[519] IBID, p. 93
[520] Bud Collins, "Free Speech and Baseball Don't Mix," Boston Globe, Apr 26, 1967, p. 24
https://www.newspapers.com/image/433949419/?terms=%22like%20talking%20to%20a%20block%20of%20cement%22&match=1

For the first time in quite a while, the '67 Red Sox infield looked sturdy around the diamond, yet Williams was shuffling players in-and-out of positions in an effort to find a place for Tony Horton, for whom he had a fixation, who could only play one position – he claimed - and that was first base. In spite of a "wobbly" early spring performance in the field by Horton, said one reporter, on March 20, he was 3-for-4 with a long home run; it was the catalyst for the Red Sox skipper to make a move that shook the sanity of the Boston media and hometown followers when the next day, inexplicably he assigned Scott to play the outfield against the Phillies. It was a moment of madness, some scribes wrote, feeling the maneuver would not be in Scott's best interest, who was already being avowed the best first baseman in both leagues. Turns out, Horton wasn't as one-dimensional as Williams was advertising as Horton was originally an outfielder. Meanwhile, Williams was needling Scott incessantly, and it was beginning to bother sports writers over his condemnation of his big first baseman.

The starting Red Sox infield in 1967. Left to right: Joe Foy, Rico Petrocelli, Mike Andrews, and George Scott (courtesy of Boston Red Sox)

Sluggers Carl Yastrzemski, George Scott and Tony Conigliaro in Winter Haven in 1967, the season of the Impossible Dream (courtesy of Boston Red Sox)

George Scott was not amused with the maneuver, feeling Williams was playing favorites with Horton, among his concerns of *"lousing up his hitting,"* he alleged to coach Eddie Popowski. It looked that way to the sports writers as well, who felt Williams was not giving them a straight explanation. The *Globe's* John Ahern speculated that *"someone in a high place likes him [Horton] very much"* to preempt the talented Scott," alleging that the first-sacker *"is being peddled around,"* to his consternation.[521]

It only got worse. On March 23, Scott's 23rd birthday, the sports page headline read, *"Red Sox Willing to Trade Scott."* He was put on waivers along with pitchers Jose Santiago and Gary Roggenburk, all three subject to trade, which made it look even more like Scott was dispensable to be replaced by Horton. The young first baseman was further shamed – as he saw it - when he was assigned to play right field against the Dodgers on the same day. *"I didn't blame Dick [Williams] for playing me in the outfield, although I didn't feel I belonged there. I blamed him for not being honest with me and not letting me know what he was doing when he kept using Tony Horton. I knew he had to see what was best for the team. I just didn't like the way he did it. [It] seemed disrespectful,"* said Scott in a later interview, touching on the underlying guarded and cautious behavior

---

[521] John Ahern, "Scott Plays RF, Stirs Trade Talk," The Boston Globe, March 22, 1967, p. 49-50
https://www.newspapers.com/image/433925266/?terms=is%20being%20peddled%20around

between them, and Williams' insensitivities toward Scott that developed almost immediately.[522] Things took a different twist with the reporters after the Dodgers game when Scott catapulted into the right field wall chasing a John Kennedy fly ball that kept slicing away from him and which he misjudged. The impact was made with such force that teammate Mike Andrews announced, in jest, that *"He [Scott] moved the wall from 330 feet to 332."* Scott was knocked senseless and had to be revived with an extra boost of smelling salts. *Boston Globe* senior writer Harold Kaese was more conciliatory than some of the other reporters by his comment that Williams may have been justified in using Scott in the outfield, nonetheless raising suspicions of his own. He was less than enamored by the appearance that the manager may have been favoring his Toronto bunch, including Horton, over other players and possibly *"from the more ugly suspicion that Yawkey wants Horton on the team,"* who was another of Yawkey's fair-haired boys, summing up his view that *"The Horton problem is real."*[523]

One major league scout did not share Kaese's sentiment, however, saying, *"Damndest experiment I ever saw or heard of. You'd think he'd thank God he got off so lucky and put an end to his foolishness."*[524] Williams' abrupt response to the rancor was, *"It should have been caught,"*

---

[522] George Scott interview: March 23, 2006
[523] Harold Kaese, "Is Yawkey Back of Scott Shift?" Boston Globe, March 24, 1967, p. 19. https://www.newspapers.com/image/433938278/?terms=yawkey&match=1
[524] John Ahern, "Scott Out of Hospital, No Fractures Found," Boston Globe, Mar 24, 1967, p. 17
https://www.newspapers.com/image/433941868/?terms=%22Dick%20williams%22%20&match=1

and that was all he was willing to say about the matter. Scott never played another game in the outfield and was back at first base upon his return from injury on March 30. Teammate Rico Petrocelli expressed sympathy for George in his book *Impossible Dream Red Sox*: "*We didn't tell it to the press, but we agreed with them. We couldn't understand why Williams was playing Scott in the outfield. Boomer was a great athlete but wasn't an outfielder. In fact, he went on to play 2,034 games in the major leagues, and not one of them was in the outfield.*"[525]

Another factor that stood out in this shuffling of players between field positions was against whom it was being done and why. As Howard Bryant pointed out, before the days of baseball unions and guaranteed contracts "*that made the players more than hired hands, it was more common for managers to tinker with players and their positions,*" except the more notable ballplayers such as Ted Williams, Mickey Mantle, Duke Snider and Eddie Mathews, as examples, who were exempt from the practice.[526] However, not in the case of future Hall of Famer Henry Aaron, an accomplished ballplayer who was often manipulated by manager Fred Haney in and out of lineups and field positions, and Henry began to ask why. Or, when a dedicated racist Solly Hemus of the Cardinals once embarrassed the first baseman, All-Star and Gold Glover Bill White by playing him in center field. In both cases, the men were black. In both cases

---

[525] Rico Petrocelli and Chaz Scoggins, "Rico Petrocelli's Tales from the Impossible Dream Red Sox," Sports Publishing, L.L.C.com, Champaign, IL, 2007, p. 50.
[526] Howard Bryant, "The Last Hero: A Life of Henry Aaron," p. 240

it was felt they were being made to look foolish by being played out of position. Dick Williams was a product of that old school of thought in many ways, and such a similarity is hard to ignore. George had his own opinions, and that was one of them.

Nothing came of the waiver initiative by the Red Sox naming George Scott in the mix. The *Globe's* Will McDonough speculated in his March 23 article that it could have been a tactic to arouse Scott purely as a means to motivate him – to "shake up the player," he wrote – where he had been resisting the manager's capricious tactics. But of course, this seemed unlikely or necessary behavior when the second-year star was batting nearly .400 at the time and fielding magnificently, very likely the best on the team, and hardly required inspiration.

Meanwhile, Dick Williams, who, labeled by one newspaper upon his death in 2011 as *"a feisty old-school baseball manager"* – this description perhaps being overly generous - often took the traditionalist role of the 1940s – 1950s in his handling of blacks; he was less willing to listen to them, such as Elston Howard, who said Williams would not only not talk to him for weeks but ignored him altogether, especially in 1968. Elston Howard was brought to the Red Sox toward the end of the '67 season, during the Sox' pennant run, not only for his baseball skills but also for his coaching qualities and dealing with young players and pitchers that invoked discussions and speculation about a possible major league manager's role for him in the near future. The Red Sox could have nurtured this to not only help the team and their negative public perception dealing with blacks but also help with the facilitation of a future managerial role of a black athlete that, in major league baseball, did not occur until 1975. Management was hoping Howard would give Dick Williams a helping hand upon his arrival with the players, especially pitchers, where that was needed and maintain team stability in the stretch run that Howard was so familiar with playing for championship Yankee teams. Howard did just that in the '67 run, helping the first Red Sox team in twenty-one years to appear in a World Series. However, in the following year, when Dick Williams seemed to be losing his composure along with his sanity, that was on full display because of a key offseason skiing injury to his '67 Cy Young pitcher Jim Lonborg, losing young superstar slugger Tony Conigliaro, who, destined for the Hall of Fame, was felled in '67 by a Jack Hamilton beanball and forced out for the entire '68 year, and a shortened career, and dealing with an overweight George Scott, leading to a poor spring training team performance and thwarting Williams' starry-eyed plans for a repeat season; Elston Howard became little more than a bench-warmer in '68 and an overlooked long-term member of Williams' infamous doghouse.

At the conclusion of the '68 season Howard announced his retirement as a player. It was well known that there was a so-called "communications gap" between Howard and Williams throughout the season, with Howard appearing in a mere 71 games for the Red Sox. The Boston sportswriters seized the opportunity to question Howard about this, sensing there was more to the story about what was going on with Williams and his players that deserved the coverage. Always the gentleman, Howard preferred to take the high road to journalist questioning with the remark, *"I don't care if he's mad at me or not...I respect him as a gentleman."* But when questioned if Williams was really a gentleman toward him, his response was less circumspect: *"In the end, he (Williams) wasn't too much of a gentleman. But I don't care to get involved with him. I've been taught too much class for that. It was just one of those things."*[527]

"Just one of those things:" As a rule, this term was a keynote self-protective defensive expression often made by cautious black athletes when dodging the difficult questions of race, especially during the troublesome racial unrest period of the 1960s and '70s. Invariably a cautious man, it was likely there was a racial element in Elston Howard's response, and maybe his best effort to be truthful at the time, as was true with other Red Sox black players who saw much more in Dick Williams' assaults than what was typically labeled by whites, and some blacks, as "treating them all the same."

Scott's appearances in the local newspapers, which were instigated by his lowbrow manager, mirrored a racial element that generally was not picked up or reported on by the local scribes. Red Sox teammate and friend Rico Petrocelli remembered quite painfully the public criticism and verbal

---

[527] Bob Sales, "Yankees to Name Howard to Coaching Staff Today," The Boston Globe, October 22, 1968, p. 35.
https://www.newspapers.com/image/434590197/?terms=Bob%20Sales&match=1

assaults brought by Williams against Scott. *"It seemed at times he just didn't like George,"* said Petrocelli, adding that Williams was unusually *"tough on him,"* which he expressed in a manner highlighting the unpleasantness and incivility of these encounters; *"all too frequent,"* blurted Rico. He was especially displeased with Williams' tactic of making Scott's punishments open issues to the team and matters of full disclosure to the public. *"They could have called him into the office,"* said Petrocelli, like they did with other Red Sox players under Williams' scrutiny and kept the matter quiet, but instead, *"they seemed to always come out in public about it [with George]."*[528]

Williams was constantly harassing George Scott, said teammate and close friend Joe LaHoud, riding him for his weight, which was always a problem for George. He was merciless in his approach with constantly unpleasant blunt sarcasm, said LaHoud, railing at him with such remarks as, *"'Did you eat a pound of potatoes last night?'"* and comparable rants that were very personal, made in the presence of the team, which predictably got to Scott's core leading to some rocky and very insecure moments for the Boomer at the end of '67 followed by a disastrous season in '68. Dick Williams' relentlessness toward George dismantled the young slugger personally, finding no refuge with the team or even with a few sports reporters. *"If you humiliated or took away some of the confidence from*

---

[528] Rico Petrocelli interview: October 17, 2008

George Scott, he became one-third the ballplayer he would be if you just patted him on the back and told him how great a job he was doing," said LaHoud.[529]

Another Red Sox teammate, Jerry Moses, who was white and who, ironically, was from Yazoo City, Mississippi, known as the "Gateway to the Delta" that was built upon a history of slavery and racial intolerance and was not far from Scott's hometown of Greenville, shared similar viewpoints to LaHoud's; he pulled no punches, showed slightly less empathy in discussing Williams' treatment of George. *"But in his own mind, he was the kind of guy who had to be built up. You can't knock him down. And Dick [Williams] would beat him down. Dick destroyed his confidence...Most great athletes have the inner strength that makes them excel. Boomer lost that in '68. Dick really hurt him,"* said Moses.[530] However, as much as he was a critic of Dick Williams, Moses also placed some of the blame on Scott himself for "allowing" the manager to get away with the abuse. *"You can't allow anyone to do that to you,"* exclaimed Moses.[531] But oh, you could indeed if you were a black from the Deep South, as was George Scott. To put it mildly, he was used to invectiveness coming from there, unlike his counterparts from the North. Any change for George, such as standing up to antagonists, would come later but it was gradual and mired in personal conflict of another age. Surely, Moses was all too familiar with the racial

---

[529] Peter Golenbock, "Red Sox Nation," quoting Joe LaHoud, p. 321
[530] IBID, quoting Jerry Moses, p. 321 & 322
[531] IBID, quoting Jerry Moses, p. 322

background of his hometown of Yazoo City and was as much in a state of racial unrest as was the rest of the Deep South while he was growing up there, similar to George Scott but from quite different perspectives, and that wasn't about to change until the late 1960s in most southern cities. The social justice and political behavior standard for him was considerably different and far more favorable to him than what Scott's experience was as a Southern black in *Jim Crow* surroundings, where civil disobedience had not yet found its footing.

"*I let him get into my head,*" said George Scott during an interview. "*I let Dick Williams get into my head, and he nearly destroyed me. I thought I would be out of baseball because of him.*"[532]

As complicated a man as he was, what was not quite as clear about Dick Williams was his predisposition toward black athletes, ballplayers and functionaries, as few as there were of the latter and whether he harbored the old style of institutionalized Yawkey-style "gentleman's agreement" form of black resistance, of which he was once a constituent from that era if nothing else, which steadfastly kept blacks out of the game until Jackie Robinson in 1947. It was difficult to say definitively, as Williams' intensity for winning – affecting all of his players alike – outdistanced if not superseded any biases he may have held, or at least made them less obvious, but the symptoms were there that would flare up every so often, albeit that he was at one time a teammate of Jackie Robinson. So was Eddie Stanky,

---

[532] George Scott interview: August 20, 2006

also of the Dodgers, who was from that era, but he changed dynamically and malevolently toward blacks once he joined the St. Louis Cardinals in 1952; the Redbirds were a racist organization until a year later when new owner August "Gussie" Busch intervened. The fact was that Williams had such a deep desire to win that little else mattered, and player sensitivities were not in his playbook. And how that would manifest into a racial element, often missed or ignored by baseball historians but not missed by many of the black ballplayers, will be discussed.

Among the hallmarks attributed to Dick Williams was a reputation he fancied for being a very tough and utterly accomplished bench jockey, which had its roots during the Deadball era; for him, it was during the 1940s - '50s period, along with other notable bench jockey entertainers such as Leo Durocher and Eddie Stanky. Throughout his baseball career, Williams took great pride in being known as the resident smartass, which was a tag he used in describing himself; he relished the sharp-tongued role, especially knowing how effective he was in mocking players, managers, coaches and the dehumanizing effect he had on them. In his autobiography, he proudly explained, *"I was a verbal hit man,"* boasting as if being said with a wry smile and with pride. *"Few in baseball had a bigger or more effective mouth. Officially, I was ranked third on baseball's list of loudmouths, behind only Leo Durocher and Eddie Stanky."*[533] He became remarkably effective in his verbal attacks until it was affecting his opponent's play and their coaching, which was his assignment by such managerial luminaries as

---

[533] Dick Williams and Bill Plaschke, No More Mr. Nice Guy, p. 50

Dodger manager Chuck Dressen and soon he was finding himself becoming more distant from the ballplayers. *"I became increasingly alienated from players who didn't understand the art of heckling and just thought I had a big mouth,"* said Williams.[534]

But there was a racial element to bench jockeying of the '40s and early part of the 1950s festering on the Dodgers ballclub as they continued to bring up black players at a pace, unlike the rest of the league, gaining the attention of other known racist clubs like St. Louis and Milwaukee seeking to exploit the situation on the ballfield. In this mix of recognized white racist ballplayers were Enos Slaughter, Joe Garagiola, and manager Eddie Stanky of the Cardinals, the latter an intrepid racist – who was once a teammate of Jackie Robinson - and Dodger regulars Preacher Roe and Billy Cox among *"several bench-warming southerners," according* to author, historian and educator Carl Prince, that included Dick Williams. *"The arrival of Jim Gilliam brought racial conflict on the Dodgers back to the surface,"* said Prince. While working out during spring training, reserve infielder Bob Morgan called out to his Dodger teammates about Gilliam, who was new to the team from the Negro Leagues, *"'How come he ain't a Dodger? He's dark enough.'"* This brought forth a response from a second-string outfielder standing nearby, *"'probably Dick Williams,'"* fearing being displaced, who responded, *"'Yeah, they're gonna run us all right out of here.'"* The "Southerners" on the team included Dick Williams, who was

---

[534] IBID, p. 54

from *"southern Illinois,"* acting like he was from the South highlighted Prince in a humorous moment.[535]

"Today, of course, nobody understands. As a manager, I wished my players would be needlers, but few wanted any part of it. Modern-day players seem to have formed friendship societies with agreements never to yell at one another. Most of them are all working together, with very few willing to make anybody mad enough to jeopardize their ass for the sake of winning. That's why some of my players hated me: because I didn't give a damn about their corporations, and I'd needle their buddies anyway. The players on all teams want to work together now so nobody loses. Which means somebody does lose – the fans," wrote Williams.[536]

There was no mistaking that some of that constitutive tension and ritual of ragging and the personal attacks came to roost in his early managerial days with the Boston club, even hastening a few players to earlier than-expected departures from the team, to cite a few, catcher Joe Azcue, John Wyatt, Joe Foy, pitcher Don McMahon and their golden boy Tony Conigliaro, come to mind, each who clashed with Williams. Tony was traded to the California Angels in October 1970, a year after Dick Williams had left the Red Sox, but Tony's tempestuous brother Billy laid some of the blame – along with Yastrzemski and Reggie Smith, who shared the

---

[535] Carl E. Prince, "Brooklyn's Dodgers: The Bums, The Borough, and The Best of Baseball, 1947-1957," Oxford University Press, New York, NY, 1996, p. 12 & 13 https://archive.org/details/brooklynsdodgers0000prin/page/12/mode/2up

[536] Dick Williams and Bill Plaschke, "No More Mr. Nice Guy," p. 52

viewpoint - for his brother being traded onto Dick Williams, who were often feuding with each other. In a backhanded compliment besides pointing out their memorable clashes, most of them reaching the press, Dick Williams commented in his autobiography, *"He was a fighter, and so am I, and that's probably why we got into so many verbal scrapes. I'm never sure who got the better of who, but I know that by having Tony Conigliaro in there fighting every day, the game of baseball was a winner."*[537] Symbolically, and adding to the divisiveness and rancor that was permeating the city over the trade, it was not a good publicity move by the Red Sox by not only trading Conigliaro but trading him to the very team that had nearly killed him in 1967, which was a direct cause for ending his promising career. There was a human dignity element to the trade that aroused the suspicious city.

Following the 1967 World Series, which the Red Sox had nearly won with a bunch of overachievers, Dick Williams now had his sights set on nothing less than a World Series title, and '68 was to be the year for that. But it wasn't to be, and Williams became a monster. He would say so himself; he was hateful that some of his key players in '67 would actually "turn" on him, speaking about it as if there was a personal side to their inaccessibility. In December 1967, his Cy Young ace Jim Lonborg badly injured his knee in a Vail, Colorado ski accident, and he would never be quite the same after that. And, he was flummoxed by his Gold Glove and All-Star first baseman, George Scott, who appeared at spring training

---

[537] IBID, p. 112

looking *"fat and sloppy,"* exclaimed Williams, and *"realized I would also be without my first baseman."*[538] He resorted to alcohol to soothe his nerves. *"I drank to relax. I drank because, under the heat of 1967's instant success, I couldn't provide an encore alone. I needed to stay sane, and the bottle, I foolishly thought, gave me that help."*[539] It led to a separation from his wife Norma, whom he verbally assaulted until she couldn't take it anymore, and she briefly left him. *"Over the next two years, I would forget just about everything. Not only my son"* - who he absentmindedly left at Fenway Park after a contentious and surprisingly difficult contract renewal discussion with Tom Yawkey, who was challenging Williams about a pay raise in spite of his remarkable performance in '67 - *"but my wife and the rest of my family. I would forget my manners, my common sense, sometimes even that I was a human being."*[540]

Former Red Sox pitcher Bill Lee, who played ten seasons for Boston, and 14 years overall in the majors finishing with Montreal in 1982, offers a spin on issues with managers of minimal player skills, who then become field managers - and that would include someone like Dick Williams - and how he observed they dealt with players. Lee was a teammate of Scott's at the end of the Williams regime in '69 and during a portion of the Don Zimmer troubled period of '77 and '78, which was nothing but anguish for Scott. Bill Lee was considered a certified maverick, counterculture intellect, proponent of the black athlete, and an antagonist of anyone of managerial

---

[538] IBID, p. 108
[539] IBID, p. 110
[540] IBID, p. 108

stature and related injustices – known for his clashes with Red Sox manager Don Zimmer – had this to say about the black athlete: *"I've seen it happen so often. A white guy with little natural ability shows some false hustle and becomes the manager's pet. Meanwhile, a gifted black athlete gets the job done with seeming ease, and he's considered a loafer, gets a bad reputation, and ends up in the manager's doghouse. Most managers are guys who scrambled and hustled to stay in the majors – guys like Billy Martin and Don Zimmer. They resent anyone to whom it comes easy. They prefer the scrappy little guys with few skills because they look at them and see themselves."*[541]

Dick Williams' attacks on George Scott for the three seasons they were together were nothing less than historic. No one suffered more under his wrath than did George, who seemed to be an object lesson in how not to manage a young and talented ballplayer. His admonishment of George in the press was disturbing to teammates and got the attention of other teams as well. Jim Fregosi, the California Angels' six-time All-Star shortstop and soon-to-be well-respected major league manager of 15 years mocked Red Sox manager Dick Williams for his stubbornness and questionable leadership: *"Are the Red Sox being run by a manager or a dietitian?"* he jested, boldly admonishing Williams for his lack of refinement and inability to deal with his team on an individual basis that would get the best from his players, such as Scott.[542] Williams benched Scott, except for two pinch-

---

[541] Bill Lee, "The Little Red (Sox) Book," p. 96
[542] Glenn Stout and Richard Johnson, Red Sox Century, p. 324

hitting appearances, in an all-important 1967 three-game series during a pennant run with California in August because of his weight, which was telling where the manager's priorities lay. Scott had the best batting record against California going into the series against the Angels and was among the top ten for average in the league, yet Williams chose to sit him down as a disciplinary measure because of weight. Scott was hitting an impressive .340 against the Angels' pitching. Dick Williams, revealing his bias against George, apparently defending his decision, asked rhetorically, *"'But what did he weigh when he hit the .340?' Scott could not recall his poundage for his various hits against the Angels,"* said sportswriter Harold Kaese, written with a bit of sarcasm.[543] Angels' pitchers, including Jim McGlothlin, were delighted he was not in the Red Sox lineup. *"I was surprised to find Scott wasn't in the batting order and happy too. He's a long ball hitter,"* said the Angels pitcher, explaining the difficulties he has had pitching to the Boomer, who had launched a few taters against him.[544] The Red Sox lost all three games. The next club the Sox would face after California was the Detroit Tigers, a formidable pennant contender that, among a handful of teams, would take Boston to the season-ending wire. Scott was back in the lineup against the Tigers and hit three home runs in the three-game series. The Tigers, who were well aware of George's benching in Anaheim, were

---

[543] Harold Kaese, "Sox Manager History Maker," The Boston Globe, Aug 16, 1967, p. 47
https://www.newspapers.com/image/433979358/?match=1&terms=Harold%20Kaese
[544] Roger Birtwell, "McGlothlin Glad Scott only Pinch Hit," The Boston Globe, Aug 12, 1967, p. 5

stunned at Williams' less than sensible maneuver and bravado – all for principle and maybe deeper meaning - with his young first baseman, making comments attributable to their manager Mayo Smith, calling the benching a joke. He admonished Williams in a similar manner to how Fregosi had expressed it: *"Nine teams have managers. The Red Sox have a dietitian."*[545]

Dubbed the "Boomer" because of his tape-measure home runs, George Scott intimidated pitchers with his powerful bat. (courtesy of Boston Red Sox)

---

[545] Harold Kaese, "Sox Manager History Maker," Boston Globe, Aug 16, 1967, p. 47

The *Globe's* Clif Keane introduced some colorful satire in his August 15 article by commenting, *"What would he (Williams) have told Babe Ruth when the slugger used to grab a half-dozen hot dogs before he played and had a shape like a barrel?"*[546] Seasoned *Globe* reporter Harold Kaese also offered some satire of his own, among his comments: *"If the Sox do not win, we can all be sporting about it and say, 'It was worth losing the pennant just to get the Boomer in shape.'"*[547] *And*, he added humorously, *"The Red Sox batting order for the rest of the season should carry the weights of players, as well as their positions."*[548]

Jim "Mudcat" Grant, who played one year (1971) for Dick Williams, who at the time was managing a strong Oakland Athletics club, was an insightful critic of "Dick," tempered with a certain amount of word-caution as he was, at the time of his interview, on the board of the Major League Baseball Players Alumni Association. He candidly had this to say, however, about Williams, pulling few punches, placing him in the same niche with Solly Hemus, a known racist: *"People like Dick (Williams) and people like Solly Hemus and other [white] people, they weren't the only ones [that displayed racist tendencies]. We [black ballplayers] were titled as being lazy and don't work hard, and all that kind of stuff – black male. That could have some resonance to it in terms of how a manager or a coach may act towards you."* Grant explained that it was a manifestation of the era. If

---

[546] Clif Keane, "Would Dick Bench Ruth?" Bostom Globe, Aug 15, 1967, p. 25
[547] Harold Kaese, "Sox Manager History Maker," Boston Globe, Aug 16, 1967, p. 47
[548] IBID

managers were accused of being racist, they would vigorously deny it; they didn't even know that they were being racist, argued Grant. *"It's really based on the way it was [then],"* he said. In other words, it was a legacy of the times when older managers and coaches, who grew up in an atmosphere of virulent racism, couldn't in good conscience pry themselves away from what had been instilled in them.[549]

---

[549] Jim Mudcat Grant interview: January 22, 2009

Chapter 11
An Impossible Nightmare

Fair or foul, Scott has become the patsy in what may become the first of many lineup changes.

Neil Singelais[550]

The absence of the Sox' ace pitcher Jim Lonborg was a big hole to fill. Adding to that the weight of slugger Tony Conigliaro's injury, who, it was to happen, would miss the entire 1968 season, dealt Dick Williams a major blow that he knew would be a setback to his ambitions of winning another pennant, which he fully expected to achieve, or the world championship he was hoping for. His inclination to take his frustrations out on those around him, instead of "managing" his emotions, which in the preseason he had promised himself and the team he would do, quickly caught up with him, and his heretofore pugnacious and accustomed behavior reassumed itself landing squarely on his young first baseman, again. *"It apparently doesn't take much to psyche the Red Sox these days,"* wrote senior sportswriter

---

[550] Neil Singelais, "Slumping Scott Benched; Jones Gets 1b Chance," The Boston Globe, July 1, 1968, p. 25-26.
https://www.newspapers.com/image/434593695/?terms=Neil%20singelais&match=1

Harold Kaese. *"They look at themselves and not seeing Lonborg is like missing the Prudential Tower on the Boston Skyline."*[551]

This was apparent early in the spring season when the Red Sox, losing the fifth of their first six spring games, began to trigger the manager's inner rage of contending with losing, which was anathema to him, this one a 5-3 10-inning loss to Cincinnati. He was fuming and was overheard shouting, *"I don't like this stuff. I want to see it stopped."*[552]

As much as they were not winning in the exhibition season, George Scott made a great start ripping the ball at a .462 pace with 6 RBIs, 5 extra-base hits, including two home runs – one a monster shot – and a 1.353 slugging percentage for the first six games. But it didn't last. Uncharacteristic of Scott, for he almost always shined in spring training, George ended the spring season batting a paltry .206, along with several teammates with similar averages, on a Boston team that ended at the bottom of the spring standings at 8-18; the worst for George was yet to come.

Meanwhile, a frustrated Dick Williams, who had just come off a horrible spring and not feeling too upbeat about the upcoming season, was in the news again, on April 4, just before the opening game. Toward the end of the spring schedule, Tony Conigliaro was experiencing vision issues from

---

[551] Harold Kaese, "Tongue Hides Stanky's Class," The Boston Globe, Mar 13, 1968, p. 49. https://www.newspapers.com/image/433810837/?terms=Red%20Sox&match=1

[552] Clif Keane, "Yaz Hitless, Conig Out, Sox Lose, 5-3," The Boston Globe, March 14, 1968, p. 50 https://www.newspapers.com/image/433818534/?terms=Red%20Sox

his '67 injury and planned to meet with an eye specialist in Boston, which he did on April 4; a day later, it was confirmed he had serious eye damage, and could not play, at the least, for the 1968 season. The impetuous Dick Williams was irked by the news from Boston, said he was unaware of Conigliaro's situation, and blurted some imprudent remarks before any medical reports were forthcoming: *"I don't think there's anything wrong with Tony's vision despite what he said when he got to Boston,"* exclaimed the Red Sox manager. *"If Tony can't get the job done, we'll take it from there."*[553]

When he learned about the results, he recanted his earlier position, which had all the earmarks of being distrustful of what Conigliaro had to say, as if his right fielder was, in baseball terminology, dogging it, but he never apologized even though it was apparent he was well out of line. One thing Dick Williams was not was an apologist.

It was implausible to the young 24-year-old Scott that the misery he would soon experience in 1968 under one Richard Hirschfeld Williams would be such a bummer, especially after being so optimistic about the upcoming season – that included his marriage to Malvina "Lucky" Pena on January 21 - forecasting often how great a season he was going to have, and receiving such preseason praise from the likes of future Hall of Famer

---

[553] Clif Keane, "Angry Tony C. Blasts Williams," The Boston Globe, Apr 4, 1968, p. 27 https://www.newspapers.com/image/434480348/?terms=Red%20Sox

Carl Yastrzemski and sports writers, the *Globe's* Harold Kaese describing Scott's early spring performance as *outstanding*.

On Opening Day in the Hub City, the *Boston Globe's* Jerry Nason wrote a thought-provoking profile on the Red Sox skipper whom he claimed was psychologically disarming, an enchanting kind of guy, with a *"sneaky fast flick of psychology,"* he said, which he used on players, news journalists, historians, and the Red Sox front office, among others, being *"A man who strives to intimidate events rather than be intimidated by them."* Nason compared him with the Boston Celtics all-time legend Red Auerbach as men who had stalwart *"win-damn it!* personalities. But that's where Nason drew the line between them, describing Williams as another breed in his statement, *"There, you'd guess, their styles part – for you never heard of Auerbach being privately cut up by his own players, in or out of season."*[554]

"He bows his proud neck with grace to only one baseball statistic, which reads Won-Lost. It is there that he sits in judgment of himself. With men like Williams that self-judgment can be harsh," says Nason, which, naturally, had every potential for setting a downdraft and repercussion effect on his players. *"This is his style. He will take it with him into the '68 season, which,*

---

[554] Jerry Nason, "Dick Employs Psych Tactics," The Boston Globe, April 10, 1968, p. 63
https://www.newspapers.com/image/434501385/?terms=jerry%20nason&match=1

with his sneaky fast psychological pitches, he has almost made us forget is fraught with potential pratfalls," said Nason.[555]

Four months later and well into the season, another journalist, freelance writer Leonard Shecter of *Life Magazine,* wrote a scathing condemnation of Dick Williams in his full-length article, "Baseball: Great American Myth," which, though unintended, as the objective was about the team, turned out to be a personal testimonial by several of Williams' players causing a hubbub throughout the Sox' organization and the city. Schecter was traveling with the Red Sox in May of that year to do a story on the '67 defending champions and, instead, found himself in a hornet's nest. It became a misguided exercise of gripes and bitter complaints by several Red Sox players about their manager and their dislike for the man, which came back to haunt them when the magazine was published hitting the store shelves and newsstands. Players scrambled, with obvious concerns about their careers, alleging they were misquoted while Schecter himself had to publicly defend what he wrote. Boston scribes, including the sportswriters, were all over it, but, characteristically, the journalistic fraternity came to the defense of Schecter, whom the Globe's Harold Kaese described as *"an experienced and able writer,"* vindicating him.[556]

---

[555] IBID
[556] Harold Kaese, "Quotes in 'Life' Probably Valid," The Boston Globe, August 8, 1968, p. 25

Ken Harrelson, who had not been performing well during the early part of the season and was unhappy, was quoted by Schecter remarking about Dick Williams: *"There's no way you can like that man. He doesn't give you a chance to like him."*[557] Harrelson was positively apoplectic at the disclosure, denying he ever said that, but the Boston Press gave their nod to Schecter as the most likely credible source. Don McMahon, a seasoned veteran pitcher, who was traded by the Red Sox to Chicago in June of the '67 season, and who later that year was 5-0 with the White Sox, and would win 42 more games in the major leagues before retiring at the end of '74, had some harsh words for Williams: *"He got an expression on his face like I smelled or something and he had it all the time I was there,"* fumed McMahon.[558] After several interviews over a span of six weeks mingling with the Red Sox, Schecter's summary view of Williams was particularly dispositive, and in his discourse, he bluntly concluded about the Red Sox skipper that *"Williams is not liked by his players"* – period.[559]

If anyone had a reason for griping about Williams among Red Sox players, it would have been George Scott, who suffered through his manager's verbal blitzes, which, though caustic in '67, became even more toxic the following year. There is no evidence, however, of anything George

---

[557] Leonard Schecter, "Baseball: Great American Myth," Life Magazine, August 9, 1968, p. 55
[558] IBID
[559] IBID

Scott might have said about meeting with the journalist, or whether he even spoke to Schecter during this inquiry.

On May 17, Dick Williams made another controversial move dispensing with his black ace relief pitcher John Wyatt, for all appearances a discard, for nothing more than cash, selling him outright to the New York Yankees and a very grateful manager Ralph Houk who planned to use the right-hander as their "number one relief pitcher." Senior *Boston Globe* sportswriter Clif Keane, a Dick Williams critic, was scratching his head at the "strategy" behind it where there appeared to be none, expressing in similar terms to his previous criticism of Dick Williams' "weight training" tactics that were foisted upon George Scott, in his article, "Why Did Red Sox Sell Wyatt?" *"When manager Dick Williams doesn't want a guy around,"* wrote Keane, *"it looks as though he leaves the Red Sox at any cost."* Asked what he knew about the transaction by a bewildered press, *"I can't say anything more than what happened,"* said General Manager Haywood Sullivan, who, though in a position of authority to oversee and coordinate the deal, and likely he did, appeared unwilling to explain what had actually happened when it was so mysterious and sudden, raising suspicions.[560]

It seems that Wyatt, among "20 others," he claimed, had been in Williams' infamous doghouse since the end of '67 when he couldn't pitch

---

[560] Clif Keane, "Why Did Red Sox Sell Wyatt?" The Boston Globe, May 19, 1968, p. 56 https://www.newspapers.com/image/434559088/?terms=%22Clif%20Keane%22%20

effectively because of arm stiffness. In other words, Wyatt was dogging it was the inference, taking on the appearance of race-norming in today's current-day parlance. Over the winter, while attending baseball meetings in Mexico City, Williams publicly discredited the pitcher, disparaging him in the press, as he was prone to do, and threatening to trade him, apparently due to Wyatt's blown saves in the championship stretch run. Wyatt had mentioned his arm trouble to Williams, who gave little regard or solace to the right-hander, according to Wyatt, but saw this purely as pitcher failure, a matter of indifference, and Wyatt became immediately expendable. Wyatt saw this as an attack on his character and went into an apoplectic rage, copping off his displeasure by boldly writing a letter to Larry Claflin of the *Boston Record-American* asking him that it be printed – to which Claflin was more than accommodating - in full defense of himself against Williams' charges and making it decidedly public, realizing it could be the end of the line for him; and it was, not long after that Wyatt predictably was let go, being sold to New York. "*'I've played for about 11 managers,'*" said Wyatt in his interview with baseball author and journalist Leonard Schecter, "*'and I never saw one like that. I been sold not because of my ability, but because of a personal thing. If that man is your enemy, forget it.'*"[561]

"*The players call Williams a 'front-runner,'*" wrote Claflin, alluding to the philosophic side of those who are at their best when they are in the lead.

---

[561] Leonard Schecter, "Baseball: Great American Myth," p. 55

"Do something good," said Red Sox pitcher Dennis Bennett, who was one of those twenty players sharing the Williams' doghouse, *"and he's all over you. But get on his bad list, and you never get off."*[562] Williams spoke about that often, the importance of being a front-runner, and how he preferred to deal with his players by applying that philosophy, stressing the importance of playing *"the guys that have the hot hand – the guys that are going good."*[563]

Williams shuffled players in-and-out of lineups, even positions, which would be his style the entire year that began in spring training. George Scott, who had all the credentials to be the best first baseman in major league baseball, was to feel the impact of Williams' maneuvering throughout the season and never could get his head around it. *"All of my life, from Little League ball all the way up, I never let anyone get into my head,"* lamented George Scott. *"Williams had me that year [in a mental state], so I just could not stay focused; my concentration was not good."*[564]

Talk quickly stirred about who was going to take over Tony Conigliaro's cleanup spot in the lineup, the power-hitting slot due to his absence, and all fingers were pointing to George Scott, but Dick Williams was at it again: he had other ideas for his big first baseman. He wanted

---

[562] Larry Claflin, "Wyatt Rips Williams with His Pen," The Sporting News, December 23, 1967, p. 28
[563] Will McDonough, "Hughes Leads Waslewski, 2-0," The Boston Globe, October 11, 1967, p. 47
[564] George Scott interview: January 21, 2006

George to adopt a shorter swing altogether and, in effect, become a different type of hitter, which was not his style, adding to his frustrations. It was Williams' passion for "Dodger ball" like he was raised on, the "bat control" method of hitting going to the opposite field, hit-and-run, and even bunt. In effect, he intended for George to become a non-threatening "base-hits" man, all six foot two and 215 pounds of him, and leave the home runs to someone else. It was a conflicting message for the Boomer, who was accustomed to employing a full swing and hitting for power, Babe Ruth-type blasts that sometimes went out of stadiums and entire ballparks. The other Williams, "Ted", who took a liking to George, felt the manager was performing a disservice to the young slugger attempting to convert him to a base-hits man. *"He [Ted Williams] told me 'Don't change your style,'"* mentioning a conversation he had with the Splendid Splinter and future Hall of Famer who was regularly giving batting tips to George. Ted spent time with the young rookie slugger in 1966 in Winter Haven, the Florida Instructional League in '66, and again in 1967, frequently emphasizing to avoid letting anyone change his batting style, which was one important reason he got to the majors in the first place.

He was made the project of Williams' coach Bobby Doerr, to whom Williams entrusted the role of batting "instructor"- certainly a prudent choice of a man who exemplified bat control with over 2000 base hits in his career and a future Hall of Famer - for the big first baseman to help him acquire the "new way" of hitting that the manager wanted from him. His tone was strident about Scott's conversion insisting something new was needed for balancing the lineup.

Boston Globe reporter Harold Kaese, a discerning senior writer and baseball columnist, wrote a gripping article on the needs and merits of a right-handed power hitter – a pure, unabashed slugger type – in Fenway batting behind Yastrzemski. In a pointed criticism of Dick Williams, the journalist questioned the manager's judgment in making the Boomer a "Dodger type" singles hitter when he had such raw natural power. *"[We] grieve its loss,"* wrote Kaese disconsolately.[565]

It was the "big swish" brand of hitting, according to Kaese, that was once favored by Red Sox brass for their little bandbox, it was often called, to slug home runs over Fenway's vaunted 37' 2" left-field wall and Scott fit the mold perfectly. He had an extended type of swing, a massive batting stroke, a sweeping over-swing that Red Sox hitting instructor Bobby Doerr was assigned to "correct" inexorably favoring a batting style that was being foisted on a troubled Scott. There were concerns by some, including journalist and baseball man Harold Kaese, about changing this type of hitter with a natural swing designed for the long ball into something much less: Doerr knew it. Doerr was well aware that the outcome of this experiment could be much more intimidating, or something in-between, quite possibly

---

[565] Harold Kaese, "Sox Could Use Howard's Bat," The Boston Globe, May 23, 1968, p. 53

leading to problems with his timing, rhythm, and, more importantly, Scott's confidence, which had forsaken him precipitously.

The general buzz around Boston was, "What's wrong with George Scott?" He was in a woeful batting slump, and it wasn't until early June that George finally had a good day against the Detroit Tigers with a three-hit performance and a couple of days after that, he was hitting well and seemed to be getting his rhythm back, hitting safely in six straight games. But then he had three straight games in which he went hitless and was immediately pulled from the lineup by his obstreperous manager, who charged him with "peeking" at the left-field wall, "so he is out of there," raged Williams, applying a disciplinary measure and replacing him with Ken Harrelson. It was a move that was rapidly evolving into a Dick Williams tactic designed for Scott to display no patience with him but instead banish him to his most dishonorable but well-populated doghouse.

Following a home series with California George participated with teammates Carl Yastrzemski and Rico Petrocelli to work on their hitting. *"The most awesome display of power I've ever seen,"* said Yastrzemski of Scott, who was blasting tape measure home run shots all over Fenway in a similar fashion to his batting prowess of 1966 and '67. *"There's nothing wrong with that man, except he's not swinging at the ball,"* said Yaz. *"He's feeling for it. Hitting is all aggressiveness. Once you make up your mind to swing, you've got to let it go…a big, strong guy like that, with his reflexes, he should hit 30 home runs by accident. Why don't they leave him alone and let him swing?"*[566]

On June 19, Scotty was back in the lineup, but this time, he was moved to third base as newcomer Ken "Hawk" Harrelson, acquired from Kansas City toward the end of '67, had been playing in his spot at first base and in contention for '68 MVP. Scott, on the other hand, was mired in a miserable batting slump, lingering around .176, and would finish the season at a harrowing .171. Scott, however, was far better the first baseman than Harrelson, which did not get by the manager, who realized to have any chance at a pennant, he would need Scotty's glove; he brought confidence to the entire infield.

---

[566] Bob Sales, "No Flag for Sox Without Scott," The Boston Globe, June 18, 1968, p. 41. https://www.newspapers.com/image/434644391/?terms=bob%20sales&match=1

George Scott returned to the Boston lineup on June 19, 1968, after spending time in manager Dick Williams' doghouse. Here he's sliding into home under tag of Detroit catcher Bill Freehan (courtesy of Boston Herald)

Harrelson had a 3-run home run that night against Detroit. Scott was 0-for-4, striking out twice, and he was fed up. He announced that evening he was going back to his "old swing" despite what his manager and instructor coach, Bobby Doerr, had to say about it. *"Just leave me alone,"* said Scott, and he'd dig himself out of the slump his way.[567] No doubt it would not sit well with Dick Williams. *"That's when the relationship took a different turn from there because I wouldn't make the change,"* said a reminiscent George Scott years later. Williams threatened him with a return to the minors

---

[567] Clif Keane, "'Just Let Me Hit' – Scott," The Boston Globe, June 20, 1968, p. 45

411

because of his stubbornness and also alleged he had spoken to owner Tom Yawkey about the matter. *"He lied,"* ranted Scott, remembering the unpleasant occasion, saying he went to Yawkey himself, who denied knowing anything about it. *"So, it was kind of tough [between us] from there,"* said a perturbed George Scott, still showing anger from the personal scarring he suffered after so many years.[568]

Once again, no doubt because of Scott's intransigence, Dick Williams was on his case as soon as he sensed an opportunity to pounce, and that happened at the end of June. George, in a string of ten games in which he hit safely in nine of them, including breaking up a no-hitter by Detroit's Denny McLain, a 31-game winner that year, was quickly benched by the manager after he failed to get a base hit going 0-for-5 in the remaining two games in June. He was replaced by Dalton Jones, who had no credentials for playing first base; it was only the second time in his five-year stint with the Red Sox that Jones played the position. Meanwhile, the team leader, Carl Yastrzemski, was struggling at the plate as well; Williams said that it would be up to Yaz himself to work out of his own hitting dilemma and, as it turned out, he would not be benched; Scott, however, was another story. *Boston Globe* reporter Neil Singelais, noting the double standard between

---

[568] George Scott interview: May 7, 2006

them, commented, *"Fair or foul, Scott has become the patsy in what may become the first of many lineup changes."*[569]

In advance of the July 26 game against Washington, in which he was 0-for-4, Scott was triggered after being frequently benched and pinch-hit for and through his torment, he unraveled before the press. *"I go 0-for-4, and I'm out of the lineup,"* he exclaimed. The Detroit Tigers, where the Red Sox played in June, and Washington Senators, where the Sox were for a three-game series in D.C., both raised the question: "What happened to George Scott?" What happened was that Scott had had enough of his manager and his tactics, reaching his breaking point; *"if I can't play for Dick Williams, I'd like to go somewhere else where I can play."*[570]

This did not go unnoticed by Red Sox brass, who were beginning to look inwardly at the manager and his methods with some reservations since there were issues developing with other players, and then there was the Leonard Schecter *Life Magazine* story published in August that cast serious shadows on the manager.

Ironies of all ironies, AL president Joe Cronin, known for his past racial transgressions while with the Red Sox, and his strained relationship with

---

[569] Neil Singelais, "Slumping Scott Benched; Jones Gets 1b Chance," The Boston Globe, July 1, 1968, p. 25
[570] Bob Sales, "Scott Wants to Play Baseball – If Not Here, Somewhere Else," The Boston Globe, July 27, 1968, p. 16
https://www.newspapers.com/image/434383100/?terms=%22George%20Scott%22&match=1

Jackie Robinson, whom he personally boycotted throughout his years in and out of baseball, including MLB's 25th anniversary tribute to Robinson's breaking the color barrier – celebrated during the World Series in October 1972, nine days before he died - on July 3 hired America's Olympic hero Jesse Owens as his "special public relations director" to help with player relations. Owens clarified that his assignment and task was to *"talk to the ballplayers and find out what's bugging them."*[571] Although Owens was cautious about disclosing that his real purpose was to address racial problems that had been percolating in both leagues, it was generally believed that the black athlete was Owens' charge and whom, in this investigation, received his greatest attention. He told the press otherwise, however, stating he was *"dealing with Negro and white players alike."*[572] Two of the men that seemed to have his greatest attention were both black, Tommy Davis of the White Sox and George Scott of the Bosox. Davis, who was an accomplished ballplayer with good credentials, was in an uncharacteristically bad slump, and *"obviously something was bothering him,"* Owens said.[573] The *something* was White Sox manager Eddie Stanky, reputed to exhibit little patience with black ballplayers, *"that seems to have been solved when there was a change in managers,"* Owens said.[574] "The

---

[571] Jerome Holtzman, "Jesse Owens Hears Players' Problems," The Sporting News, Aug 3, 1968, p. 30
[572] George Langford, "Owens Toils for A.L. as 'Watchdog,'" Chicago Tribune, July 17, 1968, p. 54
https://www.newspapers.com/image/376545573/?terms=George%20langford
[573] IBID
[574] IBID

same thing happened to Richie Allen of the Phillies," exclaimed Owens. *"And there are cases like George Scott in Boston – a great hitter who just can't seem to be able to do anything this year."*[575] On July 16, while Owens was attending a National League game, he mentioned that he planned to approach George Scott and discuss what was troubling him, including his dealings with his manager and coaches. Owens began his new role by meeting players in the first week of August, paying his first visit to White Sox Park on August 6 to begin his troubleshooting with some of the White Sox and Red Sox players, among them Davis and Scott, in the midst of a four-game series in Chicago. It was the first night of another benching of George – this one for a stretch of six games – by Williams. Scott was 6-for-17 in the previous eight games, four of them doubles, and hitting at a .353 clip before being ignominious, if not mysteriously, sat down.

"I remember [Jesse] Owens, yes. I saw him in Chicago when he came to me about problems he thought I was having in 1968. I was surprised. Didn't know they had anyone like this, said he was from the [American] league. I think he saw some other black players, too, like Tommy Davis, who was not very happy with [manager] Eddie Stanky. He asked me about Dick Williams, and I told him we weren't seeing eye to eye, and I was thinking about leaving Boston because of him. I thought he was going to talk to Williams, but don't know if he did or not."[576]

---

[575] IBID
[576] George Scott interview: January 23, 2006

Boston was in Cleveland toward the end of August for a four-game set against the Indians. Scott brought a pitiful .183 batting average with him into the series and was the subject of considerable trade talk, among them Indians' manager Alvin Dark, who would amass two pennants and a World Series title and was considered a good manager of men, thought highly of the big first baseman and expressed concern to the press before the August 20 game about how he was not only being mismanaged but also mishandled by the Red Sox, and didn't hesitate to say so speaking boldly about it. An expansion draft was due to occur in October 1969 and there was scuttlebutt that George's name was in the mix of ballplayers possibly available, though Dark felt he would be protected but willing to trade for him anyway. *"If I did take George,"* said Dark, speaking about trades likely to occur surrounding the draft, *"I would do with him what I did with Ken Harrelson. I would tell him he was going to play, and he would stay in there. He needs that kind of help."*[577] As if he were confirming his value to the Indians manager, who had spoken to Scott before the game pondering what was troubling him and to express his interest in George, Scotty stroked his third and final home run of the year off the hard-throwing world-class fast-baller Sam McDowell – who would strike out a major league-leading 283 batters that year – hit deep into Municipal Stadium's left-field seats. It was the only run scored against McDowell that night. What seemed peculiar about it was his presence in the lineup at all and the attendant timing of the clout – why

---

[577] Clif Keane, "Cleveland Likes Scott, Might Trade Catcher," The Boston Globe, August 21, 1968, p. 52
https://www.newspapers.com/image/434547610/?match=1&terms=alvin%20Dark

that game? Why did Dick Williams put him in that game when Scott had been struggling? - for all the marginal success George historically had registered against the big left-hander - looking bad at times - and Dick Williams was all-too-familiar with their history, claimed Scott in later years; it was the only game of the series in which Scott had appeared, giving the distinct impression Williams was out to publicly embarrass his first baseman, in whichever manner he could contrive to accomplish that.. *"He [Williams] sent me up to bat against Sam McDowell thinking that McDowell was going to make me look bad,"* said Scott in later years. He was convinced that putting him in the lineup against "Sudden Sam" was just another set-up by Williams, who he claimed had it in for him after he refused to cooperate with the manager's effort to tamper with his batting style and who he felt, was trying to embarrass him. *"[He wanted] in all situations to make George Scott look bad because he wanted to trade me,"* said Scott. *"But he had to convince Mr. Yawkey and Dick O'Connell because they didn't want to trade me, but Dick Williams wanted to get me out of his hair. Then, fortunately, they fired him the next year."*[578]

Alvin Dark considered a good baseball man and solid manager as perceived by smart baseball men and players alike, had racial indiscretions of his own, a one-time moment that he was having trouble shedding from his image. He and Dick Williams were contemporaries from a similar era,

---

[578] George Scott interview: January 23, 2006

Dark having retired as a player in 1960 and Williams in '64, yet Dark was the even-tempered commonplace sort of fellow while Williams stood out as tempestuous. It was unlikely Dark would harbor such a strong opinion about minority players, but it seems that he did: In 1964, while managing the San Francisco Giants, he was quoted as saying that *"Negro and Spanish-speaking players on this team...are just not able to perform up to the white players when it comes to mental alertness...you can't get Negro and Spanish players to have the pride in their team that you can get from white players,"* said Dark, and it stuck to him like glue, much like what occurred to the Dodgers' Al Campanis as late as 1987. It was a run-of-the-mill attitude seemingly shared by the majority of white ballplayers and managers of that era who saw this viewpoint as nothing more than harmless, of common knowledge, and a perfectly acceptable maxim.[579]

The mind games continued between the 39-year-old disgruntled manager and 24-year-old Scott when, on August 23 in Baltimore, Williams inserted a stupefied Carl Yastrzemki at first base, surprising everyone, in particular Yaz, and expressly insulting George Scott. It was the first time that Yastrzemski had played first base in his major league career and the third in succession of seven men who played first base that season who was not a first-sacker. The Red Sox faithful were beginning to think that their manager had lost his sensibilities, and he was now being second-guessed by

---

[579] Bryan Soderholm-Difatte, "Alvin Dark and the Persistence of Racial Stereotypes," Seamheads.com, November 20, 2014 https://seamheads.com/blog/2014/11/20/alvin-dark-and-the-persistence-of-racial-stereotypes/

baseball pundits, the media, fans, and, more than likely, even the Red Sox brass, who would eventually wrestle with their conscience whether Dick Williams was a good fit for Boston, in spite of '67.

"George Scott is storing up like Vesuvius," wrote senior sportswriter Clif Keane of the *Boston Globe*, characterized by many of the athletes he covered as a man of "brutal objectivity," a chronic needler, known as "poison pen" by many of the ballplayers, *"and somewhere near the end of the season he will erupt unless something is done to stop it."*[580]

Lack of communication was the problem specified by Keane, proceeding to embark, or wade, into his column on a discussion of this as being a manifestation of racial barriers still evident in major league baseball that prevented any such rapport, in spite of Jackie Robinson. *"But where in big league baseball do you find any communication between black and white? There isn't anymore now than there was about 25 years ago,"* said Keane. *"If the fan wants to see how much communication there is between white and Negro, let him get to the ballpark early someday while the teams are having batting practice. The black players on the Red Sox are gathered around with the black players on the opposition. Every day, there are*

---

[580] Clif Keane, "Scott Boiling at Treatment," The Boston Globe, Aug 27, 1968, p. 27 https://www.newspapers.com/image/434557218/?terms=Scott%20boiling%20at%20treatment&match=1

groups from the two teams. They meet in the outfield, at the batting cage, along the foul lines. They aren't supposed to."[581]

Keane suggested both were at fault but placed the greater weight on the manager whom, he suggested, needed to talk to Scott behind closed doors, but also on the coach, Bobby Doerr, who *"should listen to Scott, too. It isn't a one-way street."*[582]

It didn't take very long, and George Scott's "Vesuvius" did indeed erupt as Clif Keane had ably predicted. He had had a steady diet of shuffling in and out of lineups throughout the season that had unnerved him, and then on Saturday, September 7, after a game against the Angels in California, Scott became aware of Williams' plan to put shortstop Rico Petrocelli at first base the following day, the eighth Red Sox first baseman during the year, and the fourth to play the position without any previous experience there. Petrocelli was not suited for the position; he knew it, and so did George Scott. In fact, he was reticent to take the assignment, feeling completely out of his element, and it showed. Meanwhile, Scott was enraged and blasted his manager, insisting it would be the last time he would be humiliated by the man. *"All the guy is trying to do is kill everything I've*

---

[581] IBID
[582] IBID

got for the game," howled a very upset Scott, who promised to anyone who would listen he was done playing for Williams, demanding he be traded.[583]

"He's got something against me personally, and I intend to find out what it is. I've been in to talk with Dick O'Connell (Red Sox Vice President), and now I'm going in and have a talk with Mr. Yawkey about it," said Scott.[584]

Along with the turmoil surrounding the Scott-Williams matter, there were growing issues with the team, causing unrest with the club's front office that would play a part in Williams' eventual departure. Most notable was a developing conflict with their superstar Carl Yastrzemski – it wouldn't be the last - who had an unpleasant encounter with Williams on September 8 in California when he was asked to take a pitch on a 3-0 count that he thought he should have hit. Yaz was a Yawkey favorite, which gnawed at Williams, who felt he was being undermined by the Red Sox owner, which, in a manner of speaking, he likely was. Some pointed to Yastrzemski as a trouble source for the club's tension.

As for George Scott, he never regained his footing for the balance of the '68 season, and the general impression was that he would be trade bait going into the '69 season or possibly, but less likely, taken in the expansion draft.

---

[583] Neil Singelais, "Scott Demands Sox Trade Him," The Boston Globe, September 9, 1968, p. 27
https://www.newspapers.com/image/434398820/?terms=Scott%20demands%20sox%20trade%20him%22&match=1
[584] IBID

It has never been explained satisfactorily, nor has any hypothesis emerged to help elucidate in a fashion the reasons behind why Dick Williams chose to make George Scott his personal stooge, singularly dismantling his spirit and confidence, but the element of race may have played into it, which, in later years, George Scott felt in all probability was a factor. Scott stood up for himself when it was not customary for blacks to be heard. *"He didn't like my opinions or that I was willing to give them, and he didn't like that I had them,"* said Scott.[585] Whatever the motivational forces were that inspired a contemptuous Dick Williams to take apart young George Scott in that forgettable season of 1968, one truth seems to stand above all else. He may have had more to do with stripping George Scott's frame of mind and the erosion of his confidence than anything Scott may have brought upon himself. Williams nearly psychologically destroyed the young ballplayer. He became a special target of Williams' derisiveness, which was a generally accepted view by many of his teammates.

---

[585] George Scott interview: January 23, 2006

Chapter 12
A Moral Victory

"One sure man on the list – and apparently certain to stay with the Red Sox until at least partway through Spring training in February – was George Scott, who has been traded and sold about 50 times in the past couple of months. Scott is going to stay with the team."

Unattributed[586]

The '68 year ended badly for George Scott, in fact dreadfully, finishing his season batting .171 with a mere three home runs while the team finished in fourth place; but in spite of injuries and key players not performing well, there was irony afoot: Boston's fandom had actually grown since the prior year's miraculous *Impossible Dream* team performance leading to what became known, famously, as *Red Sox Nation* – whose fans would fill the stands for years to come - and drew an unprecedented number of nearly two million fans to their little bandbox known as Fenway in '68. The final game of the season against the Yankees drew a sellout crowd of over 35,000.

George did not play in either of the three season-ending games against New York, and there was a sense that Dick Williams felt he was in the

---

[586] Multimedia article, "Sox to Protect Scott," The Boston Globe, October 10, 1968, p. 51
https://www.newspapers.com/image/434561497/?terms=%22Haywood%20sullivan%22%20

driver's seat in full command and that his unceasing player maneuvering and managerial style throughout '68 would not be challenged by the Red Sox brass; but he was wrong, particularly as it had afflicted George Scott.

The writing was manifestly on the wall with Scott's eruption on September 7 after the indignancy of a hesitant Petrocelli, who had never played first base, being "rewarded" the position the next day; this was followed by the manager's heavy-handed announcement staging his plan with the press to insert Dalton Jones at first base two games later, after he had previously informed an exultant Boomer immediately following the September 9 game, which he played, that he would be the starting first baseman on Tuesday the 10th. In essence, he snapped the rug on Scott again. It was momentary, however, as three hours later, he announced that Scott would be starting at first, not Jones, who assumed a pinch-hit role on that day. Of course, he was besieged by the reporters sensing a story in the making as it was well known Williams was not accustomed to changing his mind once it was made up; it was not in his character. The press, meanwhile, surmised that a certain someone, possibly Vice President Dick O'Connell or Tom Yawkey, in either case, a Yawkey initiative, had interceded with a phone call to the West Coast demanding to play George, which they boldly put into print. Williams explained in a mellow manner, which was quite unlike him, that *"he and his coaching staff talked it over and decided on*

Scott."[587] The writers, seeing it differently, felt there could be no other reason for the sudden uncharacteristic change than the belief that someone in the Red Sox hierarchy called upon the manager to play Scott. Williams, as expected, denied it. None of the sportswriters, however, believed Williams' explanation or his outright denial. A moral victory for the Boomer, but it was not to last; there was more to come.

In a moment of apparent defiance by the Red Sox front office upon the Sox' return from their western road swing, manager Williams greeted the hometown crowd, who loved their Boomer – the ultimate crowd-pleaser – on September 13, by opening the home series with Dalton Jones at first base. In his autobiography, *No More Mr. Nice Guy*, Dick Williams admitted he was not particularly savvy nor sensitive about what was going on with Red Sox management when his attention was on the field. *"I was still fairly ignorant of any front office harm done to me – of course, I'm ignorant of just about everything that happens off the field during the season,"* said Williams.[588]

The American League expansion draft that was about to launch two new teams, the Kansas City Royals and Seattle Pilots, was underway on October 9 when the Red Sox submitted their "frozen 15" list of protected ballplayers

---

[587] Neil Singelais, "Scott Hitless – but Relaxed," Boston Globe, Sep 10, 1968, p. 29 https://www.newspapers.com/image/434399472/?terms=%22Dick%20Williams%22%20&match=1
[588] Dick Williams & Bill Plaschke, "No More Mr. Nice Guy," p. 116

to the league office in advance of the draft. After such a chaotic year between Dick Williams and his big first baseman *Herald-Traveler* sportswriter Tim Horgan speculated there would be no room for both on the Red Sox after what had transpired; *"Not now,"* he said.[589] It was fully expected that an embattled George Scott would not be on that list, but astonishingly, he was, sending a forewarning message to the startled Sox' manager, who felt the front office breathing down his neck.

The Red Sox brass had spoken with a well-intended public scolding of Boston's field management, the central focus being Dick Williams. Director of Player Personnel Haywood Sullivan, who in one instance Williams described as *"once a flunkie and now a head rat,"* had some heavy words for the on-field staff.[590]

"We intend to keep George around, and something has to be done about his present situation," expressed a critical Sullivan, who appeared to speak for more than just himself but as a likely spokesman for owner Tom Yawkey, whose one desire, perhaps flawed as it was for a man desirous of a championship team, was to have a "happy" team. *"We have to help George,"* said Sullivan. *"By that I mean myself, Dick O'Connell, the*

---

[589] Tim Horgan, "Scotty Gets to Play First, but for Whom?" Boston Herald-Traveler, September 10, 1968, p. 37
[590] Dick Williams & Bill Plaschke, "No More Mr. Nice Guy," p. 114

coaches, and Dick Williams. And George has to help himself...he's the greatest fielder that I've ever seen, and I think he can hit again."[591]

Red Sox General Manager Dick O'Connell had some words of his own to ensure that Williams and his coaching crew received the incisive message: *"Maybe he gets too much advice on his hitting,"* which went straight to the heart of Williams' apparent misguided experimentation of making Scott a singles hitter.[592] O'Connell added emphasis to his critical messaging, pointing a finger directly at the manager, suggesting that Scott was to be Dick Williams' number one "rehab assignment."

As Jim Mudcat Grant boldly postulated in his 2009 interview, Dick Williams fit a similar profile to that of the infamous Solly Hemus, who was known for his racial intolerance, along with a handful of others of that era, such as Eddie Stanky, Mike Higgins, Dixie Walker, Preacher Roe, Harry Walker, Charlie Grimm and reformed racist Bobby Bragan, among them. Along with George Scott, there were several black ballplayers who were regulars on the team; the greater numbers of them were honored with frequent membership in Dick Williams' notorious doghouse: Joe Foy, John Wyatt, Elston Howard, Reggie Smith, and Jose Santiago (Latino). If there truthfully was racism at play it may possibly have been something that

---

[591] Multimedia, "Sox to Protect Scott," Boston Globe, October 10, 1968, p. 51 https://www.newspapers.com/image/434561497/?terms=%22Haywood%20sullivan%22%20

[592] Larry Claflin, "Great Scott! What Will Bosox do With Poor George?" Sporting News, September 21, 1968, p. 29

Williams himself was unaware of, insisted Grant somewhat cryptically, but it nonetheless was likely to have occurred. As Grant put it, it was a symptom and signature of the times, a byproduct of bigoted vintage period baseball. These baseball people, often older managers and coaches who had played in the 1940s and '50s - the Robinson era – and managed between the '50s and '80s with direct access to and engagement of on-field players, would vehemently disavow they were racists if they were being accused of that not realizing that their actions clearly placed them in that nefarious role; but they remained clueless.

General Manager Dick O'Connell, whom it appeared was following the lead of his boss Tom Yawkey, arranged for his troubled ballplayer George Scott to spend the winter in Puerto Rico with the Santurce Crabbers and their new manager, future Hall of Famer Frank Robinson of the Baltimore Orioles. It was Robinson's managerial debut that would later on, in 1975, earn him the role of Major League Baseball's first black manager with the Cleveland Indians. He managed seventeen years until 2006 with five major league clubs. Scott credited Frank Robinson with restoring his self-respect and confidence while playing in Puerto Rico that he had lost under the trenchant criticism of Dick Williams, explaining that had he not had that opportunity with Robinson, it was unlikely he would have remained in baseball.

Scott thrived under Robinson's tutelage, batting .295 for Santurce with a league-leading 13 home runs and 46 RBIs over the course of 69 winter league games. Importantly, he also led the league in bases on balls, a good sign that he had his batting eye back. It was quite the transformation for the young ballplayer who had suffered badly under Williams, and it got the attention of Red Sox brass, who now viewed him as rejuvenated, more mature, with a more positive state of mind, and a much more confident ballplayer fashioned under Robinson's careful guidance.

"Having had a chance to play for Frank Robinson was the best thing that ever happened to my career because not only did he help me mentally, but he also helped me physically, and I became a better ballplayer," said a respectful George Scott. *"A lot of things probably I shouldn't have taken personally, but I did. He taught me a lot, and I always said that I had Frank Robinson to thank for the turnaround in my career."*[593]

---

[593] George Scott interview: January 23, 2006

February 28, 1969 - Scott's arrival in Winter Haven, Florida, for spring training as a Red Sox holdout looking for a raise following a successful winter ball season in Santurce, Puerto Rico (courtesy of Boston Herald)

February 27, 1969 – Unsigned George Scott standing next to Billy Conigliaro and Ken Harrelson at a batting cage. Scott signed his 1969 Red Sox contract the next day, February 28 (courtesy of Boston Public Library)

He was being designated for third base in '69, which he hadn't played since the beginning of 1966 as a rookie, which was brief. Williams was favoring Ken Harrelson at first base, who was a strong performer in '68 but who had little field range defensively and was better at first, whereas Scott was versatile. As senior sportswriter Clif Keane wrote, George was "solemn" about his new assignment, tight-lipped, not content with the switch being made of him by the manager, but he was much more circumspect about it and anxious just to be in the lineup than grouse about his new field position. Perhaps with a little help from his new mentor, Frank

Robinson, he had resigned himself to making the transition just to stay in the game. But there was no change in feelings between the two. Scott said that neither he nor Dick Williams got together before the start of spring training to straighten things out from '68; things remained cool. *"I come to the park and say hello to him, and he says hello to me,"* said Scott.[594] That was about it, nothing he didn't expect; however, he was content with that as long as he was playing.

What was uncanny about the start of '69, yet clear enough to the savvy local sportswriters, was the appearance that Dick Williams was operating under some kind of directive, or as much as a mandate, by the Red Sox brass to mend his unpleasantness – and improve his manners - that was on full display the previous year, as he was remarkably mellow all through the spring season. He was particularly laid-back about Scott, even praiseworthy about his new third sacker for whom he barely issued a good word all of '68. *"I don't care how much he weighs,"* exclaimed the suddenly sanctified manager to the astonished reporters used to something more distasteful from Williams, *"just look at him out there at third base, and you can see what I mean about how he can field the position."*[595] It was completely out of character for one Richard Hirschfeld Williams to heap praise on Scott when,

---

[594] Clif Keane, "Scott: Fun Is Over; It's Time to Get Set," The Boston Globe, March 3, 1969, p. 18
https://www.newspapers.com/image/434619989/?terms=%22Clif%20Keane%22%20

[595] Larry Claflin, "Tony C's First Homer Since 1967: What a Tonic for the Red Sox!" The Sporting News, Apr 12, 1969, p. 9

according to George, they were still not speaking, and the bitterness they felt for each other was manifestly pathological. Scott clearly had carried a few extra pounds into training camp that in previous years would have incited Williams, who not only would have lambasted him publicly but fined him and/or imposed actions even more punitive. This was a reconciliation most mysterious, reasoned the sportswriters, that had all earmarks of upper-level management's intervention remembering their condescension of Williams expressed at the conclusion of the '68 season and the recent episode of Scott's being protected by the club during the expansion draft, followed by their admonishment of Williams. To them, it was a ploy by the manager to offset any appearance of disenchantment in his "sneaky fast" psychologically disarming style as proffered by sportswriter Jerry Nason early in '68; simply overdone, they thought.

Scott working out at third base in spring training, at the position where manager Dick Williams would play him for most of the 1969 season (courtesy of Boston Herald)

With Scott batting inconsistently for the first couple of months of '69 and just under .200 by the first part of June, he was destined for the bench again until he dramatically delivered with an awesome home run at Fenway on June 6th against expansion team Kansas City Royals that rocketed halfway up the wall behind the center-field bleacher seats. It was a prodigious clout getting not only the attention of the Fenway fans but also KC's field manager, Joe Gordon. Gordon, who had a good view of the blast from where he sat, said, *"I saw it go over everything...it went over the whole business in center field."*[596]

Scott saved himself from a benching with that enormous shot and raised his average to over 50 points by the end of the month. He stroked his 6th homer the following day. For some inexplicable reason, as reporter Clif Keane and other sportswriters mused, Williams, who had stuck with his new third baseman all spring, unlike his troubling handling of him in '68, was on him again despite Scott's recent productivity. It had the appearance of the manager simply reaching his tolerance level and jump-starting his old tactics with George.

The Red Sox were in need of a good catcher and thought they had one on April 19 when, in a six-player deal, they traded with the Cleveland Indians for 1968 All-Star Joe Azcue, themselves giving up their '68 colorful All-Star and Boston "hero" Ken Harrelson. It was going to either be Harrelson or George Scott, and the Sox stuck with the Boomer. But it didn't work out. The Cuban backstop Joe Azcue, who was actually picked by Williams for the '68 All-Star team, was confident he would get plenty of playing time with Boston as their number one receiver, especially when the

---

[596] Clif Keane, "Scott's HR Ties In Tenth," Boston Globe, June 7, 1969, p. 19-20 https://www.newspapers.com/image/434637393/?terms=%22Clif%20Keane%22%20

Sox were eager for a good catcher and willing to sacrifice a solid ballplayer in Harrelson. Under this circumstance, it seemed almost irrational that Williams, who was behind the deal for Azcue, used him only sparingly, playing six games in April, starting in just eight games in May, and was benched in June. On June 11, Azcue bolted from the team, going AWOL because of his displeasure with Williams and not being played enough. Williams, in his usual unrelenting fashion, went ballistic over the situation, seeing him as nothing more than a defector, and demanded that the catcher, who went over his head, be immediately traded.

To his naïve belief, it didn't sit well with Red Sox brass and, in the long run, the Azcue affair presented cataclysmic consequences for Williams, amounting to preemptive action and maybe the first nail in the manager's coffin that was to bode destructive for the Sox manager. Neither Dick O'Connell nor Tom Yawkey was happy with him, feeling he should have made an effort to reconcile with their newly-acquired catcher - in particular, where they had given up a big-name ballplayer in Harrelson in order to get him - who had the potential to be a good hitter and spelled a suitable handler of a pitching staff with more patience. It was a sore spot, particularly for Yawkey who never adjusted to Williams' totalitarian manner of managing, and that would soon loom again. On June 15, they sent Azcue to California for Angels catcher Tom Satriano, which turned out to be a poor exchange for Boston. Williams maintained a bold stand in the face of this fiasco, exclaiming pugnaciously that he not only wanted to see Azcue leave Boston but how disappointed he was not to see that he hadn't been traded out of the

American League. All of New England was puzzled, asking why, for heaven's sake, Azcue was so hotly pursued by the team – two years in the making - even giving up on their 1968 Most Valuable Player contender to get him if they were not going to use him?

"Is Dick Williams on Way Out? Yawkey Rates Sox Manager Only as 'Good,'" wrote senior *Globe* sportswriter Clif Keane - finding himself in the midst of Red Sox turmoil once again - in the Globe's July 20 Sunday edition based on an informal session with Yawkey and O'Connell. Keane had baited Yawkey with a line of questioning asking him to rate the Red Sox skipper on a four-point scale of "fair to outstanding," and was pleasantly surprised when he got a response. "Good," said Yawkey, who should never have taken the bait. It rocked the city and incited Williams to demand an immediate audience with Yawkey, which occurred the following morning. It did not go well for Williams, who said Yawkey's explanation was bland. *"I just don't think you are doing good enough,"* which put things into perspective, concluding with a warning, *"So you never can tell what will happen between now and October,"* said Yawkey. *"Anything might occur,"* raising speculation that the Red Sox manager was on a very short leash.[597]

---

[597] Clif Keane, "Is Dick Williams on Way Out?" The Boston Globe, July 20, 1969, p. 88
https://www.newspapers.com/image/434655344/?terms=%22Dick%20Williams%22%20&match=1

Keane supposed that one of the main grievances Yawkey had about his manager was his lack of communication, coupled with his insistence on bringing his complaints about a player to the press without discussing them with his players. *"In my opinion, it's the awful aloofness Dick can have for no apparent reason. He can be fairly witty, and he is alert, so why not communicate with these men?"* wrote Keane.[598]

Williams dug himself a much deeper hole on August 1 when he clashed with Yawkey's revered superstar Carl Yastrzemski, benching and also fining him $500 for "loafing" in a West Coast game against Oakland. Williams was aware that Yastrzemski had a bad ankle that was acting up that night but asked him to play anyway in spite of the injury. When Yaz was thrown out at home plate on a play, Williams felt he should have scored; the manager started screaming as if he had lost his mind. It did not settle well with the front office, nor with his teammates, and got the attention of Tom Yawkey, becoming a trigger point for the Red Sox proprietor who, as an extoller of his talented superstar left fielder and future Hall of Famer, was provoked by the incident soon venting his displeasure with Williams. Yawkey did little to conceal his adoration for the popular Sox' slugger and unofficial team captain, who was in an extended power struggle with Williams that had its beginnings in 1967. Yawkey's penchant for showing favor or even canonizing some of his players, the leading example being Yastrzemski, got under Williams' skin, and perhaps it was justified. Not to

---

[598] IBID

be overlooked, Tom Yawkey was the boss who wrote the paychecks. During his personal encounter with Yawkey after rating his manager as merely "good," which got into the Sunday papers, Williams stuck his neck out to confront Yawkey, pointedly and disagreeably, citing the team owner's meddling with his players. His words, according to author Golenbock, were highly critical: *"Mr. Yawkey, I don't care about myself, but this doesn't help the ballclub one bit. I didn't think your coming into the locker room as often as you do helps, either. Too many times I've eaten someone out for a mistake, and then you put your arms around his shoulders as if to comfort him."*[599]

"He [Yastrzemski] was a powerful force with Mr. Yawkey," said Scott, leaving a discernable impression in that comment that the relationship was unhealthy for the team. *"Yaz and other [white] guys could survive longer if they weren't performing well. If I didn't play [well], I was gone."*[600]

On September 22, Dick Williams had his last hurrah with Boston: Dick O'Connell notified him he was being fired by the boss, Tom Yawkey, who had skipped town that day for his home in South Carolina, leaving his positively craven abdication of duties to O'Connell; he was only the messenger. In later years Dick Williams alluded to the impertinence of Yawkey's maneuver, coupling with it his deep-seated distaste for VP of player personnel Haywood Sullivan, who would later become Jean

---

[599] Peter Golenbock, "Red Sox Nation," p. 326
[600] George Scott interview: February 8, 2006

Yawkey's right-hand man, and who played a part in his dismissal: *"I felt a sudden rush of anger at the absentee [Tom] Yawkey, who had forced O'Connell to do something we both hated. I was even madder at Yawkey's bobo, Sullivan. And I was furious at anybody who thought that just two years after bringing this team its most miraculous pennant, I had become an idiot."*[601] Nothing could have been more welcoming to George Scott, who didn't hesitate to make his feelings known, complaining how much he disliked the man. Meanwhile, there were several major league managers salivating at the prospects of Scott being made available before the firing, such as Detroit's Mayo Smith, who expressed willingness to trade his All-Star first baseman Norm Cash and future 20-game winner Pat Dobson for Scott. Ralph Houk of the Yankees also expressed interest, sensing the strained relations between Williams and Scott. However, it was, ironically, Dick Williams who was sacrificed, and not the Boomer.

The conundrum in all of this was that despite Yawkey's long-standing passion for finally putting together a championship team recognizing that Dick Williams was capable of that, his good old boy nature, if not his actual personal constitution, overruled any business sensibility he was capable of mustering – unlike a St. Louis Cardinals team that had once been entrenched in racism themselves, but they turned it around – and, amid the controversy and angst that he stirred up by his actions, Yawkey astonishingly fired the acclaimed, fan popular and much-chagrined Williams with nine games

---

[601] Dick Williams & Bill Plaschke, "No More Mr. Nice Guy," p. 117

remaining in the 1969 season, only two years after winning the pennant. Yawkey wanted a "happy" team in the long run – that was his mettle - and that was not what Dick Williams was made of; they were opposites in the truest sense. He was old style and led by intimidation that was disturbing to some of his players, especially George Scott, who made no bones about his dislike for the man. Of the disgruntled Red Sox players, Scott's opinion of the ex-manager was the most scathing. *"Dick Williams didn't like me, and I didn't like him. That's it,"* he said. *"The least he could have done was stay with me the following year [1968] and let me work my way out of a slump. But he wouldn't, so I guess you know how I feel."*[602]

In his later years after baseball, Scott became more philosophic about Williams, and maybe even a bit more mature, by putting the turbulence and emotions he saw in Dick Williams behind him and being more thoughtful in his viewpoint. His explanation seemed to be pure paradox, however, but there was a distinct qualifier in his message. On the one hand, Scott viewed Williams as by far his "best" field manager, but it was said with reservation; he qualified that by saying even though he was a good baseball man, technically sound, on the other hand, he was not a good manager of people. *"He just didn't know how to adapt to different peoples, or he didn't want to,"* exclaimed malaprop-prone George Scott, wincing at the idea of

---

[602] Clif Keane, "We Just Didn't Like Each Other - Scott," The Boston Globe, September 24, 1969, p. 29
https://www.newspapers.com/image/435171979/?terms=George%20scott&match=1

bringing back bad memories.[603] In the same tone, he was also disguising, if not suppressing, particularly his remembrances of both the '68 and '69 years of just how anxious he was at the time and how pleased he was that Williams would no longer be his nemesis or at least it was what he thought. How wrong he was, however, as Williams still affected him in other ways, even after leaving the Red Sox, and it continued to have the appearance of being personal. *"I felt he favored the white guys on the team, had little to say to us black players unless it was to criticize us or throw us in his doghouse, like [John] Wyatt or Reggie [Smith]. It was for players he felt wasn't doing the job or just something about a play that a guy did that ticked him off, or even his manner; most of those guys were black, including Ellie [Elston] Howard, and that was hard to believe [considering his experience]. He just didn't talk to us for days or weeks, or even longer. Or, we'd find ourselves at the end of the bench, or, in my case, [in] the newspapers, or both,"* said Scott.[604]

The 1970 season was becalming to George Scott now that Williams was gone, rejuvenating him, and he put up good numbers batting .296 with 16 home runs, while the team finished in third place, though well behind the league-leading Baltimore Orioles by 21 games. Mild-mannered, soft-spoken Eddie Kasko took over for Dick Williams, diametrically the opposite of Williams, an intentional move by Red Sox brass who felt the

---

[603] George Scott interview: April 14, 2008
[604] IBID

team needed a calm approach to stabilize a fragmented team and Kasko was just the man to do it. There was no doubt that Red Sox management was behind this entirely, and it had an immediate and desirable effect that the front office was looking for; it was especially well-received by a beleaguered George Scott, who almost immediately regained his confidence and a renewed sense of optimism.

While Scott was in Puerto Rico over the winter under the tutelage of Frank Robinson, making a second appearance there, he had the added pleasure of being mentored by another celebrated future Hall of Famer Roberto Clemente, who had joined the San Juan team in late November. Both Santurce and San Juan shared the same stadium, Bithorn, in Mexico City. One glaring critique that stood out for Scott was Clemente's observation of George's abandonment – a manifestation of Dick Williams - of his "aggressive batting style," and he needed to get back to that if he wanted to be a good hitter, said Roberto. Clemente suggested using a bigger bat to slow his swing down which he found was to his advantage playing in Puerto Rico. George took the advice to heart, declaring, *"I'm doing it my way this year, and no one's going to change me. I feel better right now than I ever have in my life…these pitchers are going to find out it's going to be a little different with George this season,"* exclaimed a bubbly George Scott.[605]

Santurce, Puerto Rico, 1969 – L to R: Tony Perez, Frank Robinson, and George Scott (courtesy of baseball historian Jorge Colon-Delgado)

New manager Eddie Kasko strengthened Scott's resolve by announcing he would move George back to first base where he belonged, the best first baseman in baseball, promising him he would not be shuffled around like before. *"He was a players' manager. Eddie and I got along good…he was*

---

[605] Will McDonough, "Scott Batting Program: I'll Just Do it My Way," The Boston Globe, March 16, 1970, p. 24
https://www.newspapers.com/image/435365406/?terms=will%20McDonough&match=1

a good manager," said Scott of Red Sox manager Eddie Kasko, remarking on his brief experience with Kasko in 1970 and 1971, with emphasis on Kasko's laid-back hands-off manner, comparable to Eddie Popowski in his makeup.[606] He was servile in his manner and all-too-obliging, a good guy in the eyes of his players – but too good, said some, including the unabashed opinions being wielded by the intrepid Boston reporters who never slouched or ducked from a good story. This eventually led to disorder and general discontent among the player ranks who were wont to bickering amongst themselves, a chief transgressor being a certain Conigliaro – Tony's brother, Billy, in his first full season with Boston. He was a disturbing element on the Red Sox, according to several of his teammates, and a catalyst for unruly behavior among them that evolved into a discordant 1971 season. Joe Lahoud, who was thought to be an up-and-comer with the Red Sox, along with Billy Conigliaro, Tony's brother, both arriving on the parent club around the same time, immediately clashed, and it became news fodder for the Boston sportswriters, often dangling newsworthy stories about the two into an enthralled marketplace. Lahoud offered a mordant perspective describing their quarrelsome relationship in Peter Golenbock's book, *Red Sox Nation*, from an interview: *"When Hawk [Harrelson] was traded to Cleveland [April 1969], there was a new rivalry,"* said Lahoud. *"It was then that everything started cooking. A real nonhuman being by the name of Billy Conigliaro came around...What set it off was that Billy had an ego as big as Boston – no, as big as the state of Massachusetts. Mine was as big*

---

[606] George Scott interview: July 1, 2010

as Boston. And I was getting a lot of press coverage as the one who was going to fill Tony Conigliaro's shoes. Billy resented that."[607] Neither Lahoud nor Billy C. distinguished themselves as top-flight major league ballplayers; they were, perhaps, nothing but foils to each other's development, but they stood out as a catalyst to eventual skirmishes between the Red Sox notable and well-publicized cliques. Lahoud finished his baseball career in 1978 with the Kansas City Royals with an 11-year major league lifetime batting average of .223; Billy Conigliaro lasted five seasons in major league baseball, finishing with a lifetime .256 batting average.

Ken Brett, a former Red Sox pitcher, said about Billy Conigliaro, *"He was a friend of mine. He was always Tony's brother. Billy always had a little chip on his shoulder thought the Red Sox were out to get him. I don't know why, and it wasn't true, but he always thought he wasn't being treated fairly and that Tony hadn't been treated fairly."*[608] This became more palpable on October 11, 1970, when Tony Conigliaro was suddenly let go by the Red Sox, traded in a six-player deal with California, the very team that nearly killed him in 1967 from a pitch by the Angels' Jack Hamilton, who in later years confessed he was throwing spitballs that season, though nothing was said about the one that hit Tony Conigliaro. The trade did not go over well with his brother, Billy, who proceeded to make more aberrant

---

[607] Peter Golenbock, "Red Sox Nation," p. 340
[608] Peter Golenbock, "Red Sox Nation," p. 339

noise that was further unsettling to the team and to the front office, accusing Yastrzemski of the reason for his brother's banishment from the team, was the way Billy saw it.

"If you asked me today, what I regret the whole while I was in the Red Sox organization is that they let ballplayers get into their own little groups," said Scott. *"They let these guys – whichever group you were in – dictate what went on around Fenway Park. When I played [with] guys like Yastrzemski, Lonborg, Foy, Reggie [Smith], they had their little group. [Tony] Conigliaro, Bill Conigliaro, Mike Ryan, [Jose] Tartabull – we had our little group,"* implying he was in that mix. *"And the pitchers had their little group. You lost the sense of team,"* said a melancholy George Scott in a 2007 interview, recalling these troubled years, which were an integral part of Scott's Red Sox experience throughout his two tours with the club. Joe Lahoud, commenting on the state of the disreputable Red Sox clique's phenomenon and how they affected him, said, *"As a rookie coming in, the love-hate relationship between the Conigliaros and the Yastrzemskis was very noticeable to me, and as a rookie coming in, you fall someplace, or you don't fall at all."* Though Scott had identified with the Conigliaro group, according to Lahoud George did not have a cliquish bone in his body.[609]

The Red Sox began the '71 season slowly, losing three of their first four games. Scott looked particularly bad in the last of the four games against

---

[609] Peter Golenbock, "Red Sox Nation," quoting Joe Lahoud's interview with Golenbock, p. 336

Cleveland, "waiving aimlessly" at the ball, wrote the *Globe's* Clif Keane of Scott's sub-par performance. On a bus ride from the airport to the D.C. hotel, where the Sox were to play the Senators for three games, sportswriters were making overtures between themselves about whether this was going to be another seasonal flop for the Sox' first baseman. It reached Scott who exploded in a rage aimed directly at the reporters. He was not feeling good about the Boston press, who, instead of encouraging him – as he believed they should have –were assailing him with questions about his abilities and intimating he was not a reliable clutch hitter; to make matters worse, these opinions were shared with the public in their newspaper dailies. It was an eye-opener for George realizing he may have been a special target of the local sportswriters, with whom he didn't always get along. *"I think the underestimating that was going on was being done by the media, especially the media in Boston. I don't know why, but I think I do,"* said Scott, who, during a later interview, suggested there was a racist factor among a few of the Boston journalists. *"They never gave me the credit that I deserved. But when I didn't do well, they were the first ones to jump on me."*[610]

Equally disturbing was an event that occurred in Baltimore on May 23rd when Scott, in a crucial moment of an important game against the Orioles, was quickly called out on three straight strikes thrown by Dave McNally, each one further outside the strike zone than the previous one. It was clear to everyone in the ballpark but apparently not home plate third-year umpire

---

[610] George Scott interview: January 21, 2006

Bill Kunkel that none of the pitches were strikes, visible to everyone in the stands and on the field that it had the distinct appearance of partisanship, or something more personal. Scotty was enraged, as was coach Eddie Popowski, who rarely got into it with umpires, and manager Eddie Kasko, both of whom were promptly ejected. After the game, Scott commented about the incident: *"All I can say about that man is that a man who could call three strikes like that in the middle of a pennant race is a professional disgrace. He [Bill Kunkel] has no business being in this league; I couldn't reach those pitches with a broom."*[611]

The partisan Baltimore crowd of 48,856 booed loudly at the occurrence and the tumult that followed while Scott kept his cool, remaining in the game, yet he was also booed in a moment of grievous contempt displayed by the unruly crowd who took offense at the triggered Red Sox' on-field drama. Scott's answer was to raise his clenched fists as a gesture of Black Power, inciting the crowd even further. Remembering the day in a later interview, Scott expressed the view that it was a racist moment, clearly. *"I knew what it was,"* said he, *"and it smelled of racism."*[612]

Numerous interesting studies have been done on racial bias manifest in baseball's umpiring of called balls and strikes, with a 2007 conclusion of, *"Bad calls by the ump are as much a part of baseball as home run records,*

---

[611] Clif Keane, "Umpire Leaves Scott with Bad Taste at Plate," The Boston Globe, May 24, 1971, p. 21
https://www.newspapers.com/image/435596825/?terms=%22Clif%20Keane%22%20
[612] George Scott interview: January 21, 2006

rabid fans, and watery beer, but a new study shows that an umpire's decision may have a disturbing ulterior motive: racism…Major League Baseball umpires tend to call more strikes when the pitcher is of their same race; when they're not, umps call more balls."[613]

Unhealthy cliques had almost immediately formed in the club following Kasko's arrival, with factions led by the Conigliaros in one group and Yastrzemski, who was the acknowledged leader in the other soon after Williams' departure. Manager Kasko's temperament, so significantly different from a taskmaster like Dick Williams, was not well suited for this unruly group of ballplayers who seized upon his mild-mannered disposition, which was readily noted by the local sportswriters. Elements of discord surfaced early-on between Joe Lahoud and Billy Conigliaro, both outfielders competing for a spot on the starting nine, and it soon elevated to acrimonious levels of squabbling between the two. *Boston Globe* reporter Neil Singelais described the two as *"emotionally untamed youngsters."*[614]

The Red Sox put together a respectable won-loss record at 29-15 through May 28 but began to regress precipitously from there, losing the next 14 of 19 and 16 of 24 games overall through June 25; this included a

---

[613] Katie Rooney, "Are Baseball Umpires Racists?" reporting on a study done by Daniel Hamermesh, professor of economics at the University of Texas at Austin, Time Magazine, August 13, 2007

[614] Neil Singelais, "Conigliaro, Lahoud Kiss and Make Up," The Boston Globe, April 1, 1971, p. 43
https://www.newspapers.com/image/435814454/?terms=%22Neil%20Singelais%22%20&match=1

series sweep in Fenway, falling to Kansas City and another three-game sweep of them in Kansas City by the third-year Royals expansion team.

Scott's defensive magic around first base (courtesy of Boston Red Sox)

Among a handful of Red Sox outbursts and internal squabbling early in the season, often inspired by Billy Conigliaro, who was in the middle of the latest squabble on July 10 when he learned that his brother, Tony, then playing with the California Angels, had announced his retirement from baseball due to continuing problems with his damaged eye from the '67 beaning. Billy C., a quarrelsome testy sort who was always ready for battle, was stunned and erupted in the presence of the press when he heard the news immediately pointing at the team leader, Carl Yastrzemski, as the person behind his brother being traded the year before. He held nothing back, accusing the future Hall of Famer of meddling in the team: *"Yaz got rid of Johnny Pesky, Ken Harrelson and Tony [Conigliaro]...it was all because of No. 8 and nobody else,"* said Billy C. *"You can quote me because I don't care...they (the Red Sox) all listen to No. 8. He got me benched. I'm the only guy on this team who will speak up."*[615]

It was irrational behavior of the worst kind, catching manager Kasko and the Red Sox brass completely off guard now being confronted with a likely threat to team unity, whatever of that remained, said GM Dick O'Connell. Outfielder Reggie Smith, who was a close friend of Yastrzemski, said he would not play with Conigliaro again. Cooler heads carried the day while apologies were made, and Billy C. and Reggie Smith appeared in Boston's lineup in the first game following the July 13 All-Star break, in which Yastrzemski was a starter, giving the appearance that things were settled and decorum restored. They weren't resolved, however, and wouldn't be, and Dick O'Connell knew it.

After Conigliaro's rebellious tirade and the austere unstableness settling on the team, which followed these events, there was a vicariousness to the stress George Scott was experiencing from this debacle that was becoming his own personal ordeal. He was looking for peace from the bickering that was fragmenting and polarizing his team and just playing baseball as a team,

---

[615] Clif Keane, "Yaz on Spot: Kasko Praises, Billy C Criticizes," The Boston Globe, Jul 11, 1971, p. 77
https://www.newspapers.com/image/435815497/

but he was working on a short fuse himself these days, snapping at a Boston reporter who was a critic of a Billy C. misplay a month earlier. Of course, in the heat of the moment, with everyone short on patience and propriety these days, the outburst made the news, placing Scott squarely in the front office's beam, looking every bit like another one of the Red Sox malcontents poisoning the ranks.

The writing appeared to be on the wall for George that he was about to be trade bait when the Red Sox called up 23-year-old Cecil Cooper from their Double-A Pawtucket farm club on September 8 and assumed a starting role at first base on the 13th. Cooper would become a five-time All-Star and two-time Gold Glover.

The big swish – Scott's outsized home run swing about to leave for Milwaukee (courtesy of Boston Red Sox)

On October 10 the Red Sox and the lowly Milwaukee Brewers, who finished last in the Western Division of the American League, pulled off a blockbuster 10-player trade, sending 1967 Cy Young recipient Jim Lonborg, Billy Conigliaro, Joe Lahoud, Ken Brett, Don Pavletich, and the Boomer, George Scott, to the Brewers for speed merchant Tommy Harper – who, himself would eventually become involved in a significant racial matter amounting to litigation with the Red Sox – pitchers Lew Krause and Marty Pattin, and a minor leaguer. O'Connell looked upon the deal as ridding the team of a brigade of malcontents, while Milwaukee placed their emphasis and future on George Scott, who they labeled as the "key" man of the trade. *"For me, it's like a new lease on life,"* said Scott when he heard about the trade.[616] *"They [the Brewers] made him the key man in their big trade with the Red Sox,"* wrote Milwaukee sportswriter Larry Whiteside. *"Of the six players acquired from Boston – Billy Conigliaro, Joe Lahoud, Jim Lonborg, Don Pavletich, and Ken Brett were the others – Scott holds the key to what success the young Brewers hope to enjoy."*[617]

Although Scott was pleased with the transaction that got him to Milwaukee, seeing a better future there for himself, he was not in any way pleased with the manner in which the trade was done, learning of the trade from a local while jogging near his Cape Cod home. It was disrespectful, he charged to be embarrassed that way and for the Red Sox to lack the decency

---

[616] Larry Whiteside, "Scott Aiming to be Brewer Bomber," The Sporting News, November 27, 1971, p. 52
[617] IBID

to be upfront with him and inform him of the trade themselves. Dick O'Connell, caught up in the shenanigans of the ballclub and with the consequences frequently finding their way to the local newspapers, uncharacteristically slammed all six players collectively with a "good riddance" type of message, surprising the local sportswriters who could not fathom why such players as Lonborg and Scott were included in the unpleasant profile being characterized by the Red Sox general manager. In fact, it was learned later that Boston was more than reluctant to release their slugger first baseman – it was a sticking point – but they relented when Milwaukee's newly-appointed general manager Frank "Trader" Lane balked at any agreement that didn't include the big infielder. Lane described Scott as "a high caliber of player" who was destined to make the Brewers a bona fide power-hitting ballclub as well as strengthen the infield with his Gold Glove.

Chapter 13
Cultural Deprivation

"Milwaukee is one of the most racially segregated cities in the United States, and one of segregation's most meaningful engines was the historical practice of redlining. Policies limiting the options of prospective homeowners who were people of color shaped the city for nearly a century."

Leah Foltman & Malia Jones[618]

It began in the early 1930s across numerous American cities, manifested by the real estate industry and, like the rest of the country, adopted forthrightly by realtors of Milwaukee; it was called *redlining*. A practice of discrimination denying minority inhabitants and their populace the right of access to equal loans and housing opportunities. Notwithstanding the significant federal Civil Rights Act of 1964 and the Fair Housing Act of 1968, in Milwaukee, racial segregation of neighborhoods by unethical lending practices and zoning policies remained strikingly and firmly in place, continuing to flourish from the effects of "redlining" mapping of

---

[618] Leah Foltman & Malia Jones, University of Wisconsin Applied Population Lab, "How Redlining Continues to Shape Racial Segregation in Milwaukee: 1930s Lending Map Reveals the Policy Roots of Housing Discrimination," February 28, 2019 https://apl.wisc.edu/shared/tad/redlining-milwaukee#:~:text=Milwaukee%20is%20one%20of%20the,city%20for%20nearly%20a%20century.

what was considered desirable or undesirable properties, and which were qualified to receive government aid, that was implemented in 1938. According to Reggie Jackson, a prominent civic leader of Milwaukee's and Wisconsin's black community and a nationally recognized independent scholar, spoke on the effects of Milwaukee's redlining efforts post-depression: "*'Most people think it was just about blacks, but you know blacks, Jewish families, Polish families, and Italian families were all redlined in Milwaukee when they drew that map [of Milwaukee neighborhoods] in 1938,' Jackson said. "'Redlining maps didn't create segregation. It already existed. What the redlining maps did was it literally showed you, 'Okay, these are communities that these people belong to.'"*[619]

In the pre-Civil Rights era, long after the Milwaukee neighborhood maps were drawn up, neighborhoods were color-coded according to lender desirability and given grades from A to D, A being "Best" and most desirable for lenders. Washington Highlands, a distinguished upper-crust white Milwaukee neighborhood, was one of the first neighborhoods that came under the scrutiny of the redlining process and the *"first metro Milwaukee neighborhood to implement specific restrictions on the race of the people who could live there."* It had a history even before that of

---

[619] Anthony Dabruzzi, "History of Redlining Perpetuates Racial Inequality in Milwaukee," quoting Reggie Jackson of Nurturing Diversity Partners, Spectrum News, Milwaukee, WI, September 16, 2020
https://spectrumnews1.com/wi/milwaukee/news/2020/09/16/history-of-redlining-perpetuates-racial-inequality-in-milwaukee-

remaining exclusive only to the *"white race"* as specified in their property deeds.[620]

On July 30, 1967, the racial tension and long-standing unrest of Milwaukee's black population exploded that was grounded mostly in the housing discrepancies but also school desegregation, busing, and lack of economic opportunity, much like the city of Boston that occurred in the early 1970s. It was known as the *1967 Milwaukee Riot*, and, on August 29, the protestors, who were mostly black, marched out of the ghetto, gravitating to the south side of Milwaukee and into Kosciuszko Park, the latter mostly inhabited by upscale white residents. They were greeted by south-side residents, some 13,000 whites, and came under sniper fire.

"Boston received the attention and the infamy," exclaimed author Howard Bryant, *"but it was in Milwaukee where the nation's first lawsuit was filed, in 1965, challenging de facto segregation – public schools were segregated because city neighborhoods were segregated and, as such, could not be remedied without busing."*[621]

The clash in Kosciuszko Park took on the look of the Detroit racial riots – the bloodiest and most destructive of them - that began on July 23, 1967, and the Newark, New Jersey riots, the next most lethal, between July 12 and July 17 of 1967. The Milwaukee racial riots were a manifestation of what

---

[620] Leah Foltman & Malia Jones, University of Wisconsin Applied Population Lab, February 28, 2019
[621] Howard Bryant, "A Life of Henry Aaron," p. 428

was happening across the country among such cities as Flint, Michigan, South Bend, Cleveland, Boston, Cincinnati, Buffalo, Tampa, Los Angeles, and Chicago communities, to name only a small few; it was labeled "The Long, Hot Summer of 1967" amounting to 158 separate riot outbreaks countrywide.

"We saw the same thing going on in Milwaukee [with housing] that was going on in Boston," said Scott, who, unlike many of his black contemporaries, who came from northern cities and were less tolerant of abuse, was conditioned to ill-treatment growing up in the South. *"We just moved on until we could find an apartment as near to the ballpark that was also a good area to live. We didn't start griping about it,"* displaying a certain resignation not common to northern blacks.[622]

Black sportswriter Larry Whiteside, who had the experience of working as a journalist in both the cities of Boston and Milwaukee during this turbulent era, interviewed Scott in 1979 – shortly after he had left Boston for a second time to play in Kansas City – on a writing project exploring "The Black Athlete in Boston;" He touched upon Scott's housing experience in the area. *"I remember looking for an apartment in Dedham [Massachusetts],"* said Scott, *"around 1970. I knew personally that there were 10-12 vacancies. But the guy we met said they were all filled. I went someplace else and we kept on looking until we found a place. I wasn't*

---

[622] George Scott interview: January 23, 2007

going to sit and gripe and cry about it. If things didn't work out, I moved on to the next place. These things to me were to be expected," reflecting his Southern black culture of resignation that northern blacks never would tolerate.[623]

"It was quiet, innocuous Milwaukee that the frustrated locals, white and black, would call 'the most segregated city in America.' Since Milwaukee's neighborhoods were so clannish, the question of whether to bus the city's students to achieve integration was inevitable. As in Boston, Milwaukee school board officials tried every stalling tactic short of the four corners defense," wrote Howard Bryant.[624]

In spite of his delight transitioning to the Brewers feeling liberated, grateful even, with the knowledge he had been hotly pursued by other clubs when they realized that Boston had given up on him, and knowing that Milwaukee's two lynchpins in their general manager Frank Lane and field manager Dave Bristol were appreciative of his skills in Milwaukee; acclimating to the ballclub and the town was to be a period of strained adjustment for the Boomer. It started with his effort to extinguish the 25 pounds he had accumulated in the offseason. *"It weakened me,"* he said, *"I wanted to be in the best shape possible because I wanted to show Boston*

---

[623] Larry Whiteside, quoting George Scott, "Sox' Children of the 60s Look Back," Boston Globe, July 29, 1979, p. 80 https://www.newspapers.com/image/437079904/
[624] Howard Bryant, "A Life of Henry Aaron," p. 428

that they made a mistake in trading me."[625] A disconsolate message, perhaps, with his mind still in Boston, for a man who had expressed contentment at his being traded, yet there was a part of him, it seemed, that would tarry for a while knowing that Boston had rejected him. He was especially mindful of a betrayal, he claimed, that was the inspiration for his release from Boston, which was that he was accused of being in the mix of troublesome Red Sox players – that he denied - and thus was included in their public belittlement. He could never get over it.

And there was his new manager, Dave Bristol, with whom he experienced an almost immediate conflict, clashing with him on policy matters – not the club's but Bristol's own. Scott was finding it hard to adjust to the new team led by a capricious manager, in his estimation, who was displaying similar authoritarian characteristics to his castigator Dick Williams who he thought he was rid of but was looming again in Bristol. "They never hit it off," said sportswriter Larry Whiteside. There were borderline rudiments of racial threads woven into his frequent messages to Scott that George did not appreciate, and, unlike his younger days when he would relent, keeping his frustrations to himself and go silent, with several seasons under his belt and at age 28 he now chose to speak out and resist. Although it was unclear whether Bristol had a bigoted personality, there was no mistaking he was a man of strict deportment and personal rules. He

---

[625] Larry Whiteside, "Adjustment Over, Scott Blooming as Brewer," *Sporting News*, July 22, 1972, p. 18

was an unremitting "taskmaster," complained Milwaukee's outspoken, nononsense GM Frank Lane, who did not always get along with Bristol. For instance, he insisted that Scott wear his socks a certain way – his way, said Scott – rubbing George the wrong way. George viewed this as petty, with some merit in that opinion, refused to cooperate, and then brooded; Bristol fumed. *"It got out of hand,"* said Scott, *"on something as minor as this, but I couldn't believe he was being so small to make this so personal. He was insistent, and so was I."*[626] When Scott threatened, however, to take the matter to the fledgling *MLB Players Association (MLBPA)*, headed by executive director Marvin Miller, feeling he had the upper hand, the matter was soon dropped.

It was a period of adjustment for George – a "tough adjustment," said Whiteside - lasting longer than he personally had expected, and perhaps also there was a mutual feeling about that residing with the Brewers' management; his disenchantment had a trickle-down effect as well reaching his teammates who did not appreciate his attributes, which, in part, were based on lingering resentment with Boston. *"Sure, I liked playing in Boston, but I don't think people understand that I've always been a part of Milwaukee – since the day I was traded. But I wasn't sure Milwaukee had accepted me,"* said George.[627]

---

[626] George Scott interview: January 26, 2007
[627] Larry Whiteside, "Adjustment Over," p. 18

Mike Ferraro, a light-hitting reserve third baseman in his first and only season with Milwaukee, was one of those players who couldn't comprehend or find a reason to embrace the querulous ex-Red Sox star, who sensed by now he was on a club bereft of its dignity and doomed to lose. *"It was strange at first,"* said Scott, explaining with a measure of disappointment his adjustment to the club and the town after playing before large, exuberant crowds in Boston, *"I was used to playing in Boston and seeing 20,000 fans in the stands. And when I got to Milwaukee, there was only three or four thousand there. It was a struggle just to get up for games."*[628] This expression of dissatisfaction for a man who only a few short years before was in a spectacular pennant run and World Series and savoring the familiarity of playing before enthusiastic big crowds, was likely on display during this adjustment period. It led to fisticuffs on one occasion in the Milwaukee dugout between Ferraro and Scott, requiring two teammates to pull them apart. Ferraro did not take well to Scott's game intensity and offbeat language. Both men explained it away later that it was *"all a misunderstanding...that and other incidents made life very difficult for Scott."*[629]

Interestingly, reporter Whiteside, a black journalist, brought up a term he used for describing Scott's clashes with management and teammates as *cultural deprivation,* to explain his alleged failure of "clear communication"

---

[628] IBID
[629] IBID

with teammates. What was riveting about this charge, from a black journalist's perspective no less, was that in the six years he was with Boston, disagreements of this magnitude never happened. It was a period of mutual adjustment, insisted sportswriter Whiteside, between a typically conservative and reserved Midwestern city like Milwaukee and an unpolished figure like George Scott, whose behavior, they believed, was inappropriate and out of place for their kind of affable town.

On May 28, manager Dave Bristol, who was struggling with a revamped team courtesy of the Red Sox, was fired by the Brewers and replaced by Del Crandall, a Milwaukee favorite star catcher who was a member of the city's only World Series championship team, the 1957 Braves. He was the third field manager of a young Brewers-Pilots expansion team. The presence of new manager Del Crandall and his "enjoy the game" ideology had an immediate soothing effect on George, who declared he could play for the man, very much unlike how he felt about Dave Bristol. While Scott saw hope with Crandall, this relationship, as well, was to erode in a series of baffling events in the next few seasons.

The day after Bristol's firing, the Brewers avoided a four-game sweep by the Red Sox at Fenway with an 11-3 rout. Red Sox rejects George Scott and Billy Conigliaro returned literally with a vengeance on their minds, slugging three home runs, six base hits, and eight RBIs between them. Conigliaro, speaking for both himself and an avenging Scott, *"I have a lot of animosity, and I will remember what happened to me here as long as I live,"* said Conigliaro.[630]

Scott added to the gaiety of the day with some antics of his own, showing open defiance of the Red Sox organization for trading him and the Boston media for their tireless heckling of him. Upon smashing his home run, which was a bomb, *"Scott acted as though he wanted to take a few days rounding the bases."*[631] For good measure, he leaped with both feet onto the home plate in a final flourish of "so there" as if spiking the plate, drawing a resounding mock approval from the Fenway crowd, who were still upset with the Red Sox for trading their beloved first baseman.

Things began to fester with George and his manager Crandall on August 30 in a game in Milwaukee against Kansas City when umpire George Maloney called Scott out on strikes on a pitch that even the County Stadium crowd knew was a ball. Scotty was furious, feeling the umpire had taken the bat out of his hands in a crucial moment of the contest and, after that, continued to badger Maloney the rest of the game until he was thrown out. It was learned later that the reason for the ejection was that Scott had made an inappropriate gesture toward heckling fans that was seen by only a few, among them umpire Maloney and manager Del Crandall. The matter was the subject of debate in the Milwaukee papers whether Scotty would be

---

[630] Clif Keane, "Scott, Conigliaro Bomb Sox with 3 Homers, 8 RBI, 11-3," Boston Globe, May 30, 1972, p. 28
https://www.newspapers.com/image/435337078/?terms=%22George%20Scott%22
[631] IBID

fined; he was. Crandall levied Scott a $500 fine, which was a particularly stiff penalty at the time that enraged Scott even further and led to a nagging coolness between them, and once again, George found himself in conflict with a manager. He wasn't upset with a fine being levied but he was greatly annoyed at the amount of the fine. It appeared excessive for the circumstances. Crandall explained, *"I hope every time an umpire disagrees with him, he doesn't get thrown out of a game."*[632]

What provoked an emerging enmity between them was that Crandall, in Scott's view, failed to come to his ballplayer's side in defense of him when the umpire had obviously missed the call, or there was even a possible intentional motive behind the call, that was clearly recognized by the Milwaukee crowd; instead, in fact, it was the opposite. Crandall found fault with Scott for his peevish actions on the field without as much as a word of solace for his first baseman, ignoring the missed call but punctuating his behavior with a reprimand. Crandall did run on the field in the 8th inning when Scott was obviously upset, but George saw that as too little too late; further, it was only meant to calm his rage, not actually mitigate what had happened to his first baseman. Coming to a ballplayer's defense on such a call was a circumstance which, in most instances, managers would not have let a ballplayer fend for himself, if anything, to make a statement that the

---

[632] Multimedia, "Scott Seeths as Brewers Lose, 6-2," Wausau Daily Herald, Aug 31, 1972, p. 20.
https://www.newspapers.com/image/272943835/?terms=%22George%20Scott%22&match=1

team's interests were being violated by shoddy umpiring. Dick Williams was a manager who stood behind his players aggressively in instances like this, which George Scott was well aware of; Crandall's behavior was unacceptable to him. It got the better of him throughout the next couple of innings, welling up inside of him for Crandall's apparent indifference until he exploded, leading to the fine. *"I never forgot that incident with Crandall and it distanced us. He was not there for me,"* said the Boomer.[633]

George "Boomer" Scott had a very good first season with Milwaukee, finishing on the leaderboard in several categories, including a fourth Gold Glove award, and he was later honored by the Milwaukee baseball writers as 1972's Most Valuable Brewer. However, in the fall of that year, on October 5, in a sweeping front office restructuring initiative by Brewer owner Bud Selig, a new Brewers' general manager was named outspoken Jim Wilson of no-hit distinction when he was pitching with the 1954 Milwaukee Braves, replacing long-time GM Frank "Trader" Lane, whose first GM role was in 1948 with the White Sox. Promoted behind him was Jim Baumer, another controversial front office man who would eventually become an even greater headache for Scott, who was named to replace Wilson.

He and Scott were soon to clash as Baumer moved up the Brewers' ranks. Wilson, who had been the '71-'72 scouting director for the Brewers,

---

[633] George Scott interview: February 12, 2007

himself could be difficult. Brash by nature, often blurting out what bothered him – indiscreetly at times – and in the hands of the press and his players, he would occasionally and necessarily find himself walking back some parts of what he had said. He didn't align well with some of the players, notably ex-Red Sox outfielder Joe Lahoud, never one to abide by rules of restraint, and that would include their big first baseman George Scott, the Brewers' "best ballplayer," said Wilson, who George never could warm up to feeling the man was not supportive of the players nor had he displayed a winning attitude.

In particular, Scott was critical of the Brewers' GM when he traded away a good-hitting, solid veteran player in Ollie Brown in their nine-player deal with the California Angels in October 1973 in his attempt to rebuild a pitching staff he gave away a year earlier, questioning his resoluteness to put the best team on the field. *"He [Ollie Brown] had a good bat,"* complained Scott, *"but Wilson wanted to go with a young team, and I felt it hurt our chances. He also hurt us in '72 when he gave away our best pitchers [including former Cy Young pitcher Jim Lonborg] to get [Don] Money. I wasn't sure then how bad he wanted to win, which was a constant problem with Milwaukee."*[634] This was a reference to an October 31, 1972, seven-player trade with the Philadelphia Phillies when Wilson was being accused of depleting the team's pitching strength to acquire an infielder, Don Money; this was illuminated by the press and haunted him while he

---

[634] George Scott interview: February 12, 2007

finished firmly in next to last in his division, 23 games out of first. To Lahoud's point, Wilson was a guy who, when things were not going well with the team, it became the players' fault, but when they were winning, he postured with a flair for publicity that the credit owed was deserving unto one man - Jim Wilson. It rankled the players.

It all came to a head on May 30 when Del Crandall levied his second fine on Scott, this one a whopping $1,000, after missing two games because of a groin injury. The reason for the fine was never disclosed by Crandall or Milwaukee management, but there was an implicit allegation of malingering. Scott was irritated that he had been unceremoniously demoted from his cleanup position in the batting order in the two previous games, May 26 and 28, against California. The ultimate indignity was foisted on him on May 29 when Crandall had him batting 7th. Scott said nothing to Crandall of his displeasure of being dropped in the order but instead requested he sit out the game because of a nagging groin injury. He missed the May 30 contest as well, a second straight shutout loss to the Minnesota Twins, frustrating Crandall even more, who needed the big slugger's bat and who felt he was "dogging" it. Following the game, Scott openly complained about the indignity he was feeling over being slotted in the lower half of the batting order; it did not escape Crandall, and he imposed the fine; it was never revealed, however, until later when the matter was leaked to the press.

George Scott was enraged for not being believed by his manager. *"I said I was hurt, and the manager didn't believe me,"* he said later in the season. *"He fined me $1,000. In his mind, I was dogging it."*[635] With a well-earned reputation for being one of the hardest-working athletes on the ball field, shared among all American League ballplayers and managers, this slap-in-the-face assault on his pride and self-respect couldn't have been more insulting to Scott; he was greatly annoyed and reacted. He filed a grievance with the reconstituted Major League Baseball Players Association on June 18. The MLBPA, founded in 1953, was largely ineffective until 1966 when Marvin Miller, a labor union official, who some labeled a "Baseball Revolutionary," took the helm of the organization as its executive director, revitalizing its labor union purpose and function. The repercussions of this matter that was affecting Scott were far-reaching, more so than simply being a franchise or an American League problem, but one that touched all of baseball; it was at the heart of one of baseball's "most discriminating practices," wrote journalist Martin Ralbovsky, which was the arbitrary fining of ballplayers for such alleged misdeeds as malingering, discontent, and so-called "bad attitudes."[636] Baseball management was in complete charge of the process: they were judge and jury – either a player paid the fine or ran the risk of suspension. The player had no say in the matter and no opportunity to appeal. An enlightened George Scott was not

---

[635] Lou Chapman, "Brewers Back Off, Forget About Scott's Fine," Milwaukee Journal, September 29, 1973
[636] Martin Ralbovsky, "Scott Calls Brewer Bluff: Case Closed?" Milwaukee Journal, September 10, 1973, p. 15

going to stand for it; he was thoroughly prepared to file a civil suit and take it full way to the U. S. Supreme Court, if necessary, he asserted.

The matter of the fine and grievance appeared to have an opposite effect on Scotty than one would have ordinarily expected of an athlete following such tumult: instead of brooding, it invigorated him because he knew in his heart he was doing the right thing, and he proceeded to play inspirational baseball for the balance of the season. Scott returned to the lineup on May 31st, but Crandall, who would not yield, had him batting in the 7th slot, an apparent act of requital – tainted as it was - by the 43-year-old Brewer manager who continued to doubt the injury. It had all the earmarks of vintage baseball so common in its day of managers and coaches wielding their authority when they saw something they didn't like and how this was done with impunity, all the more so when it involved the black athlete.

Scotty returned to the lineup with a vengeance, plainly frustrated at the disrespect he was feeling, and at the same time determined to prove his worth to a club that had spited him by doing what suited him best and was more befitting of his own personal comfort zone: play tough, aggressive, competitive baseball. And that's what he did upon his return, going 2-for-3 in a 4-2 loss against Minnesota. He was besieged by reporters, still unaware of the fine, afterward sensing they were on the cusp of a good scoop. "I had pulled a groin [muscle]," retorted Scott, answering their pointed questions. "Today was a warm day. I came in early today, took two whirlpools, and had it wrapped real tight. It felt good. The warm weather helps," he said affirming for them that the injury was real. But he could not hide his distaste for the matter; he was clearly upset with his manager and with General Manager Wilson, whom he felt should have spoken to him, mumbling some words to the reporters about being the only $80,000 salaried player in the league batting seventh. The rift between Scott and the club had not abated and didn't appear it was going to anytime soon.[637]

On June 1, Crandall had George back in the cleanup slot, and he cracked a mammoth home run off of Chicago's knuckleballer, Wilbur Wood. It was the start of an impressive winning streak, historic for the Brewers, in which they won 15 of 16 games, ten in succession, starting on June 8 and culminating in an 8-3 drubbing of the Red Sox on June 18; Scott slugged two home runs in that game accounting for three runs. On June 10, in a game against the Angels, Scott banged his knee, injuring it enough to come out of the game. But he was back in the lineup the next day and games thereafter. "That shows character," exclaimed an opportunistic Del Crandall, whose Brewers had won six in a row, and feeling the pressure of the grievance action, shrewdly showing support for his big first-sacker with words that were meant for public consumption after their blowup just two short weeks before.

"It just happened that my injury occurred right at the same time as my being dropped in the lineup. Del Crandall thought I was making it up -

---

[637] Tom Flaherty, "Twins Make a Conformist of Colborn," Milwaukee Journal, June 1, 1973, p. 18

dogging it - because of the demotion, but I wasn't. It may have looked bad but it was legitimate, yet Del Crandall wasn't going to budge, and I wasn't either. I was being jerked around, and I had had enough of it. I remember Alex Johnson went through the same thing a few years before my situation with the Brewers."[638]

Scott was referring to the matter of 13-year black major leaguer Alex Johnson, an All-Star, 1970 MVP candidate, and American League batting champ, who in 1971, two years before his own grievance, was accused of not hustling and generally displaying a "bad attitude" by California manager Lefty Phillips who repeatedly fined him on twenty-five separate occasions amounting to $3,750. Johnson took action under Major League Baseball's *Second Basic Agreement* that was adopted in 1970, giving the players independent grievance arbitration rights. Meanwhile, baseball commissioner Bowie Kuhn placed Johnson on the 30-day "suspended list" without pay for "failure to give his best efforts toward the winning of the club's baseball games." Following the 30-day suspension and before the arbitration hearing, Kuhn took further action at the behest of the Angels by putting him on the "restricted list," which was a category normally reserved for those banned from baseball for life. The initiative meant Johnson was ineligible to play, would not be paid his salary, and accumulated no time toward a pension. The arbitration hearing, however, produced a sharp compromise: Johnson was to be placed on the disabled list with full pay and

---

[638] George Scott interview: March 20, 2007

full credit for major league service retroactive to the date of his original suspension; his earlier fines were upheld, however, to the dismay of the MLBPA and Marvin Miller.[639]

The Brewers went on a losing skid the first part of July, dropping them into 5th place again in the American League's East Division where they remained for the balance of the season, losing the last 21 of 29 games. The unrest on the team was palpable, "verbal dissonance," said one Milwaukee reporter. On August 23, an impertinent Joe Lahoud vocally went after management, Crandall and Wilson, particularly GM Jim Wilson, with whom he placed the blame for Milwaukee's failings. *Milwaukee Sentinel* sports reporter Lou Chapman highlighted Lahoud's sentiments, quoting the disgruntled ballplayer: *"He does not 'enjoy playing for Del Crandall, but I do not think it is all Crandall. The biggest problem is Jim Wilson. 'He is calling all the shots and having a big influence on Crandall.'"*[640] The biggest disturbance came from their MVP slugger George Scott, who was still smoldering and resentful over the 1972 fine levied on him by Crandall, the even greater May 30 imbroglio with Crandall and his colossal $1,000 fine, and his across-the-board treatment by the Brewers' front office. At the

---

[639] J. Gordon Hylton, "The Historical Origins of Baseball Grievance Arbitration," Marquette University Law School, Article 4, Issue 2, Spring 2001 https://scholarship.law.marquette.edu/cgi/viewcontent.cgi?article=1514&context=sportslaw

[640] Associated Press, quoting Lou Chapman of the Milwaukee Sentinel, who quotes Joe Lahoud; "Lahoud Wants Out, Puts Rap on Wilson," Fon Du Lac Reporter, Aug 24, 1973, p. 11
https://www.newspapers.com/image/285276699/?terms=Lahoud%20wants%20out&match=1

very best, their relationship approximated that of a wobbly, dispirited detente, but it wouldn't last.

Scotty was having a solid month of July: For twenty-one games through July 20, going into the mid-season All-Star break, he was batting .350. But then another incident appeared to have occurred between George and his manager, although no explanation was given, and Scott, who had been hitting well, was benched for the final two games of a three-game series [July 20-22] in Kansas City; the Brewers lost all three. Alarmed by the head-scratcher of what was taking place, Scott's obvious unhappiness, and where he had been hitting with authority, feeling that a story was brewing, the Milwaukee scribes questioned the Brewers skipper, who responded blandly laced with a tone of sarcasm: *"He doesn't feel well."* Scott expressed quite another view, however, when questioned by reporters directing them back to Crandall, with the comment: *"There are two guys who know what's wrong,"* refusing to elaborate; the inference from this seemed to point to the manager and general manager, most likely stemming from the fiasco of May 30 and his general discontent with Brewer management.[641] *"Scott hasn't been a happy man since spring training. The big guy publicly has, on several occasions complained of the treatment accorded him by the Brewer brass. When manager Del Crandall at one point put him in the seventh spot in the batting order, Scott rebelled. 'An $85,000-a-year player*

---

[641] The Sporting News, "Major Flashes," August 11, 1973, p. 24.

doesn't belong in that spot,' he complained. There have been other occasions when Scott and Crandall haven't seen eye to eye."[642]

While all this was simmering with Milwaukee's front office and on the field, it did not go unnoticed, especially by George Scott, that he wasn't picked by the American League All-Star manager Dick Williams for the American League team. It was a controversial voting system comprised of fan selections that were reinstituted in 1970, favoring local voter turnouts indulging in their favorite teams, hometown players, or who simply voted for old name popular players who were not performing at all-star levels; but there was room for all-star managers to remediate what the fans had created by making their own selections of player reserves to bring the roster up to 33 players. This, however, didn't work for George Scott, who, though in the upper-level mix of both the fan and player voting, placing 6th with the fans and tied for 4th with the players, was not named by his old nemesis Dick Williams, who saw things differently. He went, instead, with Chicago's Pat Kelly, who finished the year batting .280 with one home run and 44 RBIs, and Jim Spencer of Texas, who batted .262 with 6 home runs and 54 RBIs, for his backups. In comparison, Scott had a solid year and was among the leaders, batting .306 with 24 home runs and 107 RBIs. He also earned his 5th Gold Glove, recognized as unquestionably the best first baseman in the American League and the top defensive performer of the first-sacker

---

[642] Lou Chapman, "Unhappy Scott Makes Rivals Feel Worse," The Sporting News, Aug 18, 1973, p. 15

selections. Williams' choices were clearly a snub while carrying a grudge, and it wouldn't be the last. *"It was personal,"* said the Boomer.

At the same time, GM Wilson was scrambling, attempting to put a positive spin on the situation, but there was little room for that. Several club veterans were annoyed at the trading commotion that management conducted in '72 and '73 before the regular season, feeling they were not well-considered initiatives, and were upset with GM Wilson, whom they felt was not giving them the time of day nor were his actions in the best interest of the team. On August 20, as reported by several nationwide newspapers, Wilson let out to the press in a loosely worded remark that Scott, their best and *"highest-salaried Brewer,"* was not an "untouchable" in any trade discussions but later recanted that George was on the trading block. It was a careless remark that was unsettling to the team and particularly to George.[643] It was another personal insult by the callous Brewers that stirred Scott even more; to him, it was just another dagger thrust at him by Brewer hierarchy, adding to the already strained relations between them.

With his emotions now bubbling at the surface, he boiled over at Crandall and Wilson for the humiliation he was feeling, figuring he would be traded. Wilson became defensive, suggesting later on – as only he could - that the statement he made was taken out of context, despite the fact that

---

[643] AP News, "Lahoud Wants Out, Blames GM Wilson," Eau Claire Leader-Telegram, Aug 25, 1973, p. 3B

was what he had said. The Milwaukee fans were in an uproar over the matter, suggesting that the club get their act together and come up with a way to retain their beloved superstar. By the time of the World Series in October, in the face of numerous trade offers for Scott by other clubs, who were eager to wrap their arms around such a gem of a complete ballplayer, Wilson retreated, declaring Scott a definite untouchable.

On September 6, the *Milwaukee Sentinel* had broken the story of the May 30 debacle, the punitive action by the Brewers, and the grievance brought by George Scott; it came as a complete surprise to the city of Milwaukee. The *Sentinel* learned that the Executive Director of the Major League Baseball Players Association, Marvin Miller, was directly involved, announcing that the hearing on the grievance was to be heard on September 14. The pressure was bearing down on the Brewers, who, confronted with lasting consequences and a damaging legal battle, wavered for the first time, suggesting they might rescind the fine. Miller and Scott continued their plans to pursue the grievance, even into the civil courts, if necessary, threatened Scott. Things were beginning to look ominous for the Brewers and for baseball.

On September 8, Milwaukee officially dropped the fine, hoping to douse the action once and for all and allow them to slip away silently and unblemished from the public spotlight. Scott, once content to adjudicate, softened his stance, enabling the Brewers an enormous sigh of relief; astonishingly, he expressed satisfaction with the result, remarking that he got his "justice" after all. He could have made far more of the situation as possible legal precedent, but he chose not to – his pride was intact, and he had regained his self-respect, which at the time was of greater personal value to him than anything else he could have achieved through litigation. He was of a better mind cleansed of the hassles and, for a time, the overbearing, duplicitous Milwaukee front office, and was now ready to play baseball without constraints.

The Oakland A's, Reggie Jackson, once remarked that black ballplayers were often suspected of malingering by white managers and faced peremptory disciplinary action – which appeared to be the central issue in the George Scott case. As he punctuated in his explanation, the standard for white players was not the same: they could sit out with injuries, and barely anything was said other than tending to the injured ballplayer; black players, however, were expected to play. *"White players get hurt; they sit out. Black players get hurt; they're expected to play anyway. It's like we're animals or something. As soon as a black player says he's not feeling well, the manager says, 'Get it X-rayed.' If nothing shows up on the X-ray, the reaction is automatic. He's dogging it. That kind of thinking has been around baseball for years. It's unconsciously racist,"* said Jackson.[644]

George Scott compiled impressive year-end statistics: Milwaukee's team leader in batting average and RBIs, breaking the Brewers RBI club

---

[644] Ralbovsky, "Scott Calls Brewer Bluff"

record he had set the previous year; finishing second in the American League in both categories. He was club leader with a .487 slugging percentage, tied for fourth in the league; tied with teammate Dave May and Oakland's Sal Bando for total bases [295]; team leader in runs scored [98]; second on the team in game-winning hits [14] and home runs [24]; and the best first baseman in the American League garnering the second highest Gold Glove vote count [33-of-44] of all the candidates. He was listed among the American League's Most Valuable Player candidates by the Baseball Writers Association of America and was voted by the Milwaukee chapter of baseball writers as their MVP selection shared with teammate Dave May.

Chapter 14
Scott Keeps Booming

"George just happens to be one of the best six or seven players in the American League, but I feel as though this hasn't been said. I think it should have been. He's been under-publicized, and it's about time he gets the recognition he merits."

Del Crandall[645]

"Brewers' Great Scott Enters Champagne Class," wrote *Milwaukee Journal's* sports scribe Lou Chapman, reporting on Milwaukee's star first baseman, who had just entered the superstar payroll class after signing his new contract with the Brewers in late December. He had signed for a reported $100,000, but it was later learned the figure was closer to $115,000, making him the third-highest-paid athlete in Milwaukee sports history, behind Abdul-Jabbar and Oscar Robertson of pro basketball fame. Even superstars Hank Aaron and Warren Spahn of the great Braves teams of the '50s failed to pull down that kind of money in Milwaukee.[646]

---

[645] Lou Chapman, "Brewers Point the Spotlight at Scott," quoting Del Crandall, The Sporting News, August 24, 1974, p. 23

[646] Lou Chapman, "Brewers' Great Scott Enters Champagne Class," The Sporting News, January 12, 1974, P. 30; Lou Chapman, "Brewers Report: Long on Foam, Short on Body," The Sporting News, October 4, 1975, P. 17

He was a study in affluence, reported the media, as he strode exultantly from the County Stadium executive offices into the parking lot, wearing a fur-collared coat and black and white turtle-neck sweater and beaming a country-wide smile. *"I believe in first class and will continue that way,"* he said to reporters as he got into his Cadillac parked smartly outside the stadium.[647] It was a grand moment for the 29-year-old major league standout from the Mississippi Delta, who once picked cotton near the banks of the Mississippi River at $1.75 per hundred-pound satchels and who was all too familiar with the life of poverty and, true to his promise had extracted his impoverished mother from a life of deprivation to a level of self-respect, which, along with his baseball success, was his ultimate purpose.

Quite unexpectedly, Del Crandall, of all people who infrequently bestowed public praise on his first-sacker, at least in terms of character, began to speak of Scotty's latent "leadership" qualities and how these traits could benefit the club, a display of paradoxical behavior quite by surprise. He had been a "take-charge" guy the previous two years, argued Crandall of Scott, something Scott had assumed on his own, which, Crandall pointed out, by his usual hard work and dedication, would be exemplary for his youthful ball club. The average age of the Brewers' important middle-of-the infield and center field – upon which managers customarily build their teams - in 1974 was approaching 21 years, and some of the pitchers slated

---

[647] IBID

to make the team were just as youthful and inexperienced. *"He's on the verge – if not there already – of being the team leader,"* said the Brewer skipper of his new $115,000 man.[648] Crandall, however, was not quick to back his words of prophecy with any individual rewards or captainship appointment, reserving that decision – out of necessity - for much later.

The Brewers were now stationed in a new spring location in Sun City, Arizona, which their owner Bud Selig had negotiated for his team for the next ten years. But their exhibition season was about as inglorious as the previous year, with the Brewers winning 10 of 23 games. Scott, true-to-form, did assume his usual spring leadership role, hitting with gusto, a .396 average, a spring-best 22 RBIs, and 5 home runs; his last was a grand slam off Oakland's Bob Locker and 6 RBIs on the day.

But it was largely a disappointing season for the Brewers, who started well, gaining first place on April 13, where they remained for six games, dropped precipitously to fifth place on May 7, then climbed back into a four-way tie for first on May 13 bouncing between there and second until a month later, June 13, when they dropped to third. They had held first place, either solely or shared, a total of 20 games. But then they began a descent, reaching the bottom of the East Division on June 18-20, spent parts of August there, finally concluding their season in the same spot they finished

---

[648] Lou Chapman, "Turn-Around Brewers Turn Deaf Ears to Scott Offers," The Sporting News, November 3, 1973. P. 20.

the year before, in fifth [76-86], 15 games out of first and a two-game team improvement over 1973.

The season was marked by a series of events that still resonate today for George Scott, which he believes may have been his greatest disappointments on the playing field: They were named the "Beanball Wars" by the press because of their intensity and the extraordinary nature of the three-day debacle that began on July 14 on a sweltering 92-degree Sunday in Milwaukee's County Stadium in a doubleheader with manager Billy Martin's Texas Rangers. Martin, a man with a feisty reputation and a militant nature, was upset with what had occurred the previous day when his shortstop, Toby Harrah, was knocked down by Brewer pitching, he claimed. Martin felt it was intentional and, in earnest, unabashedly complained to the umpires and to Crandall, whom he disliked, while at home plate exchanging lineups. He openly threatened he would order his hurlers to throw at their 18-year-old rookie shortstop phenom, Robin Yount, with head-high brushback pitches. It was an ominous gesture disturbing to the umpires and to Crandall, who suspected the angry Texas manager just might carry out his threat. He was right: In the sixth inning, Texas reliever Pete Broberg, who had a sizzling fastball, began throwing dusters to young Yount, knocking him down twice. In the sixth, he did the same to Scott, who had 5 RBIs on the day, including a homer off Broberg, sending him sprawling to the dirt. Martin, who had been warned, was summarily tossed by umpire Ron Luciano. Broberg was tossed a few innings later for continuing his beanball assault on Brewer players and for his part in the matter. Billy Martin was later fined for his indiscretions by the American League and suspended for three games. Manager Del Crandall had some disparaging remarks for Martin after the twin-bill, saying Martin *"is always going to be several knockdown pitches behind everyone else when it serves his purpose."*[649] Billy Martin, as reported by the Milwaukee press - though the games were a split in the won-loss column - was largely the loser on this day: *"Fiery manager Billy Martin lost his temper, two arguments, two players and a coach Sunday [July 14, 1974]."*[650]

Boomer and the Kid

---

[649] Unattributed/AP News, "Wild Action in Milwaukee: Brushback Pitches Spark Controversy," Stevens Point Journal, July 15, 1974, p. 12
[650] IBID

This led to a "basebrawl" two days later with the Twins, as described by a reporter about the even more troublesome Minnesota event that made the Texas affair seem more like a "tea party," he maintained. The Brewers had control of the contest with a 5-2 lead through six innings and appeared to be coasting toward a win. In the seventh, Ray Corbin came on in relief and, with pinpoint control, struck out both Yount and Don Money. The next batter, Bob Coluccio, who was 3-for-3 on the day, was struck on the side of the head by Corbin's first pitch, a fastball, and staggered to the ground; he got up, began to walk toward the pitching mound, and then fell again. There appeared little doubt about what was intended by that pitch. In fact, Corbin admitted to the brushback. *"It looked like he froze,"* said the pitcher. *"I was just trying to brush him back. And he had been hitting us pretty good."*[651] Scott had been standing near the dugout, waiting to hit after Briggs, who was in the on-deck circle. What he saw enraged the big Brewers slugger, who led the charge to the infield, and Corbin, where Brewers and Twins players congregated. Twins manager Frank Quillici soon joined them, and the battle began; Scott led the skirmish, deciding to take Quillici on by knocking him to the ground, followed by several small clashes all around the infield. It was later reported to be the wildest-ever brawl noted by a consensus of players and writers, lasting a good ten minutes before it was brought under control. Scott, who figured prominently in the melee',

---

[651] Unattributed/ AP News, Eau Claire Leader-Telegram, "Brewers Pound Twins With Bats, Fists, 5-4," July 17, 1974, p. 13

explained it simply: *"I don't start at the bottom and work up. I start at the top and work down. Who's running the show? The manager is the man responsible."[652]*

Recounting the events *"like it was yesterday,"* said Scott in a much later interview, the importance of protecting the young Brewer players was paramount to him. *"All those kids were babies. Most of the managers tried to intimidate them,"* said George. *"Frank Quillici came to the back of the dugout and pointed to the head of Coluccio,"* said a still-raging Scott, speaking with an indelible memory of that day paired with his remembrance of what had happened to his friend Tony Conigliaro seven years before, Quillici denied ordering a bean ball, which was to be expected. *"Coluccio was never the same ballplayer after that,"* said Scott.[653] There's merit in what he claims: Coluccio was hitting .260 at the time but finished the year at .223. The following year, he batted .202, was sent to the minors, bounced between major and minor league ball in 1977-1978, and then left baseball for good.

The 1974 Midsummer All-Star Classic was held on July 23, 1974, in Pittsburgh and won by the National League 7-2. How the players got to be elected, and the reserves chosen was nothing but a "farce," wrote sports scribe Bob Wolf of the *Milwaukee Journal*, critical of the process and particularly of the All-Star managers. [1972 AL MVP Dick Allen was the

---

[652] IBID, p. 14
[653] George Scott interview: March 23, 2006

fan selection for starting first baseman.] But when it came time for them to name their backup players for the team many of the clubs, the Brewers among them, were stunned at the choices. The American League manager, Dick Williams, historically a George Scott antagonist, made two choices for his reserve first basemen: Future Hall of Famer Carl Yastrzemski, the Red Sox part-time first baseman, with which few could be critical. But far more startling was Williams' second choice: Kansas City's John Mayberry, an adequate fielder batting just .260 compared with George Scott and his .297 batting average, who was the superior first-sacker. It was a glaring offense made of Scotty infuriating Bud Selig, who appealed the matter, along with Williams' snub of his third baseman, Don Money, to American League President Lee MacPhail. Selig was seething, calling it "disgraceful" in his formal letter to MacPhail; the effort by Selig was of no avail, however, but to the city of Milwaukee, Selig's actions at the least brought into the open the injustice of Williams' initiatives. Don Money later was named as a reserve when Sal Bando, Williams' crony and backup selection from Oakland, came down with an injury. But in spite of his good bat – among the AL leaders - and being the hands-down best fielding first baseman in the American League, if not all of major league baseball, Scotty remained off the team.

Del Crandall was upset, too, and ranted about it shortly after the All-Star debacle that had everyone talking, including criticism of the National League's All-Star manager, Yogi Berra, for some of his All-Star choices. It was a conspicuous blunder, but more than likely, it was intentional. *"He's been underpublicized,"* said Crandall of his spectacular first-sacker. *"It's about time he gets the recognition he merits,"* he said, rating him among the six or seven best players in the league. Boston writers, in town for the Brewers-Red Sox four-game series, agreed with Crandall, complaining further that the trade sending Scott to Milwaukee was a bad one. Scott was hitting .304 at the time, positioned firmly among the ten top hitters in the American League.[654]

He was rewarded with his 6th Gold Glove – 4th consecutively – and named co-recipient with Don Money for the "Magic Glove Award," Milwaukee's own team award for fielding excellence. Fifty-five American League managers and coaches made George Scott a near-unanimous pick as best fielding first baseman. Of the 13 ballots not cast for Scott, five of them were by the Milwaukee staff which was precluded from voting for their own players. He had an American League-best 1345 putouts for first basemen and a major league-best 114 assists, helping his team tie with the Orioles as the best fielding team in the league. Only Joe Torre of the St. Louis Cardinals approached his assist total with 102. He named his glove "Black Magic," which he had stained black at a time when the conventional major league baseball glove was brown or tan in color. His range, reflexes, and instincts around first were far-and-away superior to his peers; he had a take-charge attitude chasing pop flies and scooping balls hit into the hole,

---

[654] Lou Chapman, "Brewers Point the Spotlight at Scott," The Sporting News, August 24, 1974, P. 23

and "better than any," said one sports scribe, coming in on bunts and whipping the ball to second base to start double plays; every bit the consummate first baseman.

One of the more striking moments in Milwaukee Brewers' history was the 1974 offseason acquisition of home run king Hank Aaron from Atlanta; it would turn out to be one of the most fortuitous and meaningful moments in George Scott's professional baseball career, as well. Aaron, who surpassed the legendary Babe Ruth's home run record of 714 that season, signed a contract on November 2nd to come back to Milwaukee; it was there as a member of the Braves that he cut his teeth as a pro ballplayer and excelled for 12 years, winning a World Series [1957], and became a Milwaukee and baseball legend. He and his team were beloved by the city making their 1966 departure to Atlanta a crushing blow, some Milwaukee fans declaring they would never return to the game of baseball again. It was a brilliant move by Bud Selig to woo the celebrated superstar back to the city in his waning days with Atlanta and drawing on a fan base that would surely respond well to the memorable slugger's return. His instincts proved to be flawless: Brewer mania had set in, with Aaron triggering season ticket sales in the fall and winter at a pace 20 percent ahead of the previous year, and the Brewers would set a team record, drawing 1,213,357 fans in the upcoming season, nearly a 27% increase over 1974.

Aaron became Scott's mentor; it was the perfect union, according to Scott, who stated that it was the only occasion in his major league career that anyone "at that level" spent time with him to explain the finer points of hitting.

> *"My locker was next to his, and he used to get in early, and I would get in early [also], and we'd sit around and just talk baseball. The reason that Hank was able to do that for me [be a mentor] was that when I grew up as a young boy playing baseball in the backyard, I was Hank Aaron or Willie Mays. And here I am in the major leagues in the same locker room, on the same team with this guy. It was unbelievable. You know Hank Aaron helped me out over there [Milwaukee]. He helped me out a lot. I will always say that the 1975 season was a direct tribute to Henry Aaron because Hank used to sit and talk to me about hitting, about pitchers, about setting pitchers up, and all of that. If I had had him with me for four or five years, there's no telling what I would have done in baseball."*[655]

One of the first acts by Del Crandall as players arrived for spring training in Sun City was to abide by his promise to fine anyone who reported to camp overweight. He wasted no time meting out the first of such penalties to George Scott, assessing him $700 - $50 for each extra pound - for his over-the-winter imprudence. Scott, whose coffers were more amply lined than in previous years, saw some humor in this and began bantering with the Brewers' newly-appointed general manager, Jim Baumer, not realizing his vindictive nature, while both were standing around the batting cage. 34-

---

[655] George Scott interview: January 24, 2006

year-old Baumer succeeded GM Jim Wilson in November 1974 in another Bud Selig office shakeup after Wilson left in the summer of that year to head up the new central scouting system. *"See, Jim, that's why I argued with you for the extra $2,000 on my contract. For things like this,"* whined an obviously contented Scotty. Said Baumer: *"We always get it back somehow."*[656] A moment of unconscious nascent prophesy, perhaps, that would soon surface, leading to friction between Scott and the rookie Brewer general manager, who appeared intolerant of their star first baseman and would prescribe the mood for the remainder of Scott's contract with Milwaukee.

On March 12, the day before the Brewers' exhibition opener with the Cubs, Crandall appealed to Aaron to give his team an impromptu closed-door talk on hitting and the mental preparation required of a good hitter. What better man for that than Aaron, thought the Brewer skipper; it lasted over an hour. When it ended and spilled out onto the clubhouse floor, an informal session began with the young Brewer players huddled around Aaron and Scott, spellbound as they listened intently to the two accomplished ballplayers exchanging words of wisdom about hitting. It was a profound moment as well for Scotty, a conscientious student of the game and of hitting, with whom Aaron appeared to identify like a kindred spirit. They were rooted in conversation with each other at times, as if alone, yet

---

[656] Mike Gonring, "Scott Finds Offseason Appetite Not So Fine," *Milwaukee Journal*, March 7, 197,. P. 10

in the presence of others as they embellished answers to the questions that were being raised by the Brewer youngsters. A bond was about to manifest itself between the two that would raise Scott's confidence and overall performance level to never-before-reached heights for him as a major leaguer.

Once more, Scotty led his teammates in yet another successful spring exhibition season for the big first baseman hitting an even .400 on 22 base hits; the Brewers, with a modicum of disappointment expressed by Crandall for not coming up with a better showing, finished in the middle of the American League pack at 12-12.[657] The day following the final spring game, the Brewers traveled to the Hub City for their April 8 opener with a formidable Boston Red Sox team. It was a chilly day in Boston, which did not deter a Fenway throng of over 34,000 fans who came out for the festivities: it was not only opening day, but Tony Conigliaro, Boston's own, was making a comeback attempt after a 3 ½ year absence from baseball, and it was the American League inaugural for the new Brewer, "Hammerin Hank" Aaron. It had a storybook crowd-pleasing ring to it. The Brewers were keyed up before the game, anticipating the introduction of Aaron and all the hoopla surrounding it; George Scott was in high spirits as he unveiled his new first baseman's mitt, a manufacturer-issued black model. *"Here it*

---

[657] The Milwaukee Journal reported Scott's spring statistics as batting .415 on 53 at-bats and 22 base hits. The Sporting News data and Milwaukee Journal box scores, however, show Scott with 55 at-bats on 22 base hits.

is, here it is," he hollered, *"Black Magic,"* prodding his teammates to take a look.[658] But the game fell flat for the Brewers, who couldn't overcome the four-run deficit they were dealt in the first three innings and lost 5-2. Scott, who was accustomed to hitting well against Red Sox hurler Luis Tiant, was 1-for-3, a double. The next day, the Brewers turned the tables on Boston, winning 7-4, behind newcomer Pete Broberg's pitching and clutch hitting by Scott, precipitated by a four-pitch walk to Aaron, loading the bases. Scotty promptly followed with a hard-hit two-out single, knocking in the first two runs of the game. It was to be the start of an extraordinary season for the big first-sacker from Mississippi, leveraged by the presence of a certifiable slugger, Hank Aaron, batting in front of him.

It set the stage for the long-awaited home opener in Milwaukee on April 11 against the Cleveland Indians. Over 48,000 fans, undeterred by the 40-degree football weather temperatures, filled the stands to welcome Hank Aaron back to their city, and they were rewarded with a 6-2 Brewers win, putting them into a tie for first place. The Brewers drifted between first and second through April, and then on May 1st, went into first place, where they remained for most of the month, in spite of weak bats and injuries soon to follow. By the end of May, only George Scott and their young shortstop and future Hall of Famer, Robin Yount, of the regulars, were getting base hits with any kind of consistency, helping to keep the Brewers in contention.

---

[658] Unattributed, "Crowd Pleasers Please Boston Crowd," *Milwaukee Journal*, April 9, 1975, P. 14; Scott later changed the name of his glove to "Black Beauty."

Scott was hitting .272, Yount .322; Hank Aaron was struggling at .187. The rest were languishing in the low 200s, including their 1974 All-Star, Don Money. *"Scott Hot, Brewers Not,"* was the May 9 headline of a *Milwaukee Journal* article highlighting George Scott's runs-batted-in streak of eight consecutive games that was approaching the major league record of twelve held by Joe Cronin and Ted Williams. Scotty would fall short, however, knocking in runs in nine consecutive games before being stopped on May 10 against Kansas City; he amassed 14 RBIs in that span.

In spite of being among the leaders, there were problems developing on the club with key injuries and a serious player behavioral issue involving their talented but temperamental second baseman, Pedro Garcia, who could not get along with Del Crandall, alleging, among his numerous complaints, that the manager was interfering in his personal life though that was never explained. Their dislike for each other was nearly pathological. Crandall benched Garcia on May 14 with an eye to sending him back to the minors, but owner Bud Selig overruled Crandall, concerned with accusations of bigotry, reinstating Garcia a week later despite his promise he would not interfere with the decisions of his field manager. The entire fiasco with Garcia, who one reporter labeled "the dissident," did not set well with the rest of the Brewer players, several of who lost their respect for the manager, assuming he had caved into upper management.

Underlying all of this was an apparent issue with Crandall and their hitting coach, Harvey Kuenn, about trying to change Garcia's batting style, according to former Brewer captain George Scott. *"That's why I got angry when Del Crandall and all those guys [coaches] tried to change Pedro Garcia and started messing with his head,"* declared Scott many years later. It struck a nerve with Scotty, whose earlier dealings with his former nemesis, Dick Williams, had left him with lasting emotional scars from the Red Sox manager's dogged attempts to change his own swing. *"If he loses his aggressiveness [with the bat], he may become a worse player,"* exclaimed the former slugger, still frustrated with the situation confronting Garcia and remembering his own personal struggle with Williams. *"They messed him up,"* decried Scott, still harboring vivid memories.[659]

Yount and Money went down with injuries, Yount with an ankle sprain on May 9 that benched him for ten games, and Money, the Brewers 1974 MVP, underwent hernia surgery on May 28 that disabled him for nearly a month. It would have an effect on the team. From May 17 to the end of the month, the Brewers lost 10 of 12 games – five by one run – putting them into a tailspin and into second place, 2 ½ games behind the Red Sox. During that same period, Scott, unlike the rest of his teammates, was hitting well: he was 14-for-43, a .326 pace, with 2 home runs and 11 RBIs.

The good pitching that held up the Brewers earlier in the year, led by Bill Champion and Pete Broberg, soon faded, and by the first week of June, Brewer pitching had regressed to a .406 ERA performance level, near the

---

[659] George Scott interview: January 24, 2006

bottom of the American League; furthermore, they importantly lacked a left-hander adding to their pitching woes. The bats were nearly as bad: On June 5, they were hitting a mere .238 as a team, third from the bottom. But while the Brewers were struggling, George Scott was building his own personal momentum, stroking 34 base hits – including an eleven-game streak - 22 RBIs, 7 home runs, and a .496 slugging percentage in the month of June. His RBI total of 53 was second only to Boston's Fred Lynn, who had 56.

By the first of July, the Brewers had crept back into second place, tied with the Yankees, one game behind the Red Sox, and about to play three important games with Boston in Milwaukee, starting with a doubleheader on July 2. Rick Wise, a 19-game winner for Boston that year, was on the mound in the first game and was pitching a no-hitter through eight and two-thirds innings. He had walked Bill Sharp (only his second of three) with two outs, and George Scott came to bat. *"I was trying to jam him. He's just a good hitter, that's all,"* said Wise.[660] Scotty proceeded to launch the ball well over the center-field fence breaking up Wise's no-hitter, which would have been his second in the major leagues. "He crushed it," said teammate Bobby Darwin, the on-deck hitter, who followed with a home run of his own off Wise. Boston won the game 6-3. Scott severely sprained his ankle sliding into first base in the second game and was carried from the field on

---

[660] Mike Gonring, "Scott Hurts Wise and Self," Milwaukee Journal, July 3, 1975, P. 8

a stretcher. But the Brewers managed to take two of three in the series, tying them with the Red Sox for first place.

Ordinarily, an injury like Scott's should have kept him from the lineup for days, but Scotty was back in there, missing only one game but limping decidedly, returning as the designated hitter in the first game of a doubleheader with Detroit. His penchant for playing and playing hard was on full display. He had trouble keeping his weight back on breaking balls due to the pain and was 0-for-8 in the next two games. But on July 6, he began a streak of five games in which he hit his 15th and 16th home runs and had 9 base hits at a .474 pace. By the All-Star break, he was hitting .281 with a .842 OPS and 58 RBIs.

Once again, there was controversy surrounding fan All-Star selections, and "perhaps the worst slipup of all," wrote *Milwaukee Journal* columnist Bob Wolf was banishing George Scott to sixth place in the voting behind inferior players who were not performing at his level. Gene Tenace of Oakland, the fans' selection to start at first base, was hitting .275 with 14 home runs. Baltimore's Lee May, hitting .244, placed fourth. None of the players that were voted in front of Scott approached his runs-batted-in mark, except for May, who also had 58 RBIs. Scott led the others with 16 home runs - Tenace was next with 14 - and he was far and away the best defensive first baseman in the league if not both leagues. All-Star manager Alvin Dark, who knew the true measure of the big first baseman who had been playing at an All-Star level and who, through the years, often expressed a desire to have the big guy in his own teams' lineups, selected Scott as his primary backup along with Mike Hargrove of Texas and Boston's Carl Yastrzemski.

It was a frustrating moment for Scotty when he first realized he had not been honored by the fans, and he vented to the press and anyone else who would listen that he couldn't understand the injustice of the fan balloting. *"You can't tell me the fans are voting right when I finish seventh [6th actually],"* complained Scott, frustrated over the lack of recognition of his skills and year-to-date accomplishments.[661] Relying on the consensus of other reporters and baseball minds Scott had made a reasonably sound inference; he was robbed yet again. The 46th All-Star Classic was played, fittingly, in Milwaukee and became as much a celebration of Hank Aaron, promoted theatrically by Bud Selig, as it was an All-Star event. Aaron was also an alternate selection along with Scott to represent the Brewers. When Gene Tenace was announced as the American League starting first baseman, the Milwaukee crowd reigned boos down on him as if the balloting had been his contrivance. Dark did, however, put George in the game playing first base in the top of the 7th with the American League down 3-0, but it was not a memorable occasion for Scotty, who struck out in his two plate appearances, in an American League losing cause, 6-3. It was the 4th straight American League All-Star game loss and 12th of the last 13. *"I*

---

[661] Mike Gonring, "Scott Sees Stars Over Baseball Fans' Taste in Balloting," Milwaukee Journal, July 13, 1975, P. 1

think I was just too keyed up," said Scott following the game. *"I wanted to hit one for my fans."*[662]

Reporters eager for something provocative interviewed several AL players willing to discuss the embarrassment of what had just happened to them. Among them was future Hall of Famer Reggie Jackson, who was 1-for-3 on the day. He was bitter about the loss, rambled on about their reasons for losing, and then proceeded to list his favorite team and players, placing the Boomer in the top spot. *"My favorite player in baseball is George Scott, and my favorite National League player is Johnny Bench,"* said the baseball superstar, making the Brewer first-sacker his preeminent choice of a long list of notable ballplayers.[663]

Chuck Johnson of the *Journal*, reporting on events surrounding the July 15 classic, wrote about Milwaukee's local hero Scott, declaring that he "is something," reflecting on a question asked of the big first baseman by one of the newspaper people probing him on why he was wearing "beads" around his neck. It was actually a puka shell type of necklace he wore that he began to use that year, made up of various kinds of shells and beads that gave the menacing appearance of a shark's teeth. Turning on his humorous side, Scott's quick-witted reply was: "Those are second basemen's teeth," without further explanation. This, of course, morphed into a variety of

---

[662] Bob Wolf, "AL Talks a Good Game, NL Plays a Good One," Milwaukee Journal, July 16, 1975, P. 16
[663] Mike Gonring, "All-Stars Find It's Still a National Game," Milwaukee Journal, July 16, 1975, P. 13

interpretations. Though the popular belief was that these were supposed to be Scott's mementos from his hard take-out slides of second basemen, he later explained it was symbolic of the rocket-like line drives he customarily hit to the right side of the infield, displacing infielders' teeth because of their inability to protect themselves.

The Brewers continued to be plagued by injuries. Pedro Garcia, their slick but moody second baseman, went down with a back injury on July 5 and remained out for over a month, playing sparingly after his August 11 return. One of their starters, Bill Champion, developed arm trouble and saw limited action in the second half of the season. It was another blow to an inept pitching staff that had trouble surviving the early innings. Then, one of their sluggers, Bobby Darwin, fractured his hand on August 2. And on the same day, and the day following, their promising 22-year-old outfielder Sixto Lezcano, another Latino like Garcia, ran aground with Del Crandall – who seemed to have problems with Latinos - who fined the young rookie a total of $150 for the two-day "temper tantrums," and benched him for a few games. Lezcano insisted it was unjust and he wouldn't pay the fine, whereupon the club took the money from his paycheck according to their normal practice.

In the midst of their precipitous skid, losing 19 of 31 games in July, Crandall, who had hinted more than a year before about designating George Scott a team captain, appointed him the Brewers on-field team leader on July 23. He was the Brewers' first captain in the six-year history of the team.

Scott had just clouted his 19th homer, driving in his 62nd and 63rd RBIs the day before the announcement, and was on a streak of 8 games that continued to 14 consecutively in which he hit safely, including 5 home runs in that span. He hit .313 in July with 36 base hits, 8 home runs, 67 RBIs, a slugging percentage of .574, and an OPS of .929.

The Brewers, however, were sliding further toward the bottom. On July 30, they were one game below .500, firmly in fourth place, ten games behind first-place Boston, whom they had just beaten two out of three games. Rumor was beginning to circulate that manager Del Crandall's job was at risk, causing the *Journal's* sports columnist Mike Gonring to write of the preposterousness of such a thought, choosing to place the blame with the players, not the manager. He pointed out the many problems on the club, the worst being inconsistent pitching, which would finish dead last in the American League, and a leaky defense that would finish next to the bottom. And, for a team that was hitting just about as poorly (.249; third from bottom in AL), to be just one game below .500 meant "Somebody's doing something right," exclaimed the sportswriter. That "somebody" was George Scott, who not only was hitting well – in spite of a poorly performing ballclub - but fielding in his usual Gold Glove manner.

The Brewers went into a losing spiral that spanned the final two months of the season, losing 41 of 57 games. On August 25, after losing 20 of 25, manager Del Crandall exploded, ordering a closed-door clubhouse meeting to scold his players on their shoddy performance. George Scott also held the floor over his teammates, charging them with being *"the laughing stock of baseball."*[664] Scott was himself seething sensing that an underlying reason for the Brewers' collapse was a lack of self-discipline with too much partying and general unpreparedness, which he loathed. *"The players have to play harder, the coaches have to coach harder, the manager has to manage harder, and the owner has to own harder,"* he exclaimed to a bevy of reporters, injecting some unintended humor into the stern lecture and drawing laughs, only a few weeks before when Brewer defeats were becoming commonplace.[665]

Del Crandall's days with the Milwaukee Brewers were numbered when, on September 22, in a game with Cleveland, rookie outfielder Sixto Lezcano once again locked horns with his manager by refusing to go into the game as a pinch runner, a game in which George Scott was 4-for-5 and hit his 32nd and 33rd home runs. Lezcano was immediately suspended for the remainder of the season. It was also discovered that Pedro Garcia had unilaterally decided not to make the road trip because of his bad back. It was apparent Crandall was losing control of his club.

But while the Brewers and Del Crandall were falling apart, *"Scott Keeps Booming"* was the headline of the September 25 *Milwaukee Journal* article following Scott's personal 10-3 demolition of Frank Robinson's Cleveland

---

[664] Lou Chapman, "Seething Pilot Crandall Blasts Brewers," The Sporting News, September 13, 1975, P. 16
[665] IBID

Indians by stroking his 34th homer and 4 RBIs. Losing manager Robinson threw up his hands, overwhelmed by Scott's performance. *"He's something,"* he said of Scott, echoing a similar comment made by the *Journal's* Chuck Johnson in his report on the '75 All-Star game. *"He can carry a club when he's right."*[666] The following day against Detroit, Scotty provided all that was needed to defeat the Tigers 3-0, knocking in all of the runs with two long home runs, the second (his 36th) a two-run shot that sailed high and long against the wind into the center field bleachers. He was awarded *The Sporting News* Player of the Week, in which he was 10-for-27 with 5 home runs and 13 RBIs.

The Brewers won their last four games but finished the year rooted in fifth place again, 28 games behind first-place Boston at 68-94, Crandall's worst managerial performance since coming to Milwaukee. He was fired on September 28 before the final game of the year against the Tigers. There were mixed reactions among the players and media, typical for a manager who has just been released. Milwaukee Pitcher Jim Colborn was the harshest critic, blaming Brewers' upper management for failing to back their manager.

It was another stellar year for their big first-sacker; however, perhaps the only bright light of a forgettable year for baseball in the city of Milwaukee. Scotty led his club in practically every category: 36 home runs,

---

[666] Unattributed, "Scott Top Boomer, Brewers Win," Milwaukee Journal, September 25, 1975, P. 18

176 base hits, 109 RBIs, 86 runs, 9 game-winning hits, and a .515 slugging percentage. He hit safely in 115 of his 158 games played. More significantly, he was the American League RBI and total bases leader [318], tied Reggie Jackson for most home runs, and finished fourth in slugging percentage. He topped it off by winning his 7th Gold Glove- 5th consecutive – by a near-unanimous 23-of-24 possible votes as the best defensive first baseman in the league.

Chapter 15
The Intractable Jim Baumer

"Everything George did last year he did out of sheer determination. He's a perfect example of a man driving himself to be better than he is. A lot of younger ballplayers should look up to him. I agree with George; he can be better, and I know he will be because he will drive himself to a higher level. He's that kind of player."

Hank Aaron[667]

Barely had the ink dried on the final lineup cards of the season and equipment packed and stored for another year when the Brewers rewarded Scotty with a new two-year contract through 1977 for an estimated $150,000-$160,000, placing him among the elite top 10 highest-paid major league ballplayers; in essence the lifeblood, if not, actually, *the franchise*.

But trade rumors were circulating during the World Series that George Scott might be on the block in exchange for the California Angels' All-Star strike-out artist and future Hall of Famer, Nolan Ryan. Remarkably, and quite unexpectedly, strong interest in him was being voiced by manager

---

[667] Joe Stargis, "Nobody Working Harder Than Scott in Brewers' Camp," quoting Hank Aaron, Waukesha Daily Freeman, Mar 26, 1976, p. 11
https://www.newspapers.com/image/83959992/?terms=%22Nobody%20Working%20Harder%20Than%20Scott%20in%20Brewers%27%20Camp%2C%22%20&match=1

Dick Williams and their GM Harry Dalton. Brewers' second-year GM Jim Baumer, a career minor leaguer - never the diplomat - who carelessly leaked that their only "untouchable" was young Robin Yount, and who was anxious to do some meaningful trading, in the next breath or at the very least making an attempt at circumspection he was not known for, and rescuing himself after a misstatement, declared that clubs would have to "overwhelm me," if he were to give up his Brewer MVP first baseman, the bread-and-butter of the team.

Trade talk became even more intense during the winter meetings in Hollywood, Florida between the Angels, Red Sox, and Brewers; they were working on a three-way deal that would have sent Scott to California, but it never materialized. The Red Sox tried to negotiate a separate deal for Scott, but that fell through as well. Sensing his folly for trading away the popular George Scott in '71 and then Scott's extraordinary '75 season, Red Sox GM Dick O'Connell seized the initiative to get him back to Boston. *"We tried to get Scott in a retrade,"* said O'Connell but failed this time.[668] Scotty was to remain a Brewer. *"Nobody's going to drive in runs like George,"* exclaimed the Brewers' new manager, Alex Grammas – the Brewers' second choice after Hank Aaron, who rejected their offer, in an enthusiastic

---

[668] Unattributed/ UPI, "Red Sox Bid for Scott Failed," The Boston Globe, February 3, 1976, p. 31

sigh of relief over the Brewers' retention of their big Gold Glover and slugging first-sacker.[669]

Despite his remarkable season, applauded colorfully by his mentor and teammate Henry Aaron, George Scott was in for disappointment, this one at the hands of his own peers. By a thin margin of 11 votes (95-84), the closest of the balloting among the candidates, the 214 players who participated selected the Kansas City Royals' John Mayberry as their choice for American League All-Star first baseman on *The Sporting News'* all-star team. To Scott, it was just another colossal snub, who, in the foremost categories of player performance essential to team performance, outperformed every other first baseman. He drove in the most runs, hit the most home runs, and hit for the most total bases of any other American League player, and clearly carried the Brewers throughout their miserable season; his value to the team based on fielding performance was unsurpassed. Scott, by his exploits in the field, was by far the best defensive first baseman – for which he was honored with his 7th Gold Glove – executing many game-saving plays never reaching a statistical spreadsheet, or, for that matter, that was even capable of being translated into a statistical measure. But Mayberry, whose batting statistics were similar in several areas to Scott's, was on a team that finished second; Scott played for a team that finished next to last, which carried a lot of weight in the decision.

---

[669] Lou Chapman, "Brewers Shedding No Tears Over Swap Shutout," The Sporting News, December 27, 1975, P. 50.

Even Mayberry's new skipper, Whitey Herzog, whose team won 41 of 66 games following his mid-season appointment as Royals' manager, equivocated about Scott not being chosen when doing an assessment of player balloting. *"I guess maybe Scott could feel that he should have been the [all-star] first baseman,"* said Herzog, who then neutralized any possible controversy by suggesting that his first baseman had a *"fine year,"* too and, besides, the *"vote was close."*[670] Scott, it happened, would be victimized by Herzog and his invectiveness, perhaps as much as racial bigotry, toward the ballplayer in 1979 playing for Kansas City in the last year of his major league career.

In the offseason, Boston's Fred Lynn dominated two important award categories: the *American League's Rookie of the Year* and, by an unprecedented vote, as a rookie, chosen as the American League's *Most Valuable Player*, the first rookie in either league to receive such an honor; he received 22 of 24 first-place votes from the Baseball Writers Association [BBWAA]. Scott finished eighth in the voting and was clearly frustrated, feeling he had been slighted yet again. He was provoked, leading to mercurial ranting that soon got the attention of sportswriters and fans with varied views and opinions.

"If there was a better player [than me] in baseball last year, I want to see him. There isn't another player who led the league in three categories

---

[670] Joe McGuff, "Brett's All-Star Omission a Disgrace – Herzog," The Sporting News, December 13, 1975, P. 49

like I did. I drove in more runs than anyone in the league, and the Brewers never got anyone on base for me. Now you tell me how anyone could be more valuable than a guy who drives in all the runs for a fourth [5th] place team."[671]

But George's dignity was restored momentarily when he was honored by the Milwaukee writers on January 25 at their annual Diamond Dinner event, designating him the Brewers' 1975 MVP. And he was the Associated Press' pick for their all-star team, distinctively composed of American and National League players. Scott was one of only four American Leaguers of the ten players selected and the only American League infielder.

Among the many awards George Scott received for his outstanding 1975 performance, perhaps the most curious, if not intriguing, of them was the one he received from Boston scribes at their annual writers' dinner. On January 29, four days after the Milwaukee Diamond Dinner ceremonies, the Boston writers toasted George in the Hub city with a so-called "special achievement" award for fashioning his most productive major league season." This was an unadulterated sentiment, perhaps, for Scott's remarkable achievements in that year that largely went unrecognized, yet plaudits for a man who remained a New England media and fan-favorite, who after more than four years still begrudged his absence from Boston.

---

[671] Unattributed, "Fred Lynn Was Named the Most Valuable Player," Los Angeles Times, February 11, 1976, P. E2

Once more, the spring season was interrupted by labor disputes between major league baseball owners and the Player's Association. Toward the end of October 1975, Executive Director Marvin Miller had received a terse written notice from the owners that as of December 31, they were terminating the Basic Agreement they had reached earlier and also their funding agreement for the pension plan, effective March 31, 1976. It was a significant blow to accomplishments achieved earlier between the two parties and nothing but a "hostile act," declared Miller. But before all of this was fully digested or acted upon, there came the historic *Seitz Decision* on December 23, 1975, effectively granting free agency to major league ballplayers one year after the expiration of their contracts. Seitz was summarily fired by the owners, but the die was cast in favor of the players. The owners appealed the Seitz decision twice and lost both times, leaving them with the singular decision of negotiating the best deal they could muster with the players. But the owners were still holding to some form of reserve clause language in any of their so-called bargaining, in spite of the legal decisions favoring the players, and the spring camps were shut down.

Commissioner Bowie Kuhn, realizing the risk to major league baseball by not opening the season, invoked his authority: on March 17, he announced the opening of spring camps, even while negotiations were still being worked on and no new contract had been reached. It was like a message from heaven for George Scott, who had been critical of the Association for not taking the owners' eight-year offer, a far cry from anything the players had just won on the courts. He chose to admonish them.

"I think the players should stop crying about slavery and worry about playing baseball. If they'd play as hard as they complain, they'd all be superstars," enunciated a clearly frustrated Scott, thrusting his own principled argument of how he negatively viewed some players.[672] Scott already had a two-year $160,000 contract tucked away, so he was eager to get started. No doubt his views did not sit well with his teammates, who saw this as betrayal setting the tone for the '76 season.

Start they did with drills on March 20 and with exhibition games underway four days later, more than three weeks after camps should have opened. But all was not contentment in the Brewer camp. Bud Selig, who would later become the major league's baseball commissioner, was one of the defiant owners refusing to negotiate with the Association, and his new general manager, Jim Baumer, eager to please the boss, had chosen to play hardball with the thirteen unsigned Brewer players. Baumer invoked the renewal clause of the uniform player's contract [sec. 10a] and cut several players' salaries by the maximum allowed of 20%. It was, of course, unsettling to the Brewer players, especially pitcher Jim Colborn, who cried foul. Baumer was already feeling the heat by being a principal in the firing of the popular Del Crandall and not accomplishing any trades in the offseason. Now he was bearing the wrath of his players, many who found him too tough at contract time, one who even labeled him "nasty." His knack for bluntness did not improve his standing with the players when, on

---

[672] Unattributed, "Morning Briefing," Los Angeles Times, March 5, 1976, P. D2

March 29, he accused his left-hander, Kevin Kobel, of being a "hypochondriac." Kobel, on whom the Brewers were relying, had a recurrence of arm trouble and was optioned to the minors.

Meanwhile, in spite of his windfall pay raise, the Boomer was not content while holding onto festering resentment of long duration spurred by Milwaukee upper management that included Del Crandall, Jim Wilson, Jim Baumer, and soon-to-be Brewers' new manager Alex Grammas, who subscribed to the company line. *"I didn't like the way they were running the team and the direction they were going. I couldn't understand why they seemed okay with what they had [for a team],"* said Scott.[673] Grammas, a light-hitting former infielder with a good glove, who, following his playing career in 1963, took on a new role as a third base coach in the 1970s for the "Big Red Machine," the Cincinnati Reds, where he made a name for himself at the valued position. His first order of business with the Brewers, in traditional old-fashioned managerial style, was to ban mustaches and beards and no excuses for not being punctual. One Milwaukee reporter, picking up on this rigid demeanor, raised the specter of future trouble for Grammas: *"Considering that Del Crandall's problems with Garcia and Lezcano started over the color of socks they wore, Grammas could be treading dangerous ground. When the Brewer front office decided between backing*

---

[673] George Scott interview: January 28, 2006

Crandall or his recalcitrant young players, it figured managers were easier to find than promising ballplayers."[674]

The Brewers finished an abbreviated spring season at 6-8; Scott played sparingly but still led the team with a .321 batting average, hit two home runs, and 8 RBIs, second only to Darrell Porter, who had 13. They opened the regular season on April 8 in Milwaukee in 44-degree weather, in front of a crowd of 44,868, and won 5-0 behind Jim Slaton's 4-hit pitching, and proceeded to win 8 of their next 11 games, slipping into first place on April 29. But it was downhill from there; the Brewers had fallen precipitously into 5th place three and a half weeks later. On May 27, in a tightly-pitched game against Boston, Pete Broberg made an errant pickoff throw in the dirt to first base, receiving an error that Scott couldn't handle, leading to the winning run. Broberg later made an acrimonious comment that it was a *"catchable ball,"* which aroused George Scott, who responded angrily that he didn't make alibis and he saw no reason why Broberg, a 1-4 pitcher with a *"four-point ERA,"* and who never had a winning season, should either. Broberg attempted to conciliate, offering his own interpretation, saying he was stunned by Scott's comments, and claimed he didn't mean it the way a vexed Scott had interpreted it; yet, it was difficult to see it any other way than a lame excuse. It may have been the bellwether of things to come for

---

[674] Jim Kornkven, "Grammas Works on Respect," Kenosha News, May 7, 1976, p. 23 https://www.newspapers.com/image/597122898/?match=1&terms=alex%20grammas

George navigating adversarial teammate encounters and disruptions, along with his disenchantment with the front office.

It was apparent that the labor unrest and salary disputes of the spring, leaving players rankled and very unhappy with Brewer management, were now expanding into a whole other territory: Grammas, whose club was still in 5th and a full six games out of first, realized he now had his hands full. *"He's playing no matter who's pitching,"* said Grammas, responding to Scott's suggestion that maybe another first baseman should play when Broberg was on the mound.[675] Scott's displeasure continued into another game three days later against the Indians when he complained to Grammas about being taken out for a pinch runner, Kurt Bevacqua, who scored. *"Hell no, I don't like it,"* raged the big first baseman, who scoffed at Grammas' actions which he thought insulting.[676] Scott, who had two hits on the day and was batting .242, was unquestionably agitated and clearly embarrassed, the consensus being that perhaps he was indulging in too many dogfights and too-frequent outbursts and needed to maintain his composure better.

On June 1, the Brewers reached the bottom of the division, 8 ½ games out of first, where they were to languish between fifth and sixth place for the balance of the year, losing a doubleheader to the last-place Tigers, each

---

[675] Unattributed/ AP News, "Scott Sounds Off On Pete Broberg," The La Crosse Tribune," May 29, 1976, p. 7
https://www.newspapers.com/image/513663966/?match=1&terms=pete%20broberg
[676] Mike Gonring, "Brewers Unload Pedro, Problems," Milwaukee Journal, June 24, 1976, p. 7

loss by one run on ninth-inning rallies. It was their third consecutive one-run loss to Detroit, losing in the final innings of come-from-behind victories. George Scott, who was 4-for-8 in the doubleheader, exclaimed: *"Either they're the '27 Yankees or we're the Bad News Bears."*[677] Manager Alex Grammas saw no humor in the matter, however, after the twin-bill debacle and chided them unmercifully. "He said we were all rotten," said one Brewer player. Further troubles ensued the next day when the Brewers lost their fourth straight to Detroit on another late-inning Tiger rally, when pitcher Jim Colborn, who was 2-6 and still fuming over the treatment he had received from Jim Baumer in the spring, balked at Grammas' instructions to intentionally walk a batter. Grammas dashed to the mound and gave Colborn a tongue-lashing in full view of the crowd and television audience. So much for his prophecy that he would never berate a player publicly. Nothing was going right for the frustrated rookie manager. After the game, which the Brewers lost 6-4, both Colborn —who was accused of throwing bean balls at Detroit batters – and George Scott, who was nearly beaned by Detroit's Vernon Ruhle and had to leave the game, received threatening telegrams. Three times the normal amount of Detroit policemen were at the next and final game of the series, but nothing came of it.

GM Baumer, who was criticized for not making any off-season trades on a club that was going nowhere without new blood, picked up 28-year-

---

[677] Mike Gonring, "Brewers Show Nothing, Grammas Shows Anger," Milwaukee Journal, June 2, 1976, p. 11

old Von Joshua on June 2 from the Giants for a player to be named, and on June 3 traded relief pitcher Tom Murphy and outfielder Bobby Darwin to Boston for 1975 World Series hero Bernie Carbo. Darwin and Murphy were the happiest men after learning of the trade, gloating about it in the Brewers clubhouse among their teammates, many of whom approached them with congratulatory remarks on how very lucky they were to be leaving a Brewers' sinking ship. On June 10 Milwaukee unloaded their troubled second baseman Pedro Garcia in a trade for another second baseman, 31-year-old Gary Sutherland, who was hitting .205. *"Pedro was floundering, you might say,"* said Grammas.[678]

But it wasn't over: Just before the June 15 trade deadline, rumors were swirling that California's alleged sore-armed hurler and future Hall of Famer, Nolan Ryan, was about to be traded to Milwaukee for the Boomer, George Scott. This fell through, however, when Ryan, looking like his old self, shut the Brewers down on a two-hit 1-0 shutout on the same day of the proposed trade. Baumer was also working on trading for Oakland's great reliever, another future Hall of Famer, Rollie Fingers, and talented All-Star outfielder Joe Rudi. This also fell through when the A's eccentric owner, Charlie Finley, sold them outright to Boston for $1 million each. Commissioner Bowie Kuhn later voided the deal as not being in the "best interests" of baseball.

---

[678] Mike Gonring, "Brewers Unload Pedro, Problems," Milwaukee Journal, June 11, 1976, p. 12.

Clearly frustrated at not accomplishing the swaps and buried in last place 13 games from the top, Jim Baumer began to rant after a 10-4 June 22 shellacking by the Tigers, their fourth straight loss. It was a game of numerous mental mistakes, missing cut-off men, misjudged fly balls, infield errors, and horrific pitching, looking like impostors in major league uniforms. But the blame for losing generally was laid at the feet of his big guy and Brewer MVP, George Scott, and their catcher, Darrell Porter, who was hitting .216. They are "killing us," complained Baumer, quoted in a local newspaper, who did not spare any words in criticizing his first baseman and catcher; it was a trait of his, according to one scribe, of being *"too straightforward,"* ne'er the diplomat, that would eventually lead him into trouble.[679] And trouble it turned into, quickly materializing from one George "Boomer" Scott, who was outraged at once again being Baumer's target, and for Grammas' initiative, possibly as a reaction to Baumer, of moving him to sixth in the batting order. Scott shot back. *"That's only an alibi for his own shortcomings,"* he said accusingly of Baumer.[680] He chided them both by pointing out that there were others on the team just as upset as he was but chose not to speak up. *"You hear them mumbling,"* he said.[681] *"The verdict [of losing] is misery. That's what I'm living in,"*

---

[679] Unattributed, "Boom! Scott Explodes at Brewers' Hierarchy," The Journal Times, June 24, 1976, Sec B
[680] Lou Chapman, "Irate Boomer Fires Back at Baumer, Grammas," The Sporting News, July 17, 1976, p.16
[681] Mike Gonring, "Playing 1st and Hitting 6th…George Scott?" Milwaukee Journal, June 24, 1976, P. 14

moaned Alex Grammas after a June 27 Sunday doubleheader loss to the Yankees, the Brewers' 7th and 8th losses in their last 9 games.[682]

The *Journal's* Mike Gonring described them, uproariously, as *"that traveling carnival,"* who were firmly mired in 6th place 16 ½ games out of first and six games behind 5th-place Boston.[683] Boomer took manager Grammas to task for dropping him in the batting order and for his indifferent demeanor and personal bearing in the handling of his players, which he found offensive. *"I've talked to him all season about his not handling me right, nor the other players – moving me up and down the line."*[684]

Not long after Scott's verbal tirade with management, the Milwaukee fan base, weighing Jim Baumer's harsh and intemperate critique of the Brewer slugger, thus avoiding the spotlight himself, and searching for a fall guy upon whom to publicly lay the blame for the Brewers' demise, suddenly turned on him. It was a natural fan reaction as if it was sanctioned by the club after their general manager's public evisceration of their highly-paid first baseman. On July 2, in a shut-out loss to the Red Sox, Scott, who was hitting .261 and now slotted third in the order, feeling the fan pressure, couldn't seem to do anything right – hitting into two double plays, fanning

---

[682] Unattributed/ UPI, "Brewers Not Getting Better," Waukesha Daily Freeman, June 28, 1976, p. 12
https://www.newspapers.com/image/82018368/?match=1&terms=%22alex%20grammas%22

[683] Mike Gonring, "Brewer Carnival Drops 2," Milwaukee Journal, June 28, 1976, p. 10

[684] Lou Chapman, "Irate Boomer Fires Back at Baumer, Grammas," The Sporting News, July 17, 1976, p. 16

twice and failing to advance runners, two from scoring position. The County Stadium crowd demonstrated their disapproval, booing him derisively, like a scoundrel, more loudly with each at-bat. Scotty was miffed at his performance, stating it was one of his worst, but was surprisingly conciliatory when asked how he felt about being rebuked so badly by his hometown fans, who only a year ago had cheered him so approvingly. *"That's part of the game,"* he said. *"That's life, man. Fans forget in a hurry,"* promising he'd get even; *"I'll produce,"* he said, always the optimist.[685] The acrimony was palpable and an actual turning point for George in how he viewed the club and the city for the remainder of the season, who never let up on him after that game. GM Baumer was the catalyst behind their condemnation of Scott, who seemed bent on driving him out of town. It was reminiscent of a time looking back to the '75 spring training episode at the batting cage when Baumer, not pleased that day at being ribbed by Scott about extracting more money from him during contract talks, promised the slugger, *"We always get it back somehow."*[686] The relationship was toxic, and Baumer's bigotry shone brightly.

The Brewers rallied by winning 8 of their next 10 games, including an astonishing five-game sweep of Texas, topped off by doubleheader come-from-behind victories – including Hank Aaron's dramatic 10th-inning

---

[685] Mike Gonring, "Dark Night for Scott, Brewers," Milwaukee Journal, July 3, 1976, p. 13
[686] Mike Gonring, "Scott Finds Offseason Appetite Not So Fine," p. 10.

walk-off homer, his 754th - going into the All-Star break that sent the Milwaukee fans into a state of euphoria, like they had won a championship remarked one reporter. They hadn't seen anything like this all year. *"You couldn't have any more thrills than this,"* exclaimed Grammas.[687] Scott was productive with 12 base hits for a .316 pace in the 9-day span. Nonetheless, the Brewers remained in last place, 14 ½ games behind first-place New York.

July 20 turned out to be a historic day in baseball, not because of anything the team had accomplished, since the Brewers were solidly in last place going into the game, having lost the last 5-of-6 since returning from the All-Star Game; it was the occasion of Henry Aaron's last major league four-bagger, the 755th "tater" of his long and illustrious career. George Scott, batting fourth, fittingly, preceded Aaron's blast with one of his own, lifting a 3-0 delivery by California's Dick Drago deep into County Stadium's left field bleachers, so deep (well over 400') that he stood at home plate watching its trajectory until the ball smashed into the stands. It was a mammoth shot. Barely had he sat down in the dugout when 42-year-old "Hammerin' Hank" followed with his own, ripping into a Drago hanging curve, lofting it into the left-field stands.

With two months left in the season no one could have imagined it was to be Aaron's last. Pitcher Jim Colburn related afterward that his wife mused

---

[687] Mike Gonring, "Brewers Unload Pedro, Problems," P. 12.

over dinner that evening that it could have been the last home run they would see from Henry Aaron. *"We could have seen history,"* she said. What a ridiculous thought, he retorted. How right she was.[688] Six days later, George Scott made some of his own personal history by breaking up a no-hitter for the fourth time in his major league career when he hit a single in the ninth inning off of Detroit's left-handed reliever Jim Crawford. The remarkable coincidence was that three of the four who were victimized by Scott's timely hitting were Detroit Tiger pitchers.[689]

Things were still not going well for Milwaukee losing the first five of their eight-game road swing. Their 1976 All-Star player, Don Money, had reinjured a groin muscle the week before, on July 31, and was used sparingly for the balance of the season. He was bitter about the injury angrily and quite uncharacteristically, blaming the County Stadium infield surface as the reason for it. His loss was a blow to the team. On August 4, an enigmatic Bernie Carbo refused to play the second game of a doubleheader in New York and received a "substantial fine" for his impertinence, publicly announced by Alex Grammas; it made for further unrest on the club.

---

[688] Richard Sandomir, "A Confluence of Coincidence This Weekend in Milwaukee," The New York Times, July 20, 2007
[689] The games in which George Scott foiled no-hit bids: June 4, 1968 v. Detroit, in 6th inning; June 20, 1968 v. Detroit, in 7th inning; July 2, 1975 v. Boston, in 9th inning; July 26, 1976 v. Detroit, in 9th inning.

On August 5, after Scott had led the Brewers to a 9-3 win in New York over the Yankees with a 3-for-3 performance and 3 RBIs, hitting his 11th homer and 53rd RBI, tops on the team, he sulked, not saying a word to reporters. Reporters being reporters, of course, drew their own conclusions speculating that Brewers' front office criticism of him, which was frequent, and the incessant booing by the Milwaukee crowd, disgusted at losing and looking for a reason and a culprit – and, following Baumer's lead - finally caught up with the big first baseman. The fans' contempt for him seemed to take on a life of its own, no matter how well Scott was playing, which seemed to drive a nail into him further each day. *"It's a shame,"* said Brewer player representative Mike Hegan, who sympathized with their first-sacker for what was now becoming conventional behavior among the Milwaukee fans who sided with Brewer management and Jim Baumer's influence. *"George has always gotten along well with the fans, and he's been a real boost to this franchise."*[690] Even Grammas expressed compassion for the big first baseman, who was the *"target of season-long booing that has become almost a ritualistic thing at Milwaukee County Stadium,"* wrote *Milwaukee Sentinel* senior reporter Lou Chapman.[691] Jim Baumer, who, in his illustrious and influential power position, could have remediated the situation by publicly standing up for Scott, but he was missing in action, complicit in the matter, which he himself had contrived.

---

[690] Lou Chapman, "Rough on Boomer," The Sporting News, September 4, 1976, p. 25
[691] IBID

On August 8, during a rainout in Boston, after the Brewers had lost two games there, Grammas, out of disgust that seemed palpable, ranted openly – "Pitiful," he called the team - about their poor performance in a 3-0 loss the day before. Scott could hold back no longer. Once more, he displayed his pent-up rage to anyone who would listen – and there were many willing to avail themselves - about Baumer and Grammas for being the main protagonists behind his misery, inculcating beliefs readily embraced by the fan base provoking their hostility toward him. It couldn't have helped that earlier in the year, Grammas had stripped him of the captaincy and maybe his dignity as well, with which he had been rewarded by Del Crandall. His criticism of his manager was even finite, finding fault with him for not listening to his scouting reports on the Red Sox hitters, whom he knew well. It was the utmost of indignities, he perceived, to be ignored by his manager who not only took his title away but who, in disrespect, now shunned his advice. *"I'm sick of playing in Milwaukee,"* said the angry Scott, stating he wanted to return to Boston, where he was appreciated.[692]

Following a late August three-game Brewers sweep of the Rangers in Texas, in which Scott was 6-for-10 hitting his 13th homer, reporters swarmed around Grammas to probe him on Scott's tirade about wanting to leave Milwaukee. Grammas dismissed it as just more poppycock. Scott later lamented that he was misquoted, but reporters were not going to buy it.

---

[692] Lou Chapman, "'I'm Sick of Milwaukee,' Declares Slugger Scott," The Sporting News, August 28, 1976, P. 12.

concluding that he was not long for Milwaukee. *"There seems to be little doubt that this is his last season as a Brewer,"* wrote the *Journal's* sportswriter Mike Gonring on August 27.

On August 26, Scotty went on a local radio station to clear the air with the Brewers and the city of Milwaukee in light of all the disapproval he was confronting and disputing an article written by sports reporter Lou Chapman in which Scott was to have said he wanted out of Milwaukee, preferring Boston. Although the latter controversy was never settled by that radio appearance, he did admit saying to a local Boston reporter during a swing through the Hub city, who asked about his interest in playing in Boston again, telling him, *"Damn right. Every player likes to play there."*[693] He also mentioned that the Boston area was attractive to him and his family, saying, *"My wife comes from there, and we have families and friends there,"* avoiding any comments about possible marital troubles that were soon to become public.[694] He did, however, make a point that there were problems off the field that were adding to his difficulties, alluding to an invasion of his privacy. *"It's a shame that someone goes into a guy's privacy because he's having a rough time. It's wrong, but I'd rather not talk*

---

[693] Unattributed/ AP News, "Scott Airs Many Problems," Manitowoc Herald-Times, August 27, 1976, p. 11
https://www.newspapers.com/image/293889687/?match=1&terms=%22It%27s%20a%20shame%22
[694] IBID

about it. I've been having a rough year on and off the field, but I really sympathize with the human beings doing those things."[695]

Scotty continued to play solid baseball despite his troubles, receiving the American League Player of the Week honors in mid-September, hitting .500 on a 14-for-28 hit performance, 8 RBIs, and 3 home runs. But his team was not playing well, losing all but one in that same span. During his hot streak all of Milwaukee turned out for a "Salute to Hank Aaron" night honoring him in his final year as a major leaguer. It ended up on a low note, with another Brewer loss, their 10th of the last 11 games, marked by an 11th-inning Yankees' comeback victory and another chewing out by Alex Grammas following the game. Of the 7 Brewer hits, Scott had 3 of them, including his 18th and last homer of the season on that memorable day in Milwaukee, attended by a huge turnout of 40,383 Milwaukee fans who came to applaud a baseball hero who was one of their own. Sadly, the next day's attendance was just over 6,000, a reflection of a Milwaukee attitude about their team that continued to the end of the season.

The Brewers ended the year losing 26 of their final 34 games in September-October and finished dead last in the Eastern Division at 66-95, 32 games out of first and 8 games behind 5th-place Detroit. Scott was the anomaly on a club of generally poor performers who, as a team, batted an anemic .246 with a fielding percentage of .975, third from the bottom of the

---

[695] IBID

American League in each category. He wrapped up the last 15 games of the season with 22 hits in 56 at-bats, hitting at a .393 pace. On the year, he led the club in about every important production category among the regulars with 77 RBIs, 18 home runs, 166 hits, 73 runs, and a .414 slugging percentage. He batted .274, second among the regulars. And he walked off with his 8th Gold Glove award, 6th consecutively, which was to be his last. *"Again, he was a source of teammate confidence by just being there,"* wrote the *Journal's* Lou Chapman, summing up his reasons for Scotty being the best of the American League's first basemen.[696]

But the numerous disagreements with management and the rancor the fans exhibited toward Scott and the club had taken their toll; changes were going to be made and Scott appeared destined to be one of them. Among them was a personal matter that confronted the slugger; the trouble he had been experiencing throughout the year with the Brewers seemed to have spilled over into his domestic life. On October 19, he was ordered to make temporary support payments in a pending divorce action filed by his wife, Lucky, that ultimately ended in divorce. *"I thought it was supposed to be [marriage] for life,"* said Scott in a much later interview on the matter of his marriage.[697]

---

[696] Lou Chapman, "Brooks' Long Fielding Award String Broken" The Sporting News, December 4, 1976, P. 56
[697] George Scott interview: March, 20 2006

Several clubs from both leagues were in hot pursuit of the slugging first baseman, including both of the Chicago teams, the Yankees, Cleveland, and the National League East Division champion Phillies, who made various pitches to the Brewers during and after the World Series. But the Brewers held their ground looking for *"a front-line player,"* said GM Baumer, for a player with the dynamics, production capabilities, and overall baseball skills of a George Scott. In spite of the turmoil surrounding Scott in '76 and the likelihood of an imminent trade, it still came as a surprise when, on December 6, it was announced that Scott had been traded, along with the Brewers' perplexing outfielder, Bernie Carbo, to the Red Sox in exchange for their promising young first baseman Cecil Cooper. *"I don't understand it,"* said a frustrated Frank Robinson of the Indians, who expected to work a three-way deal with the Yankees to acquire Scott. *"How could they give up Scott and Carbo for Cooper?"* said Robinson, critical of the Brewers and his perception of a bad deal.[698] Scotty, however, was delighted, saying he was returning to his "garden city" and that he felt like he was coming out of exile after five years in Milwaukee. He later said, however, that his decision to go back to Boston turned out to be a terrible mistake:

---

[698] Murray Chass, "Red Sox Deal Cooper for Scott and Carbo," The New York Times, December 7, 1976, P. 63

George Scott speaks to the press about his trade back to his "Garden City," Boston and the Red Sox (courtesy of Boston Herald)

"The only thing I was unhappy about [in Milwaukee] was the commitment that the team had to winning. At that time, I just didn't feel that the team was committed to winning. I wanted to be out [of Milwaukee]. It turned out to be the worst thing in the world for me. I could have stayed in Milwaukee and probably done some good things. I got out of Milwaukee and Yount and Lezcano, Gorman Thomas, and all those guys came of age, and they went to the World Series, and they started to win," said Scott. "I regret going back to the Red Sox in '77. I was very excited about going back. I don't think the Red Sox were that excited about having me back."[699]

---

[699] George Scott interview: March, 2006

A legacy of Milwaukee Brewers power hitters: George Scott, teammate Gorman Thomas, and Ben Oglivie (courtesy of George "Boomer" Scott)

Larry Whiteside, the black ex-*Milwaukee Journal* sportswriter, who had seen Scott play for the Brewers and was now a reporter for *The Boston Globe*, pointed out that Boston might not be getting the player they think they are for the benefit of those harkening back to their memories of him in the Hub: *"That will take some getting used to, for he is no longer the scared, backward kid out of Greenville, Miss."*[700] Scared he was not, and he proved it quickly, surprising everyone, especially Red Sox brass when he balked at the deal by demanding more money and a contract extension to play in

---

[700] Whiteside, Larry. "Returning Scott Dubs Boston His 'Garden City.'" The Sporting News. December 25, 1976. P. 47

Boston. He was miffed that once again he had been insulted by baseball management for not advising him, a 10-year major leaguer with 5 years with one club, whose contractual right it was to be consulted of any trade proposals. He later explained he was never unhappy at the thought of leaving Milwaukee; he simply wanted some security through a longer-term contract with the Red Sox, and he knew there were several Boston players who had them. On June 9, Scott lived up to his goal, consummating a deal with Boston. He did it himself, going around his agent Gary Walker, whom he had hired in the interim, and negotiated a multiple-year contract for $175,000 annually. Things were definitely looking up for George Scott.[701]

---

[701] Unattributed, "George!" Black Sports, September, 1977; varying reports ranged from a contract extension of 2 to 5 years – the most probable being 2 years

Chapter 16
Now He's Your Headache

"I played from 158 to 162 games a year [in Milwaukee] and played hard all the way. But you had guys who would tear a fingernail, and they would want to sit down. Well, no, I didn't take a liking to that. And I made it known. These guys are being paid to play baseball just like George Scott."

George Scott[702]

The personal attacks made on George Scott continued to emanate from Milwaukee even as the 1977 spring camps were about to open and teams were beginning to focus on the arrival of new players and the business of a new season. It was toxic as if he had perpetrated some sort of willful offense in the city, having the nature of a crime, causing Milwaukee brass and a few former teammates to seek reprisal.

Left-hander Bill Travers, the Brewers top pitcher in 1976 and a Massachusetts native, was among them; he was overheard speaking to fans disparagingly of Scott, saying he is now "your headache." He later explained when pressed by reporters that Scott should have been more discrete about his feelings while in Milwaukee. In fact, he himself couldn't have been more incautious in his loosely-worded offhanded manner

---

[702] Brent Frazee, "And the Old Brewer," The Journal Times, April 17, 1977, Section B, p. 13
https://www.newspapers.com/image/342687006/?terms=the%20journal%20times

speaking about George Scott as he toured the off-season luncheons and dinner circuits; he seemed to be thriving on it. It actually got the attention of his father, who was disturbed by his son's tactless discourse and scolded him for his indiscretions. Travers confessed his dad was not happy with him, sensing he was getting into dangerously negative media territory and possibly Brewers' front office disapproval: *"My dad called the other night,"* he said. *"He said, 'What the hell are you saying? You better keep your mouth shut,'"* spoken with obvious concerns about what this could lead to.[703]

However, less than circumspect himself, Travers' comments were soon followed by the equally incautious and bigoted words of the Brewers general manager, Jim Baumer, who should have known better for a man in his position, at the 24th annual January Milwaukee writers' Diamond Dinner, where George Scott frequently had been rewarded for his meritorious service with the Brewers.

Known for his impolitic nature – along with a personal distaste for the Boomer - having apologized to Scott once before for being too direct, Baumer rapped his former slugging first baseman in front of 700 guests by saying he now had a first baseman – Cecil Cooper – who speaks in terms of "we." It was an obvious dig at Scott; for that brief moment, Baumer's personal desire to be more of a diplomat and decorous general manager had

---

[703] Jim Kornkven, "Travers Tones Down Speech," *Kenosha News*, January 13, 1977, p. 27 https://www.newspapers.com/image/597196352/?terms=kenosha%20news

been abandoned. Cooper, who attended the affair and was not comfortable with Baumer's brazen aspersions spoken publicly against Scott, including that he was black, spoke later of Scott as being a bona fide superstar and one whose shoes would be difficult to fill; he acknowledged he bore the burden of carrying a Brewers team on his shoulders, as had George Scott.

Jim Slaton, another Milwaukee pitcher, chose the discretionary route by not jumping on the Brewer bandwagon that was ganging up on their departed first baseman: *"One guy can't ruin a ball club. It takes a team effort,"* he said in dismissive terms resonating with Milwaukee fans willing to see the situation more broadly and less accusatory.[704] Red Sox shortstop Rico Petrocelli, a former teammate of Scott's, who overheard the clatter being made of George, refuted what was being said. *"People who talk like that just don't know Scotty,"* he said, emphasizing Scott's fierce competitiveness and his determination to win, and how it was natural for him to complain when he's losing, which would come back to haunt him with the press. Losing was not in his vocabulary, and he was vocal about it, from management on down, if he sensed they were unwilling to carry their weight.[705]

---

[704] Lou Chapman, "Brewers Rap Departed George Scott," The Sporting News, March 26, 1977, P. 10

[705] Larry Whiteside,"Rico Happy to Be Red Sox Spare Part," The Sporting News, January 29, 1977, P. 34

He fought back: "It was very depressing looking at guys on our club who didn't want to play. We had guys who'd come into the clubhouse laughing when we'd lose. You'd see some guys who got scared when their names were in the lineup. There were guys who were happy when they didn't see their names in the lineup."[706]

Stunned by the vitriol that followed him from Milwaukee, Scott simply said that he would deal with the Brewers in the best way he knew how, and that was on the playing field. *"Any guy who tells you he's putting personal goals ahead of winning is full of baloney,"* said the new Boston arrival.[707] The Red Sox spring camp opened for the full roster on March 1. Scott made his appearance sporting mutton chop sideburns, a mustache of the makings of a Fu Manchu and looking several pounds overweight. He was at no loss for enthusiasm, making his presence known and immediately declaring that his nickname, "Boomer," had as much to do with his tongue as it did his bat. He, however, as well as several of his Red Sox teammates, were bound to clash with an old-school traditionalist manager like "Zim" in his second year with Boston; he was an oddity to them, loved by some but not by George Scott, who, of the "bad" managers he confessed he put up with, cited Don Zimmer as the worst of them, in spite of his awkward legacy with one Dick Williams. He had no respect for Zimmer, who he felt lacked management qualities.

---

[706] Lou Chapman, "Housecleaning Gives Brewers Five New Regulars," quoting George Scott, The Sporting News, December 15, 1976, P. 48
[707] Larry Whiteside, "The Boomer," The Boston Globe, April 6, 1977, p. 25

Scott sweating it out in Winter Haven (courtesy of Boston Red Sox)

Scott working the pounds off in Winter Haven (courtesy of Boston Red Sox)

The Boston press quickly sized up a possible conflict between Red Sox superstar Carl Yastrzemski and Scott, both of whom played first base, but one was better than the other. Manager Don Zimmer, in his first full year as their skipper, blithely dismissed the matter out-of-hand, saying there was no conflict at all. Scott was the best first baseman in the league, and *"that's where he'll play,"* he said.[708] What followed was described by one Boston sportswriter as the "Great Left Field Sweepstakes" extravaganza between two future Hall of Famers, Yastrzemski and Rice, who were vying for the position or be assigned as the DH, while Scott would contentedly reside at first base.

Scotty proceeded to knock the cover off the ball with 7 base hits in his first five exhibition games at a .500 pace, including a 410-foot homer. He continued to hit well throughout the spring season, finishing at .371 with 17 RBIs and 6 home runs, most of which were prodigious variety and a .710 slugging percentage. The club did just about as well, winning 17 of 27 contests; their last win on the last day of the exhibition season, a 4-2 victory over the St. Louis Cardinals on Scott's two-run homer in the eighth. The team was laced with power hitters like Fred Lynn, Butch Hobson, and future Hall of Famers Carl Yastrzemski, Carlton Fisk and Jim Rice, who were to set numerous home run records that year. They had slugged their way to 34

---

[708] Unattributed, "Phils Favored in NL," Delta Democrat Times, March 6, 1977, P. 14

spring home runs, the most since 1971 when they hit 36, and a team batting average of .285.

But there were concerns: Larry Whiteside of the *Boston Globe,* formerly a *Milwaukee Journal* reporter, wondered in words of caution if the Red Sox had purchased *"the proverbial bacon slab in the plastic pouch"* in describing Scott, who looked nothing like he did when he played previously for Boston.[709] It was merely another forewarning, a reality check, made by Whiteside, who had raised concerns earlier about what the Red Sox were getting in Scott when the trade was announced. Scott assured them he'd be ready when the opening day bell rang and to just let him work off the poundage and work out the kinks on his own. He was in jaunty spirits over the prospects of playing on such a power-laden club like the Red Sox, which he called "awesome," feeling it was the best major league team he had ever played for.

The 1977 season for the Red Sox' 76th opened on April 7 in Boston's Fenway Park, their 65th home opener, on a chilly day before a crowd of 34,790 hopeful fans. Carl Yastrzemski was playing right field for the first time in his career. Hardly anyone could get warm, said catcher Carlton Fisk, defending their pitcher, reliever Bill Campbell, who had just lost the save and the game, 5-4, to the Cleveland Indians in the 11th inning and who bore the brunt of catcalls from Fenway fans displaying their disapproval of

---

[709] Larry Whiteside, "Scott Down 10 lbs., now has 10 to go," The Boston Globe, March 21, 1977, P. 18

Boston's $1 million man. Fenway was filled with its share of harsh critics, a "howling mob of perfectionists," wrote the *Globe's* Whiteside, which would set the tone for the coming season. The Red Sox, who were picked to be a pennant contender, lost their first four games. Not only was the pitching faulty, but they also committed 10 errors, three of them, atypically and astonishingly, by their Gold Glove first baseman, George Scott. By the third week in April, they were in 5th place.

On April 24, Boston won only their fifth game, shutting out the new expansion Toronto franchise, the Blue Jays, 9-0. Scott, who had been pressing, was hitting only .222 but achieved a landmark of sorts in that game by being the first Red Sox player to hit a home run in a regular season game on Canadian soil. It was George's first homer of the season, a seventh-inning shot off Jays' starter Bill Singer. On April 26, the Red Sox were in Milwaukee. Scotty's first trip back to the city was one that once cheered but then reproved him. A good sum of the 12,676 Milwaukee partisan fans jeered Scott. At one point, someone threw a roll of toilet paper at him when he came to bat. He took it in stride until their pitcher, Jerry Augustine, who was notably wild with his pitches, shouted a scurrilous remark to the big Red Sox slugger as he ran out a grounder that couldn't be ignored. It was *"extremely uncomplimentary,"* wrote the *Globe's* sportswriter Bob Ryan, suggesting that there may have been racist content in what was said. *"He knows what he said,"* observed Scott to the questioning of reporters. *"Why should he want to do that?"*[710] When he took the field, Scott shook a disapproving finger at the Milwaukee dugout, aimed at Augustine, prompting even louder taunting of him that exploded from the crowd.

The Red Sox returned home on the 29th and swept three games from Oakland in which Scott was 5-for-8 including a home run blast that cleared Fenway's center field wall and struck the back of the bleachers, well over 430 feet. It was his fifth base hit of 14 in a twelve-game hit streak. On May 7, he broke up a no-hitter in the fourth inning off California's Frank Tanana, who had set down 14 consecutive batters, with an RBI triple. On May 16, the Red Sox, who had won 8-of-12 and were gaining momentum, won their fourth straight by beating the Angels 8-7. Scott powered the Red Sox to the win with two home runs in consecutive at-bats, raising his OPS to .864, as they slipped into a tie for first place with the Baltimore Orioles.

Milwaukee was in town on May 20 for a three-game series; the teams split the first two. Ex-Boston first baseman Cecil Cooper was 5-for-10, including a homer, his 6th, prompting the Boston press to inquire of Grammas, the Brewers' manager, what he thought of his new first-sacker. Grammas was effusive, capping his comments with a personal reference that had the bite of a back-handed slap to the departed George Scott. *"Everybody around here loves the guy,"* said Grammas excitedly and in as

---

[710] Bob Ryan, "Fans Don't Bug Scott, but Young Lefty Does," Boston Globe, April 27, 1977, p. 58

many ways as he could short of condemning Scott.[711] Scott, who was 2-for-7 with a home run, provided some excitement of his own. On the 22nd, he belted a game-winning grand slam home run into the Boston bullpen, the second of his major league career, breaking up a 10-10 tie in the eighth off a screwball thrown by lefthander Rich Folkers, which launched the Red Sox to a 14-10 win over Grammas' Brewers. The game was marked by 11 home runs, tying an American League record for two teams set by the Yankees and Tigers in 1950.[712] Scott couldn't contain himself taking a shot at his old Brewer manager, who failed to bring in a right-hander to deal with him. *"Alex must think I'm a lousy hitter,"* chortled Scott reprovingly over Grammas' presumed mistake.[713]

---

[711] Larry Whiteside, "Cooper Has No Axe to Grind," Boston Globe, May 22, 1977, p. 101
[712] The SABR Baseball List & Record Book. Editor Lyle Spatz. Scribner Publishing. New York. March 2007; the record of 11 home runs by both teams in a game has since been broken by the White Sox and Tigers in 1995, and again in 2002 by the same two teams, both times with 12 HRs.
[713] Lou Chapman, "Rodriguez Leaves Brewer Doghouse with a Rush," The Sporting News, June 11, 1977, P. 15.

Drawings of George Scott in Red Sox and Brewer uniforms re: 1977 & 1975 (courtesy of George Scott)

In June, the Red Sox, who were in third place in the first few games of the month, began to break out, moving into second place on June 8, one game behind the Yankees. Pitching that was perfectly miserable in May, the laughing stock of AL clubs, some quipped, was tightening up, allowing fewer runs, and the hitting continued to soar at a pace that was near the top of the league. But the Boston fan base, fueled by a popular local sports radio talk show, *Clif-n-Claf*, hosted by the *Globe's* senior sportswriter Clif Keane and the *Herald American's* Larry Claflin, seemed always to have something to grumble about in a rather vexatious manner, frequently acting like rabid animals not content with mere winning, but who went for the jugular for any reason they could muster, likely to arouse the extremist fan base. There were complaints about the pitching, the coaching, the manager, and the front office, to the point of ad nauseam. But most of the griping was centered on George Scott, undeserving as it was, who had made 11 errors and was "too heavy," complained the cultural milieu of Boston sports fanatics who would accept nothing less than a slicker, younger 23-year-old George Scott, beckoning an unlikely return to his more fluid and slender credentials. The fan outrage toward Scott boiled over around the same time he appeared on the *Clif-n-Claf* show, which immediately dissolved into horseplay and an embarrassing mockery of blacks depicted eating watermelon and fried chicken. Keane, whose reputation on race had been spotty, and Claflin were terribly insulting of blacks that day at Scott's expense, who, surprisingly, seemed content to go along with the racial stereotypical nonsense that had deteriorated into laughter. It was a racist moment that neither of the two journalists seemed to comprehend and who were shocked at the accusation, Claflin in particular, who staunchly defended his actions as simply good-natured teasing as the story burst onto the local television and radio audiences. He never lived it down, dying of a heart attack at age 53.

"He had a jocular relationship with the press," wrote Howard Bryant about the Boomer, George Scott, in his 2011 book *The Last Hero: A Life of Henry Aaron. "He was loud and boisterous and funny. He made them laugh, and he certainly was a character, a showman by nature. But Scott also later believed his personality and physical charisma undermined him as a serious ballplayer, and in retrospect, he would be wounded that his colorfulness fed*

into the stereotypes of the uneducated black athlete. Some of the stories of Scott's glibness bordered on the apocryphal, the by-product, he often felt, of cruel baiting by the white press to make him appear ignorant."[714]

A year or two later, on June 5, 1979, shortly before Scott's departure from the Red Sox, Keane was heard bantering with players and sportswriters in the Red Sox clubhouse and was overheard by *Herald-American* reporter Marie Brenner – who once described Fenway Park as a *"racist's paradise"* - referring to George Scott as a "bush nigger." Don Zimmer heard it as well and went into a defensive rage, knowing if this got out – especially at a time of racial unrest in Boston – it would blow the lid off of what little calm had been restored in the city. He accosted Brenner, demanding that she not write the story. George Scott heard it as well but refused to talk to Brenner since, at the time he was apprehensive about his own status on the team.

"I often played the game with the local press guys to keep them on my side, but it didn't always work out with them or me. The Boston writers were a tough bunch. A guy who was good at that was Looie [Tiant], who was smart enough to stay away from trouble. The Boston Newspaper guys tried to keep us blacks off guard, and sometimes, we were seen as clowns. I didn't like that, but it was hard to find a good balance between them."[715]

---

[714] Howard Bryant, A Life of Henry Aaron, p. 434-435
[715] George Scott interview: November 10, 2008

Bryant, in his book *Shut Out*, explored the so-called informal collaborative silent manifesto of required black athlete behavior in Boston, citing their renowned black pitcher of the '70s, Luis Tiant, who had 19 years in the Big Leagues, who got by with the press and fans, when more outspoken black athletes were given a sudden ticket out of Boston:

"Tiant would always be conflicted about race; he was a leader on the mound but was savvy enough to avoid the incendiary statements to the press that could have turned a hot city against him. That didn't mean he was anybody's fool. He just tried not to swim in the hot water… Peter Gammons [Boston Globe reporter] believed Tiant built the cultural bridges in the Red Sox clubhouse, and it was – again, an example of treating Tiant as a jester, not general – the something the pitcher never received the proper credit for."[716]

The *Globe's* Ray Fitzgerald, who characterized the Boston fans as malcontents, rose to Scott's defense, quoting Don Zimmer, who remarked that it wasn't Scott's weight that was the reason for his unusual number of errors; he was simply pressing too hard to do well for the Boston crowd, reminding the fans that Scott was a leading hitter in the spring season, and had made some sensational plays in the field. He would be back like he was in the spring, said the Red Sox manager, once he rids himself of the jitters. Whereupon Fitzgerald summed it up: *"I'll take Scott even at 33, and enough*

---

[716] Howard Bryant, Shut Out, p. 130

already with the tired chicken wing and racist watermelon jokes."[717] Scott was hitting .268 at the time of the story with 12 homers and a .874 OPS and was on a five-game hit streak, 7-for-16, and a .438 pace. On the 5th of June, he broke up a scoreless tie in the 6th inning off the Twins' Tom Burgmeier with a run-scoring single, leading to a 5-1 Red Sox win. He was 3-for-3 on the day, including his 1,700th major league base hit.

A year later, when things had settled down from the *Clif-n-Claf* debacle, Boston sportswriter Bob Ryan, described as "the quintessential American sportswriter," dedicated an entire column to the Boomer in 1978 honoring the man for his dedication and indisputable probity:

"I have a lot of respect for George Scott, a man who, I feel, never has been portrayed accurately in this town. He certainly is not sophisticated, and he has a talent for malapropism perhaps beyond compare. As a rural southern black who actually does eat and enjoy both chicken and watermelon and who takes no pains to hide it, he is an easy target for tasteless media attackers who find it easier to perpetuate a stereotype than to work at presenting the whole man. George Scott deserves better treatment...George Scott is just an honest ballplayer, and the team will be better off when he's back in the lineup."[718]

---

[717] Ray Fitzgerald, "Complaining's Name of Sox Fan's Game – But Why Pick on Scott?" The Boston Globe, June 7, 1977, P. 27
[718] Ryan, Bob, "Scott Earns his Keep," The Boston Globe, May 22, 1978, P. 22

On June 14, Scott and his teammates began a record-setting home run rampage, starting with the White Sox, establishing many major league records and, with them, a string of victories leading the Red Sox into first place in the AL East. Scotty was a big factor in that assault on opposing pitchers and established for himself a personal record achieved by only three other Red Sox players. Between June 14 and 19, he clouted six homers in 5 consecutive games, tying him with Jimmie Foxx [6/1940], Ted Williams [6/1957], and Dick Stuart [5/1963]. Jose Canseco eventually also accomplished the feat in 1995 with 5 homers.

After the June 14 game, in which Scotty blasted two homers, one that rocketed off the back wall of Fenway's center field bleachers – a tremendous clout, over 430 feet – and the other into the Red Sox bullpen, he went silent on the media, declaring he would not talk to them because of the unnecessarily harsh criticism and rude treatment he had been receiving. Though he deigned to explain, the vitriol he heard over sports radio talk shows, and particularly the brazen effrontery he experienced from Clif Keane and Larry Claflin, who in an instant made him their public pawn, had to have been behind his decision to go silent. Feigning silence was nothing new in the sports world; it had been the remedy of numerous sports stars through the ages as their way of stemming controversy and avoiding untruths.

On June 17, the start of an important three-game series against the second-place Yankees, who trailed Boston by a half-game, the Red Sox blasted four home runs in the first inning off of future Hall of Famer Jim "Catfish" Hunter to tie a club record for homers in one inning. Scott's was the fourth, a lengthy blast over everything in left that made the first two homers look "undernourished," wrote one reporter. They proceeded to annihilate the Yankees, clubbing 16 home runs and sweeping the series: 9-4, 10-4 and 11-1. It was devastating and embarrassing to anyone who was a Yankee or who followed them. *"Sixteen times a Yankee outfielder started back. Sixteen times he searched the heavens, seeking the elusive bunny ball,"* wrote the *Globe's* Ray Fitzgerald.[719]

---

[719] Ray Fitzgerald, "Martin: 'We should have played our fielders in the screen,'" The Boston Globe, June 20, 1977, P. 18

Greeted by Carlton Fisk after hitting another home run, Scott hit 33 homers in 1977 on a team that set many home run records (courtesy of Boston Herald)

During the second game, Yankees manager Billy Martin, who had all he could do to not implode himself as he watched the debacle in utter frustration from the dugout, got into it with his superstar right fielder, Reggie Jackson, by nearly coming to blows. Martin embarrassed Jackson by pulling him from the field in front of a national television audience and 34,603 screaming Fenway fans, accusing him of loafing. It upset Yankees owner George Steinbrenner, who nearly fired the pugnacious manager but later relented. It was nothing but a "Circus Maximus," declared Sox pitcher

Bill Lee, who did not endear himself to Billy Martin or the New York team with some of the things he said. The Red Sox out-homered [16-0], outslugged [.917], out-fielded with several defensive gems, and altogether completely outplayed the Yankees, who, ironically, would ultimately come back to win the 1977 American League pennant and World Series. Scott clouted three home runs in the series, passing teammate Jim Rice for the club lead with 18. *"I haven't seen hitting like that since junior high, and we were scoring 18 runs in the cow pasture,"* exclaimed a jubilant George Scott, who, at least for the moment, had broken his vow of silence to respond to a reporter who asked him if he had heard the Fenway cries of "Boomer, Boomer."[720]

The Red Sox were in the midst of a consecutive ten-game home run assault of which Scott played a major part, hitting 9 of 33 taters during the period, June 14-24. Yastrzemski hit for the next highest number [5]. Thirty-three home runs in ten consecutive games set a major league baseball record since tied by the Atlanta Braves, who accomplished the feat in 2006. In a four-game road sweep of the Baltimore Orioles, the first two were by shutouts, in which Scott hit his 19th and 20th home runs, which were tops in the league. On the 21st, a 7-0 Luis Tiant win over the Orioles, Scott was nearly beaned by a Dennis Martinez pitch in the ninth, hitting him in the hand. It appeared to be retaliatory by the Oriole hurler, who had given up

---

[720] Larry Whiteside, "Boston Leaves Yankees with a severe case of Shell-Sox," The Boston Globe, June 20, 1977, P. 26

4th inning homers to Scott and Rice and was soundly being beaten by the Sox. Scott didn't hesitate to leap to his feet and began to chase the young Nicaraguan lefthander who *"fled for the nearest friendly embassy,"* wrote the *Globe's* Bob Ryan.[721] *"Did you see the look on the kid's face? He must have thought the Schlitz bull was coming after him,"* exclaimed Sox pitcher Reggie Cleveland, laughing uproariously.[722] The two homers established a major league team record for most homers (26) in a 7-game span. Boston hammered 5 more home runs the next day, including Scott's league-leading 20th, off of future Hall of Famer Jim Palmer, one of the top pitchers in the league. By the end of the series, they had a full five-game lead over second-place New York, had won 16 of their last 18 games, and had out-homered their two closest rivals, the Yankees and Orioles, in a six-game span by a margin of 24-1. They had also set numerous other major league and American League records for consecutive game home runs: 3-games [16-MLB record], 4-games [18-AL record], 5-games [21-AL record], 6-games [24-MLB record], 8-games [29-MLB record] and 9-games [30-AL record].

They appeared invincible. The pitching was strong, and the hitting was next to outrageous, with Red Sox batters burning up the American League with base hits, like a "reign of terror," said one sportswriter, and lofting home runs out of ballparks in an unprecedented manner. It seemed like it

---

[721] Bob Ryan, "Tiant Wins 2-hitter, 7-0, but Scott steals show," The Boston Globe, June 22, 1977, P. 59
[722] Larry Whiteside, "Third Battle of Bull Run," The Boston Globe, June 22, 1977. P. 21

was not going to end; one reporter even suggested they were beyond human for their prodigious power display. And then it was on to New York and the cavernous Yankee Stadium where the Bronx Bombers and their defiant manager, who promised that the Red Sox would crumple before the season ended, lay in wait.

Inexplicably, they did just that, like a house of cards over the next nine games. On June 24, they battled the Yankees into the bottom of the 9th inning, leading 5-3, George Scott having broken up a tie in the 4th with his league-leading 21st homer off Catfish Hunter. It was the third home run of the game hit off Hunter and the seventh off him by Red Sox batters in just over a week. But the Yankees tied it with a Roy White homer in the ninth, hit off a usually reliable Bill Campbell, and they won it in the 11th on Reggie Jackson's run-scoring single. The Yankees followed up with two more wins over Boston, returning the favor of a sweep, the second game by a 5-1 score that brought an end to their incredulous home run streak. *"The most breathtaking home run tear in baseball history was over,"* wrote Thomas Boswell of the *Washington Post*. The Red Sox had hit a few balls, one by Rice that was estimated at 430 feet and came close to going out, but they were caught in the big Yankee ballpark. *"This place is like Death Valley,"* snorted a disappointed George Scott.[723] They continued to unravel by losing their next three games in Detroit and, shockingly, three straight to the

---

[723] Larry Whiteside, "Zimmer Looks at the Bright Side," The Boston Globe, June 26, 1977, P. 84

Orioles in Fenway Park, where they had humiliated Baltimore, Texas, Chicago and the Yankees in the previous homestand. On July 2, they slipped into second place, a half-game behind New York.

There was a kind of cultural cancer emerging – sinister by its makeup - through the ranks of the Red Sox pitching staff, unsettling to the team and particularly manager Don Zimmer, that became a distraction to the psychology of winning. Zimmer was a product of old-school Dodger baseball, a purist who simply did not understand nor tolerate any form of player behavior that was not of the straight-and-narrow or was in any way a departure from unadulterated baseball tradition.

Fundamentally, Red Sox pitchers disliked the man and did not try to hide their feelings about their manager. Bill Lee, nicknamed "Spaceman," a nonconformist of the highest order and a dissenter type of liberal persuasions, a Californian who had been struggling on the mound, was a principal among the group, who complained that he was simply misunderstood. He once said that if he were not a ballplayer, he would be living in a Napa Valley commune and stomping grapes. Lee and Zimmer's relationship was a tempestuous one. There was such a dislike between them it seemed pathological. In a moment of annoyance, Lee anointed Zimmer with an uncomplimentary title: "The Gerbil," which stuck. It immediately caught on with the Boston press and talk radio shows, and eventually, the Red Sox fan base who seemed to revel in maligning the Sox skipper who was now known disparagingly as "The Gerbil."

Rick Wise, another Sox hurler who was struggling, felt he was being mishandled by Zimmer, as did Ferguson Jenkins and even fan-favorite Luis "Looie" Tiant, who was never known to be a critic, or at least openly. They began to gravitate toward each other as they sought common ground, confidants of a counterculture they were, a bunch of iconoclasts who found strength in their own unity to effectively – and derisively - deal with Zimmer. Jenkins named the group, of which he was a self-appointed member, the "Buffalo Head Gang" - changed later to the "Buffalo Heads" - comprised of Jenkins, Bill Lee, Jim Willoughby, Wise and free-spirit Bernie Carbo. Jenkins reasoned that Buffaloes were the personification of ugliness and that Zimmer looked every bit the part of a buffalo; plus, they were dumb. It fitted perfectly. And their torment of Zimmer began.

In Bill Lee's 2003 publication *The Little Red (Sox) Book: A Revisionist Red Sox History*, co-written with sports author Jim Prime, there is a chapter on *"quotations of Chairman Lee,"* best described as savage satire tearing apart life and limb, humorously. He makes room, of course, for his greatest foe, Don Zimmer, devoting nearly a full page of "vignettes," he prefers to call them, poking fun at the former Red Sox manager. In one line of questioning in which he is asked about Zimmer's 15-second Preparation-H commercial, Lee's response was, *"Zimmer is a lovable guy, but he's dumb as a post. Anyone who would go out and sell hemorrhoid medication is asking for it. My advice to him would be to use bioflavones. I think we are interlinked because ever since he's been doing those commercials, my ass *has been itching."*[724] In another question-answer exchange under the same heading, Lee responded to a situation more closely aligned with on-field matters about Zimmer's doghouse, which Lee frequented. He said, *"Every manager has a doghouse, but Zimmer's doesn't have a door on it."*[725]

On July 4, the Sox erupted against the visiting Toronto Blue Jays, smashing 8 home runs and setting and tying all matters of major league home run records in the process. George Scott hit two of them after suffering through a 0-for-24 drought, lofting one into the center field bleachers and the other a tremendous blast rocketing high over the left field screen and bouncing off the facing of a building across the street from the ballpark. It was hit so high and far, wrote one reporter, with obvious hyperbole, that it was likely to have landed "six hours later" at the Esplanade three miles away. Of the eight homers, four of them were hit in just one inning, which was only the 10th time it had been accomplished in major league history, the 5th time the Red Sox had done it, and the second time they did it that season. The eight home runs in one game also tied a major league record with five other teams, and the Red Sox set a major league record of five or more home runs in a game for the 7th time in one season; the old record of six was held by the 1947 Giants. Seven of them were solo shots, which is also a major league record.

---

[724] Bill Lee with Jim Prime, "The Little Red (Sox) Book," Triumph Books, Chicago, 2003, p. 146
[725] IBID

What had not reached the record books was Scott's performance the game before, on July 3 against Baltimore, when he clouted three long blasts that were caught sensationally by Oriole outfielders, robbing him of home runs each time. One of them was caught by center fielder Al Bumbry, who chased Scott's drive to the 420-foot Fenway triangle in center and leaped over the high wall of the Red Sox bullpen to snag the home run ball. In each case, the runner on first, Carlton Fisk, advanced to second base, a rare maneuver that, in most cases, would end up with the runner being thrown out. *"All of them were out of the park,"* said Oriole right fielder Ken Singleton on Scott's drives. Both outfielders conceded they had no chance to catch Fisk going into second base because of the distance the balls were hit.[726]

Three Red Sox were elected by a vote of the fans for the American League All-Star team: Carl Yastrzemski, a perennial All-Star in his 11th Midsummer Classic; Carlton Fisk, his fifth All-Star appearance; and shortstop Rick Burleson, his first. Rod Carew of the Minnesota Twins was the unanimous choice to play first base with over 4 million votes. George Scott, who had 25 home runs, finished third to New York's Chris Chambliss in the fan balloting. He railed at the thought that the best American League players were not starting, such as Boston's Jim Rice and Larry Hisle of Minnesota, who were having better years than Richie Zisk or Reggie

---

[726] Francis Rosa, "Scott Robbed Three Times," The Boston Globe, July 4, 1977, P. 30

Jackson. And he couldn't hold back his objection to coming in third by over a million votes behind Chambliss, who had hit only 8 homers. *"You've got to blame the fans,"* he said. *"We had 90 taters sitting on the pine."*[727] Scott credited American League All-Star manager Billy Martin with making things right by picking him, Scott's third and last All-Star appearance, as a reserve over Martin's own man, Chambliss, along with Rice, Fred Lynn and Sox reliever Bill Campbell. It was another win for the National League, 7-5. Scott replaced Carew in the 7th inning, flew out his first time up against Tom Seaver, but in the bottom of the 9th launched a 385-foot home run into the right-center field Yankee Stadium bleachers off of power pitcher Rich Gossage, who would earn himself a place in the Baseball Hall of Fame. It was the only American League home run of the game and only their second extra-base hit. Scott's point was made.

Boston continued to keep pace with first-place Baltimore until July 31, when they slipped back into first by a half-game on the stellar pitching of their new rookie pitcher, Don Aase, who had been called up from Pawtucket, their Triple-A farm club. Pitching, however, was still Zimmer's main worry, and Bill Lee continued to be unquestionably his biggest personal nightmare. *"You guys ask him a baseball question, and in two minutes, he's talking about life in China,"* exclaimed the irritated Red Sox manager, who was as ready as anyone in the organization to wield the axe

---

[727] Alan Richman, "AL: No one to fear but fans themselves," The Boston Globe, July 20, 1977, P. 21

to the lefthander.[728] However, there were other issues; Scott had not hit another home run since the All-Star game, and he had made an uncharacteristic 20 errors in the field.

The Red Sox, however, began to surge again behind Aase and a rejuvenated Fergie Jenkins, winning 13 of 15 games through August 18 and holding a 3 ½ game lead over Baltimore. But it unraveled from there, the Red Sox losing five straight and falling into second place on August 23. On September 3, with Boston in second 4½ games off the lead, Don Zimmer, without explanation, dropped Scott – one of Boston's top run producers [82] with 31 homers –to 7th in the batting order. It hit him like a bolt of lightning; nothing had been said to him, and his pride was hurt. It was, once again, another slight made by a long line of field managers stripping him of his self-respect by not involving him in a decision affecting him without his knowledge or participation. *"I could not just ignore this as, to me, it was a racial matter. Other guys [on the team] knew what the plans were going to be for them, but they never spoke to me. They just did it,"* exclaimed a disturbed George Scott in later years.[729] He played a couple more games in the 7th slot, and then, on September 5, he engaged in a sit-down, announcing to Zimmer that he was "not mentally prepared to play." He said that he might have been more receptive to the idea if the manager had simply come to him to explain what he was planning to do and why.

---

[728] Ray Fitzgerald, "Is it Spaceman's last ride?" The Boston Globe, July 25, 1977, P. 17
[729] George Scott interview: May 12, 2008

"But he didn't," said Scott. At about the same time, the problems between the pitchers and Zimmer manifested itself once again. Zimmer's peculiar fiddling of his staff from day to day did not sit well with them, particularly Wise, Jenkins and Lee, who lost any remaining respect they had for the man. Scott sat out two games and then returned batting seventh. Zimmer returned him to his regular 6th position in the order on September 15, where he remained for the balance of the season. The Red Sox finished in second place, tied with Baltimore at 97-64, two games behind the Yankees. Astonishingly, the third-place team, Detroit, finished well behind the leaders 25 games in back of New York.

George Scott had a solid first year back in Boston, hitting a respectable .269, crunching 33 home runs (as the team set a club record of 213 home runs in one season), 157 base hits, 95 RBIs and a .500 slugging percentage, the second highest of his career.[730] He had an uncharacteristic year in the field, however, committing 24 errors, which was the most he had made in the majors in one season. In spite of that, he was a sentimental favorite for another Gold Glove, but he fell short, edged out by the White Sox' Jim Spencer 13 votes to 9.

---

[730] Scott hit a ball in the bottom of the 7th off Dyar Miller of the California Angels on August 10, 1977, in Fenway Park, "that all reasonable men except the four umpires" agreed was a home run, wrote The Boston Globe's Jack Craig; but the umpires ruled that it remained "in play." The ball struck the center field wall to the right of the yellow vertical line designating out-of-play [home run] territory. Second base umpire Russ Goetz, however, called the ball in-play. Scott shouted at Goetz as he rounded second twirling his arm symbolizing it was a homer. He easily legged out a triple but might have had an inside- the-park home run if he had not slowed his gait while protesting to the umpire.

Once again, reporters were speculating that Scott was on the chopping block. One Chicago reporter announced with certain conviction that any team looking to get the big first baseman had to accept Scott's remaining two years of his contract and pick up his "$450,000 salary that goes with it," which was a tall order for most clubs when the ballplayer was about to turn 34.

Chapter 17
Racial Injustice Persists After All These Years

"When you put something out for naming rights, they get the cash, they get the name. I don't have a problem with that. So, if you donate to a hospital and donate a wing, you get your name on the wing. I have no problem with that. But then you turn around and say that [Yawkey] was a great owner; I have a problem with that."

Tommy Harper[731]

A year after Tom Yawkey's death in July 1976, his venerable and beloved institution – the Red Sox – that he nurtured and over which he had reigned since he established ownership in 1933 was put up for sale. Several suitors pursued the opportunity, but Jean Yawkey, Tom's widow, who had assumed ownership of the team after her husband's death, favored the group led by ex-Red Sox trainer Buddy LeRoux. Haywood Sullivan, the Red Sox' former VP of Player Personnel, who had a close personal friendship with the Yawkeys, had joined the group. Sullivan's presence in the deal was persuasive for Jean Yawkey, who accepted the LeRoux-investor-led offer, even though it was not the highest bid. After the American League initially

---

[731] Dan Shaughnessy, "Tommy Harper Says Yawkey's Philanthropy Doesn't Outweigh the Racial Harm," The Boston Globe, Boston.com, Boston Globe Media Partners, March 13, 2018
https://www.boston.com/sports/boston-red-sox/2018/03/13/tommy-harper-yawkey-way-philanthropy-racial-harm/

rejected the proposal, they relented when Jean Yawkey joined as the third general partner with LeRoux and Sullivan. The deal was consummated on May 23 for $20.5 million.

When Jean Yawkey announced the sale of the Red Sox, her first step, done with dispatch, was to fire their general manager, Dick O'Connell, whom she personally disliked, who was the architect of the 1967 *Impossible Dream* Red Sox and a long-time favorite of her husband, Tom; she promptly elevated Haywood Sullivan as O'Connell's replacement. Sullivan, to the enormous pleasure of Don Zimmer, began dismantling the band of Buffalo Heads, one rogue member at a time; the immediate effect was positive, but ultimately, it may have proved more of a disservice to the organization than anything they had hoped to gain in the transactions, losing bench strength, weakening the farm system and forfeiting pitching depth. Sullivan, in his new role as general manager, took immediate action over the winter signing free agent pitchers Mike Torrez of the Yankees, Baltimore's Dick Drago and Minnesota's Tom Burgmeier. He shamefully practically gave away Fergie Jenkins to the Texas Rangers for little-known pitcher John Poloni and cash. Jenkins would win 18 games in 1978; Poloni never made the Red Sox roster. Boston's promising hurler Don Aase was traded to California, along with cash, for speedy infielder Jerry Remy. And the biggest acquisition of all came on March 30, 1978, toward the end of spring training, when Boston traded four players, including a Don Zimmer antagonist, Rick Wise, for Dennis Eckersley. Surprisingly, Zimmer's main nemesis, Bill Lee, who Zimmer more than once tried to convince the Red Sox to trade, remained on the team.

Manager Don Zimmer was not on sturdy ground with the Boston media and fan base that often ripped him to shreds, especially on the radio talk shows, which he was drawn to like a moth to a flame, adding to his angst. He made the comment as the spring season was about to get underway that in 1977, after making a pitching change and walking back to the dugout, the only person cheering him was his wife. *"Everybody else was booing,"* he said.[732]

On March 1, spring camp officially opened for all Red Sox player personnel; George Scott arrived having shed 20 or more pounds, he claimed; he had been wearing a rubber sweat suit whenever he exercised in the offseason, which he continued to use in spring training. Sensitive about his weight, often deriding reporters who dared ask him about it, this time, Scott openly acknowledged that weight was indeed an issue for him in 1977 and that the problem needed to be corrected. But in spite of his personal training efforts, he turned up with a cranky back when he first arrived in camp, which was to be more problematic for him early in the season, a sign that the years of major league baseball were beginning to take its toll. It failed, however, to hold him down. On March 7, in an intra-squad game, he wasted no time with the bat, ripping two impressive homers, one of them a

---

[732] Leigh Montville, "Williams casts a shadow, but Zimmer not worried," The Boston Globe, March 7, 1978, P. 27

415-foot grand slam. Their new lefthander, Poloni, acquired for Fergie Jenkins, was pummeled. *"We were just tuning up,"* said an animated Scott of his homers and of his teammates who crunched some of their own.[733] Not long into the spring season, Peter Gammons of the *Globe* declared that Scott was a "hefty problem," well over his 215 pounds listed in the Red Sox Media Guide, and maybe trade bait, but that no one was interested. He ran steadily around the ballpark every chance he got *"in that red sweat-suit,"* wrote Gammons, and managed to shed possibly 25 pounds, they thought. When performance projections were being made for each Red Sox player, "George Scott's weight" was front and center of every sportswriter's notepad.

The Red Sox had a decent spring, winning 15 of 26 exhibition games. George Scott fared well, as he often did in spring games, hitting .320 with 3 home runs, second best to Dwight Evans, 24 base hits, also second best, and 11 RBIs. But there were racial distractions brewing once again with the Red Sox: *New York Times* journalist Gerald Eskenazi, in his April 10 article, *"'Yes We Can,' Red Sox Say,"* spoke of the "tight little island" of a team the Red Sox were, who grew their own, to explain why they only had two blacks – George Scott and Jim Rice – and only two black players on the top two Red Sox farm clubs. It was a startling statistic, one that would be noticed and written about again by other baseball and newspaper critics as

---

[733] Larry Whiteside, "Poloni shelled as Peskys tumble, 26-5," The Boston Globe, March 8, 1978, P. 23

the season progressed, particularly as the Hub's spotlight fell on their budding – yet black – superstar Jim Rice, who resisted any effort by the media to put him in the middle of issues surrounding Boston and race. He had doubts about Boston, a city still simmering in racial unrest, and its little ballpark where racist behavior still percolated, and racial epithets could be heard wafting from the stands. *Providence Journal* sports columnist Bill Reynolds touched on some of this in his 2009 treatise on the '78 season and its effect on the city following four years of anti-busing rallies and racial violence in Boston. It was a *"welcome escape,"* he wrote, from the ravages that had divided the city, at least for a while.[734]

The 1978 Boston Red Sox (courtesy of Boston Red Sox)

---

[734] Bill Reynolds, '78: The Boston Red Sox, A Historic Game, and a Divided City, New American Library (New York), 2009

Before the start of the 1978 season, the Baseball Commissioner's office issued a list of active players with "glittering career statistics" that were worth watching as they approached certain career milestones. George Scott was one of the notables: 192 base hits short of reaching 2,000 and 52 RBIs short of reaching 1,000, which is certainly impressive career numbers among a mix of 10 still active veterans with such credentials. But as promising and as hopeful as things were from the outset for both the Boomer and the Boston ball club, with the latter performing as well in the first half as any Red Sox team in modern memory, there was a ghastly downside to the events of that season. Scott struggled with chronic injury for the first time in his career. The Red Sox, who appeared unbeatable at first just crushing the opposition, had found another way to disappoint their success-starved fans by losing again, but the manner in which it was done this time seemed almost surreal.

Boston lost three of its first four games but quickly gained their footing, winning eight in a row, and slipped briefly into first place on April 21 by a half-game over the Tigers, but then lost their next two of three to Cleveland and found themselves in second by the same margin. Zimmer had George Scott batting 7th, which he had more than once objected to in prior years when placed there, but this time, he offered no resistance. The Red Sox were loaded with power all up and down the lineup, and Scott's productive bat was one Zimmer was depending on, with 33 homers in '77, as well as his defensive strengths that made the infield well-balanced. Scott started slowly by hitting .233 through the first nine games but then surged with a six-game hit streak in which he was 12-for-26, raising his average to .339, third-best of the starting nine. But on April 23, after a strong 6-for-10 performance in a doubleheader against the Indians, his back went into spasm, and he was sidelined for several games; with the exception of one DH appearance, he missed 17 games, the longest period he had ever been away from the action. On May 15, he happily returned to the lineup but ran into more hard luck on that day in Kansas City. In the fourth inning, Amos Otis hit a Texas leaguer pop fly down the right field line hotly pursued by second baseman Remy, right fielder Evans and Scott. The ball, blown back by the wind, bounced off Scott's outstretched bare hand. Two innings later, the middle finger of his right hand swelled, and he was removed from the game; it was a hairline fracture. It was to be his personal nightmare for the rest of the season. He was out again for another 12 days, returning as a pinch-hitter on June 4 and then as a DH for five games, finally returning to the lineup on June 12 at home against the Angels.

The *Globe's* Bob Ryan's particularly flattering if not eulogistic article in the midst of Scott's extended absence in which he apologized for himself, and on behalf of others, in taking the talented first baseman for granted, and who, he noted, was clearly missed. Carl Yastrzemski, who replaced the Boomer at first base, was simply not in Scott's class, said Ryan, nor did anyone stop to think why third baseman Butch Hobson was making so many errors after Scott had left. Was it a mere coincidence that he was getting worse at his position? Ryan emphasized Scott's dedication to duty, his loyalty to the game and the team, and the value of not being one of those athletes who whined but who came to play every day. *"I submit that the personification of that trait is George Scott,"* wrote Ryan.[735]

The Red Sox were burning up the league by setting a club record 23-7 in May, 34-16 through the end of May and in first place three games ahead of the second-place Yankees; by the end of June, they were still in first place, 8 games in front. Scott, however, was struggling at the plate, affected by the injured finger that was healing all too slowly, preventing him from getting his accustomed grip on the bat and causing him to make adjustments in his swing, leading to bad habits at the plate. Don Zimmer was not about to put him on the DL. *"Right now, we're not going to do it. Who would we bring up?"* moaned the Red Sox skipper.[736] Unlike the month of April, when he was making good contact with the ball and went days without striking out, when he returned in June, strike-outs began to mount, as many as 5 in one game against the Yankees. He finished the month hitting .244. July wasn't much better for the Boomer. He batted .196 with only two home runs, getting his first hit in a string of 26 at-bats on July 31 against Chicago. He looked as bad at the plate as the numbers indicated; with each out, the Fenway crowd became more restless, booing him mercilessly. Dwight Evans appealed to the media, which was ravaging him, to soften their criticism of Scott, a sensitive man who was clearly affected by the crowd; it was blistering at times, and hopefully, with the aid of the Boston scribes,

---

[735] Bob Ryan, "Scott Earns His Keep," The Boston Globe, May 20, 1978, p. 22
[736] Larry Whiteside, "Scott Out for Three Weeks," The Boston Globe, May 18, 1978, P. 42

it would inspire the fans to ease up as well. The more they booed him, the tighter he got. It seemed to work: on July 31, upon singling in the 7th inning, the Fenway crowd roundly cheered. *"Sooner or later, things are going to come my way. They've got to,"* chanted the ever-optimistic Red Sox slugger with his doubtless predictions.[737]

Scott and the Red Sox put up some pretty fair numbers in August, Boston winning 19-of-29 and Scotty hitting .281 on 25 base hits. In the last nine games of the month, he was 13-for-35, hitting at a .371 clip, including three homers, topping it off on August 29 – a Jimmy Fund promotion night before 34,393 fans - with his third career grand slam off of Seattle's Glenn Abbott, sealing a Red Sox victory. Scott crushed Abbott's first pitch, which "was sent soaring somewhere near the site of *the nuclear power plant in Seabrook,"* wrote the Globe's Peter Gammons.[738] Center fielder Rupert Jones never moved. Neither did Scott until he watched it disappear into the night sky. It was a *"so there"* moment for Scotty, who had been extremely frustrated with himself, the media, and the hometown fans who were relentlessly razzing him. After his slam, the fickle fans called him out, hoping for a bow, just like old times, all the time chanting "Booma – Booma – Booma," their beloved Boomer. He never moved from the bench. Luis Tiant poked his head above the dugout instead, fooling some that it was

---

[737] Steve Marantz, "George Scott: Despite bricks and bats, he always bounces back," The Boston Globe, August 1, 1978, P. 23
[738] Peter Gammons, "Drago Starts It, Scott Finishes Off Mariners, 10-5," The Boston Globe, August 30, 1978, P. 21

Scott. He reverted at once to silence as he had done in '77 when confronted with the same treatment and the embarrassment of the radio show racial debacle. *"I'm mad at everyone,"* which was all he would say, aiming somehow to return the punishment he had absorbed for four long months and maybe restore some of his pride that had been shattered.[739]

Distinguished author Howard Bryant, a black himself from the Boston area who, rightfully, was sensitive to the city of Boston and their home club's treatment of blacks, and more than capable of sizing up the fickle fate of black players like George Scott performing in this city, who, when on a high note would applaud them but then just as quickly and irreverently throw them under the bus. Scott would often point this out as his fate for playing for the Red Sox in a racially compromised city. *"Scott, like most black players,"* said Bryant, *"was well aware of the team's notorious reputation when it came to dealing with blacks, and his early years in the minor leagues were characterized both by his heightened sensitivity to slight and the surprising relationship he forged in Winston-Salem with Eddie Popowski, the longtime Red Sox minor league manager,"* who was an anomaly in the city never finding reason to distinguish between his black and white players.[740]

---

[739] IBID
[740] Howard Bryant, "A Life of Henry Aaron," p. 434

Another bomb hit by the Boomer (courtesy of Boston Red Sox)

By September 1, the Red Sox still had a fairly comfortable 6 ½ game lead over New York, who, on August 9, had vaulted over Milwaukee into second place. The Red Sox, meanwhile, were having pitching problems: Only Dennis Eckersley was throwing well; Torrez, Tiant, and Jim Wright were ineffective, and Bill Lee had been banished to the bullpen by Zimmer. Right fielder Dwight Evans, an important Red Sox cog on offense and defense, was beaned on August 28, suffered dizzy spells and was not effective after that. The defense generally fell apart, particularly Hobson, a Zimmer favorite, who would commit 43 errors in the season.

Under contract for just one year, edgy Don Zimmer pressed Haywood Sullivan and the Red Sox for a multiyear deal. But Sullivan refused to give him an extension, insisting that any contract discussions would take place once the season had ended. It made him uneasy, and he began to press his players to improve their performance in his attempt to run away with the division title, proving his point to management that they should reconsider. He wore out his team, stubbornly stuck with original rosters, questioned injuries and fidgeted with his pitching staff constantly.

What seemed highly improbable actually happened: in July, just before the All-Star game, the Red Sox were 57-26 and up by 9 games over Milwaukee. The Yankees were 11 ½ games back. It was a very comfortable lead, and the team was playing almost flawlessly. Baseball pundits exclaimed that a division title was nearly in the bag for Boston; they could play the balance of the season at a .500 pace and win. The Yankees needed to play at a .700 pace to catch them. Catch them they did, surging at a .730 pace. The Red Sox played under .500 ball since the All-Star break, at 24-26, while the Yankees were 36-18 [.667] during the same period.

New York rode into Boston on September 7 for an important, and as it evolved, a decisive four-game series, having won 12 of their last 14 games and now only 4 games behind the first-place Red Sox. It turned into a disaster. The journalists labeled it the "Boston Massacre" because it was so one-sided. The Yankees outscored the Red Sox 42-9, winning the first two 15-3 and 13-2 and sweeping the series to land them in a tie for first place.

The Red Sox committed 12 errors, three of them by Hobson, who removed himself from the lineup two weeks later for the good of the team after committing his 43rd. George Scott was having miseries of his own stuck in the middle of another prolonged slump, and was 0-for-11. It continued through September 13, an agonizing 0-for-34. NBC color commentator Tony Kubek made an amusing but sage comment during the series, epitomizing what was taking place: *"This is the first time I've seen a first-place team chasing a second-place team."*[741]

The Red Sox trailed New York in second place, closing the gap between them and the Yankees by one game on September 23. They then matched them win-for-win for the next six games until October 1, when the Yankees lost 9-2 at the hands of the Cleveland Indians. Luis Tiant and the Red Sox shut down Toronto 5-0 that day; the two teams were suddenly tied. It seemed predestined to Red Sox fans; there was hope and joy and a certain confidence once again in the Hub. It was now all up to one playoff contest to decide who was going to be the AL East champion.

What is best remembered about that day, October 2, is that a light-hitting nondescript shortstop named Bucky Dent, a banjo hitter used primarily for his defense, with a lifetime record of only 22 home runs and hitting a mere .243 at the time, [.140 in his last 20 games] became an instant Yankee hero. Hurler Mike Torrez – a Yankee himself in 1977 – and the Red Sox played

---

[741] Glenn Stout and Richard Johnson, Red Sox Century, p. 383

a solid game leading into the sixth inning. Yankee bats were silent. Torrez had given up just two base hits, and the Red Sox enjoyed a 2-0 lead. It was beginning to look quite favorable for Boston. But in the top of the seventh, with one out, Chambliss and White reached on singles. Manager Bob Lemon, who replaced Billy Martin in July, pinch-hit Jim Spencer for sub-Brian Doyle, and he flew out.

It was Bucky Dent's turn. Torrez got two quick strikes on him; on the second pitch, he fouled off onto his ankle, which sent him hobbling for several minutes. There was a serious question about whether he would stay in the game, but he did. The next pitch by Torrez was history. With one infamous swing, his hands lodged well up on the bat handle to poke a single somewhere, he lofted a soft fly – harmless-appearing at first - that settled just over the wall – aided just enough by the wind - into Fenway's left field screen; a three-run homer; a Fenway Park homer that would not have gone out in most ballparks. He took the life from the ballpark with that hit; it went silent. It took a while for the fans to come to grips with what had happened. After the Yanks scored two more in the 8th inning, the Red Sox rallied in the ninth, pulling within one run of tying the game, but Goose Gossage shut the door, forcing Yastrzemski to pop up to end it. Boston lost 5-4, and the "Curse of the Bambino" remained intact.

"We really should have won the game. It was nothing but a pop-up," exclaimed Scott of Dent's home run, still carrying some of the frustration of that day during a much later interview. However, when it came to his

manager, Don Zimmer, he showed less tolerance. *"Well, any time that you lose [the division title] when you're 14 games up, and you're caught with a month left to play in the season, you can't just sit back and blame the players [entirely],"* said Scott, making a strong statement that Don Zimmer should have taken most of the blame for that disastrous season. *"Don Zimmer was probably one of the most over-rated of baseball people that I've ever seen,"* raged Scott in increasing decibels with each spoken word.[742]

Adding to his frustration of a bad season in which he played in just 120 games, batting .233 with 12 home runs, his wife, Lucky, who had briefly reconciled upon leaving Milwaukee, filed for divorce a second time in December. His world seemed to be coming apart.

"I know I've got a job of redeeming myself," exclaimed George Scott as he prepared for the '79 season, jogging every morning, doing calisthenics and wind sprints, and working hard to drop the extra weight during the offseason.[743] He was a virtual health fanatic, wrote one scribe while rumors still percolated that he was washed up and the Red Sox were anxious to find a suitor for their $200,000 previous season's bust.

He showed a dramatic weight loss; by the time he arrived at spring camp – where he arrived early - he was a svelte 216 pounds, down from 240 pounds, and a return to form that he displayed when he was a rookie. He

---

[742] George Scott interview: April 2006
[743] Larry Whiteside, "Scott Striving for Comeback with Red Sox," The Sporting News, January 13, 1979, P. 32

expounded to willing reporters on the miseries of his previous year, with first his back injury and then the broken finger, and how he tried to come back too soon, which contributed to his poor hitting. He had little ability to grip the bat properly, which affected his swing and power, he said. As it began to heal toward the end of the year, he noticed how much more bat control and power he had regained. *"I know what people have said about me this winter, and I also know those same people are unwilling to accept the truth. The truth is that I had a bad season because I had a broken hand."*[744] This year, it would be different, he claimed; he proved that by hitting over .400 during the spring exhibition season. But it didn't last.

Forty-one games into the season, with the Red Sox in second place 1 ½ games behind the first-place Orioles, Scott was benched, beginning with the May 26 game in Toronto. He had been hitting .260 on May 16 but began a hitless streak over a span of 25 at-bats, dropping his average to .219. A future Hall of Famer, Carlton Fisk, who had been injured in spring training and was having elbow trouble, was sitting, making only three appearances to that point. Zimmer needed his bat, and with Scott struggling as he was, the decision was easy - put Fisk in as a DH and move Yastrzemski to first. *"He [Scott] had a great spring training, and he worked hard,"* said

---

[744] Larry Whiteside, "Slimmed-down Scott Vows to Make Up for Bad Year," The Sporting News, April 1, 1979, P. 6

Zimmer. *"He did a great job. But if you've got a hitter like Fisk on the bench, why not put him in there?"*[745]

Scott was relegated to substitute duties, pinch-hitting twice at the end of May and two more times in early June. He was hitting a meager .224. The writing was on the wall, and Scott could see it. He asked to be traded. *"Don Zimmer never came and talked to me about nothing,"* raged Scott in an interview many years later. *"I don't think we had fifty words [between us] from a positive aspect."*[746] On June 13, the Red Sox traded for Houston's first baseman-outfielder, Bob Watson, who would hit .337 for the Red Sox in '79, complicating things even further for Scott. But that was quickly, if not mercilessly, resolved when, on the same day, an hour after the Watson deal, they dealt George Scott to Kansas City for Tom Poquette. Poquette was a cut-from-cloth fair-haired mid-western boy from Eau Claire, Wisconsin, and a fan-favorite in Kansas City. He had been with them during the Royals' recent division championships and had good seasons in '76 and '77 when he batted .302 and .292, respectively.

The move caused a furor within the Kansas City community; for days, the local papers carried fan responses questioning the deal of giving up on a young player for a 35-year-old .224 hitter near the end of his career. It was a risk Royals' manager Whitey Herzog was willing to accept; Herzog

---

[745] Larry Whiteside, "Scott (0-25) Benched, Yaz Moves to First Base," The Boston Globe, May 26, 1979, P. 21
[746] George Scott interview: October 10, 2007

wanted Scott for added punch in the lineup – he was a proven right-handed power hitter - and for improved defensive measures. *"George Scott is the best defensive first baseman in both leagues. And he is in excellent shape,"* said Herzog, who was the brains behind the Royals' three successive West Division championships 1976-1978, and who was looking for that extra snap he needed in his team to finally bring them a pennant. [747] Herzog was confident that with the big Gold Glove first baseman, he had his man. He understood he was sticking his neck out with the skeptical fans, and there was also a promise he knew he had to keep with his front office management for being persuaded into investing in Scott, both risks he was willing to take; however, taking on a declining George Scott would prove to be his strategic folly in a matter of a few weeks; Herzog had misjudged the situation and being the man he was known for he wasn't about to live this down entirely on his own. Someone was coming with him.

On June 26, Scott made his first appearance before the home crowd after a ten-game road trip. It was an impressive one to the delight of 24,550 Kansas City fans, who were beginning to feel exuberant about Herzog's acquisition. Scott rapped three hits – his 9th in 14 at-bats – including the game-winner in the 10th, stroking a bases-loaded walk-off single and a Royals victory, moving them within one game of the first-place Angels. Scott wrapped up the month of June hitting .382, to the delight of Herzog.

---

[747] Sid Bordman, "Royals Obtain Boston's Scott," The Kansas City Times, June 14, 1979, P. 7E

But in spite of his great pleasure in having the big first baseman, it was not enough. Whitey was looking for the big hit from Scott – the home run ball. It was one of the main reasons the Kansas City skipper had traded for him in his quest for a power hitter. Herzog actually had movies made of Scott's at-bats for him to study to reacquire his old touch and relearn how to once again hit the long ball. It was insulting to George. Scott sensed the pressure that was building of ominous undertones mirroring the days of Dick Williams' efforts at altering his hitting style, and he responded: *"I just want to hit the ball and let power take care of itself,"* he said, dismissing Herzog's ambitious program of re-indoctrination.[748] It would prove to have negative consequences, bringing matters between them to a boil later on.

The Royals' pitching was not holding up, however. After a six-game win streak June 22-28, they went into an extended swoon, losing 14 of their next 15 games, falling precipitously into 4th place on July 14, 10 games out of first. Herzog was frustrated and feeling the heat while Kansas City fans were beginning to heat up themselves, writing to the local newspapers and filling their fan columns with their own complaints, some about Scott, but most pointing fingers at Royals' brass – including Herzog, for choosing Scott over much-needed pitching – for not making a smart trade. *The Kansas City Star* posted a sports page headline on July 15: *"Despite Slump,*

---

[748] Mike McKenzie, "It's a Battle Royal for Regular First Base Job," The Kansas City Times, June 27, 1979, P. 5C

Herzog Won't Change."[749] It was in reaction to Herzog's statement that in spite of the prolonged slump, he was still sleeping well, playing golf and fishing, and there was nothing he felt he could do but to keep managing the way he always had. The day before, Herzog, however, received a boost from team owner Ewing Kauffman who made a rare visit to the clubhouse in support of the team and of a frustrated Whitey Herzog. As with the team, Scott also slumped in July, hitting his first and only Royals homer on July 31, after which he received a standing ovation from the Royals' crowd changing their frequent boos of him to cheers; it followed an eight-game span in which the Royals were 5-3, and he was 7-for-22 hitting at a .318 pace. Scott later lamented that he was frustrated that Herzog would not play him more consistently.

Teammate Amos Otis vented his own frustrations on July 22, publicly ripping the front office for sitting on their hands, complaining they needed a couple of power hitters and a power pitcher to fill the breach, which subject was an old wound dating back to the American League playoffs in '78. *The Kansas City Times* Sports reporter Mike DeArmond raised the specter of why George Scott didn't fill the bill for the hitter piece, but Otis wouldn't buy it, the argument falling on deaf ears, saying, *"They're so damn sure on the free agent thing, but they don't go out and get anybody. It's*

---

[749] Sid Bordman, "Despite Slump, Herzog Won't Change," The Kansas City Star, July 15, 1979, P. 1S

funny. It seems everybody can make a trade but us."[750] It was a scathing indictment of the Kansas City brass and no doubt sent them scurrying along with Whitey Herzog, who was feeling the pinch himself because of his personal choice of George Scott as that certain power hitter. It quickly spilled over into the clubhouse in an ugly way. According to Scott in a later interview Whitey Herzog, who clearly was frustrated, and reacting to Otis' public condemnation, held a clubhouse meeting during their series with Chicago in late July, only a few short days after Otis' criticism, in which he appeared to divest himself of any personal blame by openly berating Scott in front of the entire Kansas City team. Meanwhile, the Royals had won 2 of the three games in which Scott had four base hits. *"He [Herzog] said, 'the reason that we're not winning is because of George Scott,'"* exclaimed a still-angry Scott who was tormented by Herzog's brashness and his finger-pointing, explaining that it was largely the pitching that had broken down and that Herzog was looking for an easy target because of the pressure he was feeling that was precipitated by Amos Otis.[751] When Herzog was approached 28 years later for an interview, he was still smoldering about that day and the clubhouse incident with Scott; his response when asked about the matter was a sharp reproof of Scott said in a resounding way of *"No comment,"* as the effects of that unpleasant moment still lingered in his

---

[750] Mike DeArmond, "Otis Rips Front Office for Lack of Deals," Kansas City Times, July 23, 1979, p. 39
https://www.newspapers.com/image/677652048/?match=1&terms=whitey%20herzog
[751] George Scott interview: March 2006

subconscious mind.[752] Fred Patek, the Royals' shortstop, who witnessed the incident, explained it differently, saying it wasn't a formal meeting; it was clubhouse banter going on as they prepared for the game after pre-game practice that led to an informal session, a spontaneous moment when Herzog appeared in the clubhouse. *"He [Herzog] kind of accused George of not doing his job...It was just a big shouting match from what I can remember,"* said Patek, who was unquestionably startled, as were his teammates, by the sudden anger in the room on that day; Patek implied mildly that the entire matter seemed unnecessary, if not distracting.[753]

Apparently, it was Herzog's style to occasionally berate his players when things were not going well with the team, doing it openly in the presence of the team and reporters. Such was the case with Willie Wilson, also in 1979, who, according to one fan, was regularly being chastised by Herzog. *"He [Wilson] is constantly tearing this young player down by pointing out the mistakes he makes and what he has to do to play for K. C. in front of the other players, the press and the public. He is putting all kinds of pressure on the kid, wondering what he has to do to get the manager off his back."*[754] Wilson was black like Scott, a solid player who was an All-Star and four-time MVP candidate, and a Gold Glover who batted .315 in '79; he was a lifetime .285 hitter.

---

[752] Whitey Herzog interview: May 25 and 31, 2007
[753] Fred Patek interview: January 2008
[754] Fan Letters, "The Sporting Mind," quoting Kansas City fan Detroy R. Giles, The Kansas City Times, April 7, 1979, p. 81

Scott played sparingly in August, and then on August 17, he was put on waivers by the Royals. No team claimed him – the $200,000 contract no doubt having something to do with it – and Scott became a free agent five days later. He was picked up by the New York Yankees in August of that year, playing briefly for manager Billy Martin, but then released in November by team owner George Steinbrenner, who was in the throes of a rebuilding effort that did not include George Scott. He was now a free agent. He had a brief encounter with the Texas Rangers in the re-entry draft, who picked him up for "utility duties," but it was nothing but another insult to Scott. They made him a "take-it-or-leave-it" offer of a minor league role with their Triple-A Charleston club. Scott declined it, called it an "insult," and left the major leagues.

In the spring of 1980, Scott was still fuming over his dealings with Royals' manager Whitey Herzog and the manner in which he was released by the club, believing it was affecting his ability to succeed on the free agent market. He bitterly accused him of messing up his career, feeling he had provoked other managers into blocking his chances of being picked up by another team. His indictment of Herzog got back to the ex-Royal manager, who was fired by the team on October 2 at the conclusion of the 1979 season. He shot back at Scott's charges: *"I wonder if it ever occurred to him that George Scott might be the reason I'm out of baseball."* Bitterness between them was toxic, possessing a life of its own.[755]

The matter of Herzog's public criticism of his players was a talking point upon his discharge from the team and was covered in the local Kansas City newspapers the next day. There was an undercurrent between team owner Ewing Kauffman and Herzog. Kauffman, from time to time, referred to his manager as "Peck's Bad Boy" from a 19th-century fictional cartoon character, Henry "Hennery" Peck, popularly described as mischievous mean-spirited and of bad behavior – a "vicious little swaggerer "– that was to lead to eventual annoyance or embarrassment. The column had as its foundation a strong connection to violence and racist views. Obviously, it was bothering Herzog as he referred to it himself the day of his firing exclaiming, *"I just don't think I'm Peck's Bad Boy like they make me out to be."* The matter of Kauffman's displeasure of Herzog appeared more obvious that he was behind the firing. *"The owner of the Royals has said that Herzog is too candid when publicly criticizing his players. It is also known that Kauffman and Herzog have clashed verbally several times at social functions, the last time being in the press room at Royals Stadium after a late-season game,"* wrote sportswriter Del Black.[756] Of the players who might have been viewed as unsupportive of Herzog, who were interviewed after the firing, only one, pitcher Dennis Leonard, stood out as

---

[755] Unattributed, "Bunts and Boots," The Sporting News, April 12, 1980, P. 46
[756] Del Black, "The Herzog Story: A Package of Many Thoughts," The Kansas City Times, October 3, 1979, p. 1C

critical of one man when asked if any one particular player had a personal dislike for Herzog that might have interfered with his performance on the field. *"There's only one person that I know of,"* said Leonard. *"I wouldn't want to single out any player."* The reference was tactful but contained enough of an insinuation to point directly at George Scott.[757]

Marital problems that had plagued Scott throughout the '79 season were still afflicting him, ending in divorce in 1980. He had sat by the phone all winter waiting for that call that he had a future in major league baseball, which never came. Red Sox coach Tommy Harper, who would have his own racial problems later on with the club and who would sue them for discrimination on his being wrongfully fired, urged Scott to make an appearance at the spring camps; he would never get an invitation sitting and waiting, said Harper, who told him he had gone through the same experience. Scott took his advice and was seen traveling throughout Florida in his rented red Mustang, making appearances at several spring camps, but it was unproductive.

On May 2, 1980, just over a month into the season, and still reeling from the shock of his rejection by all major league clubs, 36-year-old George Scott signed with the Yucatan Lions of the Mexican League, which was designated Triple-A, although a brand of ball probably closer to Double-A. He made more money in Mexico that season than any amount he could have

---

[757] Mike DeArmond, "Angered Players Rally Behind Whitey," The Kansas City Times, October 3, 1979, p. 6C

made while still playing major league baseball in the States. *"Somebody told me, 'You never DH'd, you're still young enough. Go to the Mexican League and show people you can [still] play, and maybe somebody will invite you to spring training,'"* said Scott.[758] It was a whole new way of life for the ex-big leaguer accustomed to major league luxury, including first-class travel, posh hotels, fancy restaurants, and first-rate playing fields. Instead, he found shabby shanty towns and cities with houses crumbling, sweltering heat, rat-infested hotels and restaurants, lunatic fans (known to throw rattlesnakes into dugouts), and poorly lit and badly-conditioned ball fields, and oppressive 18-hour bus rides, some as much as 22 hours, to neighboring cities after which they were expected to immediately play nine-inning games.

He went to Los Mochis of the Mexican Pacific League toward the tail end of their winter season as player-manager of the Cañeros, replacing former major leaguer and Mexican legend Benjamin Papelero Valenzuela. It was where George got his feet wet, his first managerial assignment, brief as it was, where he got the idea and his taste for managing, in which he was 10-9. He also played in 18 games for them, hitting .254 [17-for-67] with one double and 10 RBIs. The Cañeros finished 8th in a ten-team circuit at 37-45.

---

[758] George Scott interview: February 28, 2008

Scott signed for the 1981 season with the Mexico City Tigers, owned by Mexico City businessman Alejo Peralta and managed by their president, who was also their field manager, Chito Garcia. It was there that Scott caught on with the Mexican people, developing his own following and peculiar identity. He became somewhat of a celebrity, residing in a local hotel – the Hotel California – not far from the Tigers' ballpark, the El Parque del Seguro Social (Social Security Park), in a $32-a-day suite that included a television, two beds and a phone. Mexican Baseball Hall of Fame sportswriter Tommy Morales befriended Scott and gave him a nickname that stuck with the media and fans: they called him "King Kong." "In the U.S., it means black and ugly," said Scott, offended at first but softened when he realized the appellation was a compliment among Mexican citizens, who viewed him as big and strong, a giant among men. Each time he made a tough play, the fans gave him a standing ovation, yelling, "King Kong en accion!" He had found his niche as "King Kong in action."

Scott had an exemplary year, pounding the ball game after game and leading the league in just about everything. He played in the Mexican League All-Star game and was 2-for-4; he finished the season batting .355, third-best behind Willie Norwood of Reynosa, who led the league at .365, and Bobby Rodriguez of the Mexico City Reds, who batted .363. Scott hit 18 home runs during the season and two more in the playoffs, which was won by Campeche, which had finished the season in second place behind Scott's Tigers. *"I wanted to go down there to prove to the major league owners that I could still play,"* said Scott, who became disillusioned when, once again, none of the major league teams sought him after such a splendid year in Mexico. *"So, I said, 'something is wrong,' and I said, 'the heck with it, I'm going to go into the coaches' part of it.'"*[759] He was coming to grips with the idea that the Mexican League was nothing more than the major league's graveyard, and he had to do something very different, like coaching and instructional duties, which he knew he was capable of if he was to reenter the major leagues, and had confidence that most likely the Red Sox, if not certainly other major league clubs, would take him on.

Garcia liked what he saw in Scott, liked the way he got along with his young ballplayers and the leadership qualities he exhibited, and formed a bond between the two. Garcia was planning to move up into the team's front office and recommended to Peralta that Scott replace him as full-time field manager. He got the job for the 1982 season; it seemed like a perfect fit. But it wasn't; Scott had trouble with his players right from the beginning, making demands on them that they perceived as unreasonable and not adjusting well to the culture of the league, which involved long bus rides accompanied by drinking as the players' only way, right or wrong, to appease their boredom and help them tolerate the extended and arduous travel. Scott was opposed to it and made no bones. Ex-major leaguer Doug Ault and Scott got into a swearing match on one occasion when Ault took beer onto the bus. The incident got back to management; Scott was fired

---

[759] George Scott interview: March 12, 2006

suddenly before the regular season was even underway and shipped off to Poza Rica, where he wound up playing for the Oilers.[760]

Announcement of George Scott playing for Poza Rica (courtesy of George "Boomer" Scott)

He played 83 games for Poza Rica in 1983 and then shifted to Veracruz, where he finished the season between the two teams batting .223 with just 5 homers. In his final season, 1984, with Veracruz, he played in 86 games,

---

[760] The Sporting News article of April 24, 1982, and former teammate's interviews, supports the view that Scott had a run-in with Doug Ault that led to his dismissal. George Scott, however, does not recall a specific incident with Ault; he does remember objecting to player drinking on the bus, and being let go in the spring by the Tigers. Scott believes his problems were with pitching coach Dick Pole who he fired for "undermining" him, he alleges, with Mexico City's management.

mostly as a DH, batting .305 on 92 base hits. He assumed managerial duties for Veracruz part-way into the season but left before it ended when Mexican League teams were struggling to pay their players because of the Mexican economy and the rapid devaluation of the peso. Mexican teams had to pay their American imports in U.S. dollars, which made it even more difficult. Scott said that Veracruz still owed him $4,000 of a $15,000 manager's contract at the time of his leaving. *"They just couldn't afford to pay me,"* said Scott.[761]

He went back to Greenville, Mississippi, to be with his mother there, in the house that he had built for her, and where it all began for George Scott; his playing days were over.

---

[761] Unattributed, "He is Still Trying to Make a Living in Baseball – But Business Isn't Booming for the Boomer: Now Pitching, Scott," The Boston Globe, March 23, 1986, p. 89& 98
https://www.newspapers.com/image/437566318/?match=1&terms=George%20Scott

Chapter 18
Stonewalled

"I'd asked to come back here. I thought being with a winner was all that counted. But you have to be a man too. I knew they [Red Sox] were racists in their thinking before. But I looked at the way things appeared to be run, and I thought they'd changed. I looked at [Jim] Rice and thought it might be different than it was before. It wasn't. It's just the same."

George Scott[762]

In the early part of September 1983, at the conclusion of the Mexican League's season that year and four years since George Scott's last day in major league baseball, Scott and his young boy George Scott III, who was then about 13, attended a Red Sox game at Fenway Park. The Red Sox had just constructed new luxury box seating along the first-base side of the park's grandstand roof, as well as sky-view seating, and installed the park's first elevator. He had picked up tickets from the team who assigned former Red Sox ballplayers to the seats that were used occasionally for celebrity events or just for their own family outings.

Scott soon had concerns, however, knowing he and his son were the only blacks that night sitting in the new privileged seating. *"It was obvious*

---

[762] Larry Whiteside, "Sox Children of the '60s Look Back," The Boston Sunday Globe," July 29, 1979, p. 80
https://www.newspapers.com/image/437079904/?terms=Larry%20Whiteside

591

to me from the looks we got that we didn't belong there. As peoples came in, we got the stare I'm used to. They didn't recognize me. Made me uncomfortable just the same. Mostly Boston business guys and their families, I think, [they were] in sweaters, jackets and some ties, but always glances at me and my son, like we were out of place and ruining their good time," said Scott. *"You see, I was not on the ballfield, where I belonged; I was in their stands."* According to George, it didn't really come as a surprise to him that he was in Boston; he knew the drill. *"That was an attitude in Boston,"* said Scott. *"I knew that from other athletes who played here like Bill Russell, Reggie Smith, [and] Earl Wilson; I was okay to them [fans] when I was playing on the field entertaining them but not welcome when off of it. I knew my place there, but it wasn't any different than what I grew up with."*[763]

Scott temporarily left his seat with son George III in hand and walked to the snack area located behind the luxury boxes, where he seated his son at a small table near the snack bar while he walked over to the bar for drinks and snacks. When he returned, he found his son in tears and a gentleman standing over him, who turned out to be Red Sox publicity director Dick Bresciani, who was admonishing the son in no uncertain terms insisting he did not belong there and he needed to leave. It was an awkward moment as Bresciani recognized George right away, suddenly realizing his mistake and trying to find moral shelter, but the damage had been done. *"The first thing*

---

[763] George Scott interview: May 17, 2008

out of my mouth to him was 'what the hell is going on?'" he claimed, to have shouted in anger, drawing the attention of those around them, who became uncomfortable. *"He's my son you're trying to kick out,"* screamed Boomer. Bresciani exclaimed, *"Boomer, I didn't know that was your son,"* with a half-hearted grin as if it was his way of apologizing and looking to get off the hook, said Scott. *"I got angry with him, said 'what, and you thought it was some nigger kid that got into your fancy place? Is that what you thought?'"* Bresciani's eyes widened, and he looked around the room in panic, realizing his image was in jeopardy, according to George, as he began to press up against the Red Sox executive who was looking for an escape. It was by then, said George, that he believed the fans who were standing around realized it was the Boomer, George Scott, who was creating the havoc. *"I swore at him,"* said Scott, *"and threatened his ass. He was shook and backed up nearly fell over a table as I had him by the shirt. He's lucky I didn't tear him apart. It caused a lot of commotion, but I thought their [fans'] looks were like we were messing up their evening."* Some acted like nothing was happening while Bresciani got himself out of there in short order. *"What he did to my son was hands-down racist, and I caught him at it. He was going to bring the hammer down on this black kid who didn't belong. All about power and Boston wealth that night; Bresciani acted like it was his white space – their white space, and he wasn't going to let my boy spoil it until he saw me,"* said Scott.[764]

---

[764] George Scott interview: April 24, 2008

He was a Red Sox institution, "Bresh." They spoke of him with the greatest of affection, sacrosanct to many, and well-supported in the community among staff, ballplayers, business leaders and sports writers. He was many things to the Red Sox organization during his 42-year legacy with the club: team historian, statistician – before statistics became popular in MLB - public relations director, publicity director, vice president emeritus, and above all, a fierce defender of the team, and of Tom Yawkey, that honored him in 2006 with his induction into the Red Sox Hall of Fame. Ironically, it was the same year George Scott received the same honor of sharing the stage together on that November night.

And yet, in spite of the accolades, in 1983, the Boomer saw another and a quite different side of Mr. Bresciani, a manifest display of Red Sox racism in full bloom that, in his words, soured his feelings about the man and a troublesome relationship soon followed. *"I never liked him, had hard disagreements with him before; I never trusted him; he was like a snake salesman,"* alleged Scott.[765]

Author Jerry Gutlon in his book *It Was Never About the Babe*, referenced a general Boston attitude among certain journalists, sportswriters and fans who insisted that Yawkey was harmless and not in any way behind Red Sox racism, they alleged; Bresciani ferried that theme well: *"I don't believe Tom Yawkey was a racist in any way,"* Bresciani was once quoted

---

[765] IBID

as having said, *"and I think it showed in the way he treated the [black] people who worked for him down South where he lived and had his estate...you couldn't be a racist and treat people that way, and be that nice to everybody,"* insisted Bresciani.[766] Former sports editor George Kimball of the *Boston Phoenix* and later the *Boston Herald* disagreed with that rationale, saying, *"It's sort of like saying that a benevolent slave-owner in the 1850s wasn't a racist because he was kind to his field hands."*[767]

Bresciani was a slick manipulator encompassing not only his finesse at being perfectly politic but from another side rarely seen. According to Scott, he was the epitome of "old-style" Red Sox racism. He simply was better at hiding it. At age 76, Bresciani succumbed to cancer in November 2014.

George Scott and Dick Williams at the 2006 Red Sox Hall of Fame ceremony (author's collection)

---

[766] Jerry Gutlon, "It Was Never About the Babe," quoting Dick Bresciani, p. 186
[767] IBID

The marital difficulties that beset him in 1979-1980 that ended in divorce, his leaving baseball and the lucrative salaries he had earned in the major leagues, plus some likely mismanagement of personal funds, led to hard times for George Scott. In 1985 Scott sold two of his Gold Gloves for $600 apiece to someone who Scott later realized had snookered him into thinking they would be placed in a "hall of fame" somewhere. He was crushed that he had been so deceived. He later also put up for sale his Kansas City Royals' game-worn shoes. Then he hooked up with a major New York memorabilia dealer, in a partnership, he said, and in 1986 spent his time poking around major league spring camps enticing players – many of them his friends – to participate with him in autograph and collectors shows in the off-season. It was a humbling experience for a man of such indomitable pride, but he persevered; it was just another episode of yearning for survival for the ex-major league slugger, All-Star and eight-time Gold Glover, who was all too familiar with hard times.

Another standout in the mix of a handful of black Red Sox players was Tommy Harper, who played for them between 1972 and 1974 and who, in his first year with them, became immediately aware of the club's suspicious and disturbing racial practices. He worked in different capacities for Boston beginning in 1977, selling advertising. In '78, the team announced that Harper was to handle "compliance by the team with affirmative action." During the 1972 spring training with Boston, Harper found Winter Haven intimidating toward minorities, so he stayed close to his hotel room. The Massachusetts Commission Against Discrimination was investigating the team for compliance purposes at the time and, according to Harper, *"He was dismissed from a front-office position in 1979 after he informed the Massachusetts Commission Against Discrimination (MCAD) that the Sox had violated their pledge [GM Bucky Harris letter of 1959] to improve the franchise's racial diversity."*[768]

In 1985, Harper was brought into their front office to work as a special assistant to GM Lou Gorman. During this stint, Harper had the courage to speak up – when other Red Sox black players, like Jim Rice, would not - about the local Winter Haven Elks Club racial practices of handing out invitations to Red Sox white players but not blacks, which had been going on for at least 13 years. It got the attention of Sox part owner and CEO Haywood Sullivan, who had a checkered past with black players, dismissed it out of hand, saying he wouldn't comment on the matter *"because there's nothing wrong, and there has been nothing wrong."*[769]

Harper was fired by the Red Sox in December 1985 and filed a formal complaint of race discrimination with the U. S. Equal Employment Opportunity Commission, which ultimately sided with Harper. Sportswriter Michael Madden laid the blame squarely in the lap of Haywood Sullivan.

---

[768] Bob Hohler, "Harper Is Still Haunted," The Boston Globe, September 21, 2014, p. C7 https://www.newspapers.com/image/444538791/?terms=Bob%20Hohler
[769] Michael Madden, "Sox Practicing Tacit Complicity?" The Boston Globe, March 15, 1985, p. 31.
https://www.newspapers.com/image/438799234/?terms=michael%20madden

Although Tommy Harper's legal matters were publicly known and of a high profile, what was not well known or made as clear, but nevertheless in evidence, was about another black ex-Red Sox ballplayer, George Scott, who during the time of Harper's legal and racial entanglement with the Red Sox, was furiously writing letters to the Red Sox hierarchy looking for work, starting at the end of 1979 when he became a free agent, and all during his time in the Mexican League and independent league baseball.

It was unmistakable that while all this was going on with Harper, who was making exponential progress in his legal dispute with the Red Sox, causing them to stir uncomfortably and well more than once, George Scott was in the throes of his own exclusionary nightmare with them; his failure to get a job with Boston that appeared to have a racial bias, that in similar ways paralleled what was going on with Harper, each being black and each contending with Red Sox resistance. Basically, they were shadowing each other in so many ways, starting with the 1971 trade between Milwaukee and Boston when Harper, still an active player, was sent to the Red Sox and Scott to the Brewers; the circumstances involving their synchronous exposure to the Elks Club – but Scott, among the few black players on the team had said nothing about it, which could be blamed on the aftereffects of his Southern culture, which was to remain silent - and both worked nearly in tandem with one another for Premiere Auto as a means of employment, if not just as a coping mechanism.

In his new role of overseeing compliance as part of his affirmative action duties, Harper, in his interview with black reporter Larry Whiteside, made it clear what in this capacity his mission was: *"I deal a lot with the players, and I make it my business to talk to all of them, especially the black ones. They tell me they've never had anybody they could sit down and talk to before."*[770]

George Scott was on the Sox ballclub in 1978 and was not having a particularly good year, not only on the field but dealing with manager Don Zimmer, along with his frequent marriage troubles to complicate things, when Harper was handling compliance matters for Boston. He did speak briefly to Harper, he said, but not in any depth; informal at best. *"Tommy Harper gave me time to iron out personal issues I was dealing with when Don Zimmer never spoke to me. I resented how Zimmer treated me as if I was invisible. He knew as a manager he should have spoken [to me], but he didn't."*[771]

The undercurrent of racial bigotry here was revealed rather dramatically in another forum when Los Angeles Dodgers Vice President of Player Personnel, Al Campanis, on April 6, 1987, disclosed unknowingly to the general public his bigotry toward blacks, and most likely in that opinion – and, from a position of power - he was speaking in behalf of major league

---

[770] Larry Whiteside, "Harper Has a Mission for Sox, Blacks," The Boston Globe, July 29, 1979, p. 77
https://www.newspapers.com/image/437079884/?terms=%22Larry%20whiteside%22
[771] George Scott interview: November 7, 2007

team management generally throughout baseball when asked why there were so few blacks in baseball front offices and managers. His cynical response was, *"I don't believe it's prejudice. I truly believe that they [blacks] may not have some of the necessities to be, let's say, a field manager or perhaps a general manager."* He was fired two days later.[772]

This revelation by Campanis may have been at least a partial explanation for why George Scott was not being treated fairly by the Red Sox in seeking a job with them, but of course, there was an immutable history of Red Sox racism he had to contend with as well.

Between 1982 and 1989, another black player, Dennis "Oil Can" Boyd, a tormented and high-strung Red Sox pitcher and Mississippi native, often frequented the local newspaper sports columns during his tenure with Boston with rants of his own about how racist the team was, wagging his finger not only at their upper-level management, but specifically at field manager Joe Morgan, who clashed with black future Hall of Famer Jim Rice, and third baseman Wade Boggs, who would later be rewarded with entry into the Baseball Hall of Fame. The matter of Wade Boggs, the consummate Red Sox All-Star and premiere hitter, rose to the surface in June 1988 when a sordid story broke concerning his affair with *Penthouse* model Margo Adams. It was all over the news, local and national, and of

---

[772] Unattributed/ Associated Press, "Campanis Resigns Post With Dodgers," The Palm Beach Post, April 19, 1987, p. C1
https://www.newspapers.com/image/130753687/?terms=al%20campanis

significant embarrassment to the Red Sox. In spite of that, the Red Sox never blinked, rewarding Boggs with a three-year contract on July 7, a year from the Margo Adams debacle, even though it was still among front-page turmoil. *"If a black player did some of the things that Boggs did with that woman,"* said J. D. Dawson of the Boston Community Schools from Mattapan, a Boston suburb, *"he would have been gone. He might have been shot,"* pointing out the double standard.[773]

Meanwhile, Boyd, a quality starting pitcher, was hospitalized for a psychiatric evaluation in 1986 after walking out on the team in an agitated state after being snubbed for the All-Stars. After a series of injuries and more incidents, Boyd's "reward," whose story was as much in turmoil as was Boggs but of another kind, was given his release by the Red Sox at the end of '89. Oil Can Boyd, according to George Scott, manifested the deepest of feelings about his racial past in the South growing up in a nearby Mississippi town of Meridian, harboring resentment even deeper, perhaps, than ballplayers like Reggie Smith, Earl Wilson and Tommy Harper, and its injustice ate him up. In 1994-1995, at age 34, he joined the Sioux City, Iowa Explorers of the independent Northern League. Sports editor Terry Hersom of the *Sioux City Journal* delved into the "Can's" past, writing an article in which he highlighted the deeply sensitive side of Oil Can's difficulties in

---

[773] Steve Fainaru, "In Racism's Shadow," The Boston Globe, August 4, 1991, p. 81 https://www.newspapers.com/image/439435669/

the majors that were grounded in his being *"tormented by the scars of racial bigotry."*[774]

George Scott, who was managing the Lynn, Massachusetts Mad Dogs in an Independent League in '97, picked up Oil Can in a salvaging effort from a Bangor, Maine Northeast League independent club. *"He told us to never be disrespected,"* said Boyd quoting a philosophical message of his father's he carried with him fervently throughout his life. *"I grew up in a racial time,"* said Boyd. *"I love all people, but I don't like a man that's judgmental of me. I absolutely can't deal with the word 'nigger.' The part of the country I come from, they call you dumb, black nigger. You're supposed to be illiterate if you're a black kid from the south,"* exclaimed an agitated and very intense Boyd to reporter Terry Hersom.[775]

Boyd had returned to the Red Sox in '89 after shoulder injuries that kept him largely out of baseball for the two previous seasons. The Sox considered him one of four Boston starting pitchers. Oil Can, who was eligible for salary arbitration, realizing his importance to the team and as a starter, was looking for a pay raise, but GM Lou Gorman was balking, instead giving him a pay cut. Boyd's agent, George Kalafatis, who realized the emotional level of his client, the "combustible Can" they called him, did his best in convincing Boston to treat the hurler with well-deserved respect

---

[774] Terry Hersom, "Oil Can Gives X's Big Lift," June 7, 1994, p. 27 https://www.newspapers.com/image/337619275/?terms=oil%20can%20boyd
[775] IBID, p. 28

to get the best from him. *"He's ready to start pitching again,"* said Kalafatis. Larry Whiteside, who interviewed Kalafatis, touched upon what Boyd was bringing to the team and the value that would be gained by dealing with his client in good faith. *"Kalafatis said he hopes the Red Sox realize the importance of a healthy Dennis Boyd. Life will be a lot more peaceful if Boyd doesn't have other things on his mind."*[776]

During the winter meetings in December, Boyd, still unsigned by the Red Sox and still being jerked around by them, went in another direction, accepting a lucrative one-year offer, with incentives, by the National League Montreal Expos, "far larger than one tendered by the Red Sox," reported the *Boston Globe*. He had a solid 1990 season with Montreal with a 10-6 won-loss record and a single season personal best 2.93 ERA.

It was a similar experience with the Red Sox Rogelio "Roger" Moret, a southpaw pitcher who had a lot of promise but, like Dennis Boyd, was high-strung, requiring careful mentoring and appeasement, and that didn't seem to be in the cards for Moret or the Red Sox. Moret played six seasons for Boston between 1970 and 1975; in his final season with them, he was 14-3, but he never adjusted to Boston, an enigma to managers Eddie Kasko and Darrell Johnson and front office management. Bill Lee, then a Montreal pitcher one year removed from Boston, *"of some flakiness"* in his own right,

---

[776] Larry Whiteside, "Boyd, Sox Sparring in Contract Talks," The Boston Globe, January 6, 1989, p. 22
https://www.newspapers.com/image/438532263/?match=1&terms=oil%20can%20boyd

wrote Larry Whiteside of the *Boston Globe* in his 1979 series "The Black Athlete in Boston," said it best when summing up what happened to Moret in Boston: *"They caused his problem by getting rid of him without dealing with it. Their attitude was that we're not going to touch it,"* said Lee.[777]

Jay Acton, a lawyer, New York literary agent, and an early pioneer that led to the incarnation of independent league baseball, was instrumental, along with Eric Margenau, in forming the Empire State League on Long Island in 1987. Miles Wolff, who developed independent professional baseball in 1993, forming the highly successful Northern League in 1993 and later the Can-Am League, of which he was commissioner, and co-authored *The Encyclopedia of Minor League Baseball*, credits Acton with paving the way for this distinctive brand of pro ball that has since found its niche throughout the U.S. and parts of Canada. Acton's new league, which played its 50-game schedule at Hofstra University in Hempstead, NY, was comprised of four teams made up of players who had exhausted their collegiate eligibility but were not drafted by major league clubs; in effect, the league gave them a second chance at being noticed by the big leagues.

George Scott paid $2,000 to join the league and was one of three black managers; it was his first managerial role in the U.S and his introduction to independent league baseball that brought him back into American-style

---

[777] Larry Whiteside, "Harper Has a Mission for Sox, Blacks," The Boston Sunday Globe, July 29, 1979 p. 77
https://www.newspapers.com/image/437079884/?match=1&terms=Larry%20Whiteside

organized baseball and nearer major league operations where he felt it would offer him leverage and a ticket back to major league baseball. His fervent ambition was nothing less than to be spotted by a major league club and take on a role with them as a coach or minor league manager, or even something less just to get his foot in the door. He had been writing letters to them for several years since he left major league baseball, but none of the clubs gave him the time of day, nor rarely the courtesy of a reply. Matt Sczesny, a highly-regarded and longtime Red Sox scout and minor league manager himself, made a point to visit Scott in Hempstead that year and was impressed. *"He's a good baseball man, George. I guess he could manage. He knows the game, and it says a lot that he's here working in these conditions,"* said Sczesny, noting the Spartan conditions of the playing field: no lights, no dugouts, no scoreboards, and a "crowd" of 20-30 scattered across a small open-air grandstand.[778] Jay Acton, believing Scott was being given the snub by the Red Sox and other clubs, expressed more anger about Scott's plight with an element of racial questioning in his voice about how he saw the matter. *"He's in first place and with a team that has about the third-best talent in the league. If you're telling me he can't be a minor-league manager or a big-league coach, then there's something wrong somewhere,"* said Acton.[779] *"What he won't do, for certain, is write any more letters,"* wrote sportswriter Kevin Paul Dupont. *"Long before the Al Campanis faux pas and the awareness that blacks were shortchanged*

---

[778] Kevin Paul Dupont, "George Scott is Managing in a Small-Time League, Hoping It'll Be...Boomer's Showcase," The Boston Globe, July 24, 1987, P. 49
[779] Jay Acton interview: May 15, 2007

after their playing careers, Scott was writing to major league teams in hopes of landing work. Responses were few. The Red Sox, said Scott, told him time and time again that they'd contact him if they made any moves. Moves were made, but offers weren't."[780]

The league MVP was George's oldest son, Dion, who played first base on his father's team, the Diggers. *"He was the best player by far,"* said Acton, who shared an anecdotal story about father and son that year as the playoffs were approaching.[781] Scott was in need of pitching. His solution: he traded his son, Dion, to one of the other teams to get what he needed. Dion was completely dumbfounded, as was Acton and others in the league. It was the quintessence of the expression, "to win at all cost," and, by his actions, the personification of a man who would do just that. But the league, a no-frills enterprise, collapsed after two years of operations. Scott managed only one year.

Scott was struggling but found shelter and some financial relief when, from 1988 through 1992, he worked for Premiere Auto Body, an automobile repair shop in Allston, Massachusetts, once known as Geneva Auto Body that, ironically, was physically located next to Fenway Park a mere 200 yards away. It was the same place where Tommy Harper worked after he was dismissed by the Red Sox at the end of 1985, leading to his racial discrimination complaint. Stan Block, the owner of the establishment,

---

[780] Kevin Paul Dupont, Boomer's Showcase, p. 49
[781] Jay Acton interview: May 15, 2007

considered his workplace a refuge for former Red Sox black players, George Scott among them, to earn some kind of steady income and a place where they could land on their feet. Block noted that it was where the local newspaper scribes congregated as in a forum, an accommodation for them provided by Block, who sympathized with the black ex-players and actually interviewed Harper in 1986 after he had filed his suit and later after the EEOC upheld his action. Block, who was particularly close to Harper, felt that Haywood Sullivan was intolerant of blacks and lurking in the shadows of the debacle surrounding Harper's termination with the Red Sox. *"She was a little bit tougher toward the black ballplayers"* than Tom Yawkey was, said Block of Jean Yawkey, who was closely aligned with Sullivan.[782] Her abrupt 1977 firing of *"the best general manager in Red Sox history,"* wrote Howard Bryant, of highly-esteemed Dick O'Connell, who was instrumental in bringing blacks into the organization, was unexplainable other than it was personal: she just didn't like O'Connell. Harper eventually settled his suit with the club in December 1986.

Scott was also doing some autograph peddling at the time, noted Block, visiting major league clubhouses, soliciting autographs and arranging shows. But this was not a successful venture. *"They were friendly towards him, but none of them really helped him…Hawk Harrelson promised him a job with the Chicago White Sox and he never came through,"* said Block. "The *Red Sox never did anything for him at all. They never really*

---

[782] Stan Block interview: October 8, 2008

recognized him. I felt bad for him because he was always sitting home waiting for some team to call him." Reggie Jackson helped Scott out *"once or twice"* when money was getting tight for him, but *"that was about it,"* said Block.[783] During this time and before, he coached amateur baseball in Boston's inner city during the summer with Brannelly's Café in the Junior Park League, comprised of collegiate and ex-minor leaguers. At this stage of his life, age 48, there was no mistaking he was an incontrovertible major league discard.

In 1993, George was hired by Ernest Austen, the Athletic Director of the Roxbury Community College, a Boston inner city school, to organize and initiate RCC's first baseball program. Scott was its first coach and designed the uniforms that are still being used today. *"George came and started the [baseball] program with his own money. He put the program on his back and got it started,"* said Edsel Neal, Scott's successor, of George's trailblazing work with the college and his personal financial investment in RCC baseball. In 1996, Scott took RCC to the National Junior College Athletic Association state championship with only a nine-player team and lost against powerhouse team Quinsigamond of Worcester, Massachusetts. *"He almost pulled off winning the state championship with [just] nine guys, and five of them were pitchers...and it was a one-run game,"* chuckled Neal admiringly over what Scott had nearly accomplished with a bare minimum

---

[783] IBID

of players.[784] Scott's last year coaching RCC was in 1997; after that, he participated in some assistant coaching duties with them until 2000.

In 1994, during George's tenure at RCC, he signed on to manage the Minneapolis Millers, an independent league club of the newly-formed four-team Great Central League started by Minnesota businessman Dick Jacobson. There were problems from the beginning. Jacobson, whose league owned all four clubs, was working on a shoestring budget and ultimately could not support the payroll. To complicate his ambitions, he was competing for business with three other local ball clubs: the major league Minnesota Twins, a well-supported St. Paul club of the highly successful independent Northern League, and another start-up club, the Minneapolis Loons of the independent six-team North-Central League. Then in August, a member of a singing group who had been staying in an Augsburg College dormitory in the Twin Cities while on tour complained she had been raped by one or more members of the Millers' baseball team who were staying at the same facility. Things rapidly deteriorated from there, with Jacobson canceling the final four games of the season, thus putting a pause on his ill-fated venture with independent baseball and a departure from the Great Central League. George Scott, whose ambition it was to get a foothold on managing in the newly-charted and burgeoning

---

[784] Edsel Neal interview: September 23, 2008

independent leagues, got, instead, nothing but disappointment and a lesson in fiscal ignominy.

Ever the optimist, in 1995, Scott took yet another chance with independent baseball, which was not without its annoyances, joining a Saskatchewan Canadian club, the Saskatoon Riot, in the newly-formed Prairie League, made up of eight teams, four American and four Canadian. Scott became discouraged with the ownership, the Ferguson brothers, right from the outset, who weren't committed to winning, he said. *"I had never been nowhere where the owners can look out [on the playing field], see that they don't have talent, and still not be willing to spend some money [for players],"* said Scott, complaining that they had a $55,000 salary cap yet a payroll of around $20,000. Asked to name some of his players, Scott retorted: *"I don't care to remember them because they were lousy."*[785] The Riot posted a 9-21 record under Scott, who became disenchanted and left the organization on July 13, midway into the season. *"If I knew then what I know today, I never would have got involved [with Minnesota or Saskatoon],"* said Scott. *"Because I wanted so bad to try to get me a job in the United States in somebody's minor league system, okay, and I was out to just do about anything to show people that I was a good manager."*[786]

And then, his third bold attempt at independent league baseball finally proved to be a positive experience and one that showcased his managerial

---

[785] George Scott interview: February 15, 2008
[786] IBID

skills and should have been his ticket back to major league baseball. In 1996, he latched onto the Massachusetts Mad Dogs, an expansion team in the second-year independent North Atlantic League, made up of six clubs from New York State, New Jersey, New Hampshire, Pennsylvania and Ontario, Canada. Jonathan Fleisig, a 31-year-old trader of energy futures on the New York Mercantile Stock Exchange and a successful businessman with ownership of two minor league hockey teams, owned the Mad Dogs, which was located in Lynn, Massachusetts. Scott had a successful year, winning 56 of 77 games – among the records set by minor league ball clubs for most victories in a season – finishing 13 ½ games in front of Catskill, the second-place club. However, they lost the league championship in a two-game playoff sweep to the Catskill's Cougars.

Mike Babcock, the Mad Dogs general manager at the time, recounted, on a disturbing note, how they lost the final game of the championship to Catskill. Mad Dogs ace hurler Jay Murphy, who had dealt with Catskill handily during the regular season, took his team into the ninth with a 2-0 lead. But it unraveled from there. The Catskill hitters started delaying tactics of stepping out of the box to distract Murphy. It did upset him; he proceeded to hit a batter, then the next batter "hit the weakest little duck fart" bloop single that scored a run, and ultimately the game was tied. The Mad Dogs then lost 4-2 in 12 innings. According to Babcock, it seemed to take the air out of the ballpark, losing to a team they were supposed to beat easily and then watching Catskill celebrate their victory on the Mad Dogs' home field to make matters worse. Babcock said that he went to work for the Catskill team a year after that as their GM, and when going through the desk drawers of his predecessor, found a DVD tape *"Gaylord Perry's Dirty Tricks of Baseball,"* which assumedly was seen, believed Babcock, by the Catskill team in preparation of that championship game. *"Everything on that Gaylord Perry tape is everything they did. They must have watched it on the way to the damn ballpark,"* said Babcock, still outraged at the thought they might have been beaten because of an opponent's contemptible tactics.[787]

George Scott was named Manager of the Year, a tribute he thought would get the attention of the Red Sox, and three of his players were picked up by major league clubs at the end of the season. Not only was the team successful on the diamond, but they also drew the most fans [52,394], leveraging them for another season, if not in the North Atlantic League, which was in jeopardy because of failing franchises, then somewhere else.

The North Atlantic League collapsed as expected, but Fleisig's Mad Dogs shifted to the third-year Northeast League in '97, one of several independent leagues in a flourishing market, joining seven other clubs, including Catskill of the defunct North Atlantic League. Scott had another good year, winning 45 of 82, finishing third in the first half but then tying for the second-half lead at 23-17. Once again, however, they lost in the playoffs 2-games-to-1 to Albany, who lost to Elmira for the league championship. The Mad Dogs had even greater attendance than the year

---

[787] Mike Babcock interview: April 29, 2008

before, drawing 72,681 fans, second only to Albany's 72,985. Things were looking financially very promising for Fleisig's and George Scott's Mad Dogs. But it didn't last. There were problems with Fraser Field, where the Mad Dogs played; it needed major repairs. Interest began to dwindle as the season wore on, and by its end, the Massachusetts club had the second lowest attendance (47,123) – a decline of over 25,500 fans – of the eight-team league. They fell to 39-45 on the year and failed to make the playoffs.

At the conclusion of the '98 season, Miles Wolff, commissioner of the thriving and quite profitable Northern League, took an unprecedented step by merging with the eight-team Northeast League, establishing two divisions [Central and Eastern] with the 16 teams. It was his desire to enter the Northeast market where there were rich prospects for establishing a foothold, already proven by the success of the Northeast League, notwithstanding the poorer performance of the Massachusetts entry. But the Mad Dogs were assimilated nevertheless with the rest of their league and joined the Eastern Division. They began the season setting a milestone by signing a woman, Tammy Holmes, to their roster; she became the first female positional player of an all-male professional baseball team. Holmes had played for two years with the all-female Silver Bullets pro team before it folded. But it was short-lived. She played in two games with the Mad Dogs, was hitless [five strikeouts] in seven at-bats, with an on-base percentage of .222, and then left the team on June 13. The Mad Dogs were 21-22 in the first half of the division, playing one game behind the North's Division Adirondack. But in the second half, they fell to last place at 20-23, and their attendance was the worst in the league at 38,528. It was the last season for the fiscally struggling Mad Dogs, who succumbed at the end of the year.

George Scott displayed his mettle with the Mad Dogs club and had proven his field manager qualifications in those four seasons; to many, he had earned his stripes for the next step of at least a coaching position in major league baseball, even if it meant starting in the minors, but it wasn't to be. He never heard from any of the major league clubs, which was startling, especially not having heard from the Red Sox, who he was closest to – or, so he thought – whom he expected was likely to give him at least a special assignment instructor role, for which he was well qualified, similar to Tommy Harper who in 2002, at age 62 – less than three years after Scott finished with the Pittsfield club - would be given such a position in Boston. It seemed George should have been offered that kind of job. He was now 58 but still within the age boundaries of playing a valuable part in major league baseball.

Tragedy befell George Scott in 2000. His mother, Magnolia, died in September, and his significant other, Edith Lawson, of Randolph, Massachusetts, with whom he had a relationship of some 20 years, died suddenly on December 19 of a heart attack while going to work as a nurse at the New England Medical Center. It was a personal blow of immense magnitude for the Boomer; first, his beloved mother, then his fiancé whom he was about to marry, died suddenly within three months of each other.

Bereft with enormous grief, he picked up the pieces of a life severely shattered and moved on. He knew no other way to deal with it; George Scott knew what it was to survive. He moved into the home he had built for his mother in Greenville, back to his Mississippi roots, along with his teenage son Brian, who was born of George's relationship with Edith.

But it wasn't over; old friend Mike Babcock, who was then the GM of the Rio Grande Valley White Wings of Harlingen, Texas, of the independent Texas-Louisiana League, pursued Scott that winter to manage the White Wings. It was only a few months after Scott's personal tragedy, but because of their friendship, Babcock knew it might be the perfect situation for George to lift him up by the bootstraps during some very dark days. The White Wings were a stable team, one of the 1994 charter members of the league, and had won the Texas-Louisiana League championship in 2000 under manager Eddie Dennis, who left the team after that. *"That left me looking for a manager…he [George Scott] was the first guy to pop into my head,"* said Babcock. It was not a good season for Scott, who had to deal with an undisciplined team, incidences of drugs among the players, and a wholesale bad experience. They finished well down the ranks of the seven-team league at 40-56. *"The cast of characters we had in Rio Grande weren't the best character type guys, and I think that took a lot out of George that season because of that. It's all about the love of the game with George,"* said Babcock.[788]

Opportunity knocked once again, however, at season's end when old friend Jonathan Fleisig approached Scott, proposing to start another independent club in 2002, the Berkshire Black Bears of Pittsfield, Massachusetts, that would join the Eastern Division of the powerful Northern League. It represented a return to a city steeped with numerous personal memories and a venerable ballpark, Wahconah, where he first made a name for himself as a 21-year-old Red Sox prospect who that year [1965] tore the league apart dramatically carrying Pittsfield to an Eastern League championship. The offer to manage again, especially there, was a no-brainer; he jumped at the chance. But once again, he ran into disappointment with a team of players who seemed less than dedicated nor unwilling to perform in a manner to which he was accustomed. *"It was almost euthanasia...because he's not a quitter,"* said Fleisig about the decision he had to make to relieve his friend, George Scott, of the indignities he was experiencing with a young ballclub of malcontents that ended in his firing.[789] *"It used to be 70% coaching and 30% recruiting; now it was 40% recruiting, 50% babysitting and 10% coaching; that wasn't George's personality,"* said Fleisig. Speaking on the caliber of the new young ballplayer that Scott was encountering, Fleisig added: *"They were all state*

---

[788] IBID
[789] Jonathan Fleisig interview: October 28, 2008

all-stars, or all-county; they were the stars of their high school team, they had been prima donnas and had their asses kissed since they were probably ten years old; they had it all...they had a chip on their shoulder...all the women love me, my mom loves me...when you talk to somebody like George when it's about team, that's tough," said Fleisig expounding on the reasons behind Scott's disenchantment with the 2002 year in Pittsfield, that concluded in a dismal 24-65 season.[790] Scott did not return in 2003; it was the end of his long and exemplary, sometimes turbulent, baseball career: 30 years professionally and 5 years of college and amateur baseball.

Tragically, George Scott succumbed to complications from diabetes on July 28, 2013, in his hometown of Greenville, Mississippi. He was 69 years of age. American sportswriter Gordon Edes of ESPN, a former historian and writer for the *Boston Globe*, and sportswriter for several other major newspapers in the course of his career, covered the story of Scott's death on July 30 in his article, *"Not a Happy Ending for Boomer."* Of the several things he had to say in his tribute of George Scott, perhaps the most vivid of these in describing George was this: *"George Scott never got over the bitterness he felt over the fact that Major League Baseball, and the Red Sox in particular, never offered him a job when his playing days were over -- as an instructor, a coach or a manager. Coupled with the slights he endured as a young player in what he perceived as a racially insensitive organization (one of his minor league teams, believing it a harmless prank,*

---

[790] IBID

once came to his hotel room dressed like Ku Klux Klan members) -- this child of the segregated Mississippi Delta was burdened by sorrows when he died in Greenville, Miss., in the home he built for his mother back in that magical year, 1967."[791]

George Scott navigated his way through flourishing Jim Crow surroundings while growing up in the Mississippi Delta – once steeped in slavery - in the town of Greenville, he called home, though temperate in its racial behavior, provided little, if any, quarter for Southern blacks who sought equality and survival there. From the Delta, and relying on his exceptional athletic skills, Scott emerged from the poverty of the Delta to make his mark in professional baseball, promising his mother he would lift her from her impoverishment, which he did. But he confronted a realm of bigotry throughout his minor and major league baseball years in the form of partisan ownership and ripples of racially intolerant field management that challenged his very existence as a black ballplayer. And, as he prophesied, his chances for continuing in professional baseball would be challenged because of his skin color once he left the major leagues, and it was, though he remained intensely hopeful against the odds. He had proved in his various experiences after the major leagues that he was a good baseball man with valued management skills, lauded by many, but major league baseball, in the forefront of those being the Boston Red Sox, who once deemed him

---

[791] Gordon Edes, "Not A Happy Ending for Boomer," ESPN, July 30, 2013 https://www.espn.com/boston/mlb/story/_/id/9520950/george-boomer-scott-died-feeling-some-resentment

"unreliable," stonewalled him from re-entering their domain; simply enough, he was looking for that one chance again, which he had achieved years before that gave him a shot at a baseball future, yet the phone never rang for him after that, and he died a tormented man.[792]

---

[792] Steve Fainaru, "In Racism's Shadow," The Boston Globe, August 4, 1991, p. 81 https://www.newspapers.com/image/439435669/

Photo Album

April 2006, George Scott in front of Greenville, MS house he built for his mother (author's collection)

April 2006, "Boomer" at the Jimmy Bellipanni Baseball Complex, home of the Delta Community College Baseball Team, Moorhead, Mississippi (author's collection)

Scott with best buddy E. T. Davis in Greenville, circa June 2006 (author's collection)

Scott at his home in Greenville, circa June 2006 (author's collection)

George Scott's Mother Has No Doubts About Her Son's Ability

By JAMES TYSON
DD-T Sports Editor

AT least one person here in the home town of Red Sox George Scott isn't surprised that the Greenville slugger is turning eyes in the American League this year.

"He should have gone to the majors last year, but he got his knee hurt," according to his mother, Mrs. Magnolia Straw.

"A ball player. That's all he's ever wanted to be," Mrs. Straw said. The sun hovering just over the River levee brought out the grey in her short black hair, making her look older than her 48 years.

"George Junior has been playing ball ever since he was just a little fellow," she said. "I've been working so hard, though, since his father died I can't remember too much about his growing up."

George was born on a farm at Longwood 20 miles south of Greenville. The 22-year-old hitting bombshell is the middle of Mrs. Straw's three children. George's older brother, Otis Scott, lives in Memphis, Tennessee, and his younger sister, Beatrice, lives just a few blocks from her mother in Greenville.

The Scotts moved to Greenville when George was a baby. George was two then when his father died and his mother went to work as a cook and a field hand. She still works parttime as a maid.

"I always had to work," Mrs. Straw recalled. "I didn't want to take them out of school. I didn't want to be the cause of their not learning anything."

"George Junior used to work in the fields when he was little." She smiled. "But he wouldn't go when he grew up a little. He didn't like no field work. He just went there when he couldn't get anything else to do."

"I wanted him to get an afternoon job and work while he was going to school," Mrs. Straw said. "But he told me he didn't have time. He was always playing ball and I thought he just wanted to get out of working."

But George did get a job and worked during the afternoons and through the summers for the Pepsi-Cola Bottling Company while he was attending Coleman High School.

George participated in all the sports at Coleman — three-year letterman in baseball, football and basketball. He had college scholarship offers in each of the sports.

"He could beat 'em all playing any of it," his mother said proudly. "He always played good. I never went to see him play, though. The first time I saw him play was when the scout man (Edward Scott) took me."

"George Junior studied more about ball while he was in school than he did his books — that ball. I think sometimes the only reason he went to school was to get to play ball," she added. "He was more interested in that than learning anything."

"That boy's just always been a ball player and he's always been big and tall. His daddy was big and George Junior is just like his daddy."

Mrs. Straw talks with a great deal of pride, though matter-of-factly, about her son's accomplishments. Before he left for spring training this year, George had convinced his mother as well as most other Greenvillians who knew him that this was his year and he was going to make the big leagues.

Mrs. Straw said that she hadn't seen her son since the last day of February when he left for Florida.

"But I'm keeping up with him," she was quick to add. "I'm looking every day in the papers to see what he has done. He gave me a little ole schedule sheet so I could follow the games."

Mrs. Straw grew tired as she sat on the pourch of her small grey rented home on Beckwith Street talking about her son. But she turned and added a final comment as she opened the door to go inside for a rest: "He says he's going to buy me a house and stop me from working. I'll sure be glad of that."

MRS. MAGNOLIA STRAW, mother of Red Sox slugger George Scott, and one of her grandaughters.

Scott's mother Magnolia [Scott] Straw interviewed in May, 1966 by local paper Delta Democrat-Times (author's collection)

1962 Negro Big Eight State Basketball Champions, the Coleman Tigers. Scott is # 44 (courtesy Andrew Jackson)

Tigers in action against Broad Street High School on Thanksgiving Day. George Scott is passing to Lott Lang.

George Scott over threw A. C. Thomas.

1962 Coleman High School Tigers football. Quarterback George Scott passing to his receivers. (courtesy Andrew Jackson)

The 1962 Colemanite, Coleman High School yearbook (courtesy Andrew Jackson)

November 16, 1967 Greenville parade honoring George Scott, an important member of the 1967 American League Champion Boston Red Sox; an unprecedented gesture celebrating a black man of the town (courtesy Andrew Jackson)

"Throw Me One, Too!"

Hometown hero, November 16, 1967 (courtesy Andrew Jackson)

George Scott Baseball Camp for Greenville's youth, 1992. L to R – E. T. Davis, George Scott, Frank Barnes, Archie Quinn. (courtesy George Scott)

Red Sox Scout Ed Scott (courtesy Ed Scott)

The 2006 Boston Red Sox Hall of Fame Induction Gala, November 9, 2006 (author's collection)

George Scott being inducted into the Red Sox Hall of Fame, at Boston Convention and Exhibition Center, November 9, 2006 (author's collection)

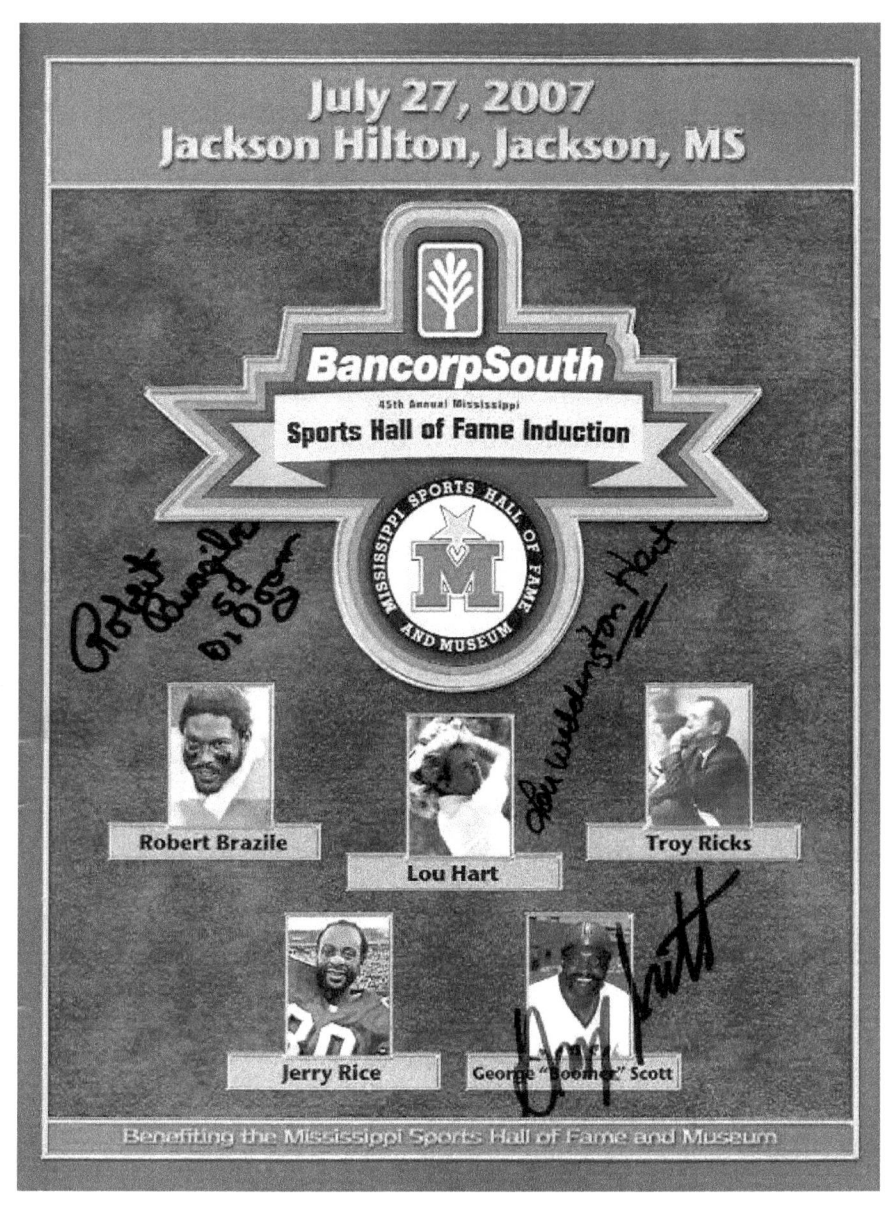

The 2007 Mississippi Sports Hall of Fame Induction of George Scott, July 27, 2007, Mississippi Sports Hall of Fame and Museum, Jackson Hilton, Jackson, Mississippi (author's collection)

George Scott with former Red Sox star pitcher, Dave "Boo" Ferris, a member of the Mississippi Sports Hall of Fame, at the 2007 induction ceremonies (author's collection)

Index

Numbers in **bold italics** indicate pages with photographs

Aaron, Henry "Hank" 186, 257, 283, 381, 481, 492-95, 499, 506-08, 520
Aase, Don 557-58, 562
Abbott, Glenn 569
Acton, Jay 604-06
Abdul-Jabbar, Kareem 481
A Wave of Terror Threatens the South 152
    see Hodding Carter Jr.
Abolitionist Movement 70
Absentee landlordism 113
Adams, Margo 600-01
Adirondack Lumberjacks *(Northern League)* 613
African Americans 75, 168, 192
Afro-American 248
Agricultural Adjustment Act (AAA) 100-102
Aguirre, Hank 350
Ahern, John 379
Alabama, state of 68, 201, 258
Albany-Colonie Diamond Dogs 612
Albany Senators 248
Allen, Dick "Richie" 415, 487
Allston MA 606
American Abolitionist 143
American Experience 27
American History Tellers 142
American League 212
American Veterans Committee 255
An American Dilemma 143
Anderson, Dick 241
Anderson, Sparky 235
Andrews, Mike **378**, 380
Anguilla MS 43, 74-75, 90
Aniston AL 201

635

Antebellum South 46, 49
Anti-busing 565
Anti-Literacy Laws 73
Aparicio, Luis 344
Arizona, state of 328
Arkansas, state of 66, 88, 258
Ashford, Emmett 354
Ashmore, Harry S. 39
Atlanta Braves 490, 550
Auerbach, Red 401
Augsburg College 609
Augustine, Jerry 539-40
Ault, Doug 588
Austen, Ernest 608
Avon MS 43, 64, 67-68, 75, 104, 129, 144
Azcue, Joe 390, 435-36

Baseball's Great Experiment 256
    see Jules Tygiel
B. F. Harbert & Co. 81
Babcock, Mike 611-12, 615-16
Babe Ruth League 188
Baltimore Orioles 326, 344, 428, 442, 448-49, 489, 498, 540, 550-51, 553, 556-59, 562, 576
Bando, Sal 488
Bangor ME 602
Barber, Steve **344**
Barlow, William 93, 126
Barnett, Ross 202
Baumer, Jim 467, 491-92, 506-07, 512-13, 516-18, 520, 523-24, 528, 533
Beanball Wars 484
Beane, Carl 4
Bell, Gary 326-27
Belzoni MS 158, 166-167, 178, 193
Bench, Johnny 500
Bennett, Dennis 333, 406
Benoit MS 162-166

Berkshire Black Bears   616
Berra, Lawrence Peter "Yogi"   488
Beulah MS   66-67
Bevacqua, Kurt   515
Big Road Blues   123
Bilbo, Theodore   33-34, 141-42
Birmingham AL   201, 230, 270
Birmingham Black Barons   214
Birmingham (White) Barons   230, 232, 270
Birtwell, Roger   246
Bithorn Stadium   443
Black activist(s)   182
Black Bayou Plantation   18-19
Black Bayou River   169
Black Codes 28, 32, 85
    see *Mississippi Black Codes*
Black lynching(s) 6, 56-57, 59-63, 170, 179, 188
Black Magic   489, 493-94
Black Migration, *see Great Migration*
Black Monday   150
Black Power   449
Black, Del   584
Blease, Coleman L.   62
Block, Stan   606-07
Blues, The   93, 122-28, 147
Bobby Henry Memorial Pool   154
Boggs, Wade   600-01
Bolivar County MS   18, 66, 112, 162-163
Bolivar County MS   66, 162
Bolling, Milt   257, 261-62
Bond, Bettie Mae (Hughes)   66
Bond, Eva Mae   111
Bond, Thomas Sr. 66
Bond, Thomas T. H., Jr.   52, 66-68, 77, 103, 110-14, 129, 139
Book Week   140
Booker Town   147
Boomer   4

Booth, Clark   235, 272, 349
Boston Baseball Writers Dinner   266
Boston Braves   212, 220, 223, 266
Boston Bruins   293
Boston Celtics   276, 299-01, 310, 401
Boston Against Busing 297
Boston Chronicle 220
Boston City Council   219
Boston Convention and Exhibition Center   3
Boston Garden   293
Boston Globe   222, 226, 243, 246-47, 251-52, 264, 287, 325, 327, 335-36, 357, 360, 363, 368, 380, 382, 396, 401, 408, 412, 450, 530, 538-39, 542, 545, 548, 564, 567, 603-04
Boston Guardian 220
Boston Herald   333, 595
Boston Herald American   542, 542
Boston infamy   458
Boston Irish majority   272, 305
Boston Phoenix   595
Boston Public Library   237
Boston racial riots   459
Boston Record-American   405
Boston, MA, City of   7-9, 36, 212-13, 271, 276, 294, 296, 305, 458-59, 565, 570

Boston Red Sox:

    13 months since hired   262
    1946 World Series   246
    a Boston massacre 572
    and then there was Bucky Dent   574
    asks to be traded   577
    being remiss 233
    black quality players   219
    bogus tryout 217
    Bresciani balks   8
    business executive 248
    Cardinals take the lead   260

caucasian in the woodpile 274
circumstantial evidence 268
complacent Red Sox 251
couldn't be racist and treat people that way 595
Cronin no friend of integration 229
dealing with Boston, a racist city 292
deftly skilled 270
didn't show similar interest in blacks 348
do something good 406
effects of Institutional racism 9
farm director 238
fragmented team 443
good riddance 455
gradualism a racial component of MLB 337
Hall of Fame dinner 3
hardly endearing to fans 325
he undermined himself 368
he was wrong 424
his inexplicable departure 356
how inaccurate the book 273
I don't think we had fifty words between us 577
immutable history of Red Sox racism 600
impossible dream team 322
infusing black talent 320
Institutional racism 9
integration issues 256
Isadore Muchnick 221
it wasn't just about race 307
Jean Yawkey takes over 562
Joe Cronin indifferent 224
knew going in they were racist 276
lost his sensibilities 418
Lucchino didn't remember 4
Mays and Piper Davis bitter 231
nary a black player on the field 275
never set well in Boston 334
no one came to his table 4
no racial element to O'Connell 292
not a good publicity move 391
nothing but a sham 222
O'Connell fired 562
on defense of Red Sox 234

on future manager Williams 309
on Robinson 226
only countrywide black journalist 335
only two black players on team 564
only white players were invited 328
outcry from the stands 223
pioneer Tom Yawkey 213
playing in Boston a risk 277
poor exchange 436
racial barriers 419
racial distractions brewing 564
racial intolerance 343
racist tryout 222
rapidly ascending the ladder 277
rates manager only as good 437
Red Sox propaganda 333
Red Sox racism in full bloom 594
Red Sox scouts 229
refuge for black ex-Red Sox players 607
segregation affair 232
showing indifference 250
signing Red Sox contract 216
slick manipulator 595
someone was yelling 223
something has to be done about Scott 426
stale Red Sox arguments 273
strange man 217
struggled with chronic injury 566
subjugation of black athlete 302
the clown 286
the king 329
the Sox' magnate 235
there is nothing wrong, and there hasn't been 597
they never did anything for him 607
they remained segregated 237
treating them all the same 384
wielded enormous power 245
would accept nothing less 543
Yawkey a mix of benevolence through charity 266
Yawkey complicated 217
Yawkey fails big chance 229
Yaz was emboldened 347

you had a chance   269

Boston school (forced) busing   36, 296-98, 306, 335
Boston School Committee   219, 296-98
Boswell, Thomas   552
Boyd, Betty Jo   146
Boyd, Dennis "Oil Can"   600-03
Boynton v. Virginia   200
Bradner Stadium   277
Bradshaw Township AR   66
Bradshaw, Clay County AR   66
Brady, SC Judge Tom P.   150
Bragan, Bobby   427
Brannelly's Café   608
Braves Field   229
Brenner, Marie   544
Bresciani, Dick "Bresh"   8-**9**, 592-95
Brett, Ken   446, 454
Brewery, the   211
Bristol, Dave   460-62, 464
Broberg, Pete   484, 494, 496, 514
Brookhaven MS   167
Brooklyn Dodgers   209-10, 219, 239, 245, 278, 336, 366, 368, 373, 388-89, 553
Brown I - see *Brown v. Board of Education of Topeka, 1954*
Brown II   34-36, 157, 172, 204, 336
Brown, Ollie   468
Brown v. Board of Education of Topeka, 1954   34-36, 39, 149-50, 155-56, 167-68, 200-01, 204, 295, 328, 336-37
Brown, David   152
Brown, John   74
Bryant, Carolyn   174, 178
Bryant, Howard   215, 219-21, 226, 229, 233, 235-37, 245, 250, 256, 270-72, 276, 286, 299, 302, 307, 310, 312, 320, 330, 335, 365, 369, 381, 460, 543, 545, 570, 607

641

Bryant, Roy 169, 175, 179
Bryant's Grocery & Meat Market 174
Buddin, Don 254
Buffalo Heads 554, 562
Buffalo NY racial riots 459
Bullitt, Alexander C. 48-51
Bullitt, Diana Moore (Gwathemy), (A. C. Bullitt's mother) 50
Bullitt, Fanny Elizabeth "Fanny" (daughter of A. C. & Irene Bullitt) 51
Bullitt, Frances Elizabeth "Fanny" (Smith) 46-47
Bullitt, Thomas Washington (A. C. Bullitt's father) 50
Bumbry, Al 556
Burgmeier, Tom 546, 562
Burleson, Rick 556
Busch, August A. "Gussie" 211, 388
Butler, Mary Ann 74
Byrd, Harry 35

Cabinet card 69
Cafardo, Nick 321
California Angels 352-53, 390, 393-94, 420, 436, 446, 468-69, 472, 506, 517, 521, 540, 562, 567, 578
Campanella, Roy 197
Campanis, Al 418, 599, 605
Campbell, Bill 538, 552, 557
Campeche Pirates 587
Can-Am League 604
Canada, Tracie 343
Canseco, Jose 547
Canton MS 68
Carbo, Bernie 517, 522, 528, 554
Carew, Rod 556-57
Carolina League 279-80, 288
Carolina University 280
Carter, Chelsea R. 343

Carter, Hodding III   155, 202
Carter, Hodding Jr.   7, 39, 139-41, 151-54, 162, 165-66, 179, 181, 193, 295
Cash, Wilbur Joseph "W. J." "Jack"   57-59, 61-64, 77, 87, 94, 97, 99-100, 108, 110-11, 113
Cash, Norm   440
Catskill Cougars   611-12
Chain gang   85
Cape Cod   294, 454
Cato Institute   101
Chambliss, Chris   556-57, 574
Champion, Bill   496, 501
Chaney, James Earl   14, 182
Chapman, Ben   245
Chapman, Lou   474, 481, 523, 525, 527
Chicago Cubs   242, 492, 528
Chicago Defender   95, 220
Chicago Housing Authority   108
Chicago IL racial riots   459
Chicago White Sox   217, 260, 403, 414, 476, 528, 547, 553, 568, 607
Chicago, Illinois   6, 95-96, 108-09, 112, 123, 145, 147, 149, 174, 177, 213
Chickasaw Indian tribe   65, 67
Choctaw Indian tribe   65, 67
Christopher, Joe   322, 327
Cincinnati OH   209
Cincinnati racial riots   459
Cincinnati Reds   212, 283, 513
Citizens' Council(s)   37-38, 148-52, 154-59, 167, 182, 184, 191-93, 200, 202, 204, 295
Civil Rights   6, 17, 37, 61, 139, 170, 173, 180, 256
Civil Rights Act of 1964   5, 28, 31, 38, 183, 456
Civil Rights Act of 1875   20
Civil Rights activist   14
Civil Rights Laws   17

Civil Rights Movement of 1960s 7, 121, 173, 181-82
Civil Rights slayings 6
Civil War 16, 19, 21-22, 28, 40, 54, 57, 68, 74, 79, 85, 94, 107
Claflin, Larry 333, 405, 542, 547
Claiborne County MS 44, 67
Clark, Alexis 132
Clarksdale MS 76, 109
Clay County AR 66
Clemente, Roberto 443
Cleveland Buckeyes 221, 225
Cleveland Indians 326-27, 416, 428, 435, 445, 448, 494, 503, 515, 528, 538, 573
Cleveland MS 85, 122
Cleveland OH 459
Cleveland, Reggie 551
Clif-n-Claf 542-43, 546
Clifton Plantation 19
Cloud Nine Lounge 325, 333, 356
Clowning 350
Coahoma County MS 18, **80**, 109
Cobb, James C. 31, 41, 45-46, 49, 59, 92, 101, 103, 123-24, 127, 131, 151, 159
Cobb, Ty 217
Coca Cola Bottling plant 193
Cohn, David L. 108-09
Colborn, Jim 504, 512, 516, 521
Coleman High School Baseball Team **208,** 211
Coleman High School 1-2, 154, 185, 188, 194, 204-**05, 06**-08, 216, 261, 300
Coleman High School ballpark **209**
College of William & Mary 47
Collins, Bud 376
Collins Cleaners 190
Collins, Eddie 218, 220-23, 230, 234, 236, 241, 243-44, 249, 258, 266-67, 269, 292, 360
Coluccio, Bob 486

Columbia University   220
Confederate states   26, 28
Congress on Racial Equality (CORE)   182, 201, 203
Conigliaro, Billy   390, **431**, 445-47, 450-54, 464-65
Conigliaro, Tony   308-09, **352**, 368, **378**, 383, 390, 398-99, 400, 406, 446-47, 487
Cooper, Cecil   453, 540
Corbin, Ray   486
Cotton States League   197
County Stadium   465, 482, 484, 520-22
Courts, Gus   167-68
Cox, Billy   389
Crandall, Del   464-65, 467, 469, 472, 474-75, 477, 481-85, 488-89, 491-93, 495-96, 501-04, 512-14, 524
Crawford, Jim   522
Crawford, Pat   211
Cronin, Joe   218, 223, 229-34, 237-46, 249-50, 258, 270, 273, 292, 360, 413, 495
Croppers, *see sharecropper(s)*
Crowe, George   212-15, 262

Daley, Arthur   346
Daniel, Pete   91
Daniels, Ruby Lee   76
Dark, Alvin   416-418, 498-99
Darwin, Bobby   497, 501, 517
Dalton, Harry   507
Davenport, Charlie   26
Davis, Edward "E. T."   186, 199, 283, **284-85**
Davis, Jefferson   26
Davis, Piper   231, 329
Davis, Spencer "Babe" (Scout)   257
Davis, Spud   211
Davis, Tommy   414-15
Dawson, J. D.   601
de facto segregation   458
    see Howard Bryant
DeArmond, Mike   580

De La Beckwith, Byron   184
Deadball Era   388
Dean, Daffy   211
Dean, Dizzy   211
Dee, Henry Hezekiah   184
Deep South   7, 22, 28, 45, 49, 58, 62, 76, 149-50, 154, 157, 201, 262, 302, 386-87
Delancy, Bill   211
Delta, *see Mississippi Delta*
Delta Cotton Plantations 48, 56
Delta Democrat-Times [DDT]   7, 38, 44, 111, 139, 153, 163, 165, 193
Delta Leader   81
Demeter, Don   325-27, 334
Democrat Party   151
Dennis, Eddie   615
Dent, Bucky   573-74
Depression, *see Great Depression*
Des Moines Register   335
Des Moines Tribune   335
Desegregation   37, 109-10, 141, 149-50, 153-54, 157, 159, 165, 171, 204, 295-97, 303, 307, 458
Detroit MI   241
Detroit racial riots   458
Detroit Tigers   217, 324-27, 334, 350, 355-56, 394, 409, 412-13, 440, 504, 515-16, 518, 522, 552, 559, 566
Diamond Dinner   510, 533
Dickins, Dorothy   117
Digby, George   229-30, 232, 262-**64**
DiMaggio, Joe   243
Diming, James   180
Dixiecrats   151
Dixie League   188
Dobson, Pat   440
Doby, Larry   227
Doerr, Bobby   407-08, 411, 420
Dogging   341-42
Dollard, John   104

Dorchester MA   36
Douglass, Frederick   70-71, 74, 143
Douthit, Taylor   211
Downey, Tom   331
Doyle, Brian   574
Drabowsky, Moe   344
Drago, Dick   521, 562
Drake University   335
Dressen, Chuck   389
Drew, Mississippi   6, 13, 173, 175-76
Driskell, Jay   62
Dupont, Kevin Paul   605
Durham NC   280
Dyer, Eddie   246

Eastern League   290
Eastland, James "Big Jim"   35, 97, 141-42
Eau Claire WI   577
Eckersley, Dennis   562, 571
Edes, Gordon   4, 617
Edwards, Charles Marcus   185
Elks Lodge   263, 597
Elliott, Debbie   180
Elmira Pioneers (*Northeast League*)   612
Emancipation Proclamation of 1863   74
Empire State League   604
Encyclopedia of Minor League Baseball   604
Encyclopedia of Southern Culture   125
    see Charles R. Wilson & Dr. William Ferris
Erie PA   223, 226
Eskenazi, Gerald   564
Europe   50, 52, 93, 96
Evans, Billy   237-44, 246
Evans, David   123, 126, 128
Evans, Dwight   564, 567-68, 571
Evansville Press   241
Ever-May Plantation   44
Evers, Medgar   5-6, 14, 178, 184

Fair Housing Act 456
Falmouth MA 286
Fanny Smith & Fanny Bullitt (steamboats) 46-47
Farmer, James 203
Father of the Blues 122
    see *W. C. Handy*
Father of the Delta Blues 128
    see *Charley Patton*
Faulkner, William 88
Faust, Drew Gilpin 27, 32
Federal Writers' Project 25
    see *Slave Narrative Project*
Feller, Bob 197
Fenway fans, see *Fenway Park*
Fenway Park 10, 217, 221-23, 229, 265, 293, 353, 392, 408, 423, 434-35, 447, 493, 538, 540, 549, 556, 569, 591, 606
Ferraro, Mike 463
Ferris, Dr. William 125
Fesley Families 90, 118, 142-44
Fesley, James 68-**70,** 71-74, 143
Fesley, Laura (Owens) 68
Fesley, Margaret 68-69, 118
Fesley, Owen 68-69, 118
Fetter, Henry D. 338-39
Field Hollers 124, 126
Fingers, Rollie 517
Finley, Charlie 517
First Ballfield 12
Fish Pond Plantation 26
Fisk, Carlton 537-38, 556, 576
Fitzgerald, Ray 545, 548
Fleisig, Jonathan 611-13, 616
Flint MI 459
Flood, Curt 214
Florida Instructional League 407

Florida, state of   258
Folkers, Rich   541
Foltman, Leah   456
Foner, Eric   30
Ford, Whitey   345-46, 350
Forest MS   20
Formisano, Ronald   297-98, 300, 304, 306
Foules, Elbert   214, **216**, 261
Forest Plantation   52
Foy, Joe   290, 311, 320-21, 335, 375, **378**, 390, 427
Foxx, Jimmie   242-43, 346, 547
Francis Williams family   66
Franklin TN   66-67
Freedmen   22, 25, 33, 40-41
Freedom Riders   6, 201-03
Freedom Rides   6, 201, 203
Freedom Summer   165, 182
Fregosi, Jim   393, 395
Frisch, Frankie   210

Galoots   334
Gammons, Peter   271-72, 545, 564, 569
Garagiola, Joe   389
Garcia, Chito   587-88
Garcia, Pedro   495-96, 501, 503, 513, 517
Gas House Gang   210
Gentleman's agreement   213, 219, 253, 387
Georgia, state of   57, 157, 258
Geneva Auto Body   606
Germany   131
Gershon, Livia   86
Gibson, Bob   214, 361, 366
Gilliam, Jim   389
Glendora MS   13, 168-69
Glennon, Eddie   232-33
Goldstone, Lawrence   20
   see Inherently Unequal

Golenbock, Peter   237-39, 308-09, 331-32, 347, 361, 364-65, 439, 445
Gonring, Mike   519, 525
Goodman, Andrew 182
Gordon, Joe   435
Gorman, Lou   597, 602
Gossage, Rich "Goose"   557, 574
Grace, Willie   226-27, **228**
Gradualism   337, 339
Graham, Lindsay   142
Graham, Renee   71
Grammas, Alex   507, 513, 515-19, 521-24, 526, 540-41
Grant, Jim "Mudcat"   396, 427-28
Great Central League   609
Great Depression   42, 96-100, 217
Great Migration   93, 105, 107, 112, 121
Great War   64
Green, Lennie   322, 334
Green, Elijah Jerry "Pumpsie"   247-50, 253-56, 275-76, 301, 313, 320, 329, 331, 335, 356-57, 362
Green v. School Board of New Kent County   36
Greene, Bryan   132
Greenville, *see Greenville, Mississippi*
Greenville Bucks   197-98
Greenville Day Care   146
Greenville High School   207
Greenville Red Sox   283
Greenville MS   2-3, 5-7, 10-15, 81, 84-85, 91, 108, 113, 115, 119, 122, 129, 137, 139, 142, 144, 146-48, 151, 154-55, 162, 176, 178, 185, 187, 191-92, 197, 200, 207, 213-15, 258, 261, 263, 277, 301, 386, 530, 590, 615, 618
Greenwood MS   14, 123, 177, 184
Grenada County MS   18
Gresham, Deloris Melton   13, 60, 175
Grimm, Charlie   427
Grossman, James R.   54

Groton School 271
Grove, Lefty 243
Guindon, Bob 278
Gutfarb, Bill 268
Gutlon, Jerry M. 197, 594
Gutman, Herbert 103

Halberstam, David 235, 275
Haller, Bill 353
Hamilton, Jack 383, 446
Handy, W. C. 122
Haney, Fred 381
Hanging Bridge of Shubuta 6
Hargrove, Mike 499
Harlingen TX 615
Harper, Tommy 263-64, 302, 337, 454, 561, 585, 596-99, 601, 606-07, 614
Harrah, Toby 484
Harrell, Billy 257
Harrelson, Ken "Hawk" 403, 409-10, 416, **431**, 435-36, 445, 607
Harrington, John 273
Harris, Bucky 250, 252-55, 597
Harrison, Roscoe 118
Harvard University 47, 76
Hayes, Alice Ruth 146
Hegan, Mike 523
Hempstead NY 604-05
Hemus, Solly 361, 381, 396, 427
Henry, Aaron 149
Henry, John 10
Herman, W. J. Bryan "Billy" 307-10, 329-30, 333-34, 343, 352-53, 355-57, 359-60, 362-63, 375
Hersom, Terry 601-02
Herzog, Whitey 509, 577-84
Hicks, George 108
Hicks, Louise Day 296-97, 305-06

Higgins, Mike "Pinky"   218, 236, 249-55, 257-59, 274, 276, 292, 310, 317-20, 329-31, 427
Hill Place Plantation   44
Hill, Samantha   70
Hirshberg, Al   250, 308
Hisle, Larry   556
Hobson, Butch   537, 567, 571
Hodges, Gil   367
Hofstra University   604
Holland, Hal   278
Holmes, Tammy   613
Hopson, Howell   106
Hopson, Richard   107
Horgan, Tim   426
Horton, Tony   326-27, 372, 377, 379-80
Houk, Ralph   404, 440
House of David   197-98
Houston Astros   217, 260, 330, 577
Howard, Elston "Ellie"   367, 382-84, 427, 442
Hughes, Bettie Mai   66
Human Geography of the South   99
Humphreys County MS   90, 93, 158, 166-167
Humphreys, Benjamin G.   22-23, 28
Hunter, Jim "Catfish"   548, 552
Hurwitz, Hy   252
Hyde Park   293

Idlewild Plantation   67, 113
Impossible Dream   423, 562
Indianola MS   6, 75, 177, 203, 295
Indian Removal Act   64-65
Inherently Unequal   20
    see Lawrence Goldstone
Institutional Racism   9
Integration   141, 154, 157, 168, 172, 204, 211, 213, 229, 233, 269, 340
International Harvester   106
Introduction of The Mind of W. J. Cash   87

Ireys, Henry T.   46-47
Irish Americans   36
Irish Catholics   298
Irvin, Monte   186, 197
Itta Bena MS   123, 177
It Was Never About The Babe   594
   see Jerry Gutlon

Jackson Advocate   134
Jackson County MS   18
Jackson Daily Clarion-Ledger   60-61
Jackson, Andrew   43, 64, **189**-90
Jackson, Dr. L. Jordan   206-07
Jackson, Reggie (Civil Rights)   457
Jackson, Reggie (Oakland A's)   479, 500, 505
Jackson, Reggie (N.Y. Yankees)   549, 552, 556-57, 608
Jackson MS   6, 37-38, 134, 178, 182, 184, 201, 202
Jackson State University   212
Jacobson, Dick   609
Japan   131
Jenkins, Ferguson "Fergie"   554, 558-59, 562, 564
Jennings, Kathleen   46, 50
Jensen, Jackie   251
Jersey Street   10
Jet Magazine   176
Jethroe, Sam   221-23, **224-25**, 226, 234, 256, 266, 269, 315
Jim Crow   2, 6-8, 11, 14, 20, 28, 31, 37, 56, 72, 88, 94, 96, 119, 121, 129, 131-32, 142-43, 148, 155, 161, 174, 185, 187, 220, 261-62, 277, 313, 332, 387, 618
Johns Hopkins   76
Johnson, Alex   473
Johnson, Andrew   27
Johnson, Charles   104, 129
Johnson, Chuck   500, 504
Johnson, Claude Otis   162-163, 166

Johnson, Darrell 603
Johnson, Lyndon 38
Johnson, Rheta Grimsley 16
Johnson, Richard 218, 222, 254, 268
Jones, Adam 10
Jones, Dalton 412, 424-25
Jones, K. C. 301
Jones, Malia 456
Jones, Rupert 569
Jones, Sam 301
Joshua, Von 517
Jurges, Billy 250-51, 331

Kaese, Harold 237, 241-46, 251, 317, 327, 360, 362, 380, 394, 396, 399, 401-02, 408
Kalafatis, George 602-03
Kansas City Athletics 322, 410
Kansas City Kansan 335
Kansas City Monarchs 221, 227
Kansas City Royals 425, 434-35, 446, 451, 459, 465, 475, 495, 508-09, 567, 577-83, 596
Kansas City Star 579
Kansas City Times 580
Kasko, Eddie 442, 444-45, 450, 603
Katie Lewis Memorial Pool 172-73
Kauffman, Ewing 580, 584
Keane, Clif 197, 222, 234-36, 252, 254, 258, 273, 325, 357-58, 396, 404, 419-20, 431, 435, 437-38, 448, 542, 544, 547
Kellum, J. W. 169
Kelly, Pat 476
Kelly, Zelma 144
Kennedy, Atty General Robert 115
Kennedy, John 347, 380
Kentucky, state of 42, 49
Key, Valdimer Orlando "V. O." 76
Keys v. Carolina Coach Company 200
Killen, Edgar Ray 183

Kimbell, Elmer   13, 168-69
King Kong   587
King, Martin Luther, Jr   5, 180-81
Kinston NC   280
Kirschner, Eddie   241
Klein, Christopher   98
Kobel, Kevin   513
Kosciuszko Park   458
Kountze, Maybray "Doc"   220, 229
Krause, Lew   454
Kuenn, Harvey   495
Kuhn, Bowie   355, 473, 511, 517
Kunkel, Bill   354, 449
Ku Klux Klan (KKK)   2, 30, 33, 35, 54, 56, 63-64, 148, 152, 154, 165, 168, 182-84, 201, 281, 618

Lacy, Sam   220, 236, 248-49
Lahoud, Joe   347, 364, 385-86, 445-47, 450, 454, 468-69, 474
Lake Washington   43, 67
Landis, Kenesaw Mountain   213
Lange, Dorothea   80
Lane, Frank "Trader"   455, 460, 462, 467
Lawson, Edith   1, 614
Lee, Bill   392, 550, 553-55, 557-59, 563, 571, 603-04
Lee, George Winston   14, 158, 166, 178
Lee, Mary   27
LeFlore County MS   57
Leland MS   151
Lemann, Nicholas   68-69, 75-76, 81, 83, 90, 95-97, 103, 105-09, 112-13, 121-22, 148-49
Lemon, Bob   574
Leonard, Dennis   584
LeRoux, Buddy   561
Lester, W. O.   165
Lezcano, Sixto   501, 503, 513
Levine, Lawrence   124

Lewis, William "Buddy"   214
Lincoln County Courthouse   167
Lincoln County MS   167
Lincoln, Abraham   26-27
Lindsey, Jim   211
Little Red (Sox) Book, The   554
    see Bill Lee
Little Rock AR   294-95
Livingston MS   68
Logan, Rayford W.   24
Lonborg, Jim   348, 368, 383, 391, 398-99, 447, 454, 468
Locker, Bob   483
London, England   53
Long-Chain Charlie   85
Long, Jordan Blumberg   233
Loughborough Plantation   19
Long Taters   1-2, 8
Longwood Landing   44
Longwood Plantation   42-44, 46-48, 50-52, 64, 68, 74, 77-**78**, 81, 90, 99, 103-04, 110-11, 113-15, 127, 129, 135, 139, 144
Longwood, *see Longwood Plantation*
Look Magazine   152
Los Angeles Angels   217, 260
Los Angeles Dodgers   599
Los Angeles CA racial riots   459
Los Mochis Cañeros   586
Louisiana, state of   57, 184, 258, 262
Louisville Colonels   238, 250, 270
Louisville KY   47, 49-50, 270
Lowenfish, Lee   336
Lucas, James   26
Lucchino, Larry   4
Luciano, Ron   484
Lucy Webb School   **145**
Lupien, Tony   239
Lynching, *see Black Lynching*

656

Lynn, Fred   509, 537, 557
Lynn MA   227, 611

Mack, Connie   242
MacPhail, Lee   488
Madden, Michael   597
Madison County MS   68-69
Magic Glove Award   489
Maglie, Sal "The Barber"   353
Mahoney, Neil   257, 259, 265, 320
Major League Baseball   14-15
Major League Baseball Players Association 396, 462, 470, 474, 478, 511-12
Maldonado, Felix **260**
Maloney, George   465
Malzone, Frank   321
Mann, Jack   274-75
Mantle, Mickey   381
Maravich, Peter "Pistol Pete"   301
Margenau, Eric   604
Marshall, Alexandra Dunbar   52
Marshall, Dunbar   52
Marshall, Fanny B. (Smith) (Bullitt) 52
Martin, Billy   484-85, 549-50, 557, 574, 583
Martin, Pepper   211
Martinez, Dennis   550
Massachusetts Commission Against Discrimination (MCAD)   249, 255, 257, 265, 596-97
Massachusetts Mad Dogs   602, 611-14
Massive Resistance   35
Mathews, Eddie   381
Mattapan MA   293
May, Dave   480
May, Lee   498
Mayberry, John   488, 508
Mayflower Café   144
Mays, Willie   186, 229-34, 239-40, 264, 275, 287

McBride, Earnest   134
McCarver, Tim   211
McComb MS   164-65
McCraw, Tommy   **324**
McCune, Dr. Frank   135
McDonough, Will   234, 247, 264, 270-73, 286, 319, 363, 365, 372, 382
McDowell, Sam   416
McFarland Publishing   1
McGlothlin, Jim   394
McLain, Denny   412
McMahon, Don   390, 403
McNally, Dave   448
Meadville MS   184
Mechanical cotton harvesting   41, 106-13
Mechanized cotton picker   106-08, 110-112, 117, 149
Medical Center Hospital   3
Melton, Beulah   169, 175
Melton, Clinton   13, 168-69, 175, 181, 184
Memphis Public Affairs Forum   152
Memphis Red Sox   214
Memphis TN   17
Mencken, H. L.   87
Meridian MS   182, 601
Mexican League   585, 590-91, 598
Mexican Pacific League   586
Mexico City   405, 443
Mexico City Reds   587
Mexico City Tigers   587
Milam, J. W.   13, 168-69, 173, 175, 179
Miller, Marvin   462, 470, 474, 478, 511
Millsaps College   37
Milwaukee school busing   458
Milwaukee segregation   458
Milwaukee WI   335, 456-58, 460, 525
Milwaukee Braves   212, 335, 389, 464

Milwaukee Brewers:

> Aaron returns to Milwaukee   490
> Aaron's last home run   521
> about to be traded for Nolan Ryan   517
> admonished in front of 700   533
> among the elite - the franchise   506
> appointed team captain   501
> begrudged his absence from Boston   510
> being jerked around   473
> both fulfillment and affliction   335
> Brewer MVP first baseman   507
> Brewers struggling   497
> by far best defensive first baseman   508
> callous Brewers   477
> consummate first baseman   490
> Crandall fired   504
> cultural deprivation   463
> deemed by Red Sox as unreliable   618-19
> dropped the fine   478
> fans' contempt and reporters' criticisms   523
> favoring owners   512
> feeling fan pressure 519
> he keeps booming   503
> he's been underpublicized   489
> his personal nightmare   567
> I wasn't sure Milwaukee had accepted me   462
> implicit allegation of malingering 469
> in his mind I was dogging it   470
> laying the blame   518
> lingering resentment with Boston 462
> looking for a front-line player   528
> navigating teammate encounters   515
> new GM Jim Wilson 467
> off-field problems   525
> owner has to "own" better   502
> personal attacks continued   532
> prescribed the mood   492
> rejected by peers   508
> returning to his "garden city"   **529**
> sick of playing in Milwaukee   524
> sliding toward the bottom   502

    Sox pick up Tommy Harper   598
    standards not the same   479
    still smoldering   474
    stripped him of his captaincy   524
    stunned at the choices   488
    team unrest was palpable 474
    the reason for fine was not disclosed   469
    they haven't seen eye to eye   476
    they jeered him   539
    they made him the key man   454
    traded for Cecil Cooper   528
    unconsciously racist   479
    vengeance on their minds 464
    verge of team leader   483
    very good first season   467
    wife Lucky files for divorce   575

Milwaukee Journal   335, 481, 487, 495, 500, 503-04, 525, 527, 530, 538
Milwaukee 1967 Racial Riots   458-59
Milwaukee Sentinel   474, 478
Mind of the South, The 57
    see Wilbur Joseph "W. J." "Jack" Cash
Ministerial Alliance   255
Minneapolis Millers   247, 254, 609
Minnesota Twins   351, 469, 471, 486, 546, 556, 562, 609
Minnesota, state of   351

Mississippi, state of:

    a stiff penalty   466
    agricultural newspaper   40
    black codes 28
    black destabilization   97
    black flight 149
    both from Mississippi   370
    broad geographic assignment   258
    caste system 120
    civil unrest 109
    could happen in Mississippi, not MA   229

county penal system   84
Delta in early to mid-19th century   16-17
Delta notable murders   164
dignity of the photograph   70
ex-slaves' on freedoms   26
human brutality   170
ignored Supreme Court   201
Jim Crow   37
just look at him at third   432
latent leadership qualities   482
like any other murder   178
loss of black labor   105
northern interference   200
not so welcoming   180
nutritional studies   117
on black marriage   76
on hostility   14
on the Old South   111
only the fittest survived   134-35
opposition to *Brown* decisions   35
plantation Negro   98
political network and voting rights   33
pressure bearing down on Brewers   478
privatization of schools   148
public opinion of Negro   22
racial justice 164
ranking on desegregation   155, 157
ratification of 13th amendment   24
record on lynching 57, 62
school desegregation   110
seditious anti-black speech   150
sharecropper living quarters   79-**80**
signing black voters   182
style of brutality   173
Supreme Court of Mississippi   164, 170
the *KKK* as continuing trend   56
two racist senators in power   139
two U. S. senators   141
vigilante groups   150
voting contrivances 183
war's effect on slaves   20
welcoming parties   201

661

    white hostility   96
    world-wide scorn   17

Mississippi Black Codes 28
Mississippi black hospitals   135
Mississippi Delta   2, 5-7, 16, 45, 72, 76, 88-89, 105-07, 165, 176, 180, 184-85, 191, 201, 482, 618
Mississippi Delta Plantations   98-99
Mississippi Legislature   23
Mississippi racism   2
Mississippi lynching   6
Mississippi River   17, 42, 47, 64, 67, 88, 128, 147, 184, 482
Mississippi River flood of 1927   88-89, 91, 94, 96
Mississippi State penitentiary system   84
    see *David Oshinsky & Parchman Farm*
Mississippi Summer Project   182
    see *Freedom Summer*
Mississippi Supreme Court   164, 170
Mississippi Valley   22
Mississippi, University of   125
Mobile AL   257
Mobley, Mamie Till   174
Money, Don   468, 486, 488-89, 495-96, 522
Money MS   174, 177
Mongrelization   38
Montgomery AL   201
Montgomery, Caroline Mosby   18
Montreal Expos   392, 603
Montville, Leigh   321
Moon, Bucklin   140
Moore, Charles Eddie   184
Moore, Vennie   82
Morales, Tommy   587
Morehead, Dave   319, 333
Moret, Rogelio "Roger"   603-04
Morgan, Bob   389
Morgan v. Virginia   200
Morgan, Joe   **9**, 600

Moses, Jerry   368-69, 386
Most Southern Place on Earth, The   31
   see James C. Cobb
Mound Bayou MS   135, 167, 177
Mt. Pleasant Plantation   266
Muchnick, Ann   222
Muchnick, Isadore   219-22
Murphy, Jay   611
Murphy, Mary Elizabeth B.   97-98
Murphy, Tom   517
My Black Place Plantation   45
My Mundle Place Plantation   44
Myrdal, Gunnar   143

NAACP   14, 132, 149, 159, 167-68, 178-79, 184, 227, 247-49, 255, 265, 296-98
Naismith Basketball Hall of Fame   300
Nashville TN   66
Nason, Jerry   251, 401-02, 433
Natchez Indian tribe   65, 67
Natchez MS   21, 26, 52-53
Natchez Trace   64, 67
National Baseball Hall of Fame   218, 220, 234, 238, 275, 365, 600
National Endowment for the Humanities   125
National Football League (NFL)   341-42
National Junior College Athletic Association   608
National League Rookie of the Year   224
National Public Radio   180
National Recovery Act, The   101
National Sportscasters and Sportswriters Association
   376
Native American(s)   65, 128
Neal, Edsel   608
Negro's Image in the South, The   23-24
   see Claude H. Nolen
Negro Leagues   214, 221, 226, 389
Negro Problem   28

Newark NJ racial riots   458
New Deal, The   75, 100-01, 110
    see Franklin D. Roosevelt
New York, state of   147, 596
New York Black Yankees   212
New York Penn League   277, 279
New York Times   346, 564
New York Times Magazine   154
New York Tribune   21
New York Yankees   244, 343, 345, 362, 367, 383, 404-05, 440, 519, 521-23, 526, 542, 547, 549-53, 559, 562, 568, 571-74, 583
Noblesse Oblige   81, 91
Nolen, Claude H.   23-24
No More Mr. Nice Guy   349, 372, 425
    see Dick Williams
North Atlantic League   612
North Carolina College of Agriculture and Mechanic Arts   54
North Carolina, state of   68
North-Central League   609
Northeast League   602, 612-13
Northeastern University   271
Northern agents   90
Northern journalism   39
Northern League   601, 604, 609, 613, 616
Norwood, Willie   587
Nowlin, Bill   267-69, 347

Oakland Athletics   396, 438, 483, 488, 540
Ocala FL   265
O'Connell, Dick   248, 252, 255-59, 292, 317, 319-22, 325-26, 328-29, 362, 417, 421, 424, 426-28, 436-37, 439-40, 452, 454-55, 507, 562, 607
Oglivie, Ben   **530**
Ohio Baseball Hall of Fame   226
Ohio River   18
Ohio Wesleyan University   337

Oklahoma, state of   65
Old South, New South   102
    see Gavin Wright
Olean NY   277-78
Olean Oilers   277-78
Origins of the Underclass   75
    see Nicholas Lemann
Oshinsky, David M.   23, 56-57, 85-86
    see Worse Than Slavery
Otis, Amos   567, 580-81
Owens, Jessie   355, 414-15
Oxford University Press   98

Palmer, Jim   551
Parchman Farm state penitentiary   6, 84-85, 123, 201-04
    see David Oshinsky
Parnell, Mel   232, 361
Patek, Fred   582
Patterson, Robert "Tut"   37, 150, 152
Pattin, Marty   454
Patton, Charley (or, Charlie)   127-28
Pavletich, Don   454
Pawtucket Red Sox   453
Pawtucket RI   453
Peckerwood(s)   175
Peck's Bad Boy   584
Peetuck   198
Pena, Malvina "Lucky"   285, 294, 400, 527, 575
Peoples Gin Company   19
Peralta, Alejo   587-88
Pepsi Cola Company   190-92
Percy, LeRoy   91
Percy, Will   91
Perez, Tony   **444**
Perini, Lou   212
Perry, Gaylord   612
Pesky, Johnny   4, 318

Petrocelli, Rico   308, 345, 369-70, **378**, 381, 384, 409, 420, 424, 534
Philadelphia Athletics   242
Philadelphia MS   14, 182-83
Philadelphia Phillies   245, 340, 377, 468, 528
Philadelphia Stars   212, 221
Philadelphia PA   209
Phillips, Lefty   473
Pittsburgh Courier   220
Pittsburgh PA   487
Pittsburgh Pirates   217, 260
Pittsfield Red Sox   257, 288, 290, 375, 614, 616-17
Planter(s), Delta   19, 40-41, 43, 45, 57-58, 63-64, 68, 73-74, 79, 87, 89-91, 94-95, 97, 101, 105, 111, 116-17, 131, 149, 151, 156, 158
Plaschke, Bill   372
    see *No More Mr. Nice Guy*
Plessy v. Ferguson of 1896   7, 34, 172, 200
    see *Brown v. Board of Education*
Pole, Dick   589
Poloni, John   562, 564
Pony League   188
Popowski, Eddie "Pop"   197, **260**, 288-90, 310, 312, 358, 362, 375, 379, 445, 570
Poquette, Tom   577
Port Gibson   44, 64, 67
Porter, Darrell   514, 518
Poza Rica Oilers   589
Powdermaker, Hortense   75, 88-89
Powell, Jim   101-02
Powers, Scott   210
Prairie League   610
Premiere Auto Body   598, 606
Prime, Jim   554
Prince, Carl   389-90
Promised Land, The   103, 105-06
    see *Nicholas Lemann*

Provenza, John   190-**92**, 193-94
Providence Journal   293, 565
Pulitzer Prize   39, 151, 193, 275, 295, 346
    see *Hodding Carter Jr.*
Puerto Rico   428, 443

Quarters, Negro Cabins, or shanties   79-**80**
    see *Sharecropper cabin or quarters*
Quillici, Frank   486-87
Quinn, Bob   217
Quinsigamond Community College   608

Race-Norming   341, 405
Race problem   95, 140
    see *Hodding Carter Jr.*
Racial acceptance   214
Racial diversity   597
Racial justice   166
Racial madness   7
Racial non-acceptance   9, 14, 336, 339
Racism   1-2, 9, 39, 77, 95, 107, 211, 214, 218, 232, 594
Ralbovsky, Martin   470
Raleigh NC   280-81
Raleigh, Union County, Kentucky   18
Ratliff, Beulah Amidon   98
Reconstruction   18, 27, 29, 41, 47, 54, 57-59, 68, 134
Red Sox Century   218, 222, 273, 302
    see *Glenn Stout & Richard Johnson*
Red Sox Hall of Fame   3-4, 8-**9**, 594-95
Red Sox Nation   237, 308, 423, 445
Redlining   303, 456-57
Reese, Harold "Pee Wee"   238-40, 243-44
Refugees   90-91, 95
Reid, Whitelaw   21-22
Remy, Jerry   **9**, 562, 567
Resident smartass   7

RetroSimba 209
Revolutionary War 18
Reynolds, Bill 293, 306, 565
Reynosa Broncos 587
Rhem, Flint 211
Rice, Jim 286, 537, 550-52, 556-57, 565, 591, 597, 600
Rickey, Branch 209, 267, 336-37
Rickwood Field 230
Riders, *see Freedom Riders*
Riggs, Lew 211
Rio Grande Valley White Wings 615
Robert T. Henry Memorial Pool 172
Robertson, Oscar 481
Robinson, Brooks 326
Robinson, Frank 428-29, 430-431, 443-**44**, 503, 528
Robinson, Jackie 9, 15, 210, 212, 219, 221-23, 226-28, 232-34, 240, 245, 256, 267, 273, 277, 287, 315, 336-40, 355, 387, 389, 414, 419, 428
Robinsonville MS 81
Rocky Mount NC 280-81
Rodriguez, Bobby 587
Roggenburk, Gary 379
Roe, Preacher 389, 427
Rolling Fork MS 43
Rollins College 337
Rolph, Stephanie R. 37-38, 150-151, 156-58
Roosevelt, Franklin D. 75, 100-01
Rosedale MS 163
Roxbury Community College 608
Roxbury MA 36, 293
Royals Stadium 584
Rudi, Joe 517
Ruhle, Vernon 516
Russell, Bill 276, 299-02, 310, 314, 334, 592
Rust Brothers 110
Ruth, George Herman "Babe" 357, 362, 396, 490

Ryan, Bob   539, 546, 551, 567
Ryan, Mike   447
Ryan, Nolan   506, 517

San Francisco Giants   418
San Juan Puerto Rico   443
Santiago, Jose   322, 325, 368, 379, 427
Santurce Crabbers   428
Sargent, Gov. Francis   306
Saskatchewan Canada   610
Saskatoon Riot   610
Satriano, Tom   436
Say Hey Kid   230
   see Willie Mays
Schwerner, Michael   182
Scott, Beatrice   75, 104, 115-**16**, 130, 137, 145, 188-89, 280
Scott, Edward "Ed" *(Red Sox Scout)* **216**, 257-59, **260**, 262, 265-66, 276, 312, 362
Scott, the family of George   42, 56, 59-60, 77, 86, 114, 115, 118, 129-30, 137, 144, 158

Scott, George "Boomer:"

    1965 Eastern League MVP   **291**
    Alex must think I'm a lousy hitter   541
    amateur free agent 312
    autograph shows   596
    ballplayer, the   1, 3
    being celebrated   **595**
    being mismanaged and mishandled   416
    block of cement   375
    Boomer with sister Beatrice   **116**
    born March 23, 1944   115
    climbed the sports ladder   207
    conflicting message for the Boomer   407
    death of   2-3, 15
    demands a trade   421
    diabetes of   2-3

dismantled the young slugger   385
Dodger type   408
driving in Greenville   10-11
effects of *Jim Crow* 14
Emmett Till   6
fawned over Yaz   348
finally, a job that showcased his managerial skills   610
first ballfield   11-**12**
first certified African-American star   321
first managerial job   586
first year of eight Gold Gloves   **371**
form of subjugation 350
former nemesis   496
found his way around Boston's racial politics   301
furiously writing letters   598
going back to his old batting style 411
going to go into a coach's role   588
got the job…then fired   588
Greenville gun shop   13
Harrell plays mentoring role   257
he hustles   **324**
Herzog was insulting   579
his arrival in the city (Boston)   299
holdout   **430-31**
I never let anyone get in my head   406
inexplicably in the outfield 377
it was personal   477
jump-starting old tactics   435
just the same   591
just to get the Boomer in shape   396
keeping a low profile   294
KKK prank   281
later known as "Boomer"   129
like Death Valley   552
loss of confidence   370
mad at everyone   570
major league discard   608
manager of the year   612
mentor   490
mockery of blacks   543
most valuable Brewer   467

670

nearer to major league operations		604-05
never offered a job	617	
newfound slugger	351	
no longer the scared, backward kid		530
no one helped	4	
no respect for Zimmer	536	
no telling what I would have done		491
number one rehab assignment	427	
on Olean	**278**	
one of O'Connell's first moves		292
patently picking on Scott	369	
personal tragedy	614	
playing days were over		590
playing for Red Sox could be troublesome		276
pleasing to be in a northern town	278	
promised a job	607	
put on waivers by Kansas City		583
race played a part	422	
racial conflict	5, 7	
racial element	1	
Red Sox HOF	3-4, 8, **9**	
reign of terror	551	
resented how Zimmer treated me		599
rife with racism	279	
Rookie of the Year	372	
rookie sensation	**352**	
Scott's Vesuvius	420	
showing disloyalty	358	
silent on the media	547	
sitting in his truck	**11**	
a line of George Scotts	74	
succumbed to diabetes complications		617
Sultan of Swat	**344**	
systemic non-acceptance	14	
take-it-or-leave-it offer	583	
tasteless media attackers	546	
the Boomer becomes the "Boomer"		321
the roster	**316**	
they weren't used to me	359	
tips from the splendid splinter		**323**
too keyed up	500	
tough-minded	285	

       traded again   577
       wanted so bad to try to get me a job   610
       we didn't belong there   592
       weight struggle   3
       what the hell is going on?   593
       what was bugging them?   414
       why don't they leave him alone   409
       why was he put in that game?   417
       willing to trade him 379
       with coach Andrew Jackson   **190**
       with coach Davis Weathersby   **196**
       won't play me   370
       wouldn't be easy for Scott 307
       you would not get well-liked   289
       youthful Scott   6

Scott, George Charles Jr.   115-**16**, 118-19, 129-30, 137, 142, 145-48, 154, 159-61, 188-89, 197, 213, 214-**16,** 217, 259

Scott, George Sr   42-43, 51, 56, 59, 68, 74-75, 77, 81-84, 86, 93-95, 97, 99, 103-04, 107-08, 114-15, 119, 120, 122-23, 125-27, 129, 132-36

Scott, George III   4, 591-92

Scott, Magnolia "Maggie" (Simon) (Gilmore)   68, 72, 74-77, 81, 83-85, 89, 102-03, 114, 115, 117-**19**, 127, 134, 136-39, 141-42, 144-47, 154, 188, 260, 277, 614

Scott, Mary (James)   90, 93-95, 99, 103

Scott, Otis Charles   75, 104, 130, 137, 145, 188

Scottsdale AZ   328, 334

Scranton, Bob   230, 232-33

Scranton Eastern League   231, 241

Sczesny, Matt   605

Seale, James Ford   184-85

Seattle Pilots   425

Seattle WA   257

Seaver, Tom   557

Second Basic Agreement   473

Segregated public buses   200

Segregation 34, 37-39, 50, 96-97, 105, 119, 150, 155-56, 172, 182, 185, 200-03, 219, 236, 458
Seitz Decision 511
Selig, Allan H. "Bud" 467, 483, 488, 490, 492, 495, 499, 512
Selma AL 298
Separate but Equal 34, 36, 171, 200
    see Plessy v. Ferguson of 1896
Separate but unequal 135
Shannon, Walter 214
Sharecropper cabin or quarters 79, **80**
Sharp, Bill 497
Sharkey County MS 43, 75, 90
Sharecropper(s) 19, 41, 47, 68, 74-76, 82-83, 86, 89, 90, 94, 96-97, 101-04, 107, 114, 115, 117, 120-22, 132, 136, 162, 174
Shecter, Leonard 402-05, 413
Sheehan, Alan 368
Sheridan Plantation 173
Shotgun house 144, 147-48
Shubuta MS 6
Shut Out 219, 365, 369, 545
    see Howard Bryant
Sidey, Hugh 45, 114-15, 118
    see Time Magazine
Silver Bullets 613
Simon families 68, 90, 118
Simon, Edd 68
Simon, Grace "Gracey" (Fesley) 68
Simon, Magnolia "Maggie" 68, 72-74, 84
Singelais, Neil 398, 412, 450
Singer, Bill 539
Singleton, Ken 556
Sinnot, Dick 305
Sioux City Explorers 601
Sioux City IA 601
Sioux City Journal 601
Skwar, Don 247

Slack, Bill 280-82
Slaton, Jim 514, 534
Slaughter, Enos 389
Slave Narrative Project 25
Slipping 114
Smith family
    see Benjamin "Ben" Smith
    see Irene Smith

Smith, Benjamin "Ben" 42-48, 64-65, 67
Smith, Benjamin "Ben" – Will & last testament 48
Smith, Berry 20
Smith, Ellison "Cotton" Ed 62
Smith, Frances Elizabeth "Fanny" *(daughter of Ben & Irene Smith)* 46-48, 50
Smith, George 322
Smith, Gerrit 74
Smith, Irene (wife of Benjamin Smith) 48-49
Smith, Lamar "Ditney" 167
Smith, Mayo 395, 440
Smith, Mrs. Benjamin 46
Smith, Reggie 257, 286-87, 302, 321, 334-37, 340-341, 348, 390, 427, 442, 452, 592, 601
Smith, Wendell 220, 236
Smithsonian Magazine 132
Snider, Duke 381
Social Darwinism 134
Social Security Park 587
Society for American Baseball Research (SABR) 210
Somerville MA 306
Sons of the American Revolution 150
South Bend IN 459
South Boston 36, 271
South Carolina, state of 28, 201, 218, 250, 258
Southie 36, 271
Spahn, Warren 481
Spencer, Jim 476, 559, 574
Sports Illustrated 274

Sportsman's Park 197-98
St. Louis Browns 209
St. Louis Cardinals 208-15, 243, 246, 260-62, 340, 361, 366, 381, 388-89, 440, 489, 537
St. Louis MO 209-10
St. Paul MN 609
Stanky, Eddie 387, 389, 414-15, 427
State Sovereignty Commission 191
Steinbrenner, George 549, 583
Stephens, Vern 232
Stephenson, Jerry 361
Stier, Isaac 21
Stockton CA 247
Stout, Glenn 218, 222, 247, 254, 273, 302, 322, 350
Strider, H. C. 179
Stuart, Dick 309, 318, 547
Sugrue, Thomas 339-40
Sullivan, Haywood 362-63, 376, 404, 426, 439-40, 561-62, 572, 597, 607
Sun City AZ 483, 491
Sunflower County MS 85
Sunflower River 17
Sutherland, Gary 517
Swann v. Charlotte-Mecklenburg Board of Education 36
Systemic non-acceptance of blacks 14

Taborian Hospital 135, 167
Tallahatchie Court House 174
Tampa FL racial riots 459
Tanana, Frank 540
Tartabull, Jose 322, 334, 447
Tallahatchie River 17, 174-75, 17
Tasby, Willie 253
Tenace, Gene 498-99
Tenant Farming 19, 25, 40, 47, 58, 75, 89-90, 94, 97-98, 101, 102, 104, 106-08, 114, 117

Tennessee, state of   65
Texas-Louisiana League   615
Texas Rangers   476, 484, 499, 553, 562, 583
Texas, state of   211, 258
Thirteenth Amendment   16, 24-25, 27-29, 32
Thomas, Gorman   529-**30**
Thomas, John   162-165
Thompson, William Hale "Big Bill"   33
Tiant, Luis "Looie"   301, 494, 544-45, 550, 554, 569, 571, 573
Tiger Stadium   350
Till, Emmett   6-7, 13, 100, 169, 173-81, 184
Time Magazine   45, 115, 118, 150-51, 153, 157
Times Picayune   50-51
Tomasik, Mark   209
Torrez, Mike   562, 571, 573-74
Toronto Canada   320
Torre, Joe   489
Toronto Blue Jays   539, 555, 573
Toronto Maple Leafs   363, 372-73, 380
Trail of Tears   65
Transatlantic Slave Trade   17
Transatlantica   138
Travers, Bill   532
Travis, Jimmy   14, 184
Triggering the Memories   206
    see *Dr. L. Jordan Jackson*
Troy, Phil   220
Truman, Harry S.   151
Trusty shooters   85
Tucker, Luther   198
Turner, Nate   73-74
Tygiel, Jules   256
    see *Baseball's Great Experiment*

UCLA   75, 300
United States Constitution   24
United States Navy   188

United Sates Supreme Court   34-36, 296, 328, 337, 471
United Sates Supreme Court "Separate but Equal" decision of 1896   97
University of North Carolina   126, 271
University of Tennessee   45
U. S. Equal Employment Opportunity Commission (EEOC)   597, 607
Up From Slavery   123
    see Booker T. Washington

Vail CO   391
Valenzuela, Benjamin Papelero   586
Vallier, Elise   138
Vance, Rupert B.   99
Vardaman, James K.   31-32, 62
Vera Cruz Aguila   589-90
Vicksburg MS   17
Villard, Oswald Garrison   61
Virginia, state of   17, 35, 50, 73
Voting Rights Act of 1965   28, 31

Wahconah Park   616
Wake Forest University   280
Wakefield, Zachary L.   34
Waldron, Ann   193
Walker, Dixie   427
Walker, Gary   531
Walker, Harry   427
Warmund, Joram   338
Warren County MS   57
Washington, Booker T.   122-23
Washington County General Hospital   3
Washington County Historical Society   46
Washington County MS   18, 42, 44-46, 51, 60, 64-65, 68, 84, 90, 115, 132, 142, 162, 204
Washington Highlands   457
Washington Nationals   214

Washington Post 552
Washington Senators 250, 413, 448
Watson, Bob 577
Weathersby, Davis 189, 194-**95, 96**
Wellsville NY 278, 308
Wessels, The 106
Western Carolina League 283
Wetherbee, Don 139
Where I Was Born and Raised 108-09
    see David L. Cohn
White Chief 31
    see James K. Vardaman
White Citizens' Council, *see Citizens' Council*
White Knights 184
White Sox Park 415
White Supremacy 28, 31-33, 37, 64, 97, 141, 157, 168, 181, 183
White, Bill 214, 381
White, Booker T. "Bukka" 122-23
White, Dorsey 13, 60
White, Hugh 156
White, Margaret Campbell 66-67
White, Roy 552, 574
White, Sammy 251
White, Wiley B. 67
Whitehead, Burgess 211
Whiteside, Larry 286-87, 303, 335-36, 356, 454, 459, 461-464, 530, 538-39, 599, 604
Whitten, John 180
Wilkerson family 42-43
Wilkerson, George Washington 18
Wilkerson, Jefferson Pinckney 18-19
Wilkerson, Peter 18, 42-43
Wilkerson, Thomas Jefferson 18
Wilkinson, Phil 218, 268

Williams, Dick   3-4, 7-**9**, 309, 347-49, 363-**71, 374**-76, 379-380, 382-96, 399, 400-09, 411-13, 415, 417-29, 432-42, 450, 461, 467, 476-77, 488, 496, 507, 536, 579, **595**
Williams, George "Bullet"   123
Williams, Irene S. (Williams) (Bullitt) - (niece of Ben & Irene Smith)   48, 50-51
Williams, John Sharpe   62
Williams, Marvin   221-22, 256
Williams, Merritt   51
Williams, Norma   348-49, 392
Williams, Ted   232, 237, 243-45, **264**, **323,** 381, 495, 547
Williamson County TN   67
Williamson, Joel   126
Willoughby, Jim   554
Wilson NC   280-81
Wilson, Charles R.   125
Wilson, Earl   248-50, 253, 302, 324-37, 355-57, 592, 601
Wilson, Jim   467-69, 472, 474, 477-78, 492, 513
Wilson, Willie   582
Winchester MA   306
Winds of Fear   140
    see Hodding Carter Jr.
Winford, Jim   211
Winston Salem NC   257, 279-80, 570
Winston Salem Red Sox   279, 282, 288, 312
Winston Salem State University   280
Winston, George T.   54-56
Winter Haven FL   310, 314-15, 324, 328, 334, 407, 596-97
Winter Haven Red Sox   356
Wise, Rick   497, 554, 559, 562
Worcester MA   608
Wolf, Bob   487, 498
Wolff, Miles   604, 613
Wood, Wilbur   472

Woodall, Larry 229-30, 232
Wooden, John 300
Woodward, C. Vann 131, 295-96
Woodward, Kenneth 337
Women Also Know History 37
World War I 93, 98
World War II 96, 105, 131-32, 134, 148, 219, 305
Worse Than Slavery 85-6
    see David M. Oshinsky
Wright, Gavin 58, 102
Wright, Jim 571
Wright, Simeon 174-75
Wrigley, Phil 213
Wyatt-Brown, Bertram 87
    see Introduction of The Mind of W. J. Cash
Wyatt, John 322, 333, 390, 404-05, 427, 442

Yale University 47, 76
Yankee Stadium 345, 552, 557
Yastrzemski, Carl 318, 321, 332, 346-49, 358, 366, 368, **378**, 390, 401-52, 408-09, 412, 418, 421, 438-39, 447, 450-52, 488, 499, 537-38, 550, 556, 567, 574, 576
Yazoo City, Mississippi Delta 117, 159, 201, 386-87
Yazoo River Basin 16
Yawkey Family 217
Yawkey Foundation 10, 268, 561
Yawkey Way 10
Yawkey, Jean 292, 439-40, 561-62, 607
Yawkey, Julia Austin 218
Yawkey, Thomas "Tom" 10, 212-13, 217-20, 222-23, 226-28, 230-31, 233-36, 238-42, 244-45, 247-55, 266-71, 273-76, 292, 317-20, 326, 330-32, 346-49, 360, 366, 368, 380, 387, 392, 412, 417, 421, 424, 426, 428, 436-441, 561, 594, 607
Yount, Robin 484-**85**, 486, 494-96, 507
Yucatan Lions 585
Zimmer, Don 392-93, 535, 537, 544-45, 553-54, 557-59, 562-63, 566, 568, 571-72, 575-77, 599
Zisk, Richie 556